Spices of the World Cookbook
by McCormick

# SPICES
## OF THE
# WORLD
### *Cookbook*

*by*

# McCORMICK

PREPARED AND TESTED BY
MARY COLLINS
IN THE KITCHENS OF
MC CORMICK

*Produced for McCormick by Penguin Books*

This edition first published 1969
Reprinted 1970, 1971, 1972, 1973, 1974, 1976, 1978 (twice),
1980, 1981, 1983

# PREFACE

———— * ————

For generations, McCormick & Company, Inc., has provided a variety of seasonings and flavorings to cooks at home and abroad. We take pleasure in sharing with you our wealth of experience in the art and science of presenting food at its very best. The *Spices of the World Cookbook* will be equally at home in your library or on your kitchen shelf, for it is both for browsing and on-the-spot use.

Designed for all who appreciate fine food, from the uncertain amateur to the seasoned chef, this volume adds new dimensions to an ancient art. Within these pages we have included the simple and the sophisticated, the foreign and the familiar—all lovingly created and tested in our McCormick kitchens and carefully tailored to North American tastes.

It is you, the reader, whose interest and many requests have made this book possible. The efforts and enthusiasm of the members of our Home Economics staff have made it an actuality.

Special thanks go to Moss Photography of San Francisco, California, for the cover photograph.

MARY COLLINS
Home Economics Director
McCormick & Company, Inc.
Baltimore, Maryland 21202

# CONTENTS

— * —

Spices of the World Cookbook
by McCormick

# BRIEF HISTORY
# OF SPICES

——— * ———

Today we take spices for granted. There they are, always handy on the spice shelf, as ordinary as our daily newspaper; and if we run out, they are as near as the neighborhood grocery or supermarket. We can scarcely imagine a time when spices weren't commonplace and familiar. Yet the fact is that in nearly all of recorded history, man's fate has been closely bound up with his hunger for these marvelous spices.

A trace of this urgency lingers in our subconscious memories. To most of us the word spices still conveys an impression of vague and wonderful adventure; and when we speak of the "spice of life," we mean something more than piquancy—we mean romance.

The first known reference to spices occurs in the scriptures of the ancient Assyrians. According to their version of the creation, which they chiseled into stone tablets 5,000 years ago, the gods who made the earth were so impressed by the difficulty of the task that they held a sort of celestial committee meeting before they began their work. And while they discussed the problems of the creation, they drank sesame seed wine.

Long before the Assyrians, men were well acquainted with spices. Archaeologists believe that the knowledge of seasoning extends back at least 50,000 years. Very likely the first experience with seasoning came when primitive men wrapped meat in leaves before cooking it on hot coals. Their purpose was to protect the meat from dirt and ashes; however, they soon learned that certain leaves imparted a pleasant new flavor to the meat.

Of course it was not only a pleasant flavor that made spices important. Primitive men often had to eat foods that were strong-tasting or even spoiled; and later on civilized men, too, suffered greatly from unpalatable diets. In the days before modern methods of preserving and refrigerating foodstuffs, spices made it possible to eat foods which otherwise would have been inedible.

In time it was discovered that certain spices also had medicinal properties, and many of the treatises written by the doctors of ancient Greece and Rome tell how to prepare herbs and spices for use as drugs. Wine mulled with spices and honey was thought to be particularly effective in the treatment of many illnesses. Indeed, spices became important in all departments of life, even in religion. Today the ceremonial meaning of spicery remains in the incense used in many churches. Incense is only spices and other aromatics that have been prepared for burning.

For tens of thousands of years men relied on the aromatic plants they could find in their own regions; and fortunately, there are few parts of the earth which do not grow at least one or two native spices or herbs. The primitive tribes which inhabited the great forests of Europe could find dill, marjoram, parsley, thyme and several other herbs growing in their area. Generally speaking, the most important spices come from the East, specifically from India, Ceylon and the Spice Islands, which include Sumatra, Java, Bali, the Moluccas and neighboring territories. Pepper, which has always been and still is the most widely used spice, is the dried berry (called a peppercorn) of a vine that is native to Sumatra.

By the time the great civilizations of ancient Greece and Asia Minor had developed, in the centuries before the birth of Christ, a flourishing spice trade had sprung up between the East and the main cities of the Mediterranean region. The spices were brought from their

2

source to various ports in India, where they were loaded on caravans for the long overland journey to Syria. Cities along the route—Persepolis, Susa, Palmyra, Damascus—became legendary outposts of romance for the boys and girls of ancient Athens and Rome. The Bible gives numerous references to the importance of the spice trade. When the Queen of Sheba visited King Solomon, her principal gifts of state were "camels that bare spices"; and when Joseph was betrayed by his brothers, he was sold to the spice traders of a passing caravan.

As the Greek and Roman colonizers spread their civilizations throughout Europe, they took their knowledge of spices with them. It is on record, for example, that the first mustard seed were brought to England by Roman soldiers in 50 B.C. Very quickly the fierce tribes of Gaul and the Celtic outlanders learned the value of these "new" spices; and when Alaric the Visigoth subjugated Rome in 410 A.D., he demanded 3,000 pounds of peppercorns as part of his price for sparing the lives of the inhabitants.

When the great civilizations of the ancient world declined, the connection between Europe and the Orient was broken; and it was not until several centuries later that the spice trade was resumed. This time the Arabs, who were expanding aggressively eastward and westward from their base on the shores of the Red Sea, controlled traffic with the Far East. In fact, the Prophet Mohammed himself had married a widow whose wealth came from the spice trade; and hence from the very beginning the Islamic Empire derived its strength from both religious and commercial considerations. For several hundred years the Moslems enjoyed a complete monopoly of the spice trade. They brought spices to such European ports as Venice and Seville, where they sold them for enormous profit. They either would not tell the Europeans where the spices came from or they invented elaborate and frightening tales of the dangers

3

surrounding their origin. This only added, of course, to the mystery and romance already associated with the spice trade.

The value of spices to Europeans in the late Middle Ages can hardly be imagined today. A handful of cardamom was worth as much as a poor man's yearly wages, and many a slave was bought and sold for a few handfuls of peppercorns.

At last, however, the Europeans rediscovered the sources of the spice trade. Beginning with Marco Polo, more and more travelers ventured eastward and found where the centers of spice-growing and spice-trading were located. European traders organized new overland routes to the East, bringing new names—Kabul, Samarkand, Trebizond, Baghdad—into the mythology of Oriental adventure. And soon the intrepid sea explorers, men like Vasco da Gama, Columbus and Magellan, discovered practical sea routes to the lands of spice, and every major European port became a center of the spice trade. For years the dockworkers of London had their pockets sewed up to prevent them from pilfering peppercorns from the cargoes they unloaded. The first pure food law in history was an English ordinance passed in 1447 preventing the adulteration of spices and so checking fraud.

With the discovery of Central America and the islands of the Caribbean, new spices were added to the world's cuisine, notably paprika, cayenne and allspice. Some of these, such as paprika, became extremely popular in Europe, and then, centuries later, were reintroduced in America by emigrants from Central Europe.

The popularity of spices during the entire period of European expansion, from the fifteenth to the eighteenth century, cannot be exaggerated. Spice cookery reached extremes of complexity, especially in puddings and meat dishes; and the combinations of spices used might seem strange to modern palates. Hot spices, such as pepper, ginger and cloves from the Orient, were frequently mixed with native herbs like fennel and coriander. Sweet seasonings, such as anise, nutmeg and mint, were often added for good measure. These were the staple seasonings of the Renaissance diet, and these same seasonings and combinations of these seasonings have survived and are widely used in spice cookery today.

As the Arab monopoly of the spice trade declined, the great colonizing nations of Europe fought for supremacy. At first the Portuguese and Spanish, whose sea captains and navigators were supreme among early voyagers, enjoyed virtual dominion, and their sphere of influence extended from India and Burma to the Philippines. In 1493 Pope Alexander VI divided the New World between Spain and Portugal. In the 1500's Spain was dominant; then England and Holland successfully challenged her.

In the late seventeenth century America benefited indirectly from the spice trade. Boston-born Elihu Yale grew up in England where he worked as a clerk for the British East India Company, which held a monopoly on all trade with India and whose ships brought the first cargo of cinnamon from the Moluccas. He eventually became governor of Madras, India, and his fortune later endowed Yale University. In the late eighteenth and early nineteenth century Americans became directly involved in the spice trade as the clipper ships of New England began to dominate world trade. Indeed, so many pepper voyages from New England to Sumatra were undertaken that in 1843 the price of pepper dropped to less than three cents a pound, a disastrous slump which affected many aspects of American business. Later the New England spice trade fell off sharply when piracy in the Java and China Seas made the long pepper voyages too dangerous. Meanwhile the spice business, like the rest of the country, was moving west. In 1835 American settlers in Texas developed chili powder by combining various ground peppers from

Mexico, thus uncovering an entire new dimension of American taste. Later in California, once the gold rush had subsided, mustard seed and some herbs were grown.

America was settled by people from many nations who, in their native lands, enjoyed dishes which were distinctively spiced. But the move to America often separated them from their source of flavoring materials. Here, a different, better or more varied food supply removed one of the previous incentives for spicing. And many times the newer generation—to its own loss—consciously tried to depart from the traditional dishes of the old country. Only in recent times has the increase in international travel created a vogue for foods seasoned with spices from everywhere in the world. World War II provided an especially keen incitement; hundreds of thousands of American soldiers brought home from the war a taste for Oriental and Mediterranean foods. For example, between 1948 and 1956 the sale of oregano in the United States increased 5200 per cent. This was primarily the effect of an extraordinary new demand for pizza and other Italian specialties. Similarly, monosodium glutamate, which in cruder form had been used for centuries in Japan, was eagerly accepted by American consumers during the 1950's.

Today modern methods of growing, curing, grinding, mixing and packaging have made available a wide variety of spices, and at a cost which permits everyone to maintain a well-stocked spice shelf. Many spices, such as basil, marjoram and tarragon, are well-known and widely enjoyed; others, such as turmeric and fenugreek, are still, for the most part, known only to commercial users. But the interest in experimenting in spice cookery prevails throughout the country, and the appetite for new dishes from foreign lands is virtually insatiable. The result is that Americans today enjoy more interesting, more varied and more satisfying food than any nation has ever known before.

# HOW TO
# USE SPICES

—— * ——

The term "spice" or "spices" is often used in a general sense to mean any aromatic flavoring material of vegetable origin, and is often used in a more specific sense, together with the terms "herb," "seed" and "condiment" as defined below.

*Spices:* Aromatic natural products which are the dried seeds, buds, fruit or flower parts, bark or roots of plants, usually of tropical origin.

*Herbs:* Aromatic leaves and sometimes the flowers of plants, usually of temperate origin.

*Seeds:* Aromatic, dried, small, whole fruits or seeds, usually of temperate origin.

*Blend:* A mixture of spices, herbs, seeds or other flavoring materials either ground or whole.

*Condiment:* Any spice, herb or seed; but more frequently a pungent, prepared mixture of seasonings sometimes in liquid form. Condiments in many forms may be served as an accompaniment to foods.

Tastes differ greatly; therefore, it is very difficult to give exacting and precise directions for seasoning. What may be the ultimate to one person may be objectionable to another. The seasoning of food must vary to suit the tastes of those whom you are serving. One important rule to remember is that seasonings should be used in small quantities, particularly if it is a new flavor, as one may always add more if desired, but it is impossible to correct or remove seasoning if too much has been used initially.

Seasonings of all kinds, as well as spices and herbs, should enhance the natural flavor of food, never overpower it. Of course, there will always be a few exceptions to any rule as is the case in dishes such as curry or chili.

Spices and herbs make it possible for you to serve food which has variety and is more appetizing in aroma, more appealing in color, tastier and more digestible. Spice and herb cookery need not be complicated nor time-consuming nor expensive. It doesn't necessarily mean preparing and serving fancy, hot, exotic dishes; although, you might find these to be fun to prepare occasionally.

Well-seasoned food, very simply, is food that has been made to taste especially good without any predominating flavor. It is food that has been given a bit of flavor variety—through the correct use of spices and herbs.

\*　　\*　　\*

**Allspice** (*Pimenta officinalis*); also called Pimento, Jamaica Pepper, or Jamaica Pimento; native to Western Hemisphere and the only major spice produced exclusively in this area; discovered by Columbus in 1494, but not recognized as a spice at that time; introduced in Europe in early 17th century; the nearly ripe fruit of evergreen tree of myrtle family; fruit or berries are sun-dried until dark reddish-brown in color; available both whole and ground; flavor resembles a blend of Cloves, Cinnamon and Nutmeg and intensifies in food on standing.

### Uses

Allspice has versatility in its uses. Whole Allspice may be used in soups, stews, pot roasts, sauerbraten, sauces, marinades, beverages, pickled beets, pickles, preserves, stewed fruit and in poaching, boiling or steaming fish or shellfish.

Use ground Allspice in cakes, cookies, candy, frostings, plum pudding, fruit pies, mincemeat, fruit, meat loaf, pot roast, chili sauce, catchup, tomato sauce, spaghetti sauce, barbecue sauce, French dressing, soups, pickled eggs, sweet potatoes and squash.

### Suggested Amounts to Use in Various Dishes

GROUND
¼ teaspoon to 1 teaspoon in angel food cake mix or other cake mixes
⅛ teaspoon to ¼ teaspoon in 2 cups sweet potatoes
1 teaspoon in 1½ to 2 cups graham cracker crumbs for pie crust
¼ teaspoon to ½ teaspoon to 1 pound powdered sugar for frosting
½ teaspoon to 1 cup coconut, toasted
½ teaspoon to 1-inch thick slice ham
2 teaspoons to 2 cups waffle mix or recipe using 2 cups flour
⅛ teaspoon to 1 pound ground beef

WHOLE
3 in 2 to 3 cups pea soup
4 to 6 for each 2 pounds fish when poaching

\* \* \*

**Anise Seed** (*Pimpinella anisum*); native to Mediterranean area, also grown in Mexico; one of the commodities taxed by Edward I for revenue to repair London Bridge; green-grey fruit or seed of plant of parsley family; available whole and in extract; unmistakable strong licorice flavor.

9

## Uses

Anise Seed may be used whole or crushed in cookies, cakes, breads, candy, cheese, applesauce, sausage, beverages, fruit pies, pickles, beef stew, fruit salads, salad dressings, appetizers, baked apples, stewed fruits, sauces and in fish and shellfish cookery.

### Suggested Amounts to Use in Various Dishes

¼ teaspoon to ½ teaspoon, crushed, in 8-inch coffee cake recipe or mix

1 tablespoon sprinkled over tops of 2 dozen cup cakes

½ teaspoon to 1 teaspoon, crushed, to 6 apples—baked or stewed

1½ teaspoons to 2 teaspoons in cookie recipe yielding about 5 dozen

¼ teaspoon to ½ teaspoon, crushed, in 2 tablespoons butter for basting 1 pound fish

¼ teaspoon to ½ teaspoon in 8-ounce package cream cheese for spread for canapés

\* \* \*

**Basil** (*Ocimum basilicum*); also called Sweet Basil; native to India, also comes from North Mediterranean countries; called "Herb of Kings" by ancient Greeks and worshiped in India; leaf of plant of mint family; available as dried leaf; has aromatic clove-like aroma.

## Uses

Basil is sometimes called the "tomato herb" and may be used in most tomato recipes. Also widely used when preparing stuffings, noodles, rice, beef stew, venison, pork, hamburger, meat loaf, duck, lobster, shrimp, fish, veal, lamb, pizza, green or vegetable salads, French dressing, soups, eggplant, potatoes, carrots, spinach, peas, eggs, cheese, jelly, barbecue sauce and blends well with other herbs in seasoning foods.

### Suggested Amounts to Use in Various Dishes

¼ teaspoon to ¾ teaspoon in ½ cup butter for spreads on bread

¼ teaspoon to ½ teaspoon in 2½ cups tomato or vegetable soup

¼ teaspoon to ½ teaspoon in 2 cups green vegetables

¾ teaspoon to 1½ teaspoons to 1½ pounds pork chops or roasts

½ teaspoon to ¾ teaspoon to 1 head cauliflower

⅛ teaspoon to ¼ teaspoon in 2 tablespoons butter for basting 1 pound fish or 1½-pound chicken

¼ teaspoon to ½ teaspoon to 6 eggs—scrambled, egg salad or eggs à la goldenrod

\* \* \*

**Bay Leaves** (*Laurus nobilis*); also called Laurel Leaves; native to Mediterranean area; ancient Greeks gave bay or laurel wreaths to winners of Olympic Games, poets and heroes; aromatic dried green leaf of evergreen tree; has a distinct, strong, pungent flavor, almost bitter; strength of flavor increases with amount used and cooking time; usually removed from food when cooking is completed.

### Uses

Bay Leaves are used in soups; chowders; pickling; steaming, boiling or poaching fish and shellfish; tomato juice; custard sauce; French dressing; marinades; water for cooking vegetables; and when preparing aspics, pot roast, sauerbraten, game, variety meats and stews.

\* \* \*

**Beef Flavor Base;** seasoned extract of beef; add to water for broth; gives flavor to sauces and gravy; decrease salt in recipe when using.

## Uses

Beef Flavor Base is an excellent base for soup and gravy. It may also be used in sauces; sour cream and onion dips; casseroles; vegetables; stew; beef pot pie; noodles; certain molded salads; spreads; dumplings; beef hash; hamburgers; meat loaf; meat balls; wild or brown rice; fried rice; liquid for simmering meat balls, Swiss or country fried steak and pot roast; spaghetti sauce and in butter or liquids for stuffings.

\* \* \*

**Bon Appétit;** a blend of seasonings which has a celery note; used to enhance most foods with the exception of sweets; decrease salt in recipe when using. Bon Appétit is an extremely versatile seasoning.

## Uses

Use in all types of meat cookery, chicken and other poultry, soups, some breads, sauces, gravies, vegetables, appetizers, eggs, cheese dishes, fish and sea food, salads, salad dressings, dips, spreads, sandwich fillings, stuffings, tomato juice, cocktail sauce and seasoned butter. May also be used at the table to sprinkle over food to taste, as salt and pepper.

### Suggested Amounts to Use in Various Dishes

1 teaspoon to 1½ teaspoons to 1 pound ground beef
½ teaspoon to 1 teaspoon to 6 eggs—stuffed, scrambled or for omelettes

12

¾ teaspoon to 1½ teaspoons to 2 cups vegetables
¾ teaspoon to 1½ teaspoons to 1½ pounds beef, veal or
  other meats
1½ teaspoons to 2 teaspoons to 1 pound dried beans or
  lentils
¼ teaspoon to ½ teaspoon to each 1 cup white sauce
½ teaspoon in 1½ to 2 cups oyster stew
Sprinkle to taste over baked potatoes, French fries,
  cottage cheese, tossed salads or sliced tomatoes.

*  *  *

**Caraway Seed** (*Carum carvi*); native to Europe; imported
chiefly from the Netherlands; recorded in 1552 B.C. in
medical papyrus of Thebes; used by ancient Greeks and
Romans in cooking; the fruit or seed of plant of parsley
family; small, brown, crescent-shaped seed; distinctive
pleasant flavor with sweet undertone; use sparingly.

### Uses

Caraway Seed gives rye bread its distinctive flavor. Also
use in sauerkraut; cabbage; corn bread; biscuits;
waffles; rice; cheese dips; cottage cheese; noodles;
cheese straws; potatoes; cookies; baked or stewed apples;
seasoned butters; cake; beef or lamb stew; marinades for
meats; potato, cream of pea and corn soup and chowders; turnips; cauliflower; coleslaw; marinated cucumbers; beets; green beans; carrots; zucchini; cabbage
rolls; and in preparing pork, lamb, spareribs, roast goose
and guinea hen.

### Suggested Amounts to Use in Various Dishes

1 teaspoon to 1 tablespoon to 2 cups corn bread, waffle
  or biscuit mix
1 teaspoon in ¼ cup melted butter for vegetables
½ teaspoon to ¾ teaspoon, crushed, to 1½ pounds pork

¼ teaspoon to 1 teaspoon to 8-ounce package noodles

1 tablespoon to 2 tablespoons to 1½ cups cheese dip

¼ teaspoon to 1 teaspoon for each pound sauerkraut

½ teaspoon to 1 teaspoon in one-crust pastry for cheese, onion, meat or vegetable pies

1 teaspoon to 2 teaspoons to 3 cups potato salad

½ teaspoon to 1 teaspoon mixed in batter of pound cake or spice cake or sprinkled over top before baking

½ teaspoon in vinegar or cream dressings for 2 cups sliced cucumbers

\* \* \*

**Cardamom** (*Elletaria cardamomum*); native to India; also comes from Guatemala and Ceylon; grown in the garden of King of Babylon in 721 B.C.; used in perfumes in ancient Greece and Rome and in cosmetic industry today; fruit or seed of plant of ginger family; small three-sided, creamy white, pithy pod, having no flavor and containing aromatic dark brown seed; available both whole and ground (decorticated—pod removed); aromatic, pungent, sweet flavor; use with discretion and is good to freshen breath.

### Uses

Cardamom is a principal spice in Danish pastry. Also use in coffee cake, sweet breads, fruit salad dressings, fruit salads, curry powder, fruit pies, cookies, cakes, pickles, pickling spice, gingerbread, punch, grape jelly, custards, puddings, sweet potatoes, squash, fruit soups, hot spiced wines, barbecue sauce, rice pudding and honey.

### Suggested Amounts to Use in Various Dishes

GROUND

Dash to ¼ teaspoon in blueberry muffin mix or recipe making 12 muffins

1 tablespoon to 2 tablespoons to 3 pounds meat for stew
  or pot roast or 3 pounds chicken for stewing
2 tablespoons to 3 tablespoons in 4 cups vegetable soup

* * *

**Chicken Seasoned Stock Base;** gives richer flavor to
foods; serves as a base for chicken soup or stock; decrease
salt in recipe when using; is a very versatile seasoning.

### Uses

Chicken Seasoned Stock Base may be used in preparing
certain molded salads, dips, spreads, vegetables, soups,
pilaf, poultry dishes, stuffed eggs, rice, noodles, creamed
dishes, biscuits, dumplings, gravy, sauces, poached eggs
and fish, curries, chicken pie, skillet dishes, casseroles, in
butter or liquid for stuffings and in water for boiling corn.

* * *

**Chili Powder;** blend of spices; Aztecs used similar
blend but Chili Powder is truly from United States; Hot
Mexican-Style Chili Powder is available in some sections; flavor earthy and slightly sweet; flavor usually
intended to dominate food rather than enhance.

### Uses

Chili Powder is a major ingredient in many Mexican or
Mexican-style dishes such as chili con carne, tamale pie,
enchiladas and tamales. It may also be used in cocktail,
cream, tomato and barbecue sauces; dips; egg dishes;
gravy; stews; hamburgers and meat loaf; salad dressings;
venison dishes; corn and corn meal dishes; some skillet
dishes; chicken dishes; cheese dishes; marinades for

meats and poultry; seasoned, toasted bread slices; guacamole; bean casseroles; eggplant and Spanish rice.

### Suggested Amounts to Use in Various Dishes

¼ teaspoon to ½ teaspoon in 2 cups cream-style corn

⅛ teaspoon to ½ teaspoon to 1 large avocado when making guacamole

1 tablespoon to 2 tablespoons for ground beef, noodle or rice skillet dishes (about 8 cups)

2 tablespoons to 3 tablespoons in 6 cups chili con carne

¼ teaspoon in 1½ cups French dressing

1 tablespoon to 2 tablespoons to 4-pound pot roast

\* \* \*

**Cinnamon** [*Cinnamomum zeylanicum* (*C. loureirii*) (*C. cassia*)]; term "cinnamon" refers to several *Cinnamomum* species grown in Southeast Asia and Indonesia, sometimes called cassia, and to another *Cinnamomum* species grown in Ceylon which is mild in flavor, rarely sold in this country, and is always called cinnamon; in 1500 B.C. Egyptian Queen Hatshepsut used Cinnamon in perfumes; Moses told by God to use Cinnamon in preparing holy anointing oil; was one of the principal spices monopolized by the Dutch in 17th century; is the dried, inner bark of evergreen tree of laurel family; reddish-brown in color; the bark is peeled from young shoots of tree biannually; available whole (called sticks or quills), ground and as Cinnamon Sugar which is ground cinnamon mixed with sugar; is the most important baking spice; distinctively sweet, mildly pungent and spicy.

### Uses

Cinnamon is one of the best known and most versatile of all spices. Whole Cinnamon is used in pickling and

18

preserving; beverages; certain apple dishes; stewed prunes, apricots and other dried fruits; cooking some vegetables; hot chocolate; mulled wine; fruit compotes and as stirrers for beverages.

Ground Cinnamon is used in preparing cinnamon toast, sweet breads, fruit soup, some vegetable and meat soups, hot chocolate, fruit punches, plum pudding, fruit cake, spice cake, apple pie, apple dumplings, applesauce, apple butter, baked apples, fruit salads, puddings, custards, sweet potatoes, squash, pumpkin pie, cookies, ice cream, French toast, doughnuts, cinnamon rolls, jams, preserves, ham glaze, ham, pork, lamb roast, lamb or beef stews, creamed chicken, spiced nuts, chocolate fudge and dessert sauces. Sprinkle over cakes; cookies; hot cereals; eggnog; milk shakes; custards; broiled grapefruit and rice, bread or tapioca puddings.

### Suggested Amounts to Use in Various Dishes

**GROUND**

1 teaspoon to 4 teaspoons in 2-layer chocolate cake recipe or mix

½ teaspoon to 1 teaspoon in chocolate pudding recipe or mix using about 2 cups milk

⅛ teaspoon to ¾ teaspoon in vanilla pudding recipe or mix using about 2 cups milk

1 teaspoon in 1 quart vanilla ice cream

1 teaspoon in 2½ to 3 cups apples for pie, apple crisp or stewed apples

¼ teaspoon to 1 teaspoon in 2 cups sweet potatoes

Dash to ⅛ teaspoon in 1 quart chicken, tomato or fruit soup

**WHOLE**

1 3-inch piece to 4 cups rhubarb

1 to 2 3-inch pieces to 3 cups stewed fruit or fruit compotes

1 to 2 3-inch pieces in 1 quart hot beverage such as cider, tea or coffee

1 to 2 3-inch pieces to 1 quart cranberries for pie, sauce, relish or salad

1 3-inch piece in making 2 cups custard sauce

1 3-inch piece in each quart spiced peaches

*   *   *

**Cloves** (*Eugenia caryophyllata*); name comes from "clou" (French) meaning nail; native to Molucca Islands, also from Zanzibar and the Malagasy Republic; courtiers required to hold Cloves in mouth when addressing emperor during Chinese Han Dynasty 206 B.C. to 220 A.D.; Constantine presented Cloves to Bishop of Rome; seed of the clove tree were stolen from the Dutch in 18th century in an attempt to break Dutch monopoly on spice trade; is the dried, unopened bud of evergreen tree of myrtle family; available whole and ground; whole Cloves resemble nails; reddish-brown in color; flavor is penetrating, sweet and pungent—almost hot; use cautiously; flavor intensifies upon standing.

### Uses

Whole Cloves are used widely for garnishes as well as flavor. Use to stud ham, fruit, fruit peels, onions or glazed pork or beef. Use in beverages, pot roast, marinades, sauces, pickling, soups, tomato juice, spiced tongue and in making pomander balls.

Ground Cloves is used in spice cakes, fruit cakes, gingerbread, plum pudding, cookies, some breads, fruit salads, chili sauce, catchup, pickling, frostings, cooked fruits, beef stew, pot roast, tomatoes, sweet potatoes, squash, green vegetables, spiced nuts, meringues, glazes, mincemeat, fruit pies, beverages, soups and in combination with other spices.

20

*Suggested Amounts to Use in Various Dishes*

**GROUND**

⅛ teaspoon to ¼ teaspoon in 4 cups rhubarb

¾ teaspoon to 6-pound pork roast

Dash to ¼ teaspoon in mincemeat or fruit pies

⅛ teaspoon in 2 cups green vegetables, squash, carrots or sweet potatoes

¼ teaspoon to ½ teaspoon in 8 cups blueberry, cherry or grape jam or jelly

½ teaspoon in cookie recipe yielding about 7 dozen cookies

½ teaspoon to 1 teaspoon in recipe yielding 12 to 14 pounds fruit cake

**WHOLE**

4 to 12 when cooking 1 cup rice

1 to 2 for each cup hot or iced tea or mulled wine

2 to 3 for each peach in making spiced pickled peaches

6 to 8 in marinade for 4 pounds meat

1 in each Kaurabiedes (Greek Easter cookie)

½ teaspoon to 1 teaspoon in 2 cups spiced cherries

\* \* \*

**Coriander** (*Coriandrum sativum*); native to Southern Europe and Mediterranean region; recorded in 1552 B.C. in medical papyrus of Thebes; Moses compared color of manna with Coriander Seed; ancient Greeks and Romans used it in love potions; is the dried fruit or seed of plant belonging to parsley family and has slight lemon flavor.

*Uses*

Use the whole Coriander Seed in punch, sweet pickles, after-dinner coffee and wassail bowl. The crushed seed are used in preparing candies; cookies; gingerbread; Danish pastry; poaching, broiling or baking fish;

chicken; curry sauces; sausage; meat loaf and hamburgers; bean, pea, lentil and vegetable-beef soups and Scotch broth; apple pie; coffee cake; sweet buns; muffins; waffles; rice pudding; bread pudding; tapioca; custards; cream cheese (especially good for filling for date bread); applesauce; stewed fruits; fruit sauces; beef or lamb stew; roast pork; pork chops; ham; stuffing for poultry and game and meat sauces.

### Suggested Amounts to Use in Various Dishes

2 teaspoons, crushed, to 3-pound chicken
¾ teaspoon, crushed, in 9- or 10-inch apple pie
½ teaspoon to 1 teaspoon, crushed, to 1 pound fish
¼ teaspoon, crushed, in 2 cups biscuit mix or recipe making 12 biscuits or muffins
1 teaspoon, crushed, to 2 pounds ground beef
¼ teaspoon, crushed, in 1 quart vegetable-beef soup
¼ teaspoon, crushed, in ¼ cup butter for 2 cups vegetables
1 whole seed in each cup demitasse coffee
6 to 10 whole seeds in marinade for 2 pounds meat

\* \* \*

**Cumin** (*Cuminum cyminum*); also Comino and Cummin; native to Mediterranean region; imported from Iran and Morocco; Babylonian and Assyrian doctors used it in drugs; used as food preservative by early Greeks and Romans; is the dried, yellowish-brown fruit or seed of plant of parsley family; available whole and ground; has an earthy and strong flavor; use sparingly.

### Uses

Cumin is used commercially as a principal ingredient in both Chili Powder and Curry Powder. Cumin Seed are

22

sometimes substituted for Caraway Seed. May be used either whole or ground in cheese and cheese dishes, rice, chili con carne, tamales, tamale pie, eggs, meat loaf and hamburgers, soup, stew, salad dressings, tomato sauce, barbecue sauce, sauerkraut, cookies, bread, marinades for shish kebab, potatoes, lentils, cabbage, dried beans of all kinds and in cooking game, wild fowl and spareribs.

### Suggested Amounts to Use in Various Dishes

⅛ teaspoon to ¼ teaspoon in cooking 1 cup rice

Dash to ¼ teaspoon to 6 eggs—stuffed or baked Mexican style

¼ teaspoon to ½ teaspoon in marinade for 1½ pounds lamb or beef

Dash to ⅛ teaspoon in 1 cup salad dressing or mayonnaise

Dash to ⅛ teaspoon in 4 cups chowders, bisques and lentil, bean, pea or chicken soup

Dash to ½ teaspoon to 3 pounds beef for pot roast or stew

Ground Cumin and Cumin Seed, whole or crushed, may be used interchangeably in many recipes.

\* \* \*

**Curry Powder;** not a single spice but a blend of many spices which will vary according to the type Curry Powder as well as to the manufacturer; basic ingredient for all curried dishes; available as Indian Curry Powder, mild, and Madras Curry Powder, hot; is golden yellow to yellow-brown in color; use sparingly at first; may be used to enhance the flavor of food as well as to dominate; has an exotic aroma; is one of the oldest spice blends; originated in India where the Indians mixed their own spices to taste, and probably varied from time to time or meal to meal. Curry in India is usually very hot.

## Uses

Both Indian and Madras Curry Powder are used to make curried beef, lamb, fish, shrimp, lobster, rice, chicken, meat pastries, meat balls, eggs, fruit, pork, veal, duck, sauce, soup, casseroles, dips and as a seasoning in salad dressings, some vegetables, dried beans, breads and marinades.

### Suggested Amounts to Use in Various Dishes

1 tablespoon to 3 tablespoons to 1 pound cubed lamb

½ teaspoon to 1 teaspoon in corn bread recipe or mix making 12 muffins

1 tablespoon to 2 tablespoons in 6 cups mixed fruit for compote

¼ teaspoon to ½ teaspoon for 6 stuffed eggs

1 teaspoon to 3 teaspoons for 2 cups creamy curry sauce

1 teaspoon in 1 cup mayonnaise, cream cheese, commercial sour cream or a combination of these for a dip

½ teaspoon to 1 teaspoon in 2 cups sea food salad

\* \* \*

**Dill** (*Anethum graveolens*); native to Europe; Dill Seed imported from India; Dill Weed grown in California; was used in drugs by Babylonian and Assyrian doctors; the dried fruit or seed and leaves of plant of parsley family; is available as seed and weed (leaves); Dill Seed are flat, oval and light brown; Dill Weed is bright green; the flavor of Dill Weed is delicate, more subtle than Dill Seed and imparts a pleasing flavor to mild or bland foods; Dill Seed have a pungent, aromatic and characteristic flavor.

### Uses

Dill Seed are used in dill pickles, Kosher dill pickles, salads, sauerkraut, green beans, egg dishes, tomato juice,

24

soups, sauces, cottage and cream cheese, stews, pickled beets, salad dressings, breads, butters and in preparing fish, shellfish and chicken.

Dill Weed is used in salads, sauces, egg dishes, tomato juice, vegetables, breads, fish and shellfish recipes, cottage or cream cheese, salad dressings, noodles, rice and may be used as a garnish.

### Suggested Amounts to Use in Various Dishes

**DILL SEED**

¼ teaspoon to 1 teaspoon to 1 head cauliflower

⅛ teaspoon to ½ teaspoon in 2 cups green vegetables

½ teaspoon to ¾ teaspoon, crushed, to 1 pound ground beef

3 tablespoons to 5 tablespoons in each quart dill pickles

¼ teaspoon to ½ teaspoon, crushed, in 2 tablespoons butter for seasoning fish, vegetables or bread

**DILL WEED**

⅛ teaspoon to 1 teaspoon in 1½ cups cottage cheese

¼ teaspoon to ½ teaspoon in 1 cup white sauce

¼ teaspoon to ½ teaspoon to 6 stuffed eggs

¼ teaspoon to ¾ teaspoon in 2 cups green vegetables

½ teaspoon to 1 teaspoon in 8-ounce package noodles

¼ teaspoon to ½ teaspoon to 3-pound chicken

½ teaspoon in 1 cup commercial sour cream

\* \* \*

**Fennel Seed** (*Foeniculum vulgare*); native to Mediterranean region; imported from India; was used in drugs by Babylonian and Assyrian doctors; grew in gardens of Charlemagne; Puritans nibbled the seed in church and called it "meetin' seed"; is the aromatic dried fruit or seed of plant of parsley family; oval and yellowish-brown; and has slight flavor of licorice.

## Uses

Fennel Seed are used in egg dishes, fish cookery, stews, breads, sea food salads, salad dressings, vegetables, cheese dishes, baked or stewed apples, pickles, soups, sauerkraut, spaghetti sauce, marinades, sautéed mushrooms, boiling shellfish, cakes, cookies and oyster dishes.

### Suggested Amounts to Use in Various Dishes

1 teaspoon to 2 teaspoons, crushed, to 1 pound fish

A few seed to ⅛ teaspoon in water when cooking artichokes, broccoli, Brussels sprouts, cauliflower, beans and lentils

¼ teaspoon to ¾ teaspoon for 4-pound pork roast

⅛ teaspoon, crushed, in 3 cups potato salad

5 to 10 seeds in ½ cup sautéed mushrooms

⅛ teaspoon to ½ teaspoon in water when boiling 1 pound shrimp

\* \* \*

**Garlic** (*Allium sativum*); probably native to Southern Europe or Central Asia; grown world over; famous in history and various parts of the world since earliest recorded days; prized as a food by ancient Greeks and Romans; was an important food in the diet of Egyptian slaves who built the Pyramids and among the legions of ancient Rome; was considered valuable as a remedy; Hippocrates warned that it was bad for the eyes but good for the body; the ancients thought the smell of garlic drove away serpents and scorpions; is a bulbous annual of the lily family; edible part is the bulbous root made of small sections called "cloves" covered by a thin white skin; is available in a number of convenient forms —Garlic Powder, Garlic Salt, Garlic Chips, Instant Minced Garlic, Garlic Juice and Liquid Garlic—which eliminate peeling and mincing of fresh garlic; dehydrated products release flavor only after they are moistened; flavor is strong and pungent; one of the most popular seasonings; a favorite seasoning in many French and Italian foods. Garlic Powder and Instant Minced Garlic may be used in any recipe calling for fresh garlic; Garlic Chips may be used in any recipe where small pieces of garlic are desirable; decrease the amount of salt called for in recipe when using Garlic Salt.

## Equivalents

⅛ teaspoon Garlic Powder, Instant Minced Garlic or Garlic Chips is equivalent to 1 average-size clove of fresh garlic

½ teaspoon Garlic Salt is equivalent to 1 average-size clove fresh garlic

## Uses

Any of the garlic products may be increased or decreased to suit individual taste.

Garlic products are excellent in tomato dishes; soups; dips; sauces; butters; gravies; salads; salad dressings; dill pickles; some vegetables; meat, poultry or fish cookery; some cheese dishes; stews; marinades and for making garlic bread. Garlic may be used in combination with onion.

## Suggested Amounts to Use in Various Dishes

GARLIC POWDER

⅛ teaspoon to ¼ teaspoon to 2 pounds pork, beef, lamb or other meats

⅛ teaspoon to ½ teaspoon in ½ cup butter for bread, vegetables and grilled meats

⅛ teaspoon to ¼ teaspoon in 3 cups tomato, barbecue or other sauces

Dash to ⅛ teaspoon in 3 cups tomato or meat stock soups

When using Garlic Powder in a recipe with a high acid content, a more distinctive garlic flavor may be obtained by moistening the Garlic Powder in water before adding. Use 2 parts water to 1 part Garlic Powder.

### GARLIC SALT

1 teaspoon to 1¼ teaspoons to 1 pound ground beef or lamb

Dash to ½ teaspoon to 6 eggs, stuffed or for omelettes

May be sprinkled to taste on broiled foods such as chicken, chops, fish, steaks and tomatoes.

### GARLIC CHIPS

⅛ teaspoon to ¼ teaspoon in each quart Kosher dill pickles or in each pint dilled green beans

⅛ teaspoon to ½ teaspoon to 3-pound chicken for stewing

Use in place of fresh garlic in soups, stews, marinades and pickling.

May be inserted into meats before roasting.

### INSTANT MINCED GARLIC

1½ teaspoons in 1 cup vinegar-oil salad dressing

Dash to ⅛ teaspoon in making 2 pints chutney or relish

⅛ teaspoon to ¼ teaspoon in each quart Kosher dill pickles or in each pint dilled green beans

### LIQUID GARLIC

Concentrated in flavor. Use sparingly—one drop or more—to suit individual taste. Excellent for dips, spreads and salads.

### GARLIC JUICE

Use Garlic Juice when a mild flavor of garlic is desired. It combines well with other ingredients, giving an even over-all hint of garlic.

½ teaspoon to 1 teaspoon in 2 cups tomato, pizza or spaghetti sauce

1 teaspoon to 2 teaspoons in ½ cup butter for garlic butter

½ teaspoon to 1 teaspoon combined with 1 tablespoon oil or melted butter for basting broiled fish, chops, chicken or steak

\* \* \*

**Ginger** (*Zingiber officinale*); native to Southeast Asia; also comes from Jamaica; one of the first Oriental spices known in Europe; Marco Polo wrote of finding Ginger in China; is the dried and peeled rhizomes (roots) of ginger plant; available whole and ground; is light buff in color and has a hot, spicy, sweet flavor; Crystallized Ginger is fresh root cooked in syrup and is used as a confection or condiment, not a spice.

### Uses

Whole Ginger is used in pickling, syrups, beverages, marinades, stewed fruit, teriyaki sauce, preserves, tea and ginger beer.

Some recipes refer to "bruised" Ginger. To bruise Ginger, pound to break skin but not root.

Ground Ginger is one of the most versatile of all spices. Use in preparing cakes; cookies; gingerbread; ginger toast; bread; rice, bread, fruit or steamed puddings; custards; whipped cream; sauces; soups; appetizers; Oriental dishes; lamb; pork; beef; veal; venison; nearly all vegetables, particularly good in sweet potatoes and carrots; pickles; chutney; preserves; conserves; baked or stewed fruits; fruit pies and salads; salad dressings; punch; chicken and other poultry; and ice cream. It is excellent in combination with other spices.

### Suggested Amounts to Use in Various Dishes

¼ teaspoon to 2 teaspoons for 1½ pounds pork
Dash to ¼ teaspoon to 2 cups sliced carrots

¼ teaspoon to 3 cups mixed fruit
¼ teaspoon to 1 cup coconut, toasted
¼ teaspoon to 1 teaspoon in 2 cups sweet potatoes
Dash to ¼ teaspoon in bread puddings and rice puddings
  yielding 4 to 6 servings
1 teaspoon to 1½ teaspoons in cookie recipe (2 cups
  flour)
⅛ teaspoon to ¼ teaspoon to 2 egg whites for meringues

Ground Ginger may be used in many recipes in place of whole Ginger—1 teaspoon ground Ginger may be substituted for 10 to 12 pieces whole Ginger about the size of shelled peanuts.

*　*　*

**Herb Seasoning;** a unique blend of a number of herbs and spices in proportions that impart a well-rounded, smooth flavor to foods; designed primarily as an all-purpose seasoning; for those who desire a warm, full-bodied flavor without an onion or garlic note.

### Uses

Herb Seasoning is a convenient seasoning to use in the preparation of meats, vegetables, breads, gravies, poultry, game, meat spreads, croutons, cheese spreads, fish, sauces, stuffings and herb butters.

### Suggested Amounts to Use in Various Dishes

¼ teaspoon to ¾ teaspoon in 2 cups tomatoes
½ teaspoon to 1 teaspoon in 2 cups biscuit mix or recipe
  making 12 biscuits
¼ teaspoon to 1¼ teaspoons in 2 cups green vegetables
¾ teaspoon to 1½ teaspoons for 1½ pounds beef
1 teaspoon in 2 cups waffle mix or recipe using 2 cups
  flour

Dash to ¼ teaspoon to 1 cup bread cubes for herb croutons

½ teaspoon to 1½ teaspoons in corn bread mix or recipe
making 12 muffins or corn sticks

\*   \*   \*

**Lemon Peel** (*Citrus limon*) and **Orange Peel** (*Citrus
sinenis*); lemon tree probably native to Northern India;
today is grown in subtropics and tropics for commercial
purpose; toward the end of the 1st century lemon trees
were grown in Mediterranean region. Orange tree
probably native to Southern China and Burma; the
sweet orange is grown in every subtropical region of the
world; was apparently unknown to Europeans prior to
the 15th century; there are many familiar varieties of
the sweet orange. Both Lemon and Orange Peel are the
dried natural rind of the fresh fruits used for juice
extraction; dried rinds are processed by milling; small
particles are sifted out; flavor of oil is restored to peel
since some oil is lost in processing; the flavor of the
dehydrated peels is very similar to that of the grated
fresh peel.

### Equivalents

It is difficult to give exact equivalents in relation to the
fresh peel. This is due to the great variance in fresh
lemons and oranges as to type of fruit, source, size,
ripeness, peel thickness, how grated, size of grate used
and how measured (loosely or packed down). Use
slightly less or equal amounts of Lemon Peel and Orange
Peel to grated fresh peel as called for in recipes.

### Uses

Lemon Peel and Orange Peel may be used in the preparation of bread or rice puddings, breads, meringue shells
and tortes, short cakes, cakes, cookies, frostings, fillings,

custards, dessert soufflés, fruit pies, pastry, pork, chicken, duckling, glazes for ham, dessert and meat sauces, stuffings and most vegetables.

### Suggested Amounts to Use in Various Dishes

LEMON PEEL OR ORANGE PEEL

1 teaspoon to 3 teaspoons to 2 cups dried prunes or other fruits

4 teaspoons in 2 cups waffle mix or recipe using 2 cups flour

½ teaspoon to 1 teaspoon Lemon Peel to 1 pound fish

¼ teaspoon to 1½ teaspoons in vanilla pudding recipe or mix using 2 cups milk

1½ teaspoons to 3 teaspoons in 2-layer cake or 8-inch coffee cake

½ teaspoon to 1½ teaspoons in 2 cups peas or carrots

1 teaspoon to 2 teaspoons for 3 pounds pork, ham, chicken or duckling

\* \* \*

**Mace** (*Myristica fragrans*); native to Molucca Islands; imported from Indonesia and West Indies; at end of 12th century Mace was mentioned in Denmark and Europe and may have been used earlier but historians are not sure; the Dutch tried to destroy half the nutmeg trees in the Moluccas but birds carried seed to other islands; a part of the fruit of the evergreen nutmeg tree; is the bright red aril or skin covering the shell of the Nutmeg and turns brownish-orange when dried; whole Mace is called blades of Mace; available ground; flavor similar to Nutmeg but more delicate; Mace and Nutmeg are the only two spices found naturally on same plant.

### Uses

Mace has a variety of uses and can be substituted for Nutmeg in recipes. Use Mace in preparing pound cake;

spice cake; devil's food cake; gingerbread; frostings; hot chocolate; puddings; custards; fruit, chiffon, custard or refrigerator pies; breads; soups; punches; pork; beef; lamb; chicken; fish; apple dishes; sauces; creamed dishes; waffles; pancakes; doughnuts; coffee cakes; Danish pastries; glazes; muffins; vegetables; fruit salads; fruit salad dressings; cream cheese spreads for fruit and nut breads and candy.

### Suggested Amounts to Use in Various Dishes

Dash to ½ teaspoon in recipe or mix making 12 muffins
⅛ teaspoon to ¼ teaspoon in chocolate pudding mix or recipe using about 2 cups milk or in 2-layer chocolate cake recipe or mix
¼ teaspoon in stewing 2 cups dried apricots
⅛ teaspoon to ¼ teaspoon in 8-inch coffee cake recipe or mix
1 teaspoon in 2 cups waffle mix or recipe using 2 cups flour
Dash in 1 package frozen spinach or about 1 cup cooked, fresh spinach
Dash to ⅛ teaspoon in 4 cups creamed chicken or tuna
Dash to ⅛ teaspoon in 2 cups white sauce
⅛ teaspoon to ¼ teaspoon in 2 cups powdered sugar for glaze
⅛ teaspoon to ¼ teaspoon in a pound cake recipe or mix

\* \* \*

**Marjoram** (*Majorana hortensis*); native to Mediterranean region; probably used by ancient Egyptians; used as medicine by Hippocrates; symbol of happiness in ancient Greece; was used in medicines in Middle Ages; is the dried, grey-green leaves of plant of mint family; available as dried leaves and ground; has a distinctively aromatic and pleasant flavor with bitter undertone; use sparingly at first and increase to taste.

## Uses

Marjoram may be used in almost any dish except sweet foods. Use it in the preparation of lamb; pork; beef; veal; venison and other game; chicken; broiled or baked fish; shellfish; practically all tomato dishes; other vegetables such as carrots, cauliflower, peas, spinach, squash, mushrooms, beans, broccoli and Brussels sprouts; pizza; spaghetti and brown sauces; stuffings; egg dishes; breads; tossed green salads; salad dressings; soups such as onion, turtle, vegetable, spinach, Scotch broth and minestrone; oyster and clam chowder; and jelly.

### Suggested Amounts to Use in Various Dishes

½ teaspoon to 1 teaspoon in 2 cups green vegetables
¼ teaspoon to ½ teaspoon to 3-pound chicken
⅛ teaspoon to ½ teaspoon for 1½ pounds pork
¼ teaspoon to ½ teaspoon for 1 pound beef or veal
Dash to ¼ teaspoon to 4 eggs—scrambled, stuffed or for omelettes
½ teaspoon in 2 cups carrots
Dash to ¼ teaspoon in 2 cups tomato sauce
¼ teaspoon for each 3 cups bread cubes for stuffing
½ teaspoon in 2 cups biscuit, waffle or corn bread mix

\* \* \*

**Mint** (*Mentha spicata*); also called Spearmint; native to Europe and Asia; was used by ancient Assyrians in rituals to the Fire-God; mentioned in New Testament; named by Greeks after mythical character Minthe; is the dried leaf of spearmint plant; available as flakes or in extract form; has an aromatic, sweet flavor with cool aftertaste.

## Uses

Use in punches, tea, sauces for desserts, sauces for lamb, mint jelly, syrups, fruit compotes, fruit soup, split pea soup, devil's food cake, frostings, ice cream and sherbet, chocolate desserts, custards, candies, hot chocolate, vegetables, lamb stew and on lamb roast.

### Suggested Amounts to Use in Various Dishes

MINT FLAKES

¼ teaspoon to ½ teaspoon, crushed, in chocolate pudding mix or recipe using about 2 cups milk

¼ teaspoon to 1 teaspoon, crushed, in 2-layer white cake recipe or mix

½ teaspoon to 1½ teaspoons, crushed, in 2-layer chocolate cake recipe or mix

¼ teaspoon to 1 teaspoon, crushed, in 2 cups peas

¼ teaspoon in lamb stew (1 to 1½ pounds meat)

¼ teaspoon to 1 teaspoon in 3 to 4 cups fruit

½ teaspoon in 1 quart tea or fruit beverages

\* \* \*

**Mustard** (*Brassica hirta*—Yellow or White; *Brassica juncea*—Brown or Black); native to Europe and Southwestern Asia; grown in temperate regions, especially California and Montana; well known since days of ancient Greece as a condiment and for medicinal uses; frequently referred to in the New Testament and in Greek and Roman writings; is an annual herb plant bearing small seed; two varieties are utilized, yellow seed and brown seed; the yellow often referred to as white and the brown as black; dry Mustard is a mixture of the two varieties; letters DSF on label, meaning "Double Superfine," indicate very fine grind and high quality; the yellow variety is used for the whole Mustard Seed; both

35

varieties are pungent in flavor; is available as Mustard
Seed and dry Mustard, often referred to as mustard flour.

## Uses

Mustard Seed are used in preparing cucumber pickles,
vegetable relishes, corned beef, boiled beef, coleslaw,
potato salad, boiled cabbage and sauerkraut. Dry
Mustard adds zip to egg and cheese dishes, salad dressings, appetizers, meats, poultry, sauces and vegetables.

### Suggested Amounts to Use in Various Dishes

DRY MUSTARD

¼ teaspoon to ½ teaspoon in 6 eggs—stuffed, scrambled
 or for omelettes

¼ teaspoon to ½ teaspoon in 1 pound ground beef

¼ teaspoon to ¾ teaspoon to 1 pound ham

½ teaspoon to 1 teaspoon in 1 teaspoon vinegar and dash
 Turmeric to make about 2 teaspoons mustard sauce
 (hotter than commercial prepared mustard)

MUSTARD SEED

2 tablespoons for 8 pints bread and butter pickles

¼ cup to ⅔ cup for 6 pints tomato or vegetable relish

\* \* \*

Nutmeg (*Myristica fragrans*); native to Molucca Islands;
now grown in hot moist climates of the tropics (Indonesia
or West Indies); reached Europe by 12th century; the
Portuguese, and then the Dutch, monopolized nutmeg
trade for centuries; Yankee traders, making and selling
wooden Nutmegs for real Nutmegs, caused Connecticut
to be known as "The Nutmeg State"; is the oval-shaped,
dried seed of an apricot-like fruit of an evergreen tree
which bears for more than fifty years; scarlet aril covering the shell of the Nutmeg is Mace; after separation

both are dried; Nutmeg is available whole and ground; flavor sweet, warm and highly spicy; commercially used to season sausage and luncheon meats.

## Uses

Nutmeg is not only appetizing in sweet foods but enhances flavor of meats and vegetables. Ground Nutmeg or the freshly grated whole Nutmeg may be sprinkled over hot and cold milk drinks, eggnog, fruits, puddings, soups and used to season meats, poultry, sea food, vegetables and sauces. Use in making cakes, cookies, doughnuts, pies, pastries, muffins, waffles and coffee cake.

### Suggested Amounts to Use in Various Dishes

¼ teaspoon to ½ teaspoon in 2-layer white or yellow cake recipe or mix

½ teaspoon to 1 teaspoon for two-crust pastry

Dash to ¼ teaspoon in 2 cups spinach, mixed vegetables, sliced carrots and most other vegetables

⅛ teaspoon to ¾ teaspoon in vanilla pudding mix or recipe using about 2 cups milk

¼ teaspoon in about 2 cups batter for muffins, coffee cakes and waffles

½ teaspoon in chocolate frosting for 2 cake layers

⅛ teaspoon to ¼ teaspoon in 1 cup heavy cream, whipped, or 1 cup powdered sugar for a glaze

Dash to ⅛ teaspoon in 4 cups creamed chicken or tuna

⅛ teaspoon for 1 pound beef

¼ teaspoon to ½ teaspoon in a pound cake recipe or mix

One whole Nutmeg, grated, equals 2 to 3 teaspoons ground Nutmeg.

* * *

**Onion** (*Allium cepa*); native to Western Asia; known to history for more than 4,000 years; was cultivated by ancient Babylonians; also part of diet of slaves who built the Pyramids in Egypt; available as Onion Powder, Onion Salt, Instant Minced Onion, Onion Flakes, Chopped Instant Onions, Shredded Green Onions and Onion Juice; the bulb of onion plant which is member of lily family; bottled Onion Juice is processed from juice squeezed from fresh onion; Shredded Green Onions obtained from green top; all other products are obtained from dehydrated onion bulb; Onion Salt, a mixture of salt and onion powder—decrease salt in recipe when using; Instant Minced Onion, Onion Flakes and Chopped Instant Onions differ only in size of particle.

Onion is probably one of the most universal seasonings. All onion products are interchangeable as far as flavor is concerned; however, Shredded Green Onions impart a milder flavor. Use Onion Powder, Onion Salt or Onion Juice for flavor only; or for both flavor and texture, use Instant Minced Onion, Chopped Instant Onions or Onion Flakes.

### Uses

Onion products may be used in the preparation of appetizers and dips, soups and chowders, stews, all meats, game, fish, shellfish, poultry, salads and salad dressings, sauces, vegetables, gravies, stuffings, cheese dishes, egg dishes, breads, casseroles, croquettes and rice dishes.

### Equivalents

1 tablespoon Onion Powder equals 1 medium-size fresh onion

1 tablespoon Instant Minced Onion equals ¼ cup minced raw onion

1 tablespoon Onion Flakes equals ¼ cup chopped raw onion

¼ cup Chopped Instant Onions equals 1 cup chopped raw onion

### Suggested Amounts to Use in Various Dishes

ONION POWDER

¼ teaspoon to 1 teaspoon in 2 cups green, yellow or white vegetables

1 teaspoon to 1 pound cooked meat for spreads

When using Onion Powder in a recipe with an extremely high acid content, a more distinctive onion flavor may be obtained by moistening Onion Powder in water before adding to the recipe; use 2 parts water to 1 part Onion Powder.

ONION SALT

1 teaspoon to 2 teaspoons in 2 cups green, yellow or white vegetables

¼ teaspoon to 1 teaspoon to 1 pound chicken, stew meat, ground meat, veal, variety meats, game, roasts, steaks or chops

INSTANT MINCED ONION

½ teaspoon to 1½ teaspoons in 1 cup vinegar-oil salad dressing

1 tablespoon to 2 tablespoons for 1 pound dried beans

1 teaspoon to 2 teaspoons in 2 cups green, yellow or white vegetables

2 teaspoons to 3 teaspoons to 1 pound ground beef, lamb or veal

1 teaspoon to 3 teaspoons to a 7-ounce can tuna for salad or spreads

ONION FLAKES

1 tablespoon to 2 tablespoons in 4 cups soup

1 tablespoon to 2 tablespoons in 2 cups barbecued beef

2 teaspoons to 2 tablespoons in 2 cups sauces and gravies

CHOPPED INSTANT ONIONS

1 tablespoon to 3 tablespoons, plain or toasted, in 1 cup
  commercial sour cream for dip
¼ cup in 6 cups chowder or chicken or vegetable soup

Particularly good as sautéed onions for French onion
soup or with liver or hamburgers. Reconstitute in ice
water for use in salads.

SHREDDED GREEN ONIONS

½ teaspoon to 1 teaspoon to 6 eggs—creamed, scrambled
  or for omelettes
1 teaspoon to 2 teaspoons for 2 cups corn, sautéed or in
  casserole
1 tablespoon in cooking 1 cup rice or noodles

May be used as a garnish.

ONION JUICE

Use Onion Juice when a mild flavor of onion is desired.
It combines well with other ingredients giving an even
over-all hint of onion.

1 teaspoon to 2 teaspoons in ½ cup commercial sour
  cream to use as dip or topping for vegetables and soup
1 teaspoon in 1½ cups oil-vinegar salad dressing

*　　*　　*

**Oregano** (Species of *Lippia*, *Origanum* and sometimes
other genera); native to Mediterranean region; another
strain of Oregano is common to Mexico; has been used
since early days of ancient Rome; the dried leaves of a
perennial plant; available as leaves and ground; flavor
strong and aromatic with pleasant bitter undertone;
sometimes referred to as "Wild Marjoram"; flavor
similar to sweet Marjoram but stronger; an essential
ingredient of Chili Powder; practically unknown in the
United States until after World War II; the increased
popularity of pizza has stimulated the use of Oregano.

40

## Uses

Oregano goes well with tomatoes and is a natural seasoning with any tomato dish. Use to season pasta sauces, tomato juice, pizza, chili con carne, barbecue sauce and vegetable soup. It is excellent in egg and cheese dishes, onions, sea food salads, stuffings for meat or poultry, sauce for fish, and on pork, lamb, chicken and fish.

### Suggested Amounts to Use in Various Dishes

GROUND

¼ teaspoon to ¾ teaspoon in 1 pound ground beef

¼ teaspoon to ½ teaspoon for 1 pound pork

LEAVES

¼ teaspoon to ¾ teaspoon to 4 eggs for egg salad

¼ teaspoon to ½ teaspoon in ½ cup butter for baked potatoes, bread or basting fish

¼ teaspoon to ½ teaspoon in 2 cups spinach, green beans or 3 cups tomatoes

1 teaspoon to 3 cups flour in making yeast bread

1 teaspoon sprinkled over top of 12- to 14-inch pizza

⅛ teaspoon to ¼ teaspoon in 2 cups tomato, spaghetti or barbecue sauce (ground Oregano may also be used)

\* \* \*

**Paprika** (*Capsicum annuum*); native to Central America; early Spanish explorers took plants back to Europe; most is imported from Spain and Central Europe, but the plant is grown commercially in California as well; Hungarian scientist won Nobel Prize for research in vitamin content of Paprika; a richer source of Vitamin C than citrus fruits; valuable vitamins in Paprika, principally C and A; the dried, stemless pod of a sweet red pepper; available ground; most Paprika consumed in the United States is mild and slightly sweet in flavor;

agreeably aromatic and bright red in color; another type, pungent and of lighter color, is Hungarian Paprika.

### Uses

Paprika is one of the three most popular seasonings. Use as a colorful garnish for any light colored food. Sprinkle on fish, meats, canapés, soups, potatoes, eggs and sauces. Used in generous quantities, Paprika is the principal seasoning in such dishes as Hungarian goulash and chicken or veal paprika and is often used in making French dressing.

### Suggested Amounts to Use in Various Dishes

½ teaspoon to 2 tablespoons in flour for dredging 3 pounds chicken or meat

¼ teaspoon to ¾ teaspoon in 1 cup vinegar-oil for French dressing

½ teaspoon in ¼ cup butter for sautéing potatoes or to season white vegetables

½ teaspoon to 1 teaspoon in 1 cup Welsh rabbit

1 teaspoon to 1 tablespoon to 3 pounds beef in Hungarian goulash

1 teaspoon to 1 tablespoon to 2 pounds veal in veal paprika

\* \* \*

**Parsley** (*Petroselinum crispum*); native to rocky shores of the Mediterranean; the curly leaf variety, chiefly grown in California, is the main source of dehydrated Parsley Flakes; plain leaf parsley is naturalized both in the United States and several European countries; used generously to flavor and garnish foods as early as the 3rd century B.C.; the colonists introduced it to America; the dried leaves of a biennial plant; available as dehydrated flakes; excellent source of Vitamin C and several minerals; pleasant mild odor and agreeable taste; blends well with all other herbs; is used both for eye and taste appeal in most food except sweets.

## Uses

This mild flavored herb is often used both in and on food. Garnish and flavor canapés, soups, tossed green salads, coleslaw, breads, herb sauces and butters, tomato and meat sauces, stuffings for fish and meats, broiled or fried fish, meats and poultry.

### Suggested Amounts to Use in Various Dishes

2 teaspoons to 4 teaspoons in 8-ounce package noodles or 3 cups cooked rice

1 teaspoon to 2 teaspoons in 2 cups waffle mix or recipe using 2 cups flour

1 teaspoon to 2 teaspoons in 2 to 3 cups tomato sauce

1 teaspoon to 2 teaspoons to 1 pound crab meat for crab cakes; 1 pint oysters for scalloped oysters; or 2 cups tuna, salmon or chicken for croquettes

½ teaspoon to 1 teaspoon in ½ cup butter for vegetables, fish or meats

¼ teaspoon to 1 teaspoon to 2 eggs—scrambled or for omelette

\* \* \*

**Pepper** (*Piper nigrum*); native to East Indies; imported from India, Indonesia, Borneo and Malaysia; is the world's most popular spice; ancient Greeks and Romans used both White and Black Pepper for cooking; in early 5th century, 3,000 pounds pepper was demanded for ransom of Rome; in 1179 A.D. Guild of Pepperers was founded in London; Marco Polo wrote of great quantities of pepper used in China; the dried fruit or berry of climbing vine which grows on spikes like currants;

43

available as whole Black Pepper (Peppercorns), ground White Pepper, ground Black Pepper, Coarse Grind Black Pepper and Cracked Black Pepper; to obtain Black Pepper, berries are picked before fully ripe and they turn black and shrivel when dried; to obtain White Pepper, berries are allowed to ripen before harvesting and the outer shell is removed, leaving greyish-white kernel; has a hot, biting and very pungent taste; White Pepper is milder in flavor than Black Pepper; has slight musty flavor.

## Uses

Peppercorns or whole Black Peppers are used in pepper mills. Grind the pepper over foods at the table or when food is being prepared. Peppercorns are also used in some salad dressings, marinades, pickling, poaching fish, soups, sauces and stews.

Ground White Pepper is especially popular in white or light colored foods where the dark specks of Black Pepper do not add to the aesthetic appearance. White Pepper may be substituted for Black Pepper in any recipe.

Black Pepper comes in three different grinds—fine, coarse and cracked. Black Pepper may be used in any dish except sweets. However, it is sometimes used in cake and is a characteristic ingredient in the German Christmas cookie, pfeffernüsse.

### Suggested Amounts to Use in Various Dishes

**PEPPERCORNS**
10 to 12 in marinade for sauerbraten, 4 pounds beef
4 to 6 in liquid for poaching 1 to 2 pounds fish
8 to 10 in liquid when boiling chicken, shrimp, pot roast
  and variety meats such as tongue

### GROUND BLACK PEPPER

⅛ teaspoon to ½ teaspoon in spice cake mix

⅛ teaspoon to ½ teaspoon to a 7-ounce can tuna for salad

¼ teaspoon to ½ teaspoon in pfeffernüsse recipe making 6 dozen cookies

### COARSE GRIND BLACK PEPPER

¼ teaspoon to ½ teaspoon in 1½ cups French or other salad dressings

⅛ teaspoon to ½ teaspoon to 4 cups bread cubes for stuffings

⅛ teaspoon to ¼ teaspoon sprinkled over 1 pound steak, chops, fish, chicken or liver before broiling

### CRACKED BLACK PEPPER

1 teaspoon to 2 teaspoons to 1 pound steak for peppered steak

½ teaspoon to 1 teaspoon in 2 cups marinade for meats

⅛ teaspoon to each individual salad bowl of chef's or tossed salad

### GROUND WHITE PEPPER

Dash to ⅛ teaspoon to 6 eggs—stuffed, scrambled, creamed or for omelettes

⅛ teaspoon to ¼ teaspoon in 2 cups mashed potatoes

¼ teaspoon in 2 cups white or light-colored sauce

⅛ teaspoon to ¼ teaspoon in 2 cups vichyssoise or other light-colored soups

⅛ teaspoon to ¼ teaspoon for 1 pound fish

⅛ teaspoon to ¼ teaspoon for 1 head cauliflower

\* \* \*

**Pepper, Red** [*Capsicum frutescens (C. annuum)*]; Red Pepper and Cayenne; native to tropical America and West Indies; known in pre-Inca days; Columbus found hot red peppers in Cuba and introduced them to Europe; fruit of pepper plant; has no relation to Black and

White Pepper; Red Pepper available crushed and ground; Cayenne available ground; ground Red Pepper and Cayenne are available as a blend; orange-red to deep red in color; has a hot, pungent flavor; use with caution; in some sections of the United States whole red pepper may be purchased as Chili Tepines.

## *Uses*

Both Cayenne and Red Pepper are widely used in Mexican and Italian dishes. Use to season meats, sea food, deviled eggs, appetizers, soups and chowders, tomato aspic, cottage and cream cheese, cheese dishes, sauces, gravy, salad dressing, pickles, poultry, game, vegetables, spaghetti sauce, tamales, curried dishes, creamed dishes, ceviche, cheese straws or wafers, dips, spreads for canapés, sauces for sea food appetizers, tomato juice cocktail, Bloody Marys, omelettes, soufflés, croquettes, tamale pie, guacamole, barbecued beef and pork.

Crushed Red Pepper is particularly important in pickling, chowders, gumbos, spaghetti sauce, pizza sauce and in making sausage.

## *Suggested Amounts to Use in Various Dishes*

CAYENNE AND RED PEPPER
Dash to ¼ teaspoon to 1 pound shrimp
Dash to ⅛ teaspoon to 6 eggs—stuffed, scrambled or for omelettes
Dash to ⅛ teaspoon in ½ cup butter for basting chicken or fish or to use over vegetables

CRUSHED RED PEPPER
⅛ teaspoon to 1 teaspoon to 1 pound ground beef
⅛ teaspoon to ¼ teaspoon in 2 cups pizza or spaghetti sauce

1 teaspoon to 2 teaspoons to 4 pints tomato relish, mixed
   pickles or dilled green beans

*A good rule to follow is to use a dash to ⅛ teaspoon in most
recipes for 4 servings unless extremely hot food is desired.
Increase to suit individual taste.*

\* \* \*

**Pickling Spice;** blend of whole and broken spices, herbs
and seeds; designed primarily for use in pickling but may
be used in other food preparation; tie Pickling Spice in
a cheesecloth bag for easy removal when used in such
dishes as pot roast, spiced fruits and vegetables.

### Uses

Pickling Spice may be used in pickles, stewed prunes,
pickled beets, pickled eggs, marinades, sauerbraten,
spiced fruits, boiled shrimp, pot roast and game cookery.

### Suggested Amounts to Use in Various Dishes

1 teaspoon to 2 teaspoons to 2 cups prunes for stewing
1 teaspoon to 1 tablespoon to 2 cups whole beets
1 tablespoon in 4 cups mixed fruits or fruit cocktail
2 tablespoons to 4 tablespoons in 1 quart water for boiling
   1 to 2 pounds shrimp
1 tablespoon to 2 tablespoons to 4-pound pot roast of beef
   or venison

\* \* \*

**Poppy Seed** (*Papaver somniferum*); native to Southwestern
Asia; imported mainly from the Netherlands, Poland
and Iran; was cultivated as a source of cooking oil by
Egyptians as early as 1500 B.C.; seed come from the
opium poppy but contain no narcotic properties; the
Dutch cultivate the best quality seed; is a uniform

slate-blue color; seed come from the pod of an annual plant which belongs to the poppy family; appears round to the eye but is actually kidney-shaped; the tiny dried seed have a pleasant, crunchy, nut-like flavor and add eye appeal and texture as well as flavor to foods; is of culinary importance especially in Slavic and Hungarian baked goods.

## Uses

Poppy Seed may be used as an ingredient in a recipe, sprinkled over the top of food before cooking or as a garnish. Use in cottage cheese, cream cheese, scrambled eggs, pie crust, cheese sticks, fruit compotes, fruit salad dressings, cookies, cakes, breads and noodles. Sprinkle over top of fruit salads, vegetables, breads, cookies, cakes and casseroles.

### Suggested Amounts to Use in Various Dishes

1 teaspoon to 3 teaspoons in recipe or mix making 12 corn bread or plain muffins

2 teaspoons to 4 teaspoons in a two-crust pastry

½ teaspoon to 1 teaspoon in ½ cup butter and stir into 8-ounce package noodles, cooked

2 teaspoons in 8-ounce package cream cheese

1 teaspoon in 1 cup fruit salad dressing

¼ cup to ⅓ cup in 2-layer white cake recipe or mix

2 tablespoons to 4 tablespoons in cookie recipe using about 3 cups flour

\* \* \*

**Poultry Seasoning**; a blend of herbs; was created primarily for seasoning stuffings but may be used in many other dishes.

48

Poultry Seasoning may be used in stuffings; roasting, broiling or frying chicken; roasting turkey; veal dishes; waffles; biscuits; meat loaf and hamburgers; gravy; creamed chicken; chicken, turkey or salmon croquettes; sautéed chicken livers; liver pâté; chicken soups; chicken and dumplings; chicken pot pie and pastry for meat pies.

*Suggested Amounts to Use in Various Dishes*

¼ teaspoon to ¾ teaspoon for 3-pound frying chicken
½ teaspoon in about 4 cups creamed chicken or turkey
½ teaspoon to 2 teaspoons to 4 cups bread cubes for stuffing
⅛ teaspoon to ¼ teaspoon for 1 pound veal

\* \* \*

**Pumpkin Pie Spice;** a blend of Cinnamon, Ginger, Allspice, Nutmeg and Cloves; a certain percentage of each is blended to bring out the finest flavor of each spice; the whole spices are placed on high speed mills and ground together; this welding of the spice particles assures a permanent smoothness of flavor not possible by merely mixing after grinding; as with all blends of spices, manufacturers have their own secret formulas.

*Uses*

Pumpkin Pie Spice is a mouth-watering blend with just the right flavor note for seasoning pumpkin pie. Excellent used in gingerbread, cookies, fruits, squash, sweet potatoes, applesauce and other apple dishes, sweet rolls, frostings, waffles, muffins, whipped cream, glazes, cakes, puddings, dessert sauces and for making toast.

¼ teaspoon to 1 teaspoon in pound cake recipe or mix

¼ teaspoon to 1 teaspoon in 1 cup flake or shredded coconut, toasted

2 teaspoons to 3 teaspoons in 1½ cups mashed pumpkin for pie

½ teaspoon to ½ cup uncooked rice for rice pudding

½ teaspoon to 1 teaspoon for 2 cups sweet potatoes, mashed or candied

½ teaspoon to 1 teaspoon for 2 cups apricots for stewing, tarts or pie

*   *   *

**Rosemary** (*Rosmarinus officinalis*); native to the Mediterranean area; present sources are Yugoslavia, France, Spain, Portugal and, to an extent, the moist climates of North Carolina, Virginia and California; an herb used extensively as early as 500 B.C.; prominent in folklore; one legend says that Rosemary will grow only in the gardens of the righteous; in *Hamlet*, Ophelia said, "There's rosemary, that's for remembrance"; even today in England Rosemary is placed on graves of English heroes; used by the colonists to scent soap; is the dried leaves from small perennial evergreen shrub of the mint family; the slender, slightly curved leaves are greyish-green in color, resembling miniature curved pine needles; distinctive, fresh, sweet pinewoods flavor; is used to great extent in perfumery.

### Uses

Rosemary, a sweet, fragrant herb, is excellent in lamb dishes, soups, stews, marinades, poached or boiled fish or sea food, Italian tomato sauce for fish, liver pâté, boiled potatoes, cauliflower, spinach, mushrooms, turnips, fruits, fruit juices, breads; and is used in preparing poultry, veal, beef, pork, wild fowl and venison. Sprinkle Rosemary over coals when barbecuing meats.

### Suggested Amounts to Use in Various Dishes

½ teaspoon to 1 teaspoon, crushed, in 1 package corn bread mix, 2 cups biscuit mix or recipe making 12 muffins or biscuits

¼ teaspoon to 1 tablespoon for a 3-pound chicken

¼ teaspoon in 4 cups mixed fruit or 2 cups fruit juice

¼ teaspoon to ½ teaspoon in 2 cups potatoes, cauliflower or tomatoes

¼ teaspoon to 1 tablespoon in 6 cups barbecue sauce

½ teaspoon, crushed, for 3- to 4-pound lamb roast or use in combination with Thyme and Sage

\* \* \*

**Saffron** (*Crocus sativus*); native to Mediterranean area; imported primarily from Spain; ancient Assyrians used Saffron for medicinal purposes; listed in medical papyrus of Thebes (1552 B.C.); Constantine presented gift of spices, including Saffron, to the Bishop of Rome; is the dried stigmas of the saffron crocus; most expensive spice in the world; requires 75,000 blossoms or 225,000 stigmas to make 1 pound; available whole; is orange-yellow in color; used as much in cooking for color as for flavor; has a pleasantly bitter flavor; use sparingly—a little goes a long way.

### Uses

Saffron is widely used in French, Spanish and South American dishes. An essential ingredient in arroz con pollo, bouillabaisse, paella and risotto. May also be used in yeast breads, rice, chicken dishes, soups, cakes, sauces and sea food dishes. The individual pieces of Saffron may

51

be used in recipes; however, it is usually crushed before using.

### Suggested Amounts to Use in Various Dishes

Dash to ¼ teaspoon, crushed, for 1 cup uncooked rice
Dash to ⅛ teaspoon, crushed, for 3-pound chicken
8 to 10 individual pieces, crushed, in 8- or 9-inch layer cake
⅛ teaspoon to 1 teaspoon in 4-cup flour recipe for bread or buns or in a package hot roll mix
Dash to ⅛ teaspoon, crushed, for 2 pounds veal

\* \* \*

**Sage** (*Salvia officinalis*); native to Mediterranean area; imported primarily from Dalmatian region of Yugoslavia; do not confuse with sagebrush of American West; was used for medicinal purposes during Middle Ages; the dried leaf of a plant of mint family; is grey-green in color; available as dried leaves, ground and rubbed; very aromatic and slightly bitter; use sparingly.

### Uses

Sage is well known for its use in stuffings for poultry, fish, game and other meats. Thousands of pounds go into the commercial making of sausage each year. Sage may also be used in soups, chowders, waffles, biscuits, lima beans, saltimbocca, onions, eggplant, sauces, tomatoes, cheese, marinades, potatoes and in preparing poultry, fish, beef, pork and veal.

### Suggested Amounts to Use in Various Dishes

¼ teaspoon to ½ teaspoon in 2 cups green vegetables
¼ teaspoon to ¾ teaspoon to 1 quart bread cubes for

stuffing for poultry, fish, pork chops, breast of veal and crown roasts

¼ teaspoon to 1 tablespoon in 6 cups barbecue sauce in combination with Rosemary and Thyme

2 teaspoons in 2 cups waffle mix or recipe using 2 cups flour

½ teaspoon to 3 pounds pork, veal, lamb, beef and other meats

¼ teaspoon to ½ teaspoon in 1 pound ground lamb

Dash to ¼ teaspoon in 3 cups soup—cream, chowder, vegetable, tomato or sea food

½ teaspoon to ¼ cup flour for dredging meats

Dash to ¼ teaspoon in ¼ cup butter for basting 1 pound fish when baking or broiling

Dash to ¼ teaspoon in 3 cups tomatoes

\* \* \*

**Savory** (*Satureja hortensis*); sometimes called Summer Savory; native to Mediterranean countries; Hippocrates speaks of its medicinal properties; used for seasoning cakes, pies and puddings in Middle Ages; is the dried, brownish-green leaves of plant of mint family; has aromatic, piquant flavor; available ground.

## *Uses*

Savory blends well with other herbs. It may be used alone or in combination with other herbs in stuffings for meat, fish or poultry; egg dishes; sauces; soups; meat loaf and hamburgers; stews; beans; cabbage; peas and tomato juice.

## *Suggested Amounts to Use in Various Dishes*

¼ teaspoon to ½ teaspoon in 2 cups green beans, Brussels sprouts, lima beans, peas or other green vegetables

¼ teaspoon to ½ teaspoon in 1 pound ground beef
Dash to ¼ teaspoon in 3 cups consommé, fish chowder
   or bean, split pea, tomato or vegetable soup
¼ teaspoon to 3 cups bread cubes for stuffing
⅛ teaspoon to 6 stuffed eggs
¼ teaspoon to ½ teaspoon for 3-pound chicken
¼ teaspoon for 1 pound of fish
Dash to ¼ teaspoon in 1½ cups brown sauce or gravy

\* \* \*

**Season-All;** blend of seasonings; an extremely versatile seasoning used to enhance flavor of most food except sweets; adds color to light-colored foods; reduce salt in recipe when using Season-All; may also be used as a garnish or at the table as one would use salt and pepper.

### Uses

Use Season-All in preparing vegetables; cheese dishes such as cheese soufflés, Welsh rabbit, cheese sauce and grilled cheese sandwiches; tomato, mushroom, barbecue and cream sauces; soups; beef; lamb; veal; variety meats; pork; poultry; game; fish; sea foods; seasoned butter; salad dressings; coleslaw and potato, chicken, tuna, salmon, shrimp, crab and macaroni salads. Sprinkle over broiled or fresh sliced tomatoes; cottage cheese; fried potatoes; corn on the cob; cheese cubes for appetizers; dips; canapés; spreads; omelettes; scrambled, fried, poached, stuffed or creamed eggs and on raw vegetables such as celery, carrot sticks, cauliflower and radishes.

### Suggested Amounts to Use in Various Dishes

2 teaspoons in ½ cup butter for breads and vegetables or
   to brush over fish or meat when broiling

1 tablespoon for 3-pound pork or beef roast
½ teaspoon to 1 teaspoon to 1½ cups cottage cheese
1 teaspoon to 1½ teaspoons in 1 pound ground beef
¾ teaspoon to 1 teaspoon in 2 cups fresh, frozen or canned vegetables
2 teaspoons to 1 tablespoon for 3-pound chicken
½ teaspoon to 1 teaspoon for 6 eggs—scrambled, stuffed or for omelettes

\* \* \*

**Sesame Seed** (*Sesamum indicum*); also known as "Benne Seed"; native to Asia; cultivated extensively in China, India and Central America; a food of the ancient Egyptians and Persians; regarded highly by Orientals as a staple food, as valuable as the soy bean; Sesame Seed signifies immortality to Brahmins; Negro slaves brought Sesame Seed to America; early Assyrians, several thousand years before Christ, believed their gods drank Sesame Wine at their conference prior to creating the earth; Sesame Seed is the dried, hulled fruit of a tropical annual herb; creamy white, smooth and slippery oval-shaped seed; rich nut-like flavor; tons of seed are utilized every year to make a rich Middle Eastern candy, Halvah; the seed is a source of a fine cooking oil and paste.

### Uses

Sesame Seed is one of the most versatile seeds. The flavor of toasted Sesame Seed resembles that of toasted almonds. Use, toasted or untoasted, in many of the same ways nuts are used. Sprinkle canapés, breads, cookies, casseroles, salads, noodles, soups and vegetables with Sesame Seed. Add to pie crust, pie fillings, candy, cakes, cookies, dumplings, cheese spreads and dips and stuffings. When recipe calls for "toasted" seed—toast Sesame Seed in 350°F. oven 15 minutes or until lightly browned before using.

## Suggested Amounts to Use in Various Dishes

1 teaspoon to 2 teaspoons, toasted, in 1½ cups flour for dumplings

1 tablespoon to 4 tablespoons, toasted, in 1 pound ground beef

1 teaspoon to 1 tablespoon, toasted, in 2 tablespoons melted butter for vegetables

2 tablespoons to 4 tablespoons, toasted, for two-crust pastry

⅓ cup, toasted, to 3 cups stuffing for poultry or pork chops

¼ cup, toasted, in pecan pie filling

Sprinkle over waffles, biscuits, muffins and rolls before baking.

\* \* \*

**Tarragon** (*Artemisia dracunculus*); native to Western and Southern Asia; is cultivated in Southern Europe, especially France, and the temperate zones of the United States; one of the most aromatic herbs and a favorite of connoisseurs for its intriguing flavor; a festive herb, often used as garnish by the French on aspic-coated meats; slender dark green leaves of a shrub-like perennial; available as dried leaves; has a somewhat astringent flavor, reminiscent of Anise; best known as the flavoring for tarragon vinegar; the flavor of Tarragon, being very aromatic, stands alone well and should be used sparingly.

### Uses

Tarragon is the distinctive flavor in Béarnaise sauce. May be used in mayonnaise; tartare, mustard and sour cream sauces; pickles; turtle soup; tuna salads and casseroles; marinades; ragouts and pot roasts. Use in preparing veal, lamb, venison and other game, chicken, duck, Cornish hens, squab, pheasant, fish, shellfish and egg dishes. Excellent sprinkled over salad greens.

## Suggested Amounts to Use in Various Dishes

¼ teaspoon to ½ teaspoon in 2 cups peas or spinach

¼ teaspoon in 2 cups soup—turtle, tomato, mushroom or fish chowders

½ teaspoon to 1 teaspoon in ½ cup butter for sautéing shellfish or as a sauce for fish

¼ teaspoon to ½ teaspoon for 2 pounds veal

¼ teaspoon to ½ teaspoon in 2 cups white sauce for creamed eggs or fish dishes

¼ teaspoon for 1 pound broiled or baked fish

1 tablespoon in 3 cups mayonnaise for green goddess salad dressing

1 teaspoon for 3-pound chicken

1½ teaspoons in Béarnaise sauce recipe using 3 egg yolks

½ teaspoon to 1 teaspoon in ½ cup butter for topping steaks and chops

1 tablespoon in 1 pint white wine vinegar to make tarragon vinegar (let stand before using)

\* \* \*

**Thyme** (*Thymus vulgaris*); native to the Mediterranean area; cultivated in Southern Europe and United States; France is the leading producer of Thyme; French Thyme and Lemon Thyme are the two varieties that are commercially important; Assyrian doctors and chemists recognized the medicinal properties of Thyme; used as a fumigant, as well as to flavor cheese and liquor by the ancient Greeks and Romans; is still used to flavor certain Scandinavian cheeses; in ancient times it was thought that Thyme would not grow well unless grown within the range of sea breezes; has a pale lavender blossom which is a favorite of the honey bee; is the greyish-green leaves of a perennial plant of the mint family; available as dried leaves and ground; has a distinctively warm, aromatic and slightly pungent flavor; commercially used to flavor Bénédictine liqueur.

Thyme, one of the most popular herbs, is used to season meat, poultry and fish. Combine Thyme with melted butter and serve over vegetables or broiled sea food or use in stuffing for fish and meats. Add to dishes made with tomato or cheese. Seasoning clam chowder with Thyme is a must. Thyme is one of the popular herbs used in making a bouquet garni.

### *Suggested Amounts to Use in Various Dishes*

GROUND

¼ teaspoon to ½ teaspoon in flour for dredging 3-pound chicken

Dash to ½ teaspoon in 3 cups clam chowder

½ teaspoon to 1¼ teaspoons to 4-pound leg of lamb— use alone or in combination with Sage and Rosemary

¼ teaspoon to ½ teaspoon in biscuit mix or recipe making 12 biscuits

¼ teaspoon to 1 tablespoon in 6 cups barbecue sauce

LEAVES

¼ teaspoon to ½ teaspoon for 1 pound liver

Dash to ¼ teaspoon in 2 cups Brussels sprouts or green beans

¼ teaspoon to ½ teaspoon for 1½ pounds round steak

¼ teaspoon to ½ teaspoon for 5-pound stewing chicken

\* \* \*

**Turmeric** (*Curcuma longa*); native to Cochin China; imported from India, Haiti, Jamaica and Peru; Turmeric is mentioned in writings of Greek physician Dioscorides (ca. A.D. 40–90); was used as a dye; today used to color butter, cheese and pickles; extensively used in East Indian cookery; rhizome or root of plant of ginger family; is washed, cleaned and sun-dried; available

ground; golden yellow color; musky odor and slightly
bitter flavor; small amount adds color to foods; a major
ingredient in Curry Powder and prepared mustard.

## Uses

Turmeric is used in egg dishes, pickles, chow-chow, rice
dishes, cream sauces, salad dressings, breads, relish,
mayonnaise, soups, noodles and in preparing chicken
and fish.

### Suggested Amounts to Use in Various Dishes

Dash to ⅛ teaspoon in 6 stuffed or scrambled eggs
Dash to ¼ teaspoon for 1 cup uncooked rice or 8-ounce
    package noodles
Dash to ¼ teaspoon in 2 cups white sauce or cheese
    sauce
⅛ teaspoon to ¼ teaspoon in ½ cup butter for basting
    chicken and sea food when broiling or baking
¼ teaspoon to ½ teaspoon in 1 cup mayonnaise or
    commercial sour cream for dressing or dunk for
    shrimp, lobster and other sea food

\* \* \*

**Vanilla** (*Vanilla planifolia*); is native to Central America
and Mexico. Mexico monopolized the profitable Vanilla
trade for three centuries. It is now produced mainly in
the Malagasy Republic (Madagascar) and neighboring
islands of Réunion and Comores. Lesser amounts come
from Java, Tahiti and Mexico. Long before Columbus
discovered America, the Aztecs enjoyed a drink called
"Xoco-Latl" made from cocoa and vanilla beans. This
was discovered by Cortez, and Vanilla was taken back
to Spain from where its use soon spread to other parts of
Europe. Vanilla is the fruit of an orchid plant; each
hand-pollinated flower becomes a long slender pod or

bean which is picked while still green. It undergoes a curing and drying process during which aroma and flavor are developed.

Pure Vanilla Extract, a delicate, subtle flavoring, is a complex mixture of natural ingredients, many of which are unknown. Imitation vanilla extract is a mixture of color and synthetic flavors, mainly vanillin. Pure Vanilla has a pleasant "bouquet" and a full, well-rounded flavor that is not present in an imitation vanilla extract. For the protection of consumers, Federal standards have now been issued to define the name Vanilla Extract and provide that no imitation flavors may be used in making pure Vanilla Extract.

### Uses

Use Vanilla to flavor most sweet foods such as eggnog, milk shakes, hot chocolate and other milk beverages; ice cream; rice, bread and other puddings; cakes; cookies; dessert or fruit sauces; custards; stewed fruits; fruit compotes; candies; glazes; frostings; whipped cream; pies; coffee; tortes; meringue shells; cheesecake; dessert soufflés; sundae toppings; cream puff and pastry fillings; muffins; coffee cakes and cream cheese filling for fruit bread.

### Suggested Amounts to Use in Various Dishes

1 teaspoon to 2 teaspoons in 2-layer cake recipe or mix

¼ teaspoon to ½ teaspoon in 1 cup heavy cream, whipped

1 teaspoon to 1½ teaspoons in 2 cups custard sauce

1 teaspoon to 1½ teaspoons in frostings for 2 cake layers

2 teaspoons to 3 teaspoons in cookie recipe making about 5 dozen

½ teaspoon to 1 teaspoon in candy recipe using 2 cups sugar

2 teaspoons in about 4 cups custard for making ice cream

The items previously discussed are merely a sampling of the many, many spices, herbs and blends available to you. After reading this section and trying the suggestions it contains, we hope you will be encouraged by the evident ease of spice and herb cookery to experiment with the many other seasonings, equally popular and useful in food preparation, which have not been mentioned here because of space limitations. Some of these are: Gumbo Filé, Hickory Smoked Salt, Italian Seasoning, Meat Tenderizer, Seasoned Meat Tenderizer, Powdered Mushrooms, Charcoal Seasoning, Salad Herbs, Seafood Seasoning, Bell Pepper Flakes, Vegetable Flakes, Barbecue Spice, Chives, Apple Pie Spice, Arrowroot and Salad Salt.

To add even greater variety in flavor, color and eye appeal, you will wish to make use of the wide variety of extracts, food colors and attractive and colorful décors.

# SPECIAL
# HELPS

——— ✳ ———

## Helpful Hints for Successful Cooking

### General

Always measure correctly. Measure liquids in a measuring cup especially designed for this purpose. These cups have head space above the one cup marking to prevent liquid from spilling over. Measure dry ingredients in nested measuring cups which do not have head space, so ingredients may be leveled with a spatula for more accurate measurement.

To measure ⅛ teaspoon of a dry ingredient, first measure a level ¼ teaspoon. Remove half of the measured ingredient.

To measure honey or molasses, first very lightly grease or oil the cup or spoon; otherwise, the measurement will be inaccurate because much of the honey or molasses will adhere to the utensil.

If a recipe calls for 1 cup chopped nuts, the nuts are chopped before measuring. In a recipe calling for 1 cup nuts, chopped, the nuts are first measured, then chopped.

When measuring brown sugar, always pack firmly into the cup.

To prevent brown sugar from hardening, store in a covered container. Insert a damp paper towel or napkin in the lid. If brown sugar has hardened, the same treatment will soften it.

When creaming butter and sugar for a cake, continue the creaming process until the mixture is light and fluffy and slightly resembles whipped cream.

When adding flour to cake batter, do not overmix.

When adding flour alternately with liquid, always start and end with the flour.

When using a glass cake pan, decrease the oven temperature 25°F.

To test for doneness insert a cake tester, skewer or toothpick in the center of the cake; when it comes out clean, the cake is done. Another test is to gently touch the center of the cake with finger. When no imprint remains, cake is done.

Arrowroot is ideal for thickening pie fillings since it becomes very clear upon thickening and does not cover any natural flavor.

After fluting the edge of pastry, press or crimp under rim in several places to prevent shrinkage.

Use 1½ to 2 cups crushed graham crackers, zwieback, gingersnaps, vanilla or chocolate wafers for an 8- or 9-inch pie.

The secret in making a perfect meringue that does not shrink nor weep:

(1) Have egg whites at room temperature.
(2) Add ¼ teaspoon Cream of Tartar to 2 to 3 whites.
(3) Beat until peaks form.
(4) Beat in sugar, adding 1 to 2 tablespoons at a time; then continue beating until sugar is dissolved and meringue forms stiff peaks.
(5) When spreading meringue over pie filling, be sure to seal meringue by spreading to crust.
(6) Bake in 400° to 425°F. oven until lightly browned.
(7) Cool in warm place free from draft.

When sauces are made in a double boiler, never allow

the water in the bottom boiler to touch the bottom of the top boiler.

If Hollandaise sauce, Béarnaise sauce or any rich butter-egg sauce separates while preparing, add 1 to 2 teaspoons boiling water, stirring briskly while adding.

To steam a pudding use a large covered kettle. Place the pudding molds on a rack. Add enough boiling water to come two thirds up the side of the mold. Be sure the top of the mold is tightly covered. Cover kettle and always keep the water boiling.

Overcooking causes custards, rice pudding and custard-type bread puddings to become watery.

Freeze carbonated drinks, fruit juices or a small amount of a punch mixture to make an ice block or ice ring to float in punch to prevent diluting.

Tie whole spices in a bag for easy removal.

Tea may tend to cloud if refrigerated. Even though the cloudiness does not affect tea flavor, it can be cleared up by adding a small amount of boiling water.

Always stir rice with a fork—helps to prevent gummy rice.

Use low heat when cooking eggs or cheese.

To hard cook eggs, cover with cold water, bring to a boil, cover and let stand, off heat, 20 to 25 minutes.

A baking dish, as referred to in this book, is shallow and usually uncovered; whereas, a casserole dish is deep and has a cover.

Vegetables will retain their original color if cooked quickly in a small amount of water and in a saucepan with a tight-fitting cover.

Strong-flavored vegetables require more seasoning than mild-flavored vegetables.

To remove a gelatine salad or dessert from a mold follow these steps:

(1) First of all, lightly oil the mold before filling.
(2) Be sure the gelatine is thoroughly set before attempting to remove. Remember, large molds require more time to set than small ones.

64

(3) Loosen around top edge with a thin spatula.
(4) Dip the mold in warm, not hot, water for a few seconds.
(5) Gently pull the molded product away from the mold on one side to let air in.
(6) Quickly turn out, upside-down, on plate.

Serve hot foods hot and cold foods cold.

## Outdoor Cooking

Start the fire early enough to have a good bed of coals before cooking begins.

A grey ash on briquets indicates they are burning.

The amount of heat depends on the number of briquets used and their distance apart. Cooking temperature may also be varied by raising or lowering the grill over the coals.

Cooking times vary due to thickness of food, heat of coals, distance from coals, outside temperature and amount of wind.

Barbecuing is not limited to expensive cuts of meat. Use Meat Tenderizer on less tender cuts for economy and variety of menu.

You will find a meat thermometer is helpful when cooking large pieces of meat on a spit. Caution should be taken when inserting the meat thermometer so the end is as near the center as possible but does not rest against the spit, the locking tines or bone.

## Cookies

Allow room for cookies to spread on baking sheet.

Remove from baking sheet as soon as removed from oven unless otherwise directed.

Remove cookies with a flat, flexible spatula.

Cool cookies on rack.

The yield will vary depending upon size of cutter used,

thickness to which dough is rolled or sliced or amount of batter dropped from spoon.

The cooking time may vary from that given in recipe due to size or thickness of cookie.

If dough is to be chilled, Chill Well. You will find it easier to work with.

When making rolled cookies, cut as many as possible on first rolling of dough. Each time the dough is rolled more flour will be worked in and the cookies will become dryer and harder.

Store crisp cookies and moist cookies in separate containers.

To mail cookies, wrap each cookie separately or use dividers between layers and rows. Fill all the empty holes and spaces and around the edges of the box with popped corn.

## Candy

**Test for Candy Making:**

*Soft Ball*—232° to 240° for fudge, panocha and fondant. Syrup makes ball in cold water which can be picked up with fingers but will not hold its shape.

*Firm Ball*—242° to 248° for caramels and caramel corn. Syrup makes ball in cold water which holds its shape when picked up.

*Hard Ball*—250° to 268° for divinity and taffy. Syrup makes ball in cold water which feels hard to the touch but is still plastic.

*Soft Crack*—270° to 290° for toffee and butterscotch. Syrup makes hard but not brittle threads rather than a ball in cold water.

*Hard Crack*—300° to 310° for brittles, lollypops and taffy apples. Syrup makes brittle threads in cold water.

A good candy thermometer is well worth its price, for it takes the "guesswork" out of candy making.

Subtract 1° for each 500 feet elevation above sea level when testing candy with a thermometer.

Use a deep, fairly heavy saucepan with straight sides rather than a shallow skillet. (Liquid evaporates too fast in a skillet.)

Cook candy at a slow, but constant, boil unless directed otherwise.

Wash down sides of pan to help prevent crystal formation and graininess.

Use any of the following methods:

(1) Wrap fork in a damp cloth and wash around sides of pan.

(2) Brush sides of pan with a pastry brush, with natural bristles, dipped in water.

(3) Cover the pan for 2 to 3 minutes after it begins to boil, being careful not to let it cook over.

To insure creaminess, cool fudge to 110° or lukewarm before stirring.

On rainy or humid days, cook candy 1° to 2° higher temperature or to a slightly firmer stage than recipe directs.

Do not worry if candy curdles while cooking. Beating will remedy this.

### Fish and Sea Food

Cook fish briefly. Fish is done when it flakes easily with a fork.

As a rule, do not turn fish when broiling or baking.

Baste fish and shellfish when baking or broiling.

For moist, tender shrimp, cook in well-seasoned, boiling water 7 minutes or until shells turn pink.

Spiced steamed shrimp, popular in many sections of the country, requires 20 to 25 minutes cooking time. Place shrimp on rack in kettle, add small amount of water and sprinkle generously with spices and herbs. Cover and steam. Shrimp is firmer and less moist which is characteristic of this cooking method.

Boil frozen rock lobster tails (it is not necessary to thaw) in boiling, salted water to cover. Allow 3 minutes longer than the ounce weight of largest lobster tail, such as 10 minutes for 7-ounce lobster tail.

### Canning

Examine jars for chips; wash well. Just before filling sterilize by boiling 10 minutes.

Spoons, funnels and other equipment used in canning and filling should also be sterilized.

Use fruits and vegetables of top quality. Be sure fresh fruits and vegetables are not overripe.

Use stone, glass or enamel container when soaking fruits or vegetables in a salt, alum or slaked lime solution.

When soaking vegetables or fruits in a solution, a plate or pie plate should be placed on top of the food and weighted down to insure the food being covered by the solution at all times . . . referred to as weighting.

Use a pure refined pickling, dairy, Kosher or rock salt. Table salt may be used; however, the brine may become cloudy.

When soaking cucumbers in a brine solution, scum will form on the top. It should be removed daily.

When whole spices are sealed in the jar with fruit or pickles, you may expect a very slightly darker product upon standing.

For best results when making jelly and preserves, work with small amounts of fruit.

Jellying stage refers to a degree of doneness in cooking jelly when two drops of the liquid will run together and flake or sheet off a spoon. When using a candy thermometer, cook jelly to about 8°F. above the boiling point of water in your locality.

Head space is the amount of space left between the top of the food and the lid.

Process refers to placing sealed jars on a rack in a large covered container with enough boiling water to come

1 to 2 inches above top of jars. Cover. Begin the timing after water has come back to a rolling boil.

The yield of a recipe will vary with the size of the vegetables or fruit being used and how compactly they are packed in the jar.

### Meat and Poultry

The most accurate way to judge the doneness of meat or poultry is with a meat thermometer. *For meat*, insert the thermometer into the thickest part, being sure the bulb does not rest on fat or bone. *For poultry*, insert thermometer so that the bulb is in the center of the inside thigh muscle or the thickest part of the breast meat. If meat thermometer is not used, test bird for doneness by moving drumstick from side to side. When it moves easily, bird is done.

MEAT ROASTING CHART

| Meat | Oven Temperature | Internal Temperature Indicated on Meat Thermometer | Approximate Time per Pound | |
|---|---|---|---|---|
| | | | Weight of Meat | Cooking Time |
| Beef | 300° to 325°F. | Rare —140°F.<br>Medium —160°F.<br>Well Done—170°F. | 6 to 8 pounds | 18 to 20 min.<br>22 to 25 min.<br>27 to 30 min. |
| Pork, Fresh | 350°F. | 185°F. | 3 to 7 pounds | 35 to 40 min. |
| Ham, Pre-cooked | 300° to 325°F. | 130°F. | 10 to 12 pounds | 12 to 15 min. |
| Ham, Smoked (uncooked) | 300° to 325°F. | 160°F. | 10 to 14 pounds | 18 to 20 min. |
| Lamb | 300° to 325°F. | 170° to 185°F. | 3 to 5 pounds | 30 to 35 min. |
| Veal | 300°F. | 170°F. | 5 to 8 pounds | 25 to 30 min. |

POULTRY ROASTING CHART

| Poultry | Oven Temperature | Internal Temperature Indicated on Meat Thermometer | Approximate Time per Pound | |
|---|---|---|---|---|
| | | | Ready-to-Cook Weight | Cooking Time |
| Turkey | 325°F. | 190°F. | 10 to 14 pounds | 4 to 5 hours |
| Chicken | 375°F. | 190°F. | 4 to 6 pounds | 2½ to 3½ hours |
| Duckling | 325° to 350°F. | 190°F. | 4 to 5 pounds | 2 to 3 hours |
| Capon | 325° to 350°F. | 190°F. | 6 to 8 pounds | 2½ to 3½ hours |
| Goose | 325°F. | 190°F. | 10 to 12 pounds | 4 to 5 hours |

When bird is stuffed, cooking time is increased slightly.

## Substitutions

It is best to use the ingredients recommended in the recipe, but the following suggestions are made if there must be substitutions.

| For | Use |
|---|---|
| 1 tbsp. arrowroot | 2 tbsp. flour<br>1 tbsp. cornstarch |
| 1 cup butter | 1 cup margarine<br>⅞ cup lard plus ½ tsp. salt<br>⅞ to 1 cup hydrogenated shortening plus ½ tsp. salt |
| 1 sq. unsweetened chocolate (1 oz.) | 3 tbsp. cocoa plus 1 tbsp. fat |
| 1 whole egg | 2 egg yolks, as in custards<br>2 egg yolks plus 1 tbsp. water, as in cookies |
| 1 cup cake flour | ⅞ cup all-purpose flour |
| 1 cup honey | 1¼ cups sugar plus ¼ cup liquid |
| 1 cup fresh whole milk | ½ cup evaporated milk plus ½ cup water<br>1 cup sour milk or buttermilk plus ½ tsp. soda. In recipes such as pancakes, biscuits and some cakes which call for baking powder omit 2 tsp. of the baking powder. |
| 1 cup sour milk or buttermilk | 1 tbsp. lemon juice or vinegar plus enough fresh whole milk to make 1 cup |
| 1 cup sugar | ¾ cup honey and omit 3 tbsp. plus 1 tsp. of the liquid. In baked products it is best to substitute honey for only one half of the sugar called for in the recipe. |
| 1 cup canned tomatoes | About 1⅓ cups cut-up fresh tomatoes simmered 10 minutes |
| 1 package active dry yeast | 1 cake compressed yeast |

## Common Food Equivalents

|  | Unit or Weight | Measure |
|---|---|---|
| Apples | 1 lb. | 3 medium (3 cups sliced) |
| Butter and other fats | 1 lb. | 2 cups |
| Butter | ¼ stick | 2 tbsp. |
|  | ½ stick (⅛ lb.) | ¼ cup |
|  | 1 stick (¼ lb.) | ½ cup |
|  | 2 sticks (½ lb.) | 1 cup |
|  | 4 sticks (1 lb.) | 2 cups |
| Cheese, Cream | 3-oz. package | 6 tbsp. |
| Cheese, grated | 1 lb. | 4½ cups |
| Chocolate, unsweetened | 1 oz. | 1 square |
| Coconut, shredded | 1 lb. | 5 cups |
| Cranberries | 1 lb. | 4 cups |
| Cream, heavy | ½ pt. (1 cup) | 2 cups whipped cream |
| Currants | 1 lb. | 3 cups |
| Dates, pitted | 1 lb. | 2½ cups |
| Eggs, whole | 3 (medium) | Approx. ½ cup |
| Egg, whites | 4 (medium) | ½ cup |
| Egg, yolks | 3 (medium) | Approx. ¼ cup |
| Flour, All-purpose | 1 lb. | 4 cups (sifted) |
| Flour, Cake | 1 lb. | 4½ cups (sifted) |
| Flour, Whole Wheat | 1 lb. | 3½ cups |
| Flour, Rye | 1 lb. | 4½ to 5 cups |
| Fruits & Peels, candied | 1 lb. | 3 cups (cut-up) |
| Gelatine, unflavored | 1 envelope | 1 tbsp. |
| Lemon, juice of | 1 | Will vary—2 to 3 tbsp. |
| Lemon Rind, grated | 1 | 1½ tsp. |
| Macaroni | 1 cup (uncooked) | 2 to 2½ cups cooked |
| Noodles or Spaghetti | 1 cup (uncooked) | 1¾ to 2 cups cooked |
| Nuts, whole (shelled) |  |  |
| almonds | 1 lb. | 3½ cups |
| pecans | 1 lb. | 4 cups |
| peanuts | 1 lb. | 3 cups |
| walnuts | 1 lb. | 4 cups |
| Orange, juice of | 1 | Approx. ½ cup |
| Orange Rind, grated | 1 | 1 tbsp. (lightly grating only the outer part of rind) |

## Common Food Equivalents

|  | Unit or Weight | Measure |
| --- | --- | --- |
| Raisins | 1 lb. | 3¼ cups |
| Rice | 1 lb. | 2 cups |
|  | 1 cup (uncooked) | 3 cups cooked |
|  | 1½ cups packaged pre-cooked | 3 cups cooked |
| Sugar |  |  |
| superfine | 1 lb. | 2 cups |
| granulated | 1 lb. | 2 cups |
| brown | 1 lb. | 2¼ cups firmly packed |
| Powdered or Confectioners' | 1 lb. | 3 cups to 5 cups; varies according to fineness of grind and way in which it is measured |

## Equivalent Measures

Dash (used frequently in
spice and herb cookery) = less than ⅛ teaspoon
3 teaspoons = 1 tablespoon
16 tablespoons = 1 cup
1 cup = ½ pint
2 cups = 1 pint
2 pints (4 cups) = 1 quart
4 quarts (liquid) = 1 gallon
8 quarts (solid) = 1 peck
4 pecks = 1 bushel
16 ounces = 1 pound

## Tablespoon Measurements

1 tbsp. = ½ fl. ounce
2 tbsp. = 1 fl. ounce
4 tbsp. = ¼ cup

```
 5 tbsp. + 1 tsp. = 1/3 cup
          8 tbsp. = 1/2 cup
10 tbsp. + 2 tsp. = 2/3 cup
         12 tbsp. = 3/4 cup
         14 tbsp. = 7/8 cup
         16 tbsp. = 1 cup
```

### Frequently Used Can Sizes

| Size | Average Contents |
|---|---|
| 8-ounce | = 1 cup |
| Buffet | = 1 cup |
| Picnic | = 1¼ cups |
| No. 300 | = 1¾ cups |
| No. 1 Tall | = 2 cups |
| No. 303 | = 2 cups |
| No. 2 | = 2½ cups |
| No. 2½ | = 3½ cups |
| No. 3 Cylinder or 46-ounce | = 5¾ cups |
| No. 10 | = 12 to 13 cups |

### Commonly Used Abbreviations

```
 tsp. = teaspoon
tbsp. = tablespoon
  pt. = pint
  qt. = quart
  pk. = peck
  bu. = bushel
  oz. = ounce or ounces
  lb. = pound or pounds
  sq. = square
 min. = minute or minutes
  hr. = hour or hours
 mod. = moderate or moderately
 doz. = dozen
```

74

# American-British Conversion Tables

### American and British Spoon Measurement

| AMERICAN | BRITISH |
|---|---|
| 1 tablespoon | 1 scant tablespoon |
| | or |
| | 1 dessert spoon (brimming) |
| 1 teaspoon | 1 scant teaspoon |

### Dry Measures

These vary according to the density of the ingredients. The following table will serve as a guide:

| INGREDIENT | AMERICAN | BRITISH |
|---|---|---|
| Baking Powder | 1 tsp. double-acting | 1½ tsp. baking powder |
| Bread Crumbs (fresh) | 1 cup | 2 oz. |
| Butter or Margarine | 1 cup (2 sticks) | 8 oz. |
| | ½ cup (1 stick) | 4 oz. |
| | ¼ cup or 4 tbsp. | 2 oz. |
| | 2 tbsp. | 1 oz. |
| Cheese | | |
| Cheddar | 1 cup (grated) | 4 oz. |
| Cream | 3-oz. packet | 3-oz. packet |
| Cottage | 1 cup | 8 oz. |
| Chocolate | 1 square | 1 oz. plain dessert or cake chocolate |
| Chocolate Chips or Chocolate Morsels | 1 cup | 6 oz. chocolate pieces |
| Coconut, flaked | 1 cup | 3 oz. |
| Coconut, desiccated | 1 cup | 2½ oz. |
| Cocoa | 1 cup | 3½ oz. |
| Dates, chopped | 1 cup | 7 oz. |
| Flour | | |
| All-Purpose such as Gold Medal | 4 cups, sifted | 1 lb. |
| | 1 cup | 4¼ oz. plain all-purpose |
| | 1 tbsp. (level) | ¼ oz. |

| INGREDIENT | AMERICAN | BRITISH |
|---|---|---|
| Cake Flour | 4½ cups, sifted<br>1 cup | 1 lb.<br>3¾ oz. plain high ratio (approx.) |
| **Fruits** | | |
| Candied Fruit | 1 cup | 7 oz. glacé cherries, peel, pineapple |
| Candied Peel | 1 cup | 5 oz. |
| Currants | 1 cup | 5½ oz. |
| Seedless Raisins | 1 cup | 5¼ oz. |
| White Raisins | 1 cup | 6 oz. Sultanas |
| Gelatine | 1 envelope<br>1 tbsp. | ¾ tbsp.<br>¼ oz. |
| Graham Crackers | 1 cup | 3½ oz. crushed digestive biscuits —no exact substitute |
| Lard | 1 cup<br>2 tbsp. | 8 oz.<br>1 oz. |
| Mincemeat | 1 cup | 10 oz. |
| **Molasses & Syrups** | | |
| Molasses | 1 cup | 8 fl. oz. or 11½ oz. black treacle |
| Maple Syrup | 1 cup | 8 fl. oz. maple syrup |
| Light Corn Syrup | 1 cup | 8 fl. oz. corn syrup or liquid glucose |
| **Nuts** | | |
| Walnuts | 1 cup | 4 oz. |
| Pecans | 1 cup | use walnuts |
| Chopped Mixed | 1 cup | 5 oz. |
| **Rice** | | |
| Uncooked | 1 cup | 6¼ oz. |
| Cooked | 1 cup | 5½ oz. |
| **Shortening (Soft White Emulsified as Crisco and Spry)** | 1 cup<br>4 tbsp.<br>2 tbsp. | 5 oz.<br>1¼ oz.<br>½ oz. |
| **Sugar** | | |
| Granulated (white) | 1 cup | 8 oz. caster sugar |
| Superfine (white fine grain) | 1 cup | 8 oz. |

cont.

| INGREDIENT | AMERICAN | BRITISH |
|---|---|---|
| Sugar *cont.* | | |
| Brown | 1 cup (packed) | 7 oz. soft brown sugar |
| Confectioner's *or* Powdered | 1 cup (sifted) | 4½ oz. icing sugar |
| Yeast | | |
| Compressed | ⅔ oz. or ⅜ oz. packets | about ½ oz. fresh |
| Dried | 1 packet | ¼ oz. dried |

## Oven Temperatures

| AMERICAN | | GAS MARK | |
|---|---|---|---|
| 225°F. – 275°F. | Very Slow | ¼, ½ | Very Slow *or* Very Cool |
| 300°F. – 325°F. | Slow | 1, 2 | Slow or Cool |
| 350°F. – 375°F. | Moderate | 3, 4, 5 | Moderate to Moderately Hot |
| 400°F. – 425°F. | Moderately Hot | 6, 7 | Hot |
| 450°F. – 475°F. | Hot to Very Hot | 8, 9 | Very Hot |
| 500°F. | | 10 | |

| FAHRENHEIT | CENTIGRADE |
|---|---|
| 225° | 107° |
| 250° | 121° |
| 275° | 135° |
| 300° | 149° |
| 325° | 163° |
| 350° | 177° |
| 375° | 190° |
| 400° | 204° |
| 425° | 218° |
| 450° | 232° |
| 475° | 246° |
| 500° | 260° |

To convert Fahrenheit temperature to Centigrade temperature, multiply the number of degrees Fahrenheit, less 32 by 5 and divide by 9.

Example:
400°F. − 32 = 368 × 5 = 1840 ÷ 9 = 204.4 or 204°C. To convert Centigrade temperature to Fahrenheit temperature, multiply the Centigrade degrees by 9 and divide by 5 and add 32.

Example:
204°C. × 9 = 1836 ÷ 5 = 367.1 + 32 = 399.1° or 400°F.

| AMERICAN | | BRITISH |
|---|---|---|
| 1 pint = 16 fluid ounces | | 1 pint = 20 fluid ounces |
| | *therefore* | |
| 2 cups | | 16 fluid ounces |
| 1½ cups | | 12 fluid ounces |
| 1 cup | | 8 fluid ounces |
| ¾ cup | | 6 fluid ounces |
| ⅔ cup | | 5½ fluid ounces |
| ½ cup | | 4 fluid ounces |
| ⅓ cup | | 2¾ fluid ounces |
| ¼ cup | | 2 fluid ounces |
| ⅛ cup | | 1 fluid ounce |

## Metric

1 ounce = approx. 28 grams
1 pound = approx. 454 grams
1 pint = approx. ½ liter

---

# Glossary of Food and Cooking Terms

*bake:* To cook by dry heat in oven; called roasting when applied to meats.

*baste:* To moisten food while it is cooking by spooning or brushing on liquid or fat.

*beat:* To stir thoroughly and vigorously.

*blanch:* To plunge into boiling water and then, in some cases, into cold water. Fruits and nuts are blanched to remove skin easily.

*blend:* To mix thoroughly.

*boiling point, to the:* The boiling point is reached when bubbles rise continuously and break at the surface. "To the boiling point" refers to the temperature reached just before bubbles begin to break surface.

*bouquet garni:* A combination of herbs tied together in thin cloth, used to season foods such as soups and stews; usually removed before serving.

*braise:* To brown in small amount of hot fat then cook slowly in covered utensil, adding a small amount of liquid.

*bread:* To coat with flour or crumbs and egg or liquid prior to cooking.

*bread crumbs:*
SOFT BREAD CRUMBS—fresh bread pulled into small pieces. FINE DRY BREAD CRUMBS—dried stale bread rolled into crumbs; may also be purchased ready-to-use. BUTTERED BREAD CRUMBS—fine bread crumbs sautéed in butter.

*bread cubes, soft:* Day-old bread cut into ½- to 1-inch cubes.

*brew:* To steep or let stand in hot water to extract the flavor, as in tea.

*broil:* To cook directly under heat or over an open fire.

*brown:* To cook in a small amount of fat until brown.

*canapés:* Small pieces of fried or toasted bread with seasoned toppings.

*caramelize:* To melt granulated sugar in skillet over medium heat, stirring constantly, until it becomes a golden brown syrup.

*champignons:* Mushrooms.

*chill:* To cool in refrigerator but not freeze.

*chopped:* Cut into small pieces with chopper or sharp knife—do not use a food grinder.

*coat:* To cover with a thin layer of flour, sugar, nuts, crumbs, Sesame or Poppy Seed, Cinnamon Sugar or a few of the ground spices.

*coats a spoon:* Refers to a degree of thickness obtained when mixture is thick enough to form a definite film on a metal spoon, as in sauces and soft custards.

*coddle:* To cook slowly and gently just below the simmering point, as eggs and fruits.

*cognac:* Brandy from the Cognac region of France.

*commercial sour cream:* Cultured, dairy soured cream.

*compote:* Fruits cooked slowly in syrup (may be spiced), during which time they retain their shape. Also refers to a stemmed dish.

*coquille:* Shell or shell dish for baking and serving foods.

*cream:* To make soft, smooth and creamy by rubbing with back of spoon or by beating with mixer; usually applied to fat and sugar.

*crêpe:* A very thin pancake of French origin.

*crisp-tender:* Cooked until just tender, but not soft nor limp.

*croquette:* Finely chopped meat or fish combined with thick white sauce, frequently cone-shaped, coated with egg and crumbs and fried until crisp.

*croutons:* Small toasted or fried cubes of bread—excellent when seasoned.

*cube:* To cut into small pieces with 6 equal sides.

*custard:* A cooked or baked sweetened mixture of milk and eggs.

*deep fat fry:* To fry food in enough fat to cover. Keep at least 3 inches between surface of fat and top of kettle. Never cover utensil while heating or frying.

*dice:* To cut into very small cubes.

*dredge:* To coat with a dry ingredient, such as flour or sugar.

*drippings:* The fat and juices obtained when cooking meats.

*drizzle:* To pour in a fine thread-like stream over a surface.

*dust:* To sprinkle or coat lightly with flour or sugar.

*filet mignon:* A slice of steak cut from the tenderloin of beef.

*filet or fillet:* A boneless strip of meat or fish.

*fines herbes:* Mixed herbs, such as Parsley, Chervil, Tarragon and Chives.

*flake:* To break into small pieces.

*fold in:* A gentle and careful combining of a light or delicate mixture with a heavier mixture.

*Grand Marnier:* Orange-flavored liqueur.

*grate:* To cut into minute particles by rubbing over grater.

*hors d'oeuvres:* Savory dainty foods served as appetizer; made from different combinations of delicacies and tidbits and served hot or cold.

*knead:* To work dough using heel of hand with a pressing motion while stretching and folding the dough.

*marinade:* A seasoned sauce, usually an oil and acid mixture, in which meats or other foods are soaked.

*marinate:* To let food stand in a marinade to season and tenderize.

*meunière:* Fish dipped in flour and sautéed in butter.

*mince:* To chop into very small bits.

*mix:* To combine ingredients by stirring.

*mousse:* A frozen dessert of sweetened and flavored whipped cream or light cream and gelatine; frozen without stirring.

*pan-fry:* To cook, uncovered, in small amount of hot fat not deep enough to cover food.

*parboil:* To cook partially in boiling salted water or other liquid.

*pare:* To cut away outside covering.

*pâté:* A paste of meat or sea food used as a spread for toast or crackers.

*peel:* To strip away outside covering.

*pilaf, pilaff, pilau or pilaw:* A dish of rice or cracked wheat, sometimes in combination with vermicelli.

*plump:* To soak in liquid or moisten thoroughly and heat in 350°F. oven until full and round.

*poach:* To simmer gently in enough hot liquid to cover, using care to retain shape of food.

*powdered sugar:* The terminology "powdered sugar" as used in the United States is referred to in many places as "confectioners' sugar" and in Canada and England as "icing sugar."

*purée:* A smooth paste, usually of vegetables or fruits,

81

made by putting foods through a sieve, food mill or
beating in a blender.

*ragout:* A well seasoned meat stew.

*ramekins:* Small oval or round individual baking dishes.

*reconstitute:* To put moisture back into dehydrated foods
by soaking in liquid.

*reduce:* To boil liquid until part of the water is evaporated.

*rice:* To force vegetables through "ricer" or fine colander
to break into small particles.

*roast:* To cook, uncovered, in oven or to cook outdoors
on spit.

*sauté:* To cook or brown in small amount of hot fat.

*scald:* To heat to just under boiling point. Used frequently in reference to heating milk.

*scaloppine:* Thin slices of meat, usually veal.

*score:* To mark food with cuts, notches or lines to prevent
curling or to make food more attractive.

*sear:* To brown surface quickly over high heat in hot
skillet or similar utensil or over grill.

*shred:* To cut or tear into small, usually long, narrow
pieces.

*simmer:* To cook slowly on top of range just below boiling
point. Small bubbles form but liquid is practically
motionless.

*skewer:* A long pin of wood or metal on which food or
meat is held while cooking; or to position food on
"skewer."

*slivered:* Sliced into long, thin pieces, usually in reference
to nuts.

*spätzle:* Dough forced through a coarse colander to form
noodles, usually used with goulash and stews.

*steep:* To soak in a liquid below boiling point to extract
flavor.

*stud:* To adorn with; for example, baked ham studded
with whole Cloves.

*suet:* White fat of beef or mutton.

*thicken:* To make a thin, smooth paste by mixing together
Arrowroot, cornstarch or flour with an equal amount

cold water. Stir into hot liquid and cook, stirring, until thickened.

*tortilla:* A thin unleavened pancake prepared from coarse corn meal.

*toss:* To gently mix ingredients with two forks or fork and spoon.

*truffle:* An edible fungus grown underground, highly prized as a delicacy, and used as a seasoning or garnish.

*whip:* To beat rapidly to incorporate air and produce expansion.

## Crab Meat Dunk

1 cup crab meat
¼ cup lime or lemon juice
1 3-ounce package cream cheese
¼ cup heavy cream
2 tablespoons mayonnaise
1 teaspoon Instant Minced Onion
⅛ teaspoon Garlic Powder

1 teaspoon Shredded Green Onions
2 dashes Cayenne or Red Pepper
1 teaspoon Worcestershire sauce
½ teaspoon salt
⅛ teaspoon MSG

Marinate crab meat in lime or lemon juice 30 minutes. Beat together cream cheese, cream, mayonnaise and seasonings until smooth and creamy. Fold in marinated crab meat. For a really attractive service, serve in a deep shell or shell-shaped bowl nested in crushed ice with an interesting arrangement of bite-size pieces of Chinese cabbage, celery, sliced cauliflowerettes, green peppers and thin, wide slices of carrot. Do not forget a basket of crackers or chips. *Makes about 1½ cups.*

## Savory Onion Rounds

¼ teaspoon Season-All
¼ teaspoon Savory
¼ teaspoon dry Mustard
Dash MSG

¼ cup mayonnaise
12 thin slices onion
12 crackers

Combine seasonings and mayonnaise. Put onion slices on crackers and spread with mayonnaise mixture. Broil until bubbly and brown. Serve hot. *Makes 12.*

---

# Guacamole

---

This avocado dip, a favorite in Mexico, is colorful, tart and delicious!

| | |
|---|---|
| 1 large ripe avocado | ½ teaspoon Chili Powder |
| ½ ripe tomato, peeled and finely chopped | ½ teaspoon salt |
| | ¼ teaspoon Black Pepper |
| ½ green pepper, seeded and finely chopped | ½ teaspoon olive oil |
| | 1 teaspoon lime juice |
| 1 teaspoon Onion Salt | ½ cup mayonnaise |

Mash avocado with a fork. Blend in remaining ingredients except mayonnaise. Spread mayonnaise over top of dip to keep it from darkening. When ready to serve, blend in mayonnaise. Serve with corn chips or use as topping for cherry tomatoes. *Makes about 2 cups.*

---

# Herb Roquefort Dip

---

| | |
|---|---|
| 1 8-ounce package cream cheese | ½ teaspoon dry Mustard |
| | ½ teaspoon Herb Seasoning |
| 1 3-ounce package Roquefort cheese | Dash Nutmeg or Mace |
| | 5 tablespoons commercial sour cream or milk |
| 1 teaspoon Beef Flavor Base | |
| 1 tablespoon hot water | |

Have cheese at room temperature. Dissolve beef flavor base in hot water. Combine all ingredients, mixing thoroughly. Serve with crackers, chips, celery or carrot sticks. *Makes about 1½ cups.*

# Quiche Lorraine

Pastry for 10-inch pie shell
4 thin slices Smithfield ham
1 cup grated Swiss cheese
5 eggs
1¼ cups milk
1¼ cups light cream

¼ teaspoon salt
⅛ teaspoon Cayenne
½ teaspoon Season-All
  or Bon Appétit
Dash Nutmeg
Dash MSG

Line a 10-inch pie plate with pastry. Cut ham into small pieces (should have about ¾ cup) and heat in frying pan for a few minutes; sprinkle over pastry. (Twelve slices bacon may be substituted for ham. Cook bacon until crisp, then crumble into small pieces.) Sprinkle cheese over ham. Beat eggs; add remaining ingredients and mix well. Pour over cheese and ham. Bake in 375°F. oven 40 minutes. You can cut Quiche Lorraine into wedges and serve as a first course or for a light luncheon. Or, cut into small squares for appetizers. *Serves 8 to 10 when cut into wedges or many more when cut into squares, depending upon size.*

# Mephisto Ham Dip

A mixture zesty enough to please the devil himself.

1 8-ounce package cream
  cheese
1 2¼-ounce can deviled ham
  or Smithfield ham spread
2 teaspoons Instant Minced
  Onion
2 teaspoons Parsley Flakes

4 teaspoons milk
1 teaspoon Powdered
  Horseradish
Dash Garlic Salt
Dash Celery Salt
Dash Black Pepper

Have cheese at room temperature. Add remaining ingredients and mix until thoroughly blended. Serve with potato chips, crisp fresh vegetables or spread on crackers and toasted bread rounds. Excellent for sandwiches too. If any dip is leftover, you may freeze it for future use. *Makes 1½ cups.*

## Cheese and Caviar Croutelettes

A different and easy-to-make appetizer—cream cheese and caviar in small pastry shells.

1 8-ounce package cream cheese
¼ teaspoon Onion Salt
⅛ teaspoon White Pepper
¼ teaspoon dry Mustard
¼ teaspoon Lemon Peel
Dash MSG

1 teaspoon lemon juice
2 tablespoons milk
4 drops Red Food Color
1 carton croutelettes (30 to 36)
2 tablespoons caviar

Have cheese at room temperature. Add onion salt, pepper, dry mustard, lemon peel, MSG, lemon juice, milk and food color. Mix until smooth and creamy. Fill croutelettes. You can make attractive shapes by using a pastry bag with tube. Top each with about ⅛ teaspoon caviar. *Makes 30 to 36.*

# Pâté de Foie en Aspic

A smooth, subtly seasoned pâté for your most elegant party.

| | |
|---|---|
| 1 pound chicken livers | ¾ cup dry white wine |
| 1 tablespoon Instant Minced Onion | or tomato juice |
| | 2 envelopes unflavored gelatine |
| 1 stalk celery, chopped | ¼ cup cold water |
| 1 Bay Leaf | 1 3-ounce package cream cheese |
| 1 teaspoon Parsley Flakes | |
| ⅛ teaspoon Thyme Leaves | ¾ teaspoon Celery Salt |
| ⅛ teaspoon Rosemary Leaves, crushed | ½ teaspoon dry Mustard |
| 1 tablespoon Chicken Seasoned Stock Base | 1 teaspoon Powdered Horseradish |
| 1 cup hot water | |

Combine first nine ingredients and ½ cup of the wine or tomato juice in a saucepan. Bring to a boil; simmer 20 minutes or until livers are tender. Remove livers; strain and reserve liquid. If necessary, add water to make 1½ cups liquid; heat and mix with gelatine which has been softened in the cold water. Stir to melt. Cover bottom of 1-quart mold with a thin layer of the gelatine mixture and chill until firm. Set aside remaining gelatine mixture. Put chicken livers through fine blade of food chopper or purée in a blender. Combine with remaining wine or tomato juice, cream cheese, celery salt, dry mustard and powdered horseradish. Mix well. Thoroughly blend chicken liver mixture with remaining gelatine mixture; pour into mold. Chill until firm. Remove from mold; serve with crackers or Melba toast. *Makes 1 quart, serving about 12 to 15 people.*

# Sesame Cheese Ball

¼ cup Sesame Seed
2 tablespoons Instant Minced Onion
1 teaspoon Beef Flavor Base
2 tablespoons lemon juice
½ pound medium sharp cheese

2 tablespoons mayonnaise
1 tablespoon catchup
1 teaspoon Worcestershire sauce
1 teaspoon dry Mustard

Toast sesame seed in 350°F. oven 15 minutes or until lightly browned. Soak onion and beef flavor base in lemon juice. Grate cheese. Mix all ingredients, except sesame seed, until well blended. Shape into ball. Spread toasted sesame seed on waxed paper; roll cheese ball in seed until outside is coated. Chill. For a festive party idea serve on a tray with a cheese knife. Surround with assorted crackers and Melba toast. Excellent when spread on toast rounds and broiled until cheese melts. Makes good sandwiches. *Makes 1 cup.*

# Chili Cheese Roll

Crunchy pecans in a cheese roll coated with spicy Chili Powder.

1 8-ounce package American cheese, grated
1 3-ounce package cream cheese

⅛ teaspoon Garlic Powder
¼ cup chopped pecans
2 tablespoons Chili Powder

Have cheese at room temperature; mix both until well blended. Stir in garlic powder and pecans. Form into a roll about 10 inches long. Spread the chili powder on waxed paper and coat the outside of cheese with the chili powder by rolling over the waxed paper. *cont.*

*cont.* Chill. Slice and serve with crackers or Melba toast. *Makes forty 1/4-inch thick slices.*

## *Tomato Juice Cocktail*

| | |
|---|---|
| 6 cups tomato juice | 1/8 teaspoon Black Pepper |
|   or 1 46-ounce can | 1 teaspoon Powdered |
| 6 whole Cloves |   Horseradish |
| 2 whole Allspice | 1 teaspoon Bon Appétit |
| 1 Bay Leaf | 1 tablespoon sugar |
| 1 tablespoon Instant Minced | Dash MSG |
|   Onion | 3 tablespoons vinegar |

Combine all ingredients except vinegar. Bring to a boil, then simmer 15 minutes. Strain. Add vinegar. Chill several hours. Serve cold. *Makes about 6 cups or 10 to 12 servings.*

NOTE:
It's fun to experiment with tomato juice. Why don't you try other combinations of spices from your spice rack?

## *Barbecued Nibblers*

| | |
|---|---|
| 1/2 cup butter | 2 cups rice cereal, bite size |
| 1 tablespoon Barbecue Spice | 2 cups corn cereal, bite size |
| 2 teaspoons Bon Appétit | 1 cup wheat cereal, bite size |
| 1/4 teaspoon Garlic Powder | 1 cup thin pretzel sticks |
| 2 tablespoons Sesame Seed, | 2 cups mixed nuts |
|   toasted | |

Melt butter in small saucepan; stir in seasonings and toasted sesame seed. (Toast sesame seed in 350°F. oven 15 minutes or until golden brown.) Pour hot seasoned butter over dry cereals, pretzel sticks and nuts. Mix thoroughly until all pieces are coated. Spread evenly in a 15½ x 10½ x 1-inch baking pan and bake in 250°F. oven 1 hour, stirring occasionally. *Makes 2 quarts.*

VARIATION:

*Curried Nibblers*—Substitute ½ teaspoon Curry Powder, ½ teaspoon Cinnamon, 2 teaspoons Onion Salt and dash Cayenne or Red Pepper for the above seasonings.

## Marjoram Meat Balls

½ cup fine dry bread crumbs
¼ cup milk
1 pound ground beef
1 teaspoon Season-All
½ teaspoon Onion Powder
½ teaspoon ground Marjoram
¼ teaspoon ground Thyme
¼ teaspoon Black Pepper
⅛ teaspoon MSG
Dash Mace
3 tablespoons oil
1 teaspoon Beef Flavor Base
¼ cup hot water

Soak crumbs in milk, then combine with ground beef, Season-All, onion powder, marjoram, thyme, pepper, MSG and mace. Shape into 30 to 36 small balls, using a rounded teaspoonful for each. Brown on all sides in hot oil. Dissolve beef flavor base in hot water; pour over meat balls. Cover and simmer 20 minutes. For extra zest, add ½ cup wine to these miniature meat balls before simmering. Serve plain or with your favorite sauce. *Makes 3 dozen.*

# Best Ever Stuffed Eggs

Subtle spices give a new and savory twist to old favorites.

6 eggs, hard cooked
¼ cup mayonnaise
2 teaspoons lemon juice
  or vinegar
½ teaspoon Chicken
  Seasoned Stock Base
⅛ teaspoon Onion Powder
⅛ teaspoon White Pepper

½ teaspoon Bon Appétit
⅛ teaspoon Savory or
  Turmeric
"Little tidbits" for toppings:
  Parsley Flakes, Paprika,
  capers, anchovies, olive
  slices or pimiento

Carefully cut hard-cooked eggs in half. You can vary
the shape by cutting the eggs crosswise instead of lengthwise. Remove yolks and mash or force through a sieve.
Add mayonnaise, lemon juice, seasoned stock base,
onion powder, pepper, Bon Appétit and savory or
turmeric. Mix thoroughly. Refill the whites, piling the
yolk mixture high. Top with parsley flakes, a dash
paprika or one of the other "tidbits." *Makes 12 halves.*

VARIATIONS:

*Dill Stuffed Eggs*—In place of Bon Appétit and savory or
  turmeric use ½ to 1 teaspoon Dill Weed, ¾ teaspoon
  Celery Salt and dash Cayenne or Red Pepper.
*Curry Stuffed Eggs*—Add ½ to 1 teaspoon Curry Powder
  to above recipe.
*Chicken or Bacon Stuffed Eggs*—To any of the above recipes
  stir in ½ cup finely minced, cooked or canned chicken
  or 3 slices bacon which has been crisp-cooked and
  crumbled.

## Bon Appétit Dip aux Herbes

Flavoring so subtle no one will be sure quite what's in it
—and everyone will want to know!

1 8-ounce package cream
    cheese
6 tablespoons milk or cream
1 teaspoon Chicken Seasoned
    Stock Base
1 tablespoon hot water
1 tablespoon Instant Minced
    Onion

½ teaspoon Bon Appétit
½ teaspoon Marjoram
    Leaves
½ teaspoon Tarragon Leaves
½ cup finely minced, cooked
    chicken, shrimp, clams
    or crab meat

Have cheese at room temperature. Beat until creamy.
Gradually stir in milk or cream and seasoned stock base
which has been dissolved in hot water. Add remaining
ingredients, mixing well. Serve with an assortment of
crisp crackers or chips. For an interesting idea use as a
filling for marinated mushrooms or bite-size tart shells.
*Makes about 1 cup.*

## Dilly of a Dip

1 cup commercial sour
    cream
1 teaspoon Dill Weed

⅛ teaspoon Onion Powder
1 teaspoon Bon Appétit
Dash MSG

Thoroughly mix together all ingredients. Refrigerate at
least 1½ hours to blend flavors. Excellent served with
crackers, chips or crisp raw vegetables. You will also find
this delicious served on hot baked potatoes. *Makes 1 cup.*

# Ceviche

Spicy and exotic lime-marinated fish bits from Mexico.

| | |
|---|---|
| 1 pound firm, white, fish fillets | 1 teaspoon Crushed Red Pepper |
| Lime juice to cover | 1 teaspoon salt |
| 3 Bay Leaves | ¼ cup sliced, stuffed olives |
| ¼ teaspoon White Pepper | ¼ cup juice from olives |
| 1 teaspoon Bon Appétit | 1 tablespoon oil |
| ⅛ teaspoon Instant Minced Garlic | ¼ cup catchup |
| ⅓ cup Chopped Instant Onions | 2 tomatoes, finely chopped |
| | 1 hot chili pepper, chopped |

Remove tissue-like skin from fish. Cut fish into very thin strips 1 inch long or into small cubes. Put in glass jar and cover with lime juice. (It will take about 1½ cups juice or 1 dozen limes, depending on size and amount of juice in limes.) Refrigerate overnight or for several hours. Drain. Combine fish with remaining ingredients. Store in refrigerator at least one hour, preferably longer. Will keep well in refrigerator for several days. When ready to serve, remove bay leaves and serve in individual dishes with a garnish of lettuce. *Serves 6 to 8.*

# Curry Dip

| | |
|---|---|
| ½ cup mayonnaise | 1 teaspoon lemon juice |
| ½ cup commercial sour cream | Dash Cayenne or Red Pepper |
| 1 teaspoon Curry Powder | Dash MSG |

Combine all ingredients, blending well. Use as a dip for shrimp, lobster and other sea food. May also be combined with flaked tuna for an interesting dip to serve with crackers. *Makes 1 cup.*

# Beef Teriyaki

1 pound tenderloin or sirloin
    beef, cut 1 inch thick
¾ cup soy sauce
¼ cup dark brown sugar,
    packed
¼ teaspoon Garlic Powder

½ teaspoon Onion Salt
2 tablespoons lemon juice
1 teaspoon ground Ginger
    or 10 to 12 pieces whole
    Ginger, about the size
    of a shelled peanut

Cut meat into bite-size cubes. Combine remaining ingredients; pour over beef cubes and let stand at room temperature one hour or in the refrigerator several hours. Thread cubes of meat onto a skewer. (Pineapple chunks may be alternated with the beef cubes.) Broil about 3 inches from heat 10 to 12 minutes, turning once, or cook over grill or hibachi. Serve hot as an appetizer or with rice as a main course. *Makes appetizers for 10 to 12.*

# Hot Canapés

1 pound ground beef
½ teaspoon MSG
½ teaspoon dry Mustard
¾ teaspoon salt
¼ teaspoon Black Pepper

⅛ teaspoon Nutmeg
1 tablespoon Instant
    Minced Onion
12 slices bread
Charcoal Seasoning

Mix ground beef with MSG, dry mustard, salt, pepper, nutmeg and onion, blending well. Cut bread into 2-inch squares or into circles 1½ to 2 inches in diameter. Arrange on baking sheet and toast on one side until golden brown. Turn bread over and spread the untoasted side of each with about 1 tablespoon of the seasoned meat. Sprinkle generously with charcoal seasoning. (Preparation up to this point may be done in advance. Cover and refrigerate until ready to broil and serve.) Broil 3 inches from heat 1 to 2 minutes. Serve immediately. *Makes about 48.*

# Curried Chicken Balls

Unusual and distinctively different are the words your guests will use to describe these delicious hors d'oeuvres.

| | |
|---|---|
| 2 pounds ground, raw chicken or turkey | 2 teaspoons salt |
| 1 teaspoon Onion Powder | 2 teaspoons lemon juice |
| 1 tablespoon Curry Powder | 2 tablespoons fine bread crumbs |
| 1 teaspoon Season-All | ¼ cup flour |
| ¼ teaspoon MSG | ¼ cup butter |
| 1 egg, lightly beaten | |

Combine all ingredients except flour and butter; mix well. Form into small, bite-size balls. Roll lightly in flour and sauté in butter 15 minutes or until golden brown on all sides. Serve in a chafing dish or candle-warmed casserole in Creamy Curry Sauce (see recipe page 399). Be sure to have plenty of toothpicks handy. *Makes about 90.*

# Tinted-Minted Pineapple

| | |
|---|---|
| 1 No. 2 can pineapple chunks | 2 tablespoons Mint Flakes |
| ½ cup vinegar | Red Food Color |
| 1 cup sugar | or Green Food Color |

Drain syrup from pineapple chunks. To the syrup add vinegar, sugar and mint flakes. Stir to dissolve sugar and bring to a boil. Cover and simmer 10 minutes. Remove from heat; keep covered and set aside to cool. Strain to remove mint flakes. To the liquid add ¼ teaspoon (about 25 drops) red or green food color; stir. Add pineapple chunks. Store in a covered dish or jar in refrigerator. You will also find this a tasty and attractive garnish for meats, especially lamb.

# Chinese Stuffed Mushrooms

The nutty flavor of toasted Sesame Seed adds elegance to these mushrooms.

1 pound mushrooms
1 tablespoon butter
2 tablespoons water
½ teaspoon Chicken Seasoned Stock Base or Beef Flavor Base
½ pound ground, cooked pork (2 to 2½ cups)
¼ teaspoon Ginger
¼ teaspoon MSG

1 tablespoon Shredded Green Onions
Dash Cayenne or Red Pepper
¼ cup minced water chestnuts
2 teaspoons soy sauce
2 tablespoons melted butter
¼ cup Sesame Seed

Select uniform-size mushrooms about 1¼ inches in diameter. Wash and remove stems. In a saucepan, combine 1 tablespoon butter, water and seasoned stock base or beef flavor base. Heat to boiling. Add mushrooms; cover and simmer 3 minutes. Remove from heat; carefully lift out mushroom caps and save liquid. Let mushrooms cool while you prepare the filling. Combine remaining ingredients except sesame seed; mix well. If mixture seems dry, add 2 to 4 tablespoons water or broth. Stuff mushroom caps and dip tops in sesame seed. (Preparation up to this point may be done in advance. Cover and refrigerate until ready to bake and serve.) Place in shallow baking pan, and add liquid in which mushrooms were cooked. Bake in 375°F. oven 25 minutes or until sesame seed are lightly browned. Serve hot. *Makes about 30.*

## Liver Pâté Bon Appétit

| | |
|---|---|
| 1 pound chicken livers | ¼ teaspoon Ginger |
| ½ cup dry white wine | ¼ teaspoon MSG |
| ½ cup water | 1 tablespoon soy sauce |
| 1 teaspoon Chicken Seasoned Stock Base | ½ cup soft butter |
| 1 teaspoon Parsley Flakes | 1 teaspoon Bon Appétit |
| 1 tablespoon Instant Minced Onion | ¼ teaspoon dry Mustard |
| | Dash Nutmeg |
| | 1 tablespoon brandy |

Combine the first nine ingredients; bring to a boil. Reduce heat and simmer 20 minutes. Cool livers in liquid; drain. Put livers through fine blade of food grinder or purée in blender. Add remaining ingredients. Beat hard until well mixed and smooth. If mixture seems too thick, add small amount of the cooking liquid. Store in refrigerator in covered container at least 24 hours to blend flavors. Serve on crisp, shredded lettuce as an appetizer or with crackers and toast as a cocktail spread. *Makes about 1¾ cups.*

## Surprise Cheese Puffs

Bite into these golden hot puffs and find a heart of stuffed olive.

| | |
|---|---|
| ½ cup butter | Dash Cayenne or Red Pepper |
| 2 cups grated sharp cheese | 1 cup sifted all-purpose flour |
| ½ teaspoon salt | 50 small stuffed green olives |
| 1 teaspoon Paprika | |

Allow butter to soften; blend with cheese, salt, paprika and cayenne. Stir in flour, mixing well. Mold 1 teaspoon of this mixture around each olive, covering it completely.

Arrange on a baking sheet and chill until firm. Bake in 400°F. oven 15 minutes. Serve hot. *Makes 50 puffs.*

NOTE: These little puffs are so easy to serve at parties as they may be made in advance, frozen on a baking sheet to keep round and stored in a plastic bag in the freezer. Bake as needed.

---

## Marinated Artichoke Hearts

| | |
|---|---|
| 1 9-ounce package frozen artichoke hearts | ¼ teaspoon Oregano Leaves |
| 2 tablespoons lemon juice | ¼ teaspoon Chervil Leaves |
| 2 tablespoons olive oil | ¼ teaspoon Tarragon Leaves |
| | ¼ teaspoon Garlic Salt |

Cook artichoke hearts following directions on package. Drain and put in small bowl. Combine remaining ingredients and pour over artichoke hearts. Chill at least 2 hours. You will find marinated artichoke hearts excellent served with egg, sea food or tossed green salad. *Serves 4.*

---

## Salted Spiced Walnuts

| | |
|---|---|
| 2 teaspoons Ginger | 4 tablespoons melted butter |
| ½ teaspoon Allspice | ½ teaspoon Garlic Salt or |
| 5 cups water | Season-All |
| 1 pound walnut halves | |

Add ginger and allspice to water; bring to boil. Drop in walnuts and boil about 3 minutes. Drain well. Spread in a shallow pan and bake in 350°F. oven 15 minutes or until lightly browned. Remove from oven and toss with melted butter and garlic salt or Season-All.

# Coquilles Saint-Jacques

This famous French dish with a bubbling-hot, delectable sauce makes an elegant first course.

6 tablespoons butter
3 tablespoons flour
¼ teaspoon dry Mustard
½ teaspoon Lemon Peel
½ teaspoon Bon Appétit
½ teaspoon Powdered
  Horseradish
2 cups light cream
½ cup sliced mushrooms

2 teaspoons Instant Minced
  Onion
½ pound scallops
½ pound cleaned, cooked
  shrimp
¼ pound crab meat
2 tablespoons dry sherry
Bread crumbs

Melt 4 tablespoons of the butter in saucepan. Add flour, dry mustard, lemon peel, Bon Appétit and powdered horseradish, then stir until well blended. Add cream. Cook, stirring, until thickened. Sauté mushrooms and onion in the remaining 2 tablespoons butter. Remove from pan with slotted spoon. To butter in pan add scallops, which have been cut into bite-size pieces, and sauté 3 minutes. Cut shrimp into small pieces. Combine sauce, mushrooms, scallops, shrimp, crab meat and sherry. Spoon into shells or ramekins; top with bread crumbs. Bake in 400°F. oven 10 minutes, then broil a few minutes until lightly browned. *Serves 8 to 10.*

# Crab-Stuffed Mushrooms

Piping hot and spicy, these will make a hit at any party.

2 dozen large, firm
mushrooms
1 tablespoon Instant Minced
Onion
2 tablespoons butter or
margarine
2 tablespoons Shredded
Green Onions
Dash Cayenne or Red
Pepper

1 tablespoon prepared English
mustard
1½ teaspoons Bon Appétit
3 tablespoons lemon juice
1 tablespoon Worcestershire
sauce
1 pound crab meat
¼ cup sherry
2 tablespoons flour
¼ cup cream

Rinse mushrooms; remove stems. Cook caps in salted
boiling water (1 tablespoon salt to 1 quart water) 2 to
3 minutes. Drain. Thinly slice tender part of stems;
sauté with minced onion in butter but do not brown.
Add remaining ingredients, mixing thoroughly. Cook
over low heat about 5 minutes. Pile the caps high with
this mixture. (Tops may be brushed with a mixture of
mayonnaise and cream, using about 2 tablespoons each.)
Place in a buttered baking dish and bake in 450°F. oven
15 minutes or until tops are delicately browned. *Makes
24.*

# Rumaki

The delightful seasoning and crisp texture are reminiscent of the South Seas.

1 pound chicken livers
1 teaspoon Season-All
¼ teaspoon Black Pepper
⅛ teaspoon Ginger
2 5-ounce cans water
  chestnuts

1 pound or about 15 slices
  bacon
Fat for deep fat frying

Cut livers into sections. Mix Season-All, pepper and ginger and sprinkle over livers. Pierce livers 2 or 3 times with fork to prevent excess popping. Slice the large chestnuts in half and cut slices of bacon in half. Wrap one section of liver and one slice of water chestnut with a strip of bacon and fasten with a toothpick. Fry in deep fat, 340°F., until golden brown, or broil if you prefer. Serve piping hot and you will want to have a bowl of Hot Chinese Mustard (see recipe page 398) close by to use as a dip. *Makes about 30.*

# Broiled Clams

4 tablespoons butter
¼ teaspoon Onion Powder
½ teaspoon Bon Appétit
½ teaspoon Lemon Peel
½ teaspoon Shredded Green
  Onions

Dash dry Mustard
Small dash Mace
Rock salt
24 clams on the half shell
2 slices bacon

Melt butter and add seasonings. Spread layer of rock salt in shallow baking pan. Arrange clams on salt. Pour ½ teaspoon of the butter mixture over each clam. Cut bacon into 24 pieces and place one piece on top of each clam. Preheat broiler and broil 4 to 5 inches from heat 4 minutes or until lightly browned and bacon is crisp. *Serves 4.*

NOTE: If fresh clams are not available, you may acquire a set of shells and use whole canned clams. You could even arrange clams in a shallow baking dish, omitting rock salt, and not use shells.

## Cheese Dip Caraway

1 8-ounce package cream cheese
½ cup commercial sour cream
2 tablespoons Caraway Seed

2 teaspoons Instant Minced Onion
1 teaspoon Season-All
1½ teaspoons Worcestershire sauce

Have cheese at room temperature; add sour cream and beat until smooth and creamy. Stir in caraway seed, onion, Season-All and Worcestershire sauce. Blend thoroughly. *Makes about 1¼ cups.*

## Marinated Mushrooms

2 tablespoons vinegar
2 tablespoons olive oil
½ teaspoon Basil Leaves
½ teaspoon Marjoram Leaves

½ teaspoon Mustard Seed
¼ teaspoon Onion Salt
1 4-ounce can mushroom crowns, drained

Combine vinegar, olive oil and seasonings. Pour over mushrooms. Chill several hours before serving. You may use the same marinade for 1 pint sliced, raw mushrooms but leave them in the marinade 24 hours. *Serves 6 to 8, allowing 4 to 5 per person.*

# Spiced Shrimp

3 tablespoons Pickling Spice
2 tablespoons Season-All
1 teaspoon Crushed Red
    Pepper
1 teaspoon salt

¼ cup vinegar
1 quart water
1 pound fresh
    or frozen shrimp

Add spices, salt and vinegar to water. Let boil 10 minutes, then add shrimp. (If you use frozen shrimp, thaw before cooking.) Boil 5 to 7 minutes or until shrimp turn pink. (Shrimp become tough when boiled too long.) Remove from heat; let stand 20 minutes, then drain. Cool, shell, devein and chill. For a buffet arrange on a tray, on a platter of cracked ice or place around a bowl of cocktail sauce. Serve as individual cocktails, or use in preparation of other dishes. *Serves 4 to 5.*

VARIATIONS:

*Oriental Spiced Shrimp*—For above spices substitute 6 Peppercorns, ½ teaspoon Onion Powder, ⅛ teaspoon Garlic Powder, ½ teaspoon Celery Seed, 2 teaspoons Parsley Flakes, 2 Bay Leaves, 1 teaspoon Curry Powder and 1 teaspoon Oregano Leaves.

*Spiced Shrimp Maison*—For even more variety, why don't you mix your own spices using a combination of any of the following: Allspice, Bon Appétit, Ginger, dry Mustard, Tarragon Leaves, Thyme Leaves, Basil Leaves, Rosemary Leaves, Coriander Seed, whole Cardamom or Fennel Seed?

# Pineapple-Grapefruit Delight

1 No. 2 can pineapple-
  grapefruit juice (2¼ cups)
2 whole Cardamom

4 whole Cloves
1 3-inch piece Cinnamon

Pour juice in a saucepan; add spices. Cover and simmer
30 minutes. Remove spices and chill juice. For a stronger
spice note, chill juice before removing spices. Serve in
small glasses before any meal, or you will find this ideal
to serve over ice cubes for a summer cooler. *Makes 2¼
cups.*

**VARIATION:**

*Pineapple-Grapefruit Refresher*—In the above recipe use
  ¼ teaspoon Mint Flakes and 5 Coriander Seeds,
  crushed, instead of whole cinnamon, cardamom and
  cloves.

# Toasted Onion Dip

The secret of this crunchy nutty flavor is Chopped Instant Onions *delicately* toasted.

1 cup commercial sour cream
2 teaspoons Beef Flavor Base
1 teaspoon Bon Appétit

2 tablespoons Chopped
  Instant Onions

Combine sour cream, beef flavor base and Bon Appétit.
Mix well and set aside. Toast onions in 350°F. oven 1
minute or until lightly browned. Add to sour cream
mixture. Allow mixture to stand at least 20 minutes
before serving. Serve with assorted crackers or chips.
*Makes 1 cup.*

# Curry Puffs

Crisp little bite-size pastries filled with an exotic curry-meat stuffing, called *Samosas* in India.

1 recipe for two-crust pastry
2 cups finely chopped
  cooked lamb
1 tablespoon Curry Powder
1 tablespoon syrup from
  chutney

1 teaspoon Season-All
¼ cup condensed cream
  of mushroom soup,
  undiluted
Fat for deep fat frying

Make pastry using your favorite recipe or package mix; roll thin. Cut out circles using a round cookie cutter 3 inches in diameter. Mix together remaining ingredients. Place 1 heaping teaspoon of the mixture on each circle of dough. Fold over to make a semicircle; thoroughly seal edges by pressing with the tines of a fork. Fry in deep fat, 375°F., 4 minutes or until golden brown. You may make these ahead of time and heat in oven when ready to serve. *Makes about 3 dozen.*

# Bologna Pinwheels

1 3-ounce package cream
  cheese
1 tablespoon milk
¼ cup finely chopped green
  olives
½ teaspoon Shredded Green
  Onions

½ teaspoon Season-All
Dash MSG
Dash White Pepper
¼ pound sliced bologna

Have cheese at room temperature; blend with milk. Stir in olives, onions, Season-All, MSG and pepper. Spread cheese mixture over bologna slices; roll tightly. Wrap in waxed paper and chill. Before serving, cut each roll into slices. *Makes about ½ cup cheese mixture or about 30 delicious bite-size pieces.*

# Celery Victor

2 bunches celery
2 cups water
½ cup wine vinegar
¾ cup oil
2 tablespoons lemon juice
1 tablespoon Chicken
  Seasoned Stock Base
4 Peppercorns
¼ teaspoon Chervil Leaves

1 teaspoon Instant Minced
  Onion
1 teaspoon Parsley Flakes
2 teaspoons Season-All
2 whole Cloves
½ teaspoon salt
8 anchovy fillets, washed
8 strips pimiento

Cut hearts of celery and tender stalks into 3-inch sections.
Place in rows in a baking dish or skillet. Combine remaining ingredients except anchovy and pimiento. Pour
over celery. Simmer 15 minutes or until celery is crisp-tender. Remove from heat; let celery cool in liquid and
chill. When ready to serve, remove celery from liquid
and place several pieces on shredded lettuce. Top with
anchovy fillets and thin strips of pimiento. *Serves 4.*

# Stuffed Celery Sticks

8 4-inch pieces celery
1 3-ounce package cream
  cheese
⅛ teaspoon dry Mustard

¼ teaspoon Paprika
¼ teaspoon Bon Appétit
1 tablespoon finely chopped
  olives

Cut tender stalks of crisp celery into 4-inch pieces. Have
cheese at room temperature; add dry mustard, paprika
and Bon Appétit. Mix until smooth and creamy. Stir in
olives. Fill celery sticks. Serve as an appetizer, on a relish
tray or with soup. *Makes about ½ cup filling.*

# Oysters Rockefeller

A version of the famous recipe created in 1889 by Antoine's Restaurant in New Orleans and named for its rich sauce.

6 tablespoons butter
6 tablespoons thawed, frozen chopped spinach
1½ teaspoons Instant Minced Onion
1 tablespoon Parsley Flakes
1 tablespoon Celery Flakes
1½ teaspoons Bon Appétit
3 Fennel Seeds, crushed

⅛ teaspoon Tarragon Leaves
⅛ teaspoon Chervil Leaves
Dash Cayenne or Red Pepper
Dash Garlic Powder
¼ cup bread crumbs
Rock salt
24 oysters on the half shell

Combine butter, spinach and seasonings. Simmer 15 minutes. Put through food mill or purée in blender. Add bread crumbs. Spread layer of rock salt in shallow baking pan. Arrange oysters on salt and spread 1 teaspoon of the spinach mixture over each oyster. Preheat broiler and broil 4 to 5 inches from heat 8 minutes or until lightly browned. *Serves 4.*

# SOUPS

— * —

## Minestrone

1 cup dried marrow beans
  or garbanzos or lima beans
7 cups water
¼ cup Chopped Instant
  Onions
1 tablespoon Parsley Flakes
3 tablespoons Celery Flakes
⅛ teaspoon Instant Minced
  Garlic
2 tablespoons Bell Pepper
  Flakes
¼ cup olive oil
¼ teaspoon Crushed Red
  Pepper
½ pound fresh spinach

2 teaspoons Beef Flavor Base
⅛ teaspoon rubbed Sage
¼ teaspoon Italian
  Seasoning
1 teaspoon ground Thyme
2 teaspoons salt
¼ teaspoon Coarse Grind
  Black Pepper
1 cup diced potatoes
2 cups tomatoes (No. 303
  can)
1 cup chopped cabbage
1 small zucchini, thinly sliced
1 cup elbow macaroni
Grated Parmesan cheese

Soak beans overnight in enough water to cover. Drain. Add the 7 cups water; cover and simmer 3 hours or until tender. Sauté onions, parsley flakes, celery flakes, garlic and pepper flakes in oil until well coated and hot but do not allow to brown. Add to beans with remaining seasonings, vegetables and macaroni. Cook over low heat 30 minutes longer. This is a thick soup; if you prefer a thinner consistency, add a little water. Serve hot with Parmesan cheese sprinkled over top of each serving. *Makes about 3 quarts.*

# French Onion Soup

Make your own savory onion soup in just 20 minutes using Chopped Instant Onions.

½ cup Chopped Instant Onions
4 tablespoons butter
4 cups hot water
2 tablespoons Beef Flavor Base

½ Bay Leaf
¼ teaspoon Black Pepper
¼ teaspoon ground Marjoram
Herb Croutons
Grated Parmesan cheese

Brown onions in melted butter over low heat to prevent burning. Add hot water, beef flavor base, bay leaf, pepper and marjoram. Simmer 20 minutes. Serve piping hot topped with Herb Croutons (see recipe page 274) and grated Parmesan cheese. *Serves 4.*

# Vichyssoise

One of the top-ranking favorites of all summer soups. Serve chilled with a sprinkling of Chives.

3 cups sliced potatoes
3 cups water
2½ teaspoons Chicken Seasoned Stock Base
1 teaspoon Onion Powder
3 tablespoons butter

1 cup light cream
1 cup milk
¼ teaspoon Celery Salt
¼ teaspoon White Pepper
¼ teaspoon Bon Appétit
Chives

Wash, peel and slice potatoes (takes about 2 large potatoes). Add water and seasoned stock base. Bring to boil and cook until potatoes are very tender. Force through a fine sieve or purée in a blender, including the liquid. Combine with remaining ingredients except chives. Heat 10 minutes, but do not allow to boil. Chill. Serve in bowls placed in crushed ice. Top each serving with chives. *Makes 6 cups.*

# Chicken or Turkey Soup

Chicken or turkey carcass
Meat from carcass (about
   1 cup)
3 tablespoons Vegetable
   Flakes
¼ cup Chopped Instant
   Onions
6 Peppercorns

5 whole Cloves
Dash Nutmeg or Mace
1 Bay Leaf
Water
1 tablespoon Chicken
   Seasoned Stock Base
1 cup long grain rice

Remove meat from carcass. For full flavor, you should have about 1 cup meat, but the more, the better. Crack bones, and put in a large saucepan along with any remaining skin. Add vegetable flakes, onions, peppercorns, cloves, nutmeg or mace, bay leaf and enough water to cover bones. Bring to boil. Reduce heat and simmer, covered, 2 hours. Cool slightly and strain. Spoon off excess fat if you wish. To the broth add seasoned stock base, the chicken or turkey meat and rice. Add salt if needed. Simmer 20 to 25 minutes. Serve hot. *Makes 6 to 8 servings.*

# Tomato Soup Oregano

1 10½-ounce can condensed
   cream of tomato soup
2½ cups tomatoes (No. 2 can)
½ teaspoon Bon Appétit
¼ teaspoon ground Oregano

¼ teaspoon Onion Powder
½ teaspoon sugar
4 tablespoons commercial
   sour cream

Combine all ingredients, except sour cream, in saucepan. Cut tomatoes into small pieces. Simmer 20 minutes. Top with sour cream just before serving. Good served with stuffed celery. *Serves 4.*

# Quick Curry Soup Indienne

½ teaspoon Indian or
Madras Curry Powder

1 10½-ounce can cream of
chicken or cream of
mushroom soup

Add curry powder to soup; prepare following directions on can. For added interest and flavor, you may like to serve a tray of condiments with curry soup—a few suggestions:

| | |
|---|---|
| Crumbled crisp bacon | Slivered toasted almonds |
| Herb seasoned croutons | Parmesan cheese |
| Finely chopped fresh onions | Thinly sliced water chestnuts |

*Makes 4 5-ounce servings.*

# Swedish Fruit Soup

You will find this chilled blend of puréed fruits topped with cream a refreshing summer favorite.

2 cups mixed dried fruit
(peaches, apricots,
pears)
1 cup dried apples
1 cup pitted prunes
1 No. 303 can red tart
pitted cherries
¼ cup raisins or currants
2 quarts water

½ cup sugar
1 3-inch piece Cinnamon
1 teaspoon Lemon Peel
¼ teaspoon Mace
⅛ teaspoon Cardamom
⅛ teaspoon Allspice
⅛ teaspoon Nutmeg
Whipped cream or
commercial sour cream

Combine all ingredients, except whipped cream or sour cream, in large saucepan. Bring to a boil; reduce heat and simmer, covered, 1 hour or until fruit is tender. Remove cinnamon; rub cooked fruit with liquid through a fine sieve or purée in blender. Chill. Serve cold topped with whipped cream or sour cream. *Makes 2½ quarts.*

112

# Lentil Soup

1½ cups lentils
7 cups water
1 tablespoon salt
½ teaspoon Coarse Grind
  Black Pepper
1 tablespoon Celery Flakes
1 teaspoon Basil Leaves

¼ cup Chopped Instant
  Onions
1 teaspoon Marjarom Leaves
2 carrots, sliced thin
½ pound ham hock
6 frankfurters
Sherry, optional

Rinse lentils. Place in a large kettle with water, seasonings, carrots and ham hock. Cover and boil gently 2 hours. Cut frankfurters into ¼-inch slices; add to soup and cook 10 minutes longer. Lentil soup traditionally is a thick, hearty potage, a meal in itself. However, you may personally prefer a thinner soup; if so, thin with water to your taste. Serve steaming hot. For a real gourmet touch let each person add sherry to taste. *Makes 3 quarts.*

# Oyster Stew

6 oysters with liquor
2 tablespoons butter
⅛ teaspoon MSG
½ teaspoon Bon Appétit
¼ teaspoon Paprika
¼ teaspoon salt

Dash White or Black
  Pepper
¼ teaspoon Worcestershire
  sauce
1 cup milk (use part cream
  if desired)

Shuck oysters if in shell. Check for bits of shell. Heat butter until it sizzles, but do not let it brown. Add oysters with liquor, seasonings and Worcestershire sauce. Heat until edges of oysters curl slightly. Add milk. Heat thoroughly, but do not boil. Serve hot topped with a dash of paprika. *Serves 1.*

# Mulligatawny

The most famous soup of India, spicy-hot, tantalizingly good.

¼ cup butter
1 3-pound chicken, cut in pieces
1 tablespoon Instant Minced Onion
3 quarts boiling water
1 tablespoon Vegetable Flakes
1 tablespoon Curry Powder

¼ teaspoon MSG
1 teaspoon Turmeric
¼ cup Chicken Seasoned Stock Base
⅛ teaspoon Mace
½ teaspoon Parsley Flakes
¼ teaspoon Black Pepper
6 tablespoons flour

Melt butter in large saucepan or Dutch oven. Add chicken pieces and onion; cover and simmer over low heat 20 minutes. Add remaining ingredients except flour. Simmer 40 minutes or until chicken is tender. Remove chicken and strain stock. Return stock to saucepan. Remove chicken from bones; chop meat and add to stock. Simmer 15 minutes. Make a thin, smooth paste by mixing together the flour with an equal amount of water. Then stir into the soup; continue cooking until thickened. Remove excess fat, if you wish. Serve piping hot. *Makes 3 quarts.*

# Cream of Zucchini Soup

A soup as delicately green and fresh as springtime.

3 cups sliced zucchini (4 small zucchini or 1 pound)
½ cup water
1 tablespoon Instant Minced Onion
1 teaspoon Season-All
½ teaspoon Parsley Flakes
2 teaspoons Chicken Seasoned Stock Base

2 tablespoons butter
2 tablespoons flour
⅛ teaspoon White Pepper
⅛ teaspoon MSG
¼ teaspoon Bon Appétit
1 cup milk
½ cup light cream
Commercial sour cream
Paprika

Combine zucchini, water, onion, Season-All, parsley flakes and 1 teaspoon of the seasoned stock base. Cook until zucchini is tender and only a small amount of water is left. Mash, put through sieve or purée in blender. In a saucepan melt butter; add flour, the remaining seasoned stock base, pepper, MSG and Bon Appétit. Blend well. Add milk and cream; simmer, stirring until thickened. Stir in zucchini, mixing well. If soup is thicker than you like, add additional milk. Serve topped with a spoon of sour cream garnished with paprika. *Makes about 4 cups.*

# Lobster Bisque Elégante

An epicurean delight, delicately spiced.

4 frozen rock lobster tails,
weighing about 8 ounces
each
3 cups water
1 tablespoon Chicken
Seasoned Stock Base
1 tablespoon Onion Flakes
6 Coriander Seeds
1 Bay Leaf

1 tablespoon Vegetable
Flakes
3 Peppercorns
5 tablespoons butter
5 tablespoons flour
1 teaspoon Bon Appétit
1 teaspoon salt
3 cups milk
1 cup light cream

Bring enough water to a boil to cover lobster tails; add
1 teaspoon salt to each 1 quart of water. Drop frozen
lobster tails into water and boil 11 minutes (or 3 minutes
plus the weight of the largest lobster tail). Remove meat
from lobster shells and dice; set aside. Crush shells and
put in saucepan. Add the 3 cups water, seasoned stock
base, onion flakes, coriander seed, bay leaf, vegetable
flakes and peppercorns. Simmer 30 minutes; strain.
Melt butter; stir in flour, Bon Appétit and salt. Cook
until bubbly. Remove from heat and add milk. Simmer
over low heat, stirring constantly, until thickened. Stir
in lobster stock, lobster meat and cream. Do not allow
it to boil. Serve piping hot. *Makes 7 to 8 cups.*

# New Orleans Shrimp Gumbo

2 pounds shrimp
4 tablespoons butter
1 tablespoon Instant Minced Onion
1½ cups chopped celery
1 tablespoon Bell Pepper Flakes
¼ teaspoon Instant Minced Garlic
4 cups fresh or frozen sliced okra

2 tablespoons flour
4 teaspoons Chicken Seasoned Stock Base
4 cups water
3½ cups tomatoes (No. 2½ can)
½ pound cubed, cooked ham
1 Bay Leaf
1 teaspoon Thyme Leaves
1 tablespoon Gumbo Filé
Hot steamed rice, optional

Cook and clean shrimp; cut into bite-size pieces. Heat butter (you may use bacon drippings if you like) in large kettle or Dutch oven. Add onion, celery, pepper flakes and garlic; sauté lightly. Dredge okra with flour. If you are using frozen okra, thaw it first. Add okra to kettle; continue to sauté for a few minutes. Add seasoned stock base, water, tomatoes, ham, bay leaf and thyme leaves. Lower heat; cover and simmer 1 hour. Add shrimp and cook 15 minutes longer. Remove from heat. Mix 4 to 5 tablespoons of the hot soup with the gumbo filé, then add to the soup. Stir about 5 minutes or until thickened. Do not cook after gumbo filé is added. Serve in soup bowls. In New Orleans a spoonful of hot cooked rice is always placed in the center of each serving. Sprinkle with additional gumbo filé if you like. *Serves 8.*

# New England Clam Chowder

| | |
|---|---|
| 3 slices bacon | 1 teaspoon salt |
| 2 cups diced potatoes | 2 cups water |
| 2 tablespoons Instant Minced Onion | 1 quart milk |
| 2 teaspoons Bon Appétit | 1 7½-ounce can minced clams |
| ¼ teaspoon White Pepper | 4 tablespoons flour |

Cut bacon into ½-inch pieces; fry over low heat until crisp. Add potatoes, onion, Bon Appétit, pepper, salt and water. Bring to a boil; reduce heat and simmer 10 minutes. Stir in milk; heat but do not allow to boil. Add clams, including liquid. Make a thin, smooth paste by mixing together the flour with an equal amount of water. Then stir into chowder; continue cooking over low heat until thickened. Remember, do not let it boil. Serve piping hot. *Serves 6 to 8.*

# Bouillabaisse

Saffron is the secret ingredient in this exquisite fish soup from the French Riviera.

| | |
|---|---|
| 1 carrot | 1 Bay Leaf |
| 1 pound tomatoes | ¼ teaspoon Thyme Leaves |
| 4 7-to 8-ounce rock lobster tails | ⅛ teaspoon Fennel Seed |
| 1 pound each perch, cod, rock, sole, red snapper | 1 teaspoon Orange Peel |
| ½ cup Chopped Instant Onions | 5 teaspoons Bon Appétit |
| ¼ teaspoon Instant Minced Garlic | ¼ teaspoon Black Pepper |
| 2 teaspoons Parsley Flakes | ⅓ cup olive oil |
| 24 individual pieces Saffron | 1 8-ounce bottle clam juice |
| | 1 tablespoon lemon juice |
| | French bread |
| | Water |

118

Peel and cut carrot into small cubes; peel, seed and chop tomatoes. Cut lobster tails into large pieces. Cut fish into 2-inch pieces. Put all ingredients except perch, cod and French bread in a large saucepan or kettle. Cover with water; boil hard 8 minutes. Add perch and cod and boil 8 minutes longer. Remove fish to large bowl or platter. Cut French bread into ¼-inch slices and put in bottom of soup tureen. Pour broth over bread. Serve the soup in soup plates and the fish on side plates. *Serves 8 to 10.*

---

## Golden Cream of Carrot Soup

---

2 cups thinly sliced carrots
  (4 to 5 large carrots)
½ cup water
1 teaspoon Bon Appétit
3 teaspoons Chicken
  Seasoned Stock Base

1 tablespoon lemon juice
4 tablespoons butter
2 tablespoons flour
¼ teaspoon Ginger
⅛ teaspoon Onion Powder
2 cups milk

Combine carrots, water, ½ teaspoon of the Bon Appétit, 1 teaspoon of the seasoned stock base and the lemon juice. Cook until carrots are tender and liquid is reduced to about 1 tablespoon. Melt butter; add flour and the remaining seasonings, stirring until smooth. Add milk and simmer, stirring until thickened. Mash carrots, put through sieve or purée in blender. Add to milk mixture and stir until well blended. Add additional milk or cream to get the consistency you like. Serve hot. *Makes about 4 cups.*

# Scotch Broth

Here is a delicious recipe you will find in very few cookbooks, and one you will want to add to your collection.

STOCK:

| | |
|---|---|
| 4 pounds lamb, meat and bones | 2 tablespoons Celery Flakes |
| 9 cups water | ½ teaspoon Thyme Leaves |
| 2 teaspoons salt | 12 Peppercorns |
| 1 tablespoon Season-All | 2 whole Cardamom |
| | 1 Bay Leaf |

Combine all ingredients and simmer slowly 3 to 4 hours. Strain. *Should make 2 quarts stock.*

SOUP:

| | |
|---|---|
| ¼ cup butter | Dash Garlic Powder |
| 2 tablespoons Instant Minced Onion | ½ cup barley |
| 1 large carrot, diced small | 3 tablespoons flour |
| ½ cup finely diced celery | 2 quarts lamb stock |
| | 1 cup cream |

Melt butter in 3- to 4-quart saucepan. Add onion, carrot, celery and garlic powder. Sauté 5 minutes. Do not allow to brown. Add barley and flour. Cook 2 minutes longer. Add hot lamb stock; mix well and simmer slowly 1½ hours. Stir in cream and simmer 10 minutes more before serving. *Makes 5 bowls or 10 cups.*

# Manhattan Clam Chowder

2 slices bacon
2 tablespoons Chopped
Instant Onions
1 tablespoon Bell Pepper
Flakes
2 tablespoons Celery Flakes
5 cups boiling water
3 whole Cloves
1 whole Cardamom
1 Bay Leaf
⅛ teaspoon Garlic Powder

1 tablespoon Season-All
½ teaspoon Thyme Leaves
¼ teaspoon Coarse Grind
Black Pepper
¼ teaspoon MSG
1 cup finely diced carrots
2 cups diced potatoes
1 cup canned tomatoes
2 cups minced clams
2 tablespoons butter
2 tablespoons flour

Cut bacon into ½-inch pieces; fry in large saucepan or kettle until brown and crisp. Add onions, pepper flakes and celery flakes; continue cooking until onions brown lightly. Add water. Tie cloves, cardamom and bay leaf in cheesecloth bag; drop into soup. Add garlic powder, Season-All, thyme leaves, pepper, MSG, carrots, potatoes, tomatoes and the liquid drained from clams. Simmer 40 minutes. Sauté clams in butter but do not brown. Add to soup and simmer 10 minutes. Make a thin, smooth paste by mixing together the flour with an equal amount of water. Then stir into chowder; continue cooking until thickened. Remove bag of spices. Serve hot. *Makes 9 cups.*

# Old-Fashioned Vegetable Soup

3 pounds soup bones
2 quarts water
1 Bay Leaf
2 cups tomatoes
    (No. 303 can)
1 cup sliced carrots
½ cup chopped celery
2 cups diced potatoes
2 cups sliced okra
2 cups whole kernel corn

¼ cup Chopped Instant
    Onions
2 tablespoons Season-All
1 teaspoon Celery Salt
½ teaspoon Black Pepper
¼ teaspoon Thyme Leaves
½ teaspoon Savory
¼ teaspoon MSG
1 tablespoon Beef Flavor
    Base

Put soup bones in a large saucepan or Dutch oven; add water and bay leaf. Bring to a boil and simmer 45 minutes, then add remaining ingredients and simmer, covered, 3 hours. Remove bones. Serve piping hot. Extra soup may be frozen and reheated as needed. *Makes 3 quarts.*

# Consommé Royale

2 10½-ounce cans consommé
2 Bay Leaves
6 whole Cloves
4 Peppercorns

3 whole Allspice
⅛ teaspoon Lemon Peel
Thin slices of avocado
    or fresh mushrooms

Combine consommé, bay leaves, cloves, peppercorns, allspice and lemon peel. Heat just to the boiling point. Remove the whole spices. For an elegant touch float very thin slices of avocado or mushroom on each serving. Serve with herb seasoned bread sticks. *Serves 4 to 6.*

## Tomato-Vegetable Soup

½ cup Vegetable Flakes
2½ cups tomatoes (No. 2 can)
2 cups water
1 tablespoon Beef Flavor Base
½ teaspoon Black Pepper
¼ teaspoon Powdered Horseradish

¼ teaspoon dry Mustard
1 Bay Leaf
¼ teaspoon Thyme Leaves
1 teaspoon Season-All
1 teaspoon sugar
½ teaspoon Dill Seed, crushed
½ teaspoon Oregano Leaves

Combine all ingredients and simmer 30 minutes or longer. Remove bay leaf. You may prefer more powdered horseradish—adjust to your own taste. This is a quick 'n' easy soup to make. *Makes 4 cups.*

## Egg Drop Soup

1 egg
⅓ cup flour
1 tablespoon water

7 teaspoons Chicken Seasoned Stock Base
6 cups boiling water

Beat egg with fork; add flour and the 1 tablespoon water and continue beating until smooth. Dissolve seasoned stock base in the boiling water. Drop the egg mixture, in a thin stream, from a spoon into the boiling broth. Move spoon slowly back and forth for even distribution. Do not stir soup until egg is cooked. For a change, use Beef Flavor Base in place of chicken seasoned stock base. *Makes 6 1-cup servings.*

# Chicken Corn Soup

1 3- to 4-pound chicken
6 cups water
3 teaspoons Chicken
  Seasoned Stock Base
1 teaspoon salt
10 individual pieces Saffron
2 cups noodles
2 cups whole kernel corn

½ teaspoon Parsley Flakes
1 teaspoon Shredded Green
  Onions
¼ teaspoon Black Pepper
⅛ teaspoon Celery Salt
Dash MSG
2 hard-cooked eggs

Cut chicken in pieces. Cook in water with seasoned stock base, salt and saffron about 1½ hours or until tender. Remove chicken from stock; take meat off the bones and cut into bite-size pieces. (Save the breast for other uses if desired.) Return cut-up chicken to stock and bring to a boil. Add noodles, corn, parsley flakes, onions, pepper, celery salt and MSG. Simmer 15 minutes. Chop eggs and add to soup. *Makes 2½ quarts.*

## Buffet Turkey Loaf

2 envelopes unflavored
  gelatine
1 cup water
1 teaspoon Chicken
  Seasoned Stock Base
3 cups chopped, cooked
  turkey
½ cup chopped celery
¼ cup sliced stuffed olives

1 cup commercial sour cream
½ cup white wine
¼ cup mayonnaise
1 teaspoon lemon juice
½ teaspoon Season-All
⅛ teaspoon Onion Powder
½ teaspoon salt
Dash Paprika

In a small saucepan soften gelatine in water. Add seasoned stock base and heat until gelatine melts. Cool. Then combine with remaining ingredients. Pour into a 1½-quart mold. Chill until firm; then remove from mold. This loaf is particularly good garnished with slices of olive and surrounded with asparagus topped with pimiento strips. *Serves 6.*

# Chef's Salad Bowl

½ head lettuce or romaine
1 bunch endive or escarole
2 carrots
1 cucumber, sliced
1 Italian onion, sliced
  and separated

1 avocado, sliced
2 tomatoes, cut into wedges
8 radishes, sliced
Salad Herbs
Salad Salt
Cracked Black Pepper

Tear salad greens into bite-size pieces. Make carrot curls. Put salad greens, carrot curls, cucumber, onion, avocado, tomatoes and radishes in salad bowl. Sprinkle generously with salad herbs, salad salt and cracked black pepper or freshly ground black pepper from pepper mill. Toss lightly with Roquefort, Italian, French or your own special herb-blended salad dressing. Serve immediately. *Serves 6 to 8.*

# Crab Salad

1 teaspoon Bon Appétit
¼ teaspoon White Pepper
⅛ teaspoon dry Mustard
Dash MSG
Dash Cayenne or Red
  Pepper
Dash Ginger

2 teaspoons lemon juice
½ cup mayonnaise
1 pound crab meat
1 cup chopped celery
½ cup chopped stuffed olives
Paprika

Blend together Bon Appétit, pepper, dry mustard, MSG, cayenne, ginger, lemon juice and mayonnaise. Pick over crab meat to remove bits of shell. Combine mayonnaise mixture, crab meat, celery and olives. Chill. Serve on crisp lettuce; sprinkle top with paprika. Serve with side dish of mayonnaise if desired. *Serves 4 to 6.*

# Curried Sea Food Salad

1 cup flaked tuna (7-ounce can)
1 cup chopped, cooked shrimp
½ cup chopped celery
¼ cup sliced ripe olives
½ cup mayonnaise
2 tablespoons lemon juice
½ teaspoon Curry Powder
½ teaspoon Bon Appétit
¼ cup Parsley Flakes
2 tablespoons water
3 cups cold, cooked rice
2 tablespoons French dressing

Chill tuna and shrimp. Add celery and olives. Blend together mayonnaise, lemon juice, curry powder and Bon Appétit; add to tuna mixture and toss lightly. Soak parsley flakes in the water about 5 minutes, then toss with rice and French dressing. Transfer to serving plate. Spoon tuna-shrimp mixture over rice. You may garnish with water cress or radish roses. *Serves 4 to 6.*

# Tarragon Tuna Salad

2 7-ounce cans tuna
1 cup diced celery
¼ cup India or sweet relish
½ teaspoon Season-All
¼ teaspoon White Pepper
½ teaspoon dry Mustard
¼ teaspoon Tarragon Leaves
1 teaspoon Parsley Flakes
1 tablespoon Instant Minced Onion
1 tablespoon lemon juice
1 cup mayonnaise

Drain and flake tuna; add celery and relish. Combine remaining ingredients; mix well. Add to tuna; mix thoroughly. Serve on crisp lettuce. Garnish with sliced hard-cooked eggs, tomato wedges or thin slices of avocado. May also be used as filling for sandwiches. *Serves 4 to 6.*

# Garden Vegetable Salad

1 10-ounce package frozen
   lima beans
1 10-ounce package frozen
   peas
4 medium-size carrots
2 medium-size potatoes
1 cup cooked, diced beets
1 cup chopped celery
½ cup salad oil

¼ cup white vinegar
Dash Garlic Powder
Dash MSG
1 tablespoon Bon Appétit
1 teaspoon Instant Minced
   Onion
¼ teaspoon White Pepper
½ teaspoon dry Mustard
⅔ cup mayonnaise

Cook lima beans and peas as directed on package; drain. Slice carrots and cook in salted water until tender; drain. Cook potatoes in salted water; peel and dice. Put all vegetables in bowl and toss gently. Combine remaining ingredients except mayonnaise; mix well. Pour over vegetables and toss until vegetables are coated. Chill several hours. Stir in mayonnaise. Serve in crisp lettuce cups. *Serves 6 to 8.*

# Piquant Tomato Aspic

An attractive and delicious tomato aspic.

2 envelopes unflavored
   gelatine
¼ cup cold water
4 cups tomato juice
3 tablespoons Celery Flakes
4 tablespoons Onion Flakes
3 Bay Leaves

3 whole Cloves
6 Peppercorns
4 whole Allspice
½ teaspoon Basil Leaves
2 tablespoons brown sugar
1 teaspoon Season-All
3 tablespoons lemon juice

Add gelatine to the cold water; set aside to soften. In a saucepan combine tomato juice, celery flakes, onion flakes, bay leaves, cloves, peppercorns, allspice, basil leaves, brown sugar and Season-All. Bring to a boil, then simmer 15 minutes. Strain; add softened gelatine and lemon juice, stirring until gelatine melts. Pour into a 1½-quart mold. Chill until firm. Remove from mold; garnish with salad greens and cottage cheese. *Serves 6 to 8.*

## Caesar Salad

A man's salad—superb with steak.

2 small heads romaine
  lettuce, thoroughly chilled
Herb Croutons
½ teaspoon Season-All
⅛ teaspoon MSG
¼ teaspoon dry Mustard
Freshly ground Black Pepper
Dash Garlic Powder
1 tablespoon lemon juice
½ teaspoon Worcestershire
  sauce
⅛ teaspoon sugar
6 tablespoons olive oil
2 tablespoons wine vinegar
1 2-ounce can anchovy fillets
1 egg, coddled (see below)
¼ cup grated Parmesan
  cheese

Wash romaine; remove outside leaves. Break the tender leaves crosswise into pieces about 1 inch wide. Store in plastic bag in refrigerator until ready to use. Make Herb Croutons (see recipe page 274). When ready to serve, place romaine in large wooden salad bowl. In a small mixing bowl combine seasonings, lemon juice, Worcestershire sauce, sugar, oil, vinegar and 3 anchovy fillets which have been mashed or minced. Mix thoroughly. Break coddled egg over greens, then pour salad dressing over all and toss lightly. Sprinkle with cheese and croutons and toss again lightly. Serve immediately on chilled salad plates. Top each serving with 2 anchovy fillets. Excellent with roast beef as well as steak. *Serves 4 to 6.*

NOTE:
To coddle egg, cook whole egg in hot but not boiling water 2 minutes.

129

# Shrimp Salad

1 pound cooked, cleaned shrimp
½ cup chopped celery
2 hard-cooked eggs, chopped
⅔ cup mayonnaise

1 teaspoon Bon Appétit
⅛ teaspoon Tarragon Leaves
¼ teaspoon White Pepper
Dash Cayenne or Red Pepper

Reserve about 6 shrimp for garnish and cut remaining shrimp into bite-size pieces. Add celery and eggs. Combine remaining ingredients; spoon over shrimp. Mix gently. Chill. Garnish with whole shrimp and lemon slices. *Serves 4 to 6.*

# Creamy Coleslaw

½ cup commercial sour cream
1 tablespoon vinegar
1 teaspoon Season-All
1½ tablespoons sugar
½ teaspoon dry Mustard
¼ teaspoon Ginger

½ teaspoon Celery Seed
Dash White Pepper
4 cups finely shredded cabbage
¼ cup minced green pepper
Paprika

Combine sour cream with the next seven ingredients. Refrigerate 20 minutes, allowing seasonings to blend. Spoon over cabbage and green pepper, tossing lightly. Sprinkle with paprika. *Serves 4 to 6.*

VARIATION:

*Coleslaw Bon Appétit*—Use ½ cup mayonnaise, 1 tablespoon vinegar, 1 tablespoon cream, ½ teaspoon Bon Appétit, ⅛ teaspoon Onion Salt, ½ teaspoon sugar, ¼ teaspoon dry Mustard, dash Cayenne and ½ teaspoon Celery Seed in place of the first eight ingredients in the above recipe. Proceed as above.

# Chicken Salad

It's the seasoning that makes this chicken salad memorable.

2 cups cubed, cooked
  chicken
1 cup chopped celery
¼ cup chopped pickle
1 hard-cooked egg, chopped
½ cup mayonnaise
1 tablespoon lemon juice
½ teaspoon Season-All

½ teaspoon dry Mustard
⅛ teaspoon MSG
Dash Nutmeg
⅛ teaspoon White Pepper
¼ teaspoon salt
Paprika
Capers, optional

Toss chicken with celery, pickle and egg. Mix together
mayonnaise, lemon juice and seasonings except paprika.
Add to chicken. Mix well. Serve on crisp lettuce, or use
to fill tomato or avocado halves. Garnish each serving
with paprika and three or four capers. May be used for
sandwiches. *Makes 4 to 6 servings.*

# Cucumbers in Sour Cream

Cool and refreshing.

2 cups thinly sliced, pared
  cucumbers
½ teaspoon salt
½ cup commercial sour
  cream
2 teaspoons vinegar
½ teaspoon sugar

2 teaspoons Instant Minced
  Onion
½ teaspoon Dill Weed
Dash Cayenne
  or Chili Powder
Cracked Black Pepper

Place cucumber slices in a bowl; sprinkle with salt and
cover with cold water. Refrigerate 30 minutes; drain
well. Combine sour cream, vinegar, sugar, onion, dill
weed and cayenne. Add cucumber slices to sour cream
and toss lightly. Chill at least 1 hour before serving.
Sprinkle with cracked black pepper. *Serves 4.*

# Egg Salad

6 hard-cooked eggs
¼ cup finely chopped celery
¼ cup finely chopped pickle
¼ cup mayonnaise
1 teaspoon vinegar

¼ teaspoon dry Mustard
1 teaspoon Season-All
⅛ teaspoon White Pepper
Dash Onion Powder
Dash MSG

Chop eggs; add celery and pickle. Combine remaining ingredients, mixing well. Add to eggs and mix carefully. Serve as a salad on crisp lettuce or as a filling for sandwiches. *Makes 2 cups.*

VARIATION:

*Fiesta Egg Salad*—To the above recipe, add ⅛ teaspoon ground Cumin or crushed Cumin Seed.

# Dill Macaroni Salad

1 8-ounce package elbow
  macaroni or salad
  macaroni
1 cup chopped celery
½ cup thinly sliced green
  pepper
¼ cup thinly sliced carrots
2 tablespoons chopped
  pimiento
½ cup mayonnaise

1 tablespoon vinegar
1 tablespoon sugar
2 tablespoons Instant
  Minced Onion
1 teaspoon Dill Weed
2 teaspoons Season-All
¼ teaspoon dry Mustard
⅛ teaspoon White Pepper
Dash Cayenne or Red
  Pepper

Cook macaroni as directed on the package. Drain and cool. Add celery, green pepper, carrots and pimiento. Mix remaining ingredients; spoon over macaroni and toss to mix thoroughly. Chill. Serve in bowl or on salad plates in crisp lettuce cups. *Serves 6 to 8.*

132

# Champagne Salad

**CHAMPAGNE LAYER:**

1 envelope unflavored
  gelatine
2 tablespoons water
1 cup champagne

¾ cup water
3 drops Red Food Color
1 pint fresh strawberries

Soften gelatine in the 2 tablespoons water, then set over hot water to melt. Combine champagne, the ¾ cup water and food color. Stir in melted gelatine. Pour into 2-quart mold and chill until almost set. Carefully push about one half of the strawberries, pointed end first, into gelatine mixture. Chill until firm, then add Spiced Cheese Layer.

**SPICED CHEESE LAYER:**

1 8-ounce package cream
  cheese
1 teaspoon Lemon Peel
½ teaspoon Ginger
Dash Mace
Dash Cardamom
1 8½-ounce can crushed
  pineapple, drained

¾ cup reconstituted
  frozen limeade
3 drops Green Food Color
¼ cup toasted slivered
  almonds
1 envelope unflavored
  gelatine
2 tablespoons water

Have cheese at room temperature. Add lemon peel, ginger, mace and cardamom and beat until fluffy. Add pineapple, limeade, food color and almonds. Mix well. Soften gelatine in water; set over hot water to melt. Add gelatine to cream cheese mixture, mixing well. Spread over Champagne Layer. Chill until firm. Remove from mold. Garnish with crisp lettuce and the remaining fresh strawberries. *Serves 8.*

# Beet Surprise Salad

Who would think of adding cinnamon and cloves to beet salad? Yet it's this little touch that gives this salad mold excitement.

| | |
|---|---|
| 1 3-ounce package lemon gelatin | ¼ teaspoon salt |
| | 6 whole Cloves |
| 1 tablespoon Powdered Horseradish | 12 whole Allspice |
| | 1 3-inch piece Cinnamon |
| 1 No. 303 can diced or julienne beets | ⅓ cup wine vinegar |
| | ⅔ cup dry white wine or water |
| 1 tablespoon brown sugar | |

Combine gelatin and powdered horseradish in large bowl. Drain liquid from beets into measuring cup; add enough water to make 1 cup. Pour into saucepan; add brown sugar, salt and spices. Heat to boiling; reduce heat and simmer 1 minute. Strain into gelatin-horseradish mixture and stir until gelatin dissolves. Add vinegar, wine and drained beets. Pour into 1½-quart ring mold or 6 individual molds. Chill until firm, then remove from mold. Serve on shredded greens. *Serves 6.*

# Layered Orange-Cranberry Mold

A two-tiered mold pretty enough to grace any party table, and exquisitely flavored.

CRANBERRY LAYER:

2 envelopes unflavored
gelatine
¼ cup cold water
1 1-pound can whole
cranberry sauce
2 tablespoons lemon juice

¼ teaspoon Allspice
⅛ teaspoon Mace
or Nutmeg
1 cup ginger ale
1 cup orange sections

Soften gelatine in cold water; melt over hot water. Combine remaining ingredients, then stir in melted gelatine. Pour into 2-quart mold. Chill until firm.

CHEESE-NUT LAYER:

1 envelope unflavored
gelatine
2 tablespoons cold water
1 cup orange juice
1 3-ounce package cream
cheese

½ teaspoon Ginger
½ cup pecan pieces
½ cup heavy cream
½ cup commercial sour
cream

Soften gelatine in cold water; melt over hot water. Gradually mix orange juice into cream cheese. Add ginger and nuts; mix well. Stir in gelatine. Combine heavy cream and sour cream and whip until stiff; fold into gelatine mixture. Pour over cranberry layer. Chill until firm. Remove from mold; garnish with crisp greens and orange sections. *Makes 8 to 10 servings.*

# Fresh Fruit Medley

| | |
|---|---|
| 1 grapefruit | 2 apples |
| 2 oranges | 2 bananas |
| 1 pint fresh strawberries | ¼ cup lemon juice |
| 1 cantaloupe or other melon | ½ teaspoon Ginger |
| 1 fresh pineapple | Dash Mace |
| 2 pears | Dash Cardamom |

Peel and section grapefruit and oranges. Remove caps from strawberries. Cut melon in half; remove seed. With ball cutter, cut balls from the melon. Peel pineapple, remove core and cut into bite-size pieces. Peel and slice pears, apples and bananas and dip in a mixture of lemon juice, ginger, mace and cardamom. Combine all of the fruit and mix gently. Pour remaining lemon juice mixture over all. You may serve plain, or with a dressing, such as Poppy Seed Dressing, Celery Seed Dressing or a whipped cream dressing. *Serves 6 to 8.*

# Frozen Bing Cherry Salad

| | |
|---|---|
| 1 No. 2 can pitted Bing cherries | 1 teaspoon Lemon Peel |
| 1 buffet can pineapple tidbits | ½ teaspoon Ginger |
| 4 ounces cream cheese | ⅛ teaspoon Mace |
| ½ cup commercial sour cream | 1 teaspoon pure Vanilla Extract |
| 2 tablespoons sugar | 4 drops Red Food Color |
| ⅛ teaspoon salt | 1 cup miniature marshmallows |

Drain cherries and pineapple. Have cream cheese at room temperature, then beat until fluffy. Add sour cream, sugar, salt, lemon peel, ginger, mace, vanilla and food color; mix well. Carefully stir in cherries, pineapple and marshmallows. Pour into ice cube tray or a 1-quart mold. Freeze. Remove from mold; slice and serve on crisp lettuce. *Makes 6 servings.*

# Party Pink Fruit Salad

A cool, refreshing summer salad.

1 8-ounce package cream
  cheese
½ cup mayonnaise
½ teaspoon Allspice
½ teaspoon Orange Peel
¼ teaspoon Cloves
Dash Nutmeg
Few drops Red Food Color

1 No. 303 can fruit cocktail
1 orange
¼ cup maraschino cherries
½ cup chopped pecans
  or walnuts
1 cup miniature
  marshmallows
1 cup heavy cream

Have cheese at room temperature; add mayonnaise, spices and food color, mixing thoroughly. Drain fruit cocktail; peel and section orange and cut cherries into halves. Add fruits, nuts and marshmallows to cheese mixture. Mix carefully. Whip cream; fold into fruit mixture. Spoon into freezer trays or 1½-quart mold. Freeze. Remove from mold; slice and serve on crisp lettuce. *Serves 8 to 10.*

# Waldorf Salad

3 cups diced apples
½ cup chopped celery
½ cup chopped walnuts
  or pecans
¼ cup raisins
½ teaspoon Lemon Peel
¼ teaspoon dry Mustard

¼ teaspoon Ginger
⅛ teaspoon Mace
Dash Cardamom
2 teaspoons lemon juice
½ cup mayonnaise
1 tablespoon light cream

Put diced apples, celery, nuts and raisins in bowl. Combine remaining ingredients; toss with apple mixture. Serve in lettuce cups. *Serves 6 to 8.*

## Sweet-Sour Cucumbers with Onions

2 cups thinly sliced, pared
  cucumbers
½ teaspoon salt
1 cup thinly sliced onions
¼ cup vinegar
1 tablespoon water

1 tablespoon sugar
½ teaspoon Dill Weed
¼ teaspoon Cracked Black
  Pepper
Dash Cayenne

Place cucumber slices in a bowl; sprinkle with salt and cover with cold water. Refrigerate 30 minutes; drain well. Add onions. Combine vinegar, the 1 tablespoon water, sugar, dill weed, cracked black pepper and cayenne. Pour over cucumbers and onions; toss lightly. Chill 1 hour or longer, tossing occasionally, before serving. *Serves 4.*

## Country Kitchen Potato Salad

No picnic table is complete without this summertime favorite.

4 cups diced, cooked
  potatoes
2 hard-cooked eggs, chopped
½ cup chopped celery
¼ cup chopped pickle
⅔ cup mayonnaise
1 tablespoon vinegar

1 tablespoon Instant Minced
  Onion
2 teaspoons Bon Appétit
⅛ teaspoon MSG
¼ teaspoon White Pepper
1 teaspoon dry Mustard

Put potatoes, eggs, celery and pickles in bowl. Blend together remaining ingredients and gently mix with potato mixture. Chill. *Serves 6.* *cont.*

*Potato-Fennel Salad*—To the above recipe, add ¼ teaspoon crushed Fennel Seed.

---

## Tuna and Tomato Mold

---

This is an impressive and delicious salad for a buffet supper or luncheon.

2 envelopes unflavored
  gelatine
1½ teaspoons Beef Flavor
  Base
1¾ cups tomato juice
1 teaspoon sugar
¼ teaspoon ground Oregano
½ teaspoon dry Mustard
1 teaspoon Powdered
  Horseradish
1 tablespoon lemon juice

¼ cup water
¼ cup mayonnaise
½ cup commercial sour
  cream
½ teaspoon Lemon Peel
1 teaspoon Shredded
  Green Onions
¼ cup chopped stuffed
  olives
¼ cup chopped celery
1 7-ounce can tuna, flaked

Mix 1 envelope of the gelatine with beef flavor base and ¾ cup of the tomato juice. Heat, stirring, until gelatine melts. Remove from heat; add remaining tomato juice, sugar, oregano, dry mustard, powdered horseradish and lemon juice. Mix well, then pour into a 1-quart mold. Chill until firm. Meantime, soften the remaining envelope of gelatine in the ¼ cup water; melt over boiling water. Remove from heat. Stir in mayonnaise and sour cream, blending thoroughly. Gently stir in remaining ingredients. Spoon this mixture over top of tomato layer and return to refrigerator. Chill until firm. Remove from mold and garnish with salad greens. *Serves 5 to 6.*

139

# Creamy Roquefort Dressing

½ pound Roquefort cheese
½ cup mayonnaise
½ cup light cream
  or commercial sour cream
2 teaspoons lemon juice

¼ teaspoon dry Mustard
Dash MSG
Dash White Pepper
Dash Garlic Salt

Crumble cheese; add remaining ingredients and mix thoroughly. If a thinner dressing is desired, add additional cream or milk. *Makes about 1 pint.*

# Cardamom Cream Dressing

Cardamom makes a wonderful difference in this creamy dressing for fruit salad.

4 egg yolks
¼ cup vinegar
1 tablespoon sugar
1 tablespoon butter
¼ teaspoon dry Mustard
⅛ teaspoon ground
  Cardamom

¼ teaspoon salt
Dash White Pepper
½ pint heavy cream
1 cup miniature
  marshmallows
½ cup chopped pecans

Beat egg yolks lightly; add vinegar, sugar, butter and seasonings. Mix well. Cook over low heat or in double boiler, stirring constantly, until thick, about 3 minutes. Remove from heat; cool. When ready to serve, whip cream. Fold whipped cream, marshmallows and nuts into the cooled mixture. Serve with fruit salads. *Makes about 2½ cups.*

# Celery Seed Dressing

1 teaspoon Celery Seed
½ cup sugar
1 teaspoon Onion Salt
1 teaspoon Paprika

1 teaspoon dry Mustard
¼ cup vinegar
1 cup salad oil

Put celery seed, sugar, onion salt, paprika and dry mustard in small mixing bowl. Add alternately 1 tablespoon vinegar and ¼ cup oil until vinegar and oil are used up, beating hard after each addition. Continue beating for 5 minutes or until dressing thickens. Serve on fruit salad, avocado salad, sliced tomatoes or use on head lettuce. *Makes about 1½ cups.*

# Lamaze Dressing

1 cup mayonnaise
1 cup chili sauce
¼ cup India relish
1 hard-cooked egg, chopped
½ pimiento, chopped
¼ green pepper, finely chopped
2 tablespoons finely chopped celery

1 teaspoon vinegar
1 teaspoon dry Mustard
½ teaspoon Shredded Green Onions
⅛ teaspoon Paprika
¼ teaspoon Black Pepper
½ teaspoon Season-All
⅛ teaspoon Turmeric
1 teaspoon A-1 sauce

Combine all ingredients, mixing well. Chill before using. If full recipe is not used at once, keep in refrigerator in tightly covered jar. This dressing is especially good with shrimp, crab or lobster, and may be used on tossed salad and some sandwiches. *Makes about 3 cups.*

## Green Goddess Dressing

1 2-ounce can anchovy fillets
Dash Garlic Powder
⅛ teaspoon Onion Powder
1 tablespoon Shredded
  Green Onions
1 tablespoon Parsley Flakes

1 tablespoon Tarragon
  Leaves
1 tablespoon Chives
3 cups mayonnaise
¼ cup wine vinegar
Dash MSG

Mash anchovies. Add remaining ingredients, blending well. Let stand 30 minutes or longer for flavors to blend. Serve with salad greens. You may toss chicken, shrimp or crab meat with the greens. *Makes about 3½ cups.*


## Poppy Seed Dressing

½ cup sugar
1 teaspoon salt
1 teaspoon dry Mustard
½ teaspoon Onion Powder

⅓ cup cider vinegar
1 tablespoon lemon juice
1 cup salad oil
1½ tablespoons Poppy Seed

Combine sugar, salt, dry mustard, onion powder, vinegar and lemon juice. Stir until sugar dissolves. Add oil slowly, beating well. Dressing thickens as oil is added. Stir in poppy seed. Store in refrigerator. Just before serving, shake to mix well. Especially delicious with fruit or avocado salad. *Makes about 1⅔ cups.*


## Ginger Cream Dressing

½ teaspoon Ginger
½ pint heavy cream

¼ cup chopped dates
¼ cup chopped nuts

Add ginger to cream; whip until stiff. Fold in dates and nuts. Serve with fruit salads. *Makes about 2 cups.*

---

## Honey Spice Dressing

½ cup French dressing
1 tablespoon honey
½ teaspoon Cinnamon

¼ teaspoon ground Cloves
⅛ teaspoon Ginger

Combine all ingredients and mix well. Excellent on fruit salads. *Makes about ½ cup.*

---

## French Dressing

½ cup vinegar
  (wine, cider or malt)
¾ teaspoon salt
Dash MSG

¼ teaspoon White Pepper
½ teaspoon dry Mustard
1½ cups olive or salad oil

Combine all ingredients in jar; cover and shake vigorously. Set aside or chill 30 minutes or longer to allow flavors to blend. Shake well when ready to use. *Makes about 2 cups.*

VARIATIONS:

*American French Dressing*—To the above recipe add 2 teaspoons sugar, 1 teaspoon Paprika and ¼ teaspoon Garlic Powder.

*South-of-the-Border Dressing*—To above recipe for French Dressing add 2 teaspoons sugar, 1 teaspoon Paprika, ¼ teaspoon Chili Powder, ¼ teaspoon Dill Seed, 1 teaspoon Celery Salt and 6 Coriander Seeds, crushed.

*Herb French Dressing*—Be creative. To the above recipe add one or a combination of the following: Curry

143

Powder, Powdered Horseradish, Basil Leaves, Tarragon Leaves, Marjoram Leaves, Parsley Flakes, Oregano Leaves, Dill Weed, Italian Seasoning or Salad Herbs.

NOTE: Reduce oil to 1 cup for a lighter bodied or less oily dressing.

## Italian Dressing

¼ teaspoon Oregano Leaves
⅛ teaspoon Garlic Powder
⅛ teaspoon White Pepper
¼ teaspoon dry Mustard
½ teaspoon Chives
½ teaspoon Parsley Flakes
1 teaspoon Season-All

1 teaspoon Instant Minced Onion
Dash Cayenne or Red Pepper
½ teaspoon sugar
½ cup wine vinegar
1 cup olive oil

Combine all ingredients in jar; cover and shake vigorously. Chill 1 hour for flavors to blend. Shake well when ready to serve. *Makes 1½ cups.*

## Roquefort Dressing

¼ pound Roquefort cheese
1 teaspoon Worcestershire sauce
1½ teaspoons Bon Appétit
½ teaspoon Black Pepper
½ teaspoon Paprika

½ teaspoon dry Mustard
⅛ teaspoon MSG
Dash Cayenne
¼ cup vinegar
1 cup salad oil

Crumble cheese, then mix together all ingredients in a pint jar. Shake well. Keep in covered jar in refrigerator. Shake again before using. *Makes about 1½ cups.*

# MEATS

———— * ————

## *Ris de Veau à la Crème*

Sweetbreads in a delicate cream sauce enriched with sherry.

2 pair sweetbreads
2 tablespoons lemon juice
1½ teaspoons salt
4 tablespoons butter
⅛ teaspoon White Pepper
¼ teaspoon MSG

⅛ teaspoon Onion Powder
½ cup sherry
¾ cup light cream or
   half and half
1 tablespoon flour

Soak sweetbreads in ice water 1 hour. (If using frozen sweetbreads, thaw just before cooking.) Drain and cover with fresh cold water. Add lemon juice and 1 teaspoon of the salt and bring slowly to a boil. Simmer 10 minutes, then quickly plunge them into ice cold water to cool. Remove tubes and connecting tissues. Cut slices diagonally about 1 inch thick. Sauté in butter 4 minutes or until sweetbreads just begin to brown. Turn and sauté other side. Sprinkle with the remaining ½ teaspoon salt, pepper, MSG and onion powder. Add Sherry; cover and simmer 5 minutes. Add cream and simmer 15 minutes longer. Make a thin, smooth paste by mixing together the flour and an equal amount of water. Stir into sweetbreads and continue cooking, stirring, until thickened. Serve hot on toast. *Makes 4 servings.*

# Beef Stroganoff

2 pounds beef, sirloin or
 tenderloin
2 tablespoons butter or
 margarine
1 tablespoon Instant Minced
 Onion

1 teaspoon Season-All
½ teaspoon salt
Dash Nutmeg
¼ cup sherry
1 cup commercial sour cream

Cut beef into bite-size strips; sauté in butter until brown.
Add onion, Season-All, salt, nutmeg and sherry. Cover
and simmer about 20 minutes. Remove from heat and
allow to cool. Have sour cream at room temperature.
Stir into the cooled beef mixture and heat over very low
heat or in double boiler until hot, being careful not to
allow it to boil. (Boiling will cause a sour cream mixture
to separate, resulting in a curdled appearance.) For
parties or buffets or even table service, you may want to
heat and serve in a chafing dish or a candle warmer type
dish. Serve with white or wild rice or buttered noodles.
*Serves 4.*

# Herb Steak

1 pound round steak
2 tablespoons flour
1 teaspoon Season-All
2 tablespoons salad oil

1 10½-ounce can condensed
 cream of mushroom soup
¾ cup water
1 tablespoon Herb Seasoning

Cut steak into serving-size pieces. Combine flour and
Season-All; pound into steak. Brown meat on both sides
in hot oil in heavy skillet. Add remaining ingredients.
Cover; simmer 45 minutes, or bake in 350°F. oven 1
hour. Excellent served with hot Buttered Noodles with
Dill or with Poppy Seed (see recipe page 233). *Serves 3 to 4.*

# Glazed Boiled Beef

| | |
|---|---|
| 1 4-pound beef brisket | 1 teaspoon Season-All |
| 2 teaspoons Meat Tenderizer | 20 whole Cloves |
| 2 tablespoons Celery Flakes | Water |
| ¼ teaspoon Coarse Grind Black Pepper | ½ cup brown sugar, packed |

Pierce meat deeply with long-tined fork. Sprinkle meat tenderizer on all surfaces. Let stand 30 minutes at room temperature. Put in deep kettle; add celery flakes, pepper, Season-All and 6 to 8 whole cloves. Cover with water. Cover kettle and simmer very slowly 2 hours or until meat is tender. (Do not boil.) Remove meat from broth and place in shallow roasting pan. Score fat in diamond shapes. Sprinkle lightly with brown sugar and stud with remaining whole cloves. Bake in 400°F. oven 20 minutes. Slice and serve hot with a horseradish or mustard sauce. *Serves 6 to 8.*

# Hamburger De Luxe

| | |
|---|---|
| 2 pounds ground round steak | Dash Nutmeg |
| 1 egg | ¼ teaspoon Black Pepper |
| 1 tablespoon Worcestershire sauce | ½ teaspoon Onion Powder |
| 1 tablespoon soy sauce | 1 teaspoon Beef Flavor Base |
| 1 teaspoon Bon Appétit | ½ cup hot water |
| ½ teaspoon dry Mustard | Fat for searing |

Mix meat, egg and seasonings thoroughly. Dissolve beef flavor base in water and gradually mix into beef. Do not overmix. Shape into 4 to 8 patties. Sear quickly on both sides in a little fat in hot skillet; finish cooking to desired degree of doneness over low heat. Serve thin patties on split and toasted hamburger buns and thick patties as a dinner entrée. *Makes 8 hamburgers or 4 hamburger steaks.*

# Herbed Minute Steaks

Marinating in a wine and herb sauce before grilling does wonders for minute steaks.

1 cup salad oil
½ cup red wine (Burgundy or Bordeaux) or ¼ cup wine vinegar
½ teaspoon Garlic Powder
½ teaspoon Onion Powder
½ teaspoon Bon Appétit
Dash Nutmeg
¼ teaspoon MSG
¼ teaspoon Black Pepper
½ teaspoon salt
½ teaspoon Oregano Leaves
½ teaspoon Basil Leaves
6 minute or cube steaks
½ cup commercial sour cream
Paprika

Combine all ingredients, except steaks, sour cream and paprika, in glass or enameled flat pan; mix well. Add steaks and marinate 1 hour, turning steaks several times. Remove from marinade; pan fry in hot skillet, or broil just until browned on each side. Top each steak with a spoon of sour cream and sprinkle with paprika. *Serves 6.*

# Hungarian Goulash

Paprika, lots of it, gives this Hungarian stew its distinctive flavor.

¼ cup Chopped Instant Onions
3 tablespoons shortening
3 pounds beef shoulder (cut into 1½-inch cubes)
1 tablespoon Paprika
½ teaspoon Coarse Grind Black Pepper
2 teaspoons Season-All
6 Anise Seeds
Dash Cayenne
1 green pepper
2 tomatoes
4 tablespoons tomato purée
1 cup water
3 slices bacon

Brown onions in hot shortening; remove. Add beef and brown on all sides. Combine paprika, pepper, Season-All, anise seed and cayenne; sprinkle over meat. Add browned onions. Chop green pepper into medium-size pieces. Peel and cut tomatoes into wedges. Add green pepper, tomatoes, tomato purée and water to meat; stir. Lay bacon strips over top. Cover and simmer 2 hours or until meat is tender. Add more water if necessary. Serve over noodles or spätzle. *Serves 4 to 6.*

---

## *Peppered Tenderloin*

---

A gourmet steak, peppery, pungent, with a zesty sauce.

6 slices beef tenderloin
  (cut 1 inch thick)
½ teaspoon salt
⅛ teaspoon Garlic Salt
¼ teaspoon MSG
Coarse Grind Black Pepper
3 tablespoons butter

1 teaspoon flour
½ teaspoon Beef Flavor Base
¼ cup hot water
2 tablespoons sauterne
¼ teaspoon Shredded Green
  Onions

Trim off most of the outside fat. Slash remaining fat, about 1 inch apart, to prevent curling. Season steak with a mixture of salt, garlic salt and MSG. Sprinkle coarse grind black pepper generously over each side and press down with knife. Sauté in butter about 4 minutes on each side. Remove meat to heated serving platter. To essence in skillet add flour and beef flavor base, stirring to mix well; then add hot water, sauterne and shredded green onions. Bring to a boil and spoon sauce over steak. Serve immediately. You will find these steaks excellent served with wild rice and sautéed mushrooms. *Serves 6.*

# Meat Loaf Baked in Sauce

2 pounds ground beef
1 medium-size potato
2 eggs, lightly beaten
¼ cup melted butter
1 teaspoon Powdered
  Horseradish
2 tablespoons Instant Minced
  Onion

⅛ teaspoon Garlic Powder
¼ teaspoon Black Pepper
¼ teaspoon MSG
1 tablespoon Season-All
3 tablespoons catchup
¼ cup milk or
  water

For a good meat loaf, have fresh-ground beef. Scrub uncooked potato and grate, peel and all. (You should have about 1 cup after grating.) Mix all ingredients well, being careful not to overmix. Shape into a loaf in a shallow baking pan. Spoon sauce, recipe below, over loaf. Bake in 350°F. oven 1 hour and 15 minutes. *Serves 6 to 8.*

### ZESTY TOMATO SAUCE:

2 teaspoons Beef Flavor Base
1 cup hot water
1 6-ounce can tomato paste
½ cup chili sauce
2 teaspoons Instant Minced
  Onion

¼ teaspoon ground Oregano
⅛ teaspoon ground
  Marjoram
Dash Nutmeg
¼ teaspoon Black Pepper
1 teaspoon sugar

Dissolve beef flavor base in hot water. Add to remaining ingredients and mix well. You will find this makes a thick sauce; and if you prefer a thinner sauce, add ¼ to ½ cup additional water.

150

# Old-Fashioned Sauerbraten

An old, old recipe—well worth the time it takes to prepare.

1 4-pound chuck roast
2 teaspoons salt
¼ teaspoon Black Pepper
½ teaspoon MSG
2 cups water
2 cups cider or wine vinegar
½ cup Chopped Instant
   Onions
3 Bay Leaves
12 Peppercorns
6 whole Cloves

2 tablespoons Celery Flakes
¼ teaspoon Thyme Leaves
1 teaspoon Mustard Seed
1 large carrot, sliced
¼ cup sugar
Flour
2 tablespoons oil
¼ cup seedless raisins,
   plumped
18 dark, old-fashioned
   gingersnaps, crushed

Rub beef with salt, pepper and MSG; place in large bowl or crock with water, vinegar, onions, bay leaves, peppercorns, cloves, celery flakes, thyme leaves, mustard seed, carrot and sugar. (One half cup dry red wine may be added to marinade if desired.) Cover and marinate in refrigerator 3 days. Turn several times. When ready to cook, remove meat from marinade, dry and dust with flour; brown on all sides in hot oil. Add marinade. Cover and simmer slowly 3 hours or until tender. Lift meat onto hot platter. Keep hot in warm oven. Strain the stock. Add raisins and gingersnaps; cook, stirring, until thick. Pour part of the gravy over the meat and serve the remaining gravy in a side dish. Serve with Potato Dumplings (see recipe for Potato Dumplings page 153). *Serves 4 to 6.*

## Pot Roast aux Herbes

Pot roast simmered in an aromatic blend of herbs and spices.

| | |
|---|---|
| 1 4-pound boneless chuck or rump roast of beef | 1 piece whole Ginger |
| 2 tablespoons flour | 1 teaspoon Oregano Leaves |
| 5 teaspoons Bon Appétit | ½ teaspoon Marjoram Leaves |
| 1 teaspoon Cracked Black Pepper | 2 Bay Leaves |
| | 3 whole Allspice |
| ½ teaspoon dry Mustard | ¼ teaspoon MSG |
| 2 tablespoons shortening | 2 teaspoons Beef Flavor Base |
| | 1 cup water |

Dredge roast with mixture of flour, Bon Appétit, pepper and dry mustard. Brown on all sides in hot shortening in large skillet or Dutch oven. Add remaining ingredients. Cover and simmer 2½ hours or until tender. If desired, add small whole white onions, potatoes, celery and carrots during the last 45 minutes of cooking. *Serves 6 to 8.*

## Sauerbraten with Potato Dumplings

A shortened version of the German classic, some think just as good.

| | |
|---|---|
| 2 cups wine vinegar | 2 teaspoons Celery Flakes |
| 2 cups water | 2 teaspoons Pickling Spice |
| 1 teaspoon salt | 1 5-pound chuck roast |
| ¼ teaspoon Black Pepper | ½ cup sugar |
| 3 tablespoons Chopped Instant Onions | 18 dark, old-fashioned gingersnaps, crushed |

Combine vinegar, water, salt, pepper, onions, celery flakes and pickling spice to make marinade. Place meat in this mixture, making sure it is covered with liquid.

Cover; let stand 2 hours. Add sugar. Place over heat and simmer, covered, 3 hours or until tender. Remove meat to platter. Keep hot. Strain liquid to remove spices. Return liquid to cooking pan; stir in gingersnap crumbs to thicken gravy and simmer 20 minutes. Serve with Potato Dumplings, recipe below. *Serves 6 to 8.*

POTATO DUMPLINGS:

2 cups riced potatoes (about 3 medium-size potatoes)
1 egg, beaten
½ cup dry bread crumbs, not toasted
⅛ teaspoon Onion Salt

¼ teaspoon White Pepper
¼ teaspoon MSG
½ teaspoon salt
Flour
Herb Croutons

After potatoes are boiled, peel and put through ricer or coarse sieve. Add egg, bread crumbs, onion salt, pepper, MSG and salt, mixing well. Add 3 to 4 tablespoons flour to potato mixture until the consistency is that of dough but not too sticky. Roll into 1½-inch balls, putting an Herb Crouton (see recipe page 274) in center of each. Gently drop into rapidly boiling, salted water. Cook 8 minutes or until dumplings change in appearance and begin to look fluffy. *Makes 16 to 18 dumplings.*

---

## Spiced Baked Ham Slice

---

1 ham slice (1 inch thick)
2 teaspoons whole Cloves
1 teaspoon dry Mustard

½ teaspoon Allspice
⅓ cup brown sugar, packed
¼ cup vinegar

Slash outside fat about 1 inch apart to prevent curling. Stick whole cloves around edge of ham. Mix remaining ingredients; pour over ham slice in shallow pan or baking dish. Bake in 350°F. oven 1 hour. Serve with green peas and broiled grapefruit slices, bananas or peach halves sprinkled with Cinnamon or Nutmeg. *Serves 4 to 5.*

# Oven Braised Short Ribs

5 pounds short ribs of beef
3 tablespoons shortening
1 tablespoon Instant Minced Onion
1/8 teaspoon Garlic Powder
1 tablespoon Bon Appétit
1 teaspoon Herb Seasoning
1/4 teaspoon ground Thyme

1 Bay Leaf
1/2 teaspoon Black Pepper
1 teaspoon Beef Flavor Base
1 cup hot water
6 medium-size potatoes, peeled
6 medium-size carrots, peeled

Brown short ribs on all sides in hot shortening. Add seasonings and beef flavor base dissolved in the hot water. Cover. Bake in 350°F. oven 2½ hours or until tender. Drain off excess fat. Add potatoes and carrots; cover and bake 45 minutes to 1 hour longer. Thicken liquid for gravy if desired. *Serves 4.*

# Meat Loaf with Mushrooms

1 pound ground beef
1/2 pound ground pork
1/2 pound ground veal
2 eggs, beaten
2 tablespoons Instant Minced Onion
2 teaspoons Powdered Horseradish
2 teaspoons salt

1/2 teaspoon dry Mustard
1 teaspoon Season-All
1/2 cup soft bread crumbs
1/2 cup chopped celery
1 4-ounce can mushroom crowns
1/4 cup mushroom liquid or water

Mix together all ingredients until blended, being careful not to overmix. Shape into loaf in shallow baking pan, or put in 9¼ x 5¼ x 2¾-inch loaf pan. Bake in 375°F. oven 1½ hours. *Serves 6 to 8.*

# Roast Whole Tenderloin

Pungently flavored tenderloin, roasted to a crusty brown outside, delicate pink inside and marvelously juicy.

1 4-pound beef tenderloin
¼ cup lemon juice
¼ cup oil
1 teaspoon Coarse Grind
   Black Pepper
1 teaspoon Herb Seasoning

2 teaspoons Bon Appétit
1 teaspoon Powdered
   Horseradish
¼ teaspoon Mace
⅛ teaspoon Garlic Powder

Marinate tenderloin in mixture of lemon juice and oil 30 minutes to 1 hour, turning once or twice. Remove meat from marinade. Combine seasonings and rub over meat. Roast in 450°F. oven 45 minutes for rare, or until meat thermometer registers desired degree of doneness. (See Meat Roasting Chart.) *Serves 6 to 8.*

# Rolled Rib Roast Royale

1 4- to 5-pound rolled rib
   or rib eye beef roast
3 teaspoons Bon Appétit
⅛ teaspoon Garlic Powder
¼ teaspoon Onion Salt

½ teaspoon Powdered
   Mushrooms
½ teaspoon Black Pepper
¼ teaspoon dry Mustard
1 teaspoon salt

Wipe roast with damp cloth. Combine seasonings and rub thoroughly into meat. Place on rack in pan. Insert a meat thermometer into the center of the thickest part. Roast in 325°F. oven 2 hours for rare, or until meat thermometer registers desired degree of doneness. Serve on platter garnished with parsley and spiced crab apples. *Serves 8 to 10.*

# Sesame Steaks

Add the nutty flavor of sesame seed and a delicious oriental marinade—and steak becomes exotic.

1 pound sirloin steak, cut
 ½ inch thick
1 teaspoon lemon juice
1 tablespoon salad oil
¼ cup soy sauce
1 tablespoon brown sugar

1 teaspoon Onion Powder
¼ teaspoon Black Pepper
¼ teaspoon Garlic Salt
¼ teaspoon Ginger
1 tablespoon Sesame Seed
Dash MSG

Cut steak into 3 or 4 serving-size pieces; place in flat baking dish. Combine remaining ingredients; pour over steak, being sure to coat all sides. Let stand 1 hour or longer, turning once or twice. Broil 3 inches from heat a few minutes on each side to desired degree of doneness. Serve with rice. *Serves 2 to 3.*

# Swiss Steak

½ teaspoon salt
2 teaspoons Season-All
Dash Garlic Powder
¼ teaspoon dry Mustard
½ teaspoon Black Pepper
½ cup flour
3 pounds round steak, cut
 ¾ inch thick

¼ cup shortening
3 tablespoons Instant Minced
 Onion
1 green pepper, sliced
½ teaspoon Basil Leaves
⅛ teaspoon MSG
2 cups tomatoes
 (No. 303 can)

Mix salt, Season-All, garlic powder, dry mustard, pepper and flour; pound well into steak. Cut meat into serving pieces. Brown on both sides in hot shortening. Add onion, green pepper, basil leaves, MSG and tomatoes. Cover. Bring to boil; reduce heat and cook slowly 1½ hours or until tender. If you would like a variation in flavor, substitute ½ teaspoon Italian Seasoning for basil leaves. *Serves 5 to 6.*

# Roast Leg of Lamb

| | |
|---|---|
| 1 6-pound leg of lamb | 1 teaspoon ground Thyme |
| 2 teaspoons Season-All | ¼ teaspoon Onion Powder |
| ¼ teaspoon Black Pepper | Dash Garlic Powder |
| ⅛ teaspoon Nutmeg | 2 teaspoons salt |

Wipe lamb with a damp cloth. Combine remaining ingredients and rub over entire surface of meat. Place, fat side up, on rack in a shallow baking pan. Insert a meat thermometer into the center of the roast. Roast in 300°F. oven 30 to 35 minutes per pound or until meat thermometer indicates desired degree of doneness. Remove lamb to a hot platter. Gravy may be made from drippings in pan. Serve very hot with any of the following accompaniments: mint jelly or sauce, currant jelly, minted pear halves or pineapple slices, chutney or peach halves filled with mint jelly. *Serves 8.*

# Herb-Roasted Rack of Lamb

| | |
|---|---|
| ¼ teaspoon ground Thyme | ½ teaspoon Season-All |
| ¼ teaspoon Black Pepper | ½ teaspoon salt |
| ⅛ teaspoon Onion Powder | 1 8-rib rack of lamb |
| ¼ teaspoon MSG | (about 2½ pounds) |

Combine seasonings and rub on lamb. Place on rack in shallow pan, fat side up. Bake in 325°F. oven 30 minutes per pound or to desired degree of doneness. Serve hot. Excellent with Wheat Pilaf (see recipe page 238) and mint jelly. *Serves 4.*

# Lamb in Gingered Cranberry Sauce

Tart, spicy and luscious sauce—and it becomes even better with reheating.

2 pounds lean lamb, cubed
2 teaspoons Season-All
¼ teaspoon Black Pepper
⅓ cup Chopped Instant
   Onions
Dash MSG
⅛ teaspoon Garlic Powder

1 6-ounce can tomato paste
1 cup red Burgundy
1½ cups water
¾ cup whole cranberry sauce
¼ teaspoon Ginger
¼ teaspoon ground Oregano

Trim off small pieces of fat from lamb and fry a few minutes to grease skillet. Add lamb cubes and brown on all sides; pour off excess fat. Add Season-All, pepper, onions, MSG, garlic powder, tomato paste, wine and water. Cover and simmer 45 minutes. Add cranberry sauce, ginger and oregano and simmer 45 minutes longer or until meat is tender. Add additional water if sauce becomes too thick. Serve hot over rice. *Serves 4 to 6.*

# Crown Roast of Lamb

Festive and very special for grand occasions; a succulent crown of lamb delicately spiced with Cardamom and Orange Peel.

¼ teaspoon dry Mustard
⅛ teaspoon Cardamom
½ teaspoon Orange Peel
1 teaspoon Bon Appétit
½ teaspoon ground
   Marjoram

½ teaspoon Black Pepper
¼ teaspoon MSG
2 teaspoons salt
1 14-rib crown roast of lamb
   (about 3 pounds)
Stuffing

Combine seasonings and rub over roast. Place on rack in shallow roasting pan. Fill center with Basic Bread

Stuffing (see recipe page 202). Roast in 325°F. oven 2 hours (about 35 minutes per pound), or until meat thermometer registers 170°F. to 185°F., depending upon desired degree of doneness. You may roast the crown roast of lamb without the stuffing and when ready to serve, fill center with cooked minted peas or a combination of cooked carrots and potato balls. *Serves 6 to 7.*

VARIATIONS:

*Herbed Crown Roast*—Instead of marjoram in above recipe, use ½ teaspoon of one of the following: Thyme, Rosemary or Herb Seasoning. Substitute Season-All for Bon Appétit.

*Gingered Crown Roast*—Add 1 teaspoon Ginger to seasonings suggested in above recipes.

## Swedish Meat Balls

| | |
|---|---|
| ½ cup dry bread crumbs | ⅛ teaspoon Allspice |
| ¼ cup cream or evaporated milk | 1 teaspoon Season-All |
| | ¼ teaspoon Black Pepper |
| 1 pound ground beef | ¼ teaspoon Garlic Salt |
| 1 egg | ¼ cup shortening or oil |
| 2 teaspoons Instant Minced Onion | ½ teaspoon Beef Flavor Base |
| | ¼ cup hot water |

Soak crumbs in cream, then combine with beef, egg and seasonings. Shape into balls 1½ inches in diameter. Brown on all sides in hot shortening; pour off excess fat. Dissolve beef flavor base in hot water; add to meat balls. Cover and simmer 20 minutes. *Serves 6.*

# East Indian Lamb Curry

The true flavor of the East is captured in this famous curry.

| | |
|---|---|
| 2 pounds lean lamb, cubed | 1 teaspoon sugar |
| ¼ cup flour | 1 cup water |
| 3 tablespoons shortening | 2 tablespoons lemon juice |
| ¼ cup Chopped Instant Onions | 1 tart apple, peeled and diced |
| 2 teaspoons salt | 2 tablespoons grated or flake coconut |
| ¼ teaspoon MSG | 2 tablespoons seedless raisins or currants |
| ¼ teaspoon dry Mustard | |
| 4 tablespoons Indian or Madras Curry Powder | Dash Nutmeg |

Dredge meat in flour and brown on all sides in hot shortening. Add onions to skillet; sauté a few minutes but do not brown. Add remaining ingredients; mix well. For a mild curry, decrease amount of curry powder used; for hot curry, increase the amount. Cover. Simmer 45 minutes or until meat is tender. Serve with rice and an assortment of condiments. *Serves 4.*

# Lamb Shanks Divine

| | |
|---|---|
| 4 lamb shanks | 1 teaspoon Sage Leaves, crumbled |
| 2 tablespoons flour | |
| 1½ teaspoons Season-All | ½ teaspoon Oregano Leaves |
| ½ teaspoon Black Pepper | ½ teaspoon Celery Salt |
| ¼ teaspoon MSG | 2 tablespoons lemon juice |
| 2 tablespoons shortening | 1 8-ounce can tomato sauce |
| ½ cup Instant Minced Onion | ½ cup water |
| ½ teaspoon Garlic Salt | |

Roll lamb shanks in flour seasoned with Season-All, pepper and MSG; brown in hot shortening. Combine remaining ingredients; pour over meat. Cover and simmer gently 1½ hours or until tender. *Serves 4.*

# Ragout of Lamb Rosemary

2 pounds lean lamb, cubed
1 tablespoon oil
¼ teaspoon Rosemary Leaves
½ teaspoon Mint Flakes
¼ teaspoon Instant Minced
  Garlic
¼ cup Chopped Instant
  Onions
1 teaspoon Season-All
1 teaspoon Celery Salt

1 teaspoon Beef Flavor Base
½ teaspoon sugar
1 Bay Leaf
Dash MSG
2 cups water
3 potatoes
3 carrots
2 tablespoons butter
2 tablespoons flour

Slowly brown lamb on all sides in oil. Add seasonings and water; gently simmer 1½ hours or until lamb is almost tender. Peel potatoes and carrots. Cut potatoes into quarters and carrots into 2-inch pieces; add to stew. Simmer 40 minutes or until vegetables are tender. In a separate pan, melt butter; add flour and cook until flour is brown, stirring constantly. Stir into stew and cook a few minutes longer to thicken gravy slightly. You might like to serve with noodles, dumplings or hot biscuits. *Serves 4 to 6.*

---

# Clove-Studded Broiled Ham

1 center cut ham slice
  (1½ inches thick)
Whole Cloves
2 tablespoons lemon juice

2 teaspoons brown sugar
1 teaspoon Lemon Peel
½ teaspoon Powdered
  Horseradish

Slash outside fat about 1 inch apart to prevent curling. Broil 3 to 4 inches from heat about 7 minutes. Turn. Stud edge of ham slice with whole cloves. Brush with mixture of lemon juice, brown sugar, lemon peel and powdered horseradish. Broil 7 minutes or until ham is lightly browned. For added color, garnish with tinted pineapple cubes. *Serves 4 to 6.*

# Pork Chops à l'Orange

4 loin or rib pork chops
    (1½ inches thick)
¼ teaspoon Black Pepper
½ teaspoon Paprika
2 teaspoons Season-All
Dash MSG

¾ cup orange juice
1 tablespoon sugar
¼ teaspoon Curry Powder
10 whole Cloves
½ teaspoon Orange Peel
Flour to thicken

Rub pork chops with mixture of pepper, paprika, Season-All and MSG. Brown chops on both sides in heavy skillet, no fat added. Combine orange juice, sugar, curry powder, cloves and orange peel; pour over chops. Cover; reduce heat and simmer 1 hour or until tender. Remove chops to warm platter. Thicken remaining liquid with flour. Spoon sauce over chops or serve in a small bowl. *Serves 4.*

# Stuffed Pork Chops

6 double-rib pork chops
3 cups bread cubes
1 teaspoon Poultry Seasoning
1 teaspoon Bon Appétit
¼ teaspoon Black Pepper
1 tablespoon Instant Minced
    Onion
½ cup finely diced celery

⅓ cup melted butter
⅛ teaspoon Black Pepper
¾ teaspoon Season-All
¼ teaspoon Ginger
¼ teaspoon dry Mustard
2 tablespoons shortening
¼ cup water

Have pocket cut in each chop. Toss together bread cubes, poultry seasoning, Bon Appétit, the ¼ teaspoon pepper, onion, celery and butter. Fill each pocket with ½ cup of the stuffing; close opening with toothpicks. Combine the remaining seasonings and rub well over chops. Brown both sides in hot shortening in skillet. Add water. Cover skillet or transfer to covered casserole, and bake in 350°F. oven 1 hour or until tender. *Serves 6.*

# Veal Scaloppine

1 pound veal, cut for
  scaloppine
2 tablespoons flour
2 tablespoons salad oil
1½ teaspoons Season-All
½ teaspoon Garlic Powder
¼ teaspoon Black Pepper
¼ teaspoon Nutmeg

1 tablespoon Instant Minced
  Onion
1 4-ounce can sliced
  mushrooms
2 tablespoons chopped green
  pepper
1 tablespoon lemon juice
¾ cup water

Dredge veal with flour. Sauté on both sides in hot oil
until well browned. Add remaining ingredients, including liquid from mushrooms. (If a more piquant scaloppine is desired, you may increase lemon juice to 2 tablespoons.) Cover and simmer 10 minutes. Serve from
platter attractively garnished with tomato wedges,
potato cakes or parsley or Paprika rimmed slices of
lemon. *Serves 2 to 4.*

# Wiener Schnitzel

6 5-ounce veal cutlets
⅓ cup flour
1 teaspoon Season-All
¼ teaspoon Black Pepper
½ teaspoon Nutmeg
2 eggs, beaten

2 tablespoons water
1 cup fine dry bread crumbs
½ cup butter
1 tablespoon Parsley Flakes
2 tablespoons lemon juice
2 tablespoons butter

Pound veal until ¼ inch thick. Dredge with mixture of
flour, Season-All, pepper and nutmeg. Dip in mixture
of egg and water, then in bread crumbs. Let dry 30 minutes. Brown veal on both sides in the ½ cup butter,
cooking about 15 minutes. Remove veal to hot platter.
To skillet add parsley flakes, lemon juice and the 2 tablespoons butter, stirring to blend with pan drippings.
Pour sauce over veal. *Serves 6.*

# Pork Mandarin

Orange, honey and spices give distinctive flavor.

| | |
|---|---|
| 2 teaspoons salt | 1 5-pound pork loin roast |
| ¼ teaspoon MSG | ½ cup orange juice |
| ¼ teaspoon ground Thyme | ½ cup honey |
| 1 teaspoon Bon Appétit | Orange slices |
| 1 teaspoon Orange Peel | Whole Cloves |
| ½ teaspoon dry Mustard | 1 11-ounce can Mandarin |
| ½ teaspoon Ginger | orange sections, drained |

Combine seasonings and rub over meat. Place on rack in roasting pan; bake in 325°F. oven 2½ hours (30 minutes per pound) or until meat thermometer registers 185°F. After 40 minutes, baste 2 or 3 times with orange juice, using about one half of it. During the last 45 minutes, combine remaining orange juice with honey and baste several times with this mixture. After removing meat to platter, surround the glazed roast with orange slices studded with whole cloves and lettuce cups filled with Mandarin orange sections. *Serves 6 to 8.*

# Indonesian Spareribs

| | |
|---|---|
| 3 pounds spareribs | 1 tablespoon Instant Minced |
| ¾ teaspoon Hickory Smoked | Onion |
| Salt | 1 teaspoon MSG |
| ¼ teaspoon Black Pepper | ½ teaspoon Ginger |
| 1 tablespoon Coriander Seed, | ¼ cup salad oil |
| crushed | 1 tablespoon brown sugar |
| 1 tablespoon Cumin Seed, | ¼ cup soy sauce |
| crushed | ¼ cup lime or lemon juice |

Cut spareribs into serving-size pieces. Place on rack in shallow pan. Combine remaining ingredients, mixing well. Spoon or brush sauce over ribs to coat all sides. Bake in 325°F. oven 1½ hours or until ribs are tender and browned, basting with sauce several times. *Serves 4 to 6.*

---

## Sweet-Sour Pork

---

| | |
|---|---|
| 2 pounds lean pork | ½ teaspoon Ginger |
| 1 cup water | 1 green pepper |
| 6 whole Cloves | 1 carrot |
| ¼ cup butter or margarine | ¼ cup onion slices |
| 1 cup brown sugar, packed | 2 tablespoons butter or |
| ¼ cup Arrowroot | margarine |
| ¼ cup soy sauce | 2 tablespoons soy sauce |
| ¼ cup vinegar | 2 tablespoons cornstarch |
| 1½ cups pineapple juice | ½ cup shortening |
| ½ teaspoon Onion Powder | |

Cut pork into pieces about ¾ inch thick and 2 inches long. Place in pan with water and cloves and bring to a boil. Reduce heat and cook 25 minutes or until tender. Pour off any remaining water. Cool meat. While meat is cooking combine the next 8 ingredients; cook over low heat until thickened, stirring constantly. (These two steps may be completed in advance; store meat and sauce in refrigerator until needed.) Cut green pepper into large pieces and the carrot into thin slices; sauté along with onion in the 2 tablespoons butter 1 to 2 minutes, stirring once or twice. Remove from skillet. Mix the 2 tablespoons soy sauce and cornstarch until smooth. Pour over the cooled pork; toss to coat pieces of pork. Heat shortening in skillet and fry pork until crisp and brown. Combine meat, vegetables and sauce (if sauce was made ahead of time, heat before using). Serve piping hot with rice as a side dish. *Serves 4 to 6.*

# Honey-Glazed Pork Shoulder

| | |
|---|---|
| 1 4- to 5-pound fresh pork shoulder | ¼ teaspoon MSG |
| 2 teaspoons salt | 2 tablespoons honey |
| 1 tablespoon Season-All | ½ teaspoon Ginger |
| ⅛ teaspoon Garlic Powder | ½ teaspoon Powdered Horseradish |
| ¼ teaspoon Black Pepper | |

Thoroughly rub pork shoulder with mixture of salt, Season-All, garlic powder, pepper and MSG. Place, fat side up, on rack in shallow pan. Roast in 325°F. oven 40 minutes per pound or until meat thermometer registers 185°F. Carefully remove skin and score fat in diamond pattern. Pour mixture of honey, ginger and powdered horseradish over scored fat and return meat to oven. Roast 20 minutes longer or until well glazed. *Serves 4 to 6.*

# Golden Clove Glazed Ham

| | |
|---|---|
| ½ ready-to-eat ham (about 8 pounds) | ⅛ teaspoon ground Cloves Whole Cloves |
| ½ cup brown sugar, packed | |

Place ham, fat side up, on rack in roasting pan. Bake in 325°F. oven 1½ hours. Carefully remove skin. Score fat by cutting into diamond shapes. Combine brown sugar and ground cloves. Spread this mixture over scored fat and stud each diamond with a whole clove. Increase temperature to 375°F. and bake ham 30 minutes longer or until well glazed. *Serves 10 to 12.*

VARIATIONS:

*Curry Glazed Ham*—In above recipe, increase brown sugar to 1 cup, use 2 teaspoons Curry Powder in place of ground cloves and combine with ¼ cup pineapple juice.

166

*Orange Glazed Ham*—In above recipe, use 1 tablespoon Orange Peel in place of ground cloves.

*Honey Glazed Ham*—Instead of brown sugar and ground cloves in above recipe, combine ¼ cup honey, 1 teaspoon Powdered Horseradish, 1 teaspoon dry Mustard and ½ teaspoon Lemon Peel; spoon over scored fat side of ham as above.

# Veal Parmigiana

| | |
|---|---|
| 1 6-ounce can tomato paste | ⅛ teaspoon MSG |
| 1 can water | 1 tablespoon brown sugar |
| ½ teaspoon Italian Seasoning | 1 teaspoon Worcestershire |
| ¼ teaspoon Oregano Leaves | sauce |
| ⅛ teaspoon Garlic Powder | 1 tablespoon butter |
| 1 teaspoon Season-All | |

Mix all ingredients together. Cook until thickened, stirring constantly. Set aside.

| | |
|---|---|
| 2 pounds veal cutlets | ½ cup olive oil |
| 2 teaspoons Season-All | ¼ cup grated Parmesan |
| ¼ teaspoon Black Pepper | cheese |
| 2 eggs | ½ pound Mozzarella cheese |
| 1 cup fine dry bread crumbs | |

Have cutlets sliced ½ inch thick and cut into serving-size pieces or leave whole. Add Season-All and pepper to eggs; beat lightly. Dip cutlets into egg mixture, then into bread crumbs. Brown on both sides in hot oil. Place cutlets in 8 x 13 x 1¾-inch baking dish. Pour sauce over meat and sprinkle with Parmesan cheese. Cover, using aluminum foil if necessary, and bake in 350°F. oven 30 minutes or until tender. Remove cover and top with slices of Mozzarella cheese. Continue baking until cheese melts. *Serves 4 to 6.*

# Osso Bucco

Braised veal shanks—a speciality of Milan.

6 tablespoons butter or margarine
4 veal shanks, cut about 3 inches in length
1 tablespoon Season-All
½ teaspoon Coarse Grind Black Pepper
3 tablespoons flour
1 teaspoon Italian Seasoning
¼ teaspoon Garlic Powder

1 tablespoon Parsley Flakes
1 tablespoon Celery Flakes
2 small carrots, diced
½ teaspoon Lemon Peel
3 tablespoons tomato paste or 1 cup canned tomatoes
1 cup hot water
1 teaspoon Beef Flavor Base
Parmesan cheese

Melt butter in deep skillet. Rub veal shanks with Season-All and pepper; dredge with flour. Brown slowly in butter; add remaining ingredients except cheese. Cover. Bring to a boil; reduce heat and simmer 1½ hours or until meat is very tender but not falling from the bone. Turn shanks over while cooking and add small amount of water if necessary. Remove cover; if sauce is still quite thin, cook uncovered to reduce liquid, or thicken with flour, by stirring in a smooth, thin paste made by mixing together equal amounts of flour and water, using 1 to 2 tablespoons of each. Serve hot over Buttered Noodles with Poppy Seed (see recipe page 233). Grated Parmesan cheese and extra sauce may be passed at the table. *Serves 4.*

# *Veal Birds*

1½ pounds veal steak,
  cut about ¼ inch thick
2 teaspoons Bon Appétit
½ teaspoon salt
Dash MSG
¼ teaspoon dry Mustard

Bread Stuffing
2 tablespoons butter
1 cup water
2 tablespoons flour
1 cup light cream

Cut veal steak into 3 x 5-inch pieces; pound to flatten slightly. Season with a mixture of Bon Appétit, salt, MSG and dry mustard. Spread each piece with Bread Stuffing; roll up and fasten with toothpick. Brown on all sides in hot butter. Transfer to a 2-quart baking dish. Add water to the skillet and scrape brown particles from bottom of skillet as it simmers. Pour over meat and bake, uncovered, in 350°F. oven 30 minutes. Blend flour with cream until smooth, then pour over meat. Bake 30 minutes longer. Remove toothpicks before serving. *Serves 4 to 5.*

BREAD STUFFING:

1½ cups soft bread crumbs
1 tablespoon Instant Minced
  Onion
1 tablespoon Parsley Flakes
⅛ teaspoon rubbed Sage

⅛ teaspoon Poultry Seasoning
¼ teaspoon Black Pepper
½ teaspoon Beef Flavor Base
¼ cup hot water
1 tablespoon melted butter

Combine bread crumbs and seasonings. Dissolve beef flavor base in hot water. Pour over bread crumbs along with melted butter, tossing well.

# Veal Cutlets Viennese

| | |
|---|---|
| 2 pounds veal cutlets | ¼ teaspoon MSG |
| 2 tablespoons butter or margarine | ¼ teaspoon Onion Powder |
| | ½ teaspoon Black Pepper |
| 1 tablespoon Powdered Mushrooms | ¼ cup white wine or water |
| | 1 cup commercial sour cream |
| 1 tablespoon Season-All | Grated Parmesan cheese |

Sauté cutlets in butter until well browned on each side. Combine seasoning; sprinkle over both sides of meat. Place in a baking dish. Mix wine with drippings in the frying pan; pour over meat. Cover dish (use foil if it does not have its own cover) and bake in 350°F. oven 45 minutes. Remove cover, spoon sour cream over meat; sprinkle with Parmesan cheese. Continue baking, uncovered, 15 to 20 minutes longer. Serve from the baking dish with sauce spooned over meat. Excellent with noodles which have been tossed with butter and any of the following: Poppy Seed, Dill Weed, Caraway Seed or toasted Sesame Seed. *Serves 4.*

# Stuffed Breast of Veal

| | |
|---|---|
| 1 4- to 5-pound breast of veal | 2 teaspoons Instant Minced Onion |
| 1 tablespoon Season-All | |
| 1½ teaspoons salt | ¾ teaspoon Celery Seed |
| 3 cups soft bread cubes | 1 teaspoon Marjoram Leaves |
| ½ cup seedless raisins | 3 tablespoons butter, melted |
| 1½ cups chopped tart apples, peeled | 1 teaspoon Beef Flavor Base |
| | 3 cups hot water |
| 1 teaspoon Orange Peel | 3 tablespoons flour |

Have pocket cut in breast of veal. Wipe meat with damp cloth. Combine Season-All and 1 teaspoon of the salt; lightly rub inside of meat with one half this mixture. Toss together the remaining ½ teaspoon salt, bread

170

cubes, raisins, apples, orange peel, onion, celery seed, marjoram leaves and butter. Fill pocket with stuffing. Close opening with skewers then lace shut. Place meat on rack in roasting pan. Combine the remaining Season-All and salt mixture, beef flavor base and 1 cup of the water and pour over meat. Cover and roast in 350°F. oven 2 hours, basting occasionally. Uncover and continue roasting 30 minutes longer or until tender. Remove meat to warm serving platter. Stir flour into drippings in pan and cook about 1 minute. Add the remaining 2 cups water; cook over medium heat, stirring, until gravy thickens. *Serves 5 to 6.*

# Saltimbocco

A Roman delight, zesty with sage.

| | |
|---|---|
| 2 pounds veal cutlet, very thinly sliced | ½ pound prosciutto (Italian ham), sliced thin |
| 2 teaspoons Bon Appétit | 6 tablespoons sweet butter |
| ¼ teaspoon Black Pepper | ½ teaspoon Beef Flavor Base |
| ½ teaspoon rubbed Sage | ¼ cup hot water |
| ⅛ teaspoon MSG | 2 tablespoons dry white wine |

Cut veal into serving-size pieces. Sprinkle with mixture of Bon Appétit, pepper, sage and MSG. Place a slice of prosciutto on each piece of veal; fasten with a toothpick or small skewer. Melt 4 tablespoons of the butter in large skillet. Sauté meat 2 to 3 minutes on each side, ending with the prosciutto side up. Remove to hot platter. To the drippings in skillet add beef flavor base, water and the remaining butter, stirring to mix well. Heat until butter is melted, then add wine and simmer 2 to 3 minutes. Spoon sauce over meat. Serve immediately with sautéed mushrooms and zucchini. You will find this recipe good for the chafing dish. *Makes 6 servings.*

# Beef Stew

| | |
|---|---|
| 2 pounds chuck, cut into 1-inch cubes | ⅛ teaspoon Tarragon Leaves |
| ¼ cup shortening | ½ teaspoon Parsley Flakes |
| 1 Bay Leaf | 2 teaspoons Beef Flavor Base |
| 1 teaspoon salt | 2 cups water |
| 1 tablespoon Season-All | 4 carrots |
| ¼ teaspoon Black Pepper | 4 potatoes |
| ½ teaspoon Marjoram Leaves | 4 small onions |
| | ¼ cup flour |

Brown meat in hot shortening. Add seasonings and water. Cover and simmer 1½ hours or until meat is almost tender. Peel carrots and cut into 1-inch pieces. Peel and quarter potatoes. Peel onions. Add vegetables to stew and continue cooking 30 minutes or until vegetables are tender. Make a thin, smooth paste by mixing together the flour and an equal amount of water; stir into stew and cook, stirring occasionally, until thickened. *Serves 4 to 6.*

# Lamb Kebabs

| | |
|---|---|
| 2 pounds lean lamb | ⅛ teaspoon Thyme Leaves |
| 2 teaspoons Season-All | Dash Allspice |
| ½ teaspoon Coarse Grind Black Pepper | 2 tablespoons lemon juice |
| ½ teaspoon Oregano Leaves | ¼ cup oil |
| 1 teaspoon Instant Minced Onion | 3 medium-size tomatoes |
| | 1 large green pepper |
| ⅛ teaspoon MSG | 12 small onions |
| | 2 tablespoons melted butter |

Cut meat into 2-inch cubes. Combine seasonings, lemon juice and oil; pour over meat. Cover and marinate in refrigerator 1 hour, turning meat several times. Quarter tomatoes, cut green pepper into 1-inch squares and

172

remove outer skin of onions. Brush vegetables with melted butter. Thread the meat, tomatoes, green pepper and onions onto skewers alternating meat with vegetables. Broil 4 inches from heat 8 minutes, turn and continue broiling 6 minutes longer or until meat is nicely browned. Brush with marinade several times while broiling. Serve with rice or Wheat Pilaf (see recipe page 238). *Serves 4.*

---

## *Veal Paprika*

---

2 pounds cubed veal
¼ cup butter
¼ cup Chopped Instant
  Onions
1 teaspoon Season-All
½ teaspoon salt
1 tablespoon Paprika

¼ teaspoon Black Pepper
1 tablespoon Parsley Flakes
1½ cups water
½ pound mushrooms, sliced
2 tablespoons butter
1 cup commercial sour cream

Brown veal in the ¼ cup butter. Add onions, Season-All, salt, paprika, pepper, parsley flakes and water. Cover and simmer 1 hour or until meat is tender. Sauté mushrooms in the 2 tablespoons butter and add to veal during the last 15 minutes of cooking time. Remove from heat; stir in sour cream. Reheat, but do not allow it to boil. If you prefer a thicker sauce, make a thin, smooth paste using 2 tablespoons water and 2 tablespoons flour or 1 tablespoon Arrowroot. Stir in and continue heating very carefully until thickened. Serve over buttered noodles or rice. *Serves 4 to 5.*

# Spiced Tongue

1 3- to 4-pound beef tongue
1 tablespoon Celery Flakes
2 tablespoons Chopped
    Instant Onions
½ teaspoon MSG
10 Peppercorns

2 tablespoons salt
2 Bay Leaves
8 whole Cloves
10 whole Allspice
¼ teaspoon Crushed Red
    Pepper

Cover tongue with water; add seasonings. Cover and simmer until tongue is tender, allowing 1 hour per pound. Cool slightly; remove from liquid. Cut off bones and gristle from large end of tongue; split skin lengthwise on underside and peel off. Slice tongue at a slant. You may serve either hot or cold, but you will find it especially good served cold for buffet or picnic dinner. *Serves 8 to 12.*

# Country Style Venison Steak

2 tablespoons flour
2 teaspoons Season-All
¼ teaspoon Black Pepper
⅛ teaspoon MSG
Dash Nutmeg
2 pounds venison round
    steak, cut ½ inch thick

3 tablespoons oil
2 tablespoons Chopped
    Instant Onions
2 carrots, sliced
1 teaspoon Beef Flavor Base
1½ cups hot water

Combine flour, Season-All, pepper, MSG and nutmeg. Pound this seasoned flour into both sides of steak. Brown on both sides in hot oil in a heavy skillet. Add onions, carrots and beef flavor base which has been dissolved in water. If you like to cook with wine, replace about one half of the water with red wine. Cover and simmer 1½ hours or until tender. *Serves 4.*

# Zesty Stuffed Frankfurters

1 pound frankfurters
¼ pound grated sharp cheese
½ teaspoon Powdered Horseradish
½ teaspoon dry Mustard
1 teaspoon Worcestershire sauce

Dash Onion Powder
1 8-ounce can tomato sauce
½ teaspoon sugar
1 teaspoon Instant Minced Onion
1 teaspoon Chili Powder

Make a slit lengthwise in each frankfurter. Mix together cheese, powdered horseradish, dry mustard, Worcestershire sauce and onion powder. Stuff frankfurters with cheese mixture; place in shallow baking dish. Combine remaining ingredients and pour over top. Bake in 350°F. oven 30 minutes. *Serves 4 to 5.*

# Kidneys in Sherry Sauce

12 lamb kidneys
4 slices bacon
1 tablespoon Instant Minced Onion
3 tablespoons flour
Dash MSG

1 teaspoon Bon Appétit
⅛ teaspoon Black Pepper
2 teaspoons Beef Flavor Base
2 cups water
1 tablespoon Sherry Extract

Scald kidneys 3 minutes; rinse in cold water. Skin, quarter and remove white portion from kidneys. Cut bacon slices into four or five pieces; fry until golden brown. Add onion and kidneys to bacon and brown lightly, about 2 minutes. Stir in flour, MSG, Bon Appétit and pepper. Add beef flavor base and water, stirring to dissolve beef base. Cover and simmer 25 minutes or until kidneys are tender. Just before serving, stir in the sherry extract. Serve on fluffy rice or hot buttered toast. *Serves 4.*

# POULTRY

— * —

## *Arroz con Pollo*

The renowned Saffron rice and chicken dish which is a meal in itself.

1 3-pound chicken
1 tablespoon Season-All
¼ teaspoon Black Pepper
¼ cup flour
½ cup olive oil
1 medium-size green pepper
½ cup Chopped Instant Onions
2 cups tomatoes (No. 303 can)
1 4-ounce can sliced mushrooms
2 cups rice, washed and drained
4 cups water

1 tablespoon chopped pimiento
⅛ teaspoon Instant Minced Garlic
1 Bay Leaf
5 teaspoons Chicken Seasoned Stock Base
⅛ teaspoon Cayenne or Red Pepper
¼ teaspoon Coarse Grind Black Pepper
⅛ teaspoon crushed Saffron
½ cup sherry or water
1 10-ounce can green peas
Parsley Flakes

Cut chicken in pieces; dredge with mixture of Season-All, pepper and flour. Brown in hot olive oil in skillet. Place browned chicken in a 4-quart casserole. Chop green pepper and sauté with onions in remaining hot oil until onions are lightly browned. Add tomatoes, mushrooms including liquid, rice, water, pimiento, seasonings and sherry. Mix thoroughly and pour over chicken. Cover and bake in 375°F. oven 40 minutes. Add drained peas

and continue baking, covered, 15 to 20 minutes longer.
Garnish with parsley flakes. Serve hot. *Serves 6.*

## Broiled Chicken

Here the herbs put new zest into an old stand-by.

| | |
|---|---|
| 2 2-pound broiling chickens,<br>cut in half lengthwise | 1 tablespoon Season-All |
| ½ cup melted butter | ¼ teaspoon MSG |
| 1 teaspoon salt | ½ teaspoon Onion Powder |

Break wing, thigh and leg joints so chicken will remain
flat while broiling. Put, skin side down, on broiler rack.
Combine remaining ingredients and brush over chicken.
Broil 5 to 7 inches from heat 15 minutes. Turn chicken
and brush with seasoned butter; broil 15 minutes longer.
Continue turning and basting chicken every 15 minutes
until drumstick is tender and shows no pink when cut.
Total cooking time is about 45 minutes. *Serves 4.*

VARIATIONS:

*Herb Broiled Chicken*—Substitute 2 teaspoons Italian Seasoning, 2 teaspoons salt, 1 tablespoon Bon Appétit
and ½ teaspoon Paprika for above seasonings.

*Chili Broiled Chicken*—Substitute 2 teaspoons salt, 1 tablespoon Chili Powder and ¼ teaspoon MSG for above
seasonings.

*Smoky Chicken*—Substitute 1½ teaspoons salt, 2 teaspoons
Hickory Smoked Salt and ½ teaspoon Paprika for
above seasonings.

*Coriander Broiled Chicken*—Crush 2 teaspoons Coriander
Seed and add to seasonings in Broiled Chicken recipe.

# Chicken en Casserole

1 3-pound chicken, cut in
  pieces
⅓ cup flour
2 teaspoons Bon Appétit
2 teaspoons Black Pepper
½ teaspoon salt
½ cup butter or margarine
1 tablespoon Celery Flakes
Dash MSG

2 tablespoons Instant Minced
  Onion
1 tablespoon Bell Pepper
  Flakes
¼ teaspoon Nutmeg
1 4-ounce can mushrooms
  with liquid
1 8-ounce can tomato sauce
1 cup water

Dredge chicken in mixture of flour, Bon Appétit, pepper
and salt. Brown in butter. Transfer the chicken to a
baking dish. To butter in skillet stir in 2 tablespoons of
the flour mixture and the remaining ingredients; mix
well. Simmer 5 minutes. Pour over chicken; cover and
bake in 350°F. oven 45 minutes or until tender. *Serves 4.*

# Chicken Cacciatore

A famous Italian dish with a rich, hearty taste.

1 3-pound frying chicken
¼ cup flour
½ cup olive oil
2 tablespoons Instant Minced
  Onion
2 tablespoons Bell Pepper
  Flakes
⅛ teaspoon Instant Minced
  Garlic

⅛ teaspoon Allspice
3 teaspoons Season-All
¼ teaspoon Black Pepper
1 teaspoon Italian Seasoning
¼ teaspoon Crushed Red
  Pepper
3½ cups tomatoes (No. 2½
  can)
½ cup white wine or water

Cut chicken in pieces. Dredge with flour; brown in oil
until golden on all sides. Drain off oil. Add seasonings,
tomatoes and wine or water; cover and simmer slowly
45 minutes or until chicken is tender. Makes a superb
meal when served with hot toasted Italian bread and
crisp tossed salad. *Serves 4.*

# Chicken Italienne

1 3-pound frying chicken
¼ cup butter or margarine
1 teaspoon Italian Seasoning
2 teaspoons Season-All
½ teaspoon salt
⅛ teaspoon Garlic Powder
¼ teaspoon Black Pepper
1 cup milk
1 cup canned tomatoes or tomato juice
1 tablespoon flour
2 tablespoons water

Cut chicken in pieces. Brown on all sides in butter. Combine seasonings, milk and tomatoes; pour over chicken. Cover and simmer 45 minutes or until chicken is tender. Remove chicken to serving dish. Blend flour and water together; add to liquid in skillet. Simmer over low heat, stirring, until sauce thickens. Pour over chicken. *Serves 4.*

# Baked Chicken Oriental

1 3-pound chicken
¼ cup flour
2 teaspoons Season-All
¼ teaspoon Black Pepper
¼ cup melted butter
2 tablespoons pineapple juice
2 teaspoons soy sauce
1 teaspoon Chicken Seasoned Stock Base
2 teaspoons Instant Minced Onion
¼ teaspoon Ginger
¼ teaspoon MSG
Dash Cardamom

Cut chicken in pieces; dredge with mixture of flour, Season-All and pepper. Place in greased 2-quart shallow baking dish. Combine remaining ingredients; pour over chicken. Cover and bake in 375°F. oven 1 hour. Remove cover and bake 30 minutes longer, basting several times. *Serves 4.*

# Turkey Creole

¼ cup shortening
¼ cup flour
½ cup chopped celery
½ cup chopped green pepper
⅛ teaspoon Instant Minced Garlic
1 teaspoon Shredded Green Onions
1 teaspoon Season-All
1 teaspoon salt
¼ teaspoon Coarse Grind Black Pepper
½ teaspoon ground Marjoram
⅛ teaspoon Cayenne
2 cups tomatoes (No. 303 can)
1 cup tomato juice
2 cups cubed cooked turkey

Heat shortening in large skillet. Add flour, stirring constantly until smooth and lightly browned. Add celery and green pepper; sauté 5 minutes, stirring constantly. Add remaining ingredients except turkey; simmer 15 minutes, stirring frequently. Add turkey and simmer 20 minutes longer. Serve hot over rice. *Serves 6.*

# Roast Pheasant

1 2- to 3-pound pheasant
2½ teaspoons Season-All
¼ teaspoon Black Pepper
⅛ teaspoon Mace
Dash Cloves
2 slices onion
1 Bay Leaf
1 slice lemon
2 tablespoons chopped celery leaves
4 slices bacon
¼ cup melted butter

Clean pheasant. Combine Season-All, pepper, mace and cloves; rub inside cavity and over outside of bird. Place onion, bay leaf, lemon and celery leaves inside cavity. Close opening with skewers; lace shut. Fold wings back and under body and tie legs together. Place pheasant, breast side up, on rack in an open roasting pan; cover breast with bacon slices. Roast in 350°F. oven until tender, about 30 minutes per pound, basting frequently with melted butter and pan drippings. *Serves 2 to 3.*

# Chicken Tarragon

1 3-pound chicken
¼ cup flour
1 tablespoon Season-All
¼ teaspoon MSG
¼ teaspoon Black Pepper
¼ teaspoon Paprika
¼ cup butter or margarine

1 teaspoon Brandy Extract
2 teaspoons Instant Minced
  Onion
1 teaspoon Tarragon Leaves
½ cup dry white wine or
  water

Cut chicken in pieces; dredge with mixture of flour, Season-All, MSG, pepper and paprika. Brown in hot butter. Sprinkle browned chicken with brandy extract, onion and tarragon leaves; add wine or water. Cover and simmer 45 minutes or until tender. *Serves 4.*

# Herb Chicken

1 3-pound chicken
¼ cup flour
1 tablespoon Season-All
¼ teaspoon Black Pepper
½ teaspoon Paprika
½ teaspoon Herb Seasoning
¼ cup butter or margarine

2 teaspoons Instant Minced
  Onion
1 teaspoon Parsley Flakes
½ teaspoon Thyme Leaves
½ cup dry white wine or
  water

Cut chicken in pieces; dredge with mixture of flour, Season-All, pepper, paprika and Herb Seasoning. Brown in hot butter. Sprinkle onion, parsley flakes and thyme leaves over chicken; add wine or water. Cover and simmer 45 minutes or until chicken is tender. *Serves 4.*

# Chicken Curry in Papaya

Exotic, delectable and different.

⅓ cup butter or margarine
2 tablespoons Instant Minced Onion
1 stalk celery, chopped
1 tart apple, peeled and diced
5 tablespoons flour
1 tablespoon Curry Powder
¼ teaspoon Garlic Powder
½ teaspoon dry Mustard
2 teaspoons Season-All
1 Bay Leaf

3 whole Cloves
4 teaspoons Chicken Seasoned Stock Base
2½ cups hot water
4 cups cooked chicken, cut into bite-size pieces
¼ cup cream or milk
2 tablespoons chopped chutney
3 papayas

In a 3-quart saucepan melt butter; add onion, celery and apple and cook about 10 minutes, stirring occasionally. Mix together flour, curry powder, garlic powder, dry mustard and Season-All; stir into apple mixture along with bay leaf and cloves. Dissolve seasoned stock base in water and stir into apple mixture; cook, stirring, until sauce thickens. Reduce heat and simmer 30 minutes. Add chicken, cream and chutney and cook 5 minutes longer. Cut 3 papayas in half. Carefully remove seed, being sure not to leave one. Fill papaya halves with curried chicken. Arrange in baking dish and bake in 350°F. oven 25 minutes. Serve with rice and chutney. *Serves 6.*

VARIATION:

*Chicken Curry in Avocado*—Instead of papaya halves, use 4 large firm but ripe avocados. *Serves 8.*

# Creamed Chicken Supreme

1 8-ounce can water chestnuts
¼ cup butter or margarine
¼ cup flour
1 teaspoon Chicken Seasoned Stock Base
1 teaspoon Season-All
⅛ teaspoon Nutmeg
Dash Mace
Dash Poultry Seasoning
Dash White Pepper
2½ cups milk
2 cups cubed cooked chicken
1 tablespoon chopped pimiento
2 tablespoons thinly sliced green pepper

Drain water chestnuts; slice thin. Melt butter in saucepan; blend in flour, seasoned stock base and other seasonings. Cook over low heat until mixture is smooth and bubbly. Remove from heat and stir in milk. Bring to a boil and cook 1 minute, stirring constantly. Add chicken, water chestnuts, pimiento and green pepper. Reduce heat to low. Continue cooking 10 to 15 minutes, stirring occasionally. Serve hot in patty shells or over waffles, toast or rice. *Serves 4 to 6.*

# Oven Fried Chicken

1 3-pound chicken, cut in pieces
½ cup melted butter
1 teaspoon salt
¼ teaspoon Black Pepper
1 teaspoon Season-All
⅛ teaspoon Onion Powder
½ teaspoon Dill Weed
¼ teaspoon Paprika
Flour

Clean and dry chicken. Dip in mixture of melted butter, salt, pepper, Season-All, onion powder, dill weed and paprika. Dredge in flour and place, skin side down, in shallow baking pan. Spoon any remaining seasoned butter over chicken. Cook in 425°F. oven 30 minutes. Turn chicken and continue cooking 15 minutes or until tender and brown. *Serves 3 to 4.*

# Chicken Rosemary

The delicate taste of Rosemary gives this dish its distinction.

| | |
|---|---|
| 1 3-pound chicken | 1 tablespoon Rosemary |
| 1 tablespoon flour | Leaves |
| 5 tablespoons oil | 1/4 teaspoon Black Pepper |
| 1 teaspoon Garlic Salt | 1 tablespoon vinegar |
| 1 tablespoon Season-All | |

Cut chicken in pieces and dredge with flour. Heat 2 tablespoons of the oil in a skillet; brown chicken on all sides. Remove chicken from skillet. Brush 1 tablespoon of the oil over bottom of a shallow baking dish and place pieces of browned chicken close together in dish, skin side down. Combine garlic salt, Season-All, rosemary leaves, pepper and the remaining oil; brush over chicken. Drizzle with vinegar; cover and marinate in refrigerator several hours before baking. Bake, covered, in 350°F. oven 45 minutes. Remove cover and turn chicken, skin side up, then continue baking 20 minutes or until tender. *Serves 4.*

# Chicken Kiev

| | |
|---|---|
| 3 chicken breasts, boned | 3/4 cup flour |
| 2 teaspoons Season-All | 2 eggs, beaten |
| 1/4 teaspoon Black Pepper | 1/2 cup milk |
| 1/8 teaspoon Onion Powder | 1 1/2 cups toasted bread |
| 1/2 teaspoon Savory | crumbs |
| 6 tablespoons chilled butter | Fat for frying |

Cut boned chicken breasts in half lengthwise and pound to flatten. Sprinkle with mixture of Season-All, pepper, onion powder and savory. Place 1 tablespoon of the chilled butter in center of each piece of breast; fold edges over butter, envelope fashion. Carefully seal the edges with toothpicks. Flour the stuffed breasts; dip in egg beaten with milk and roll in bread crumbs. Again flour, dip in egg and roll in bread crumbs. Fry in 3 to 4 inches of fat, 375°F., 12 minutes or until golden brown. Remove toothpicks and serve hot. *Serves 6.*

## Stuffed Roast Capon

| | |
|---|---|
| 1 6-pound capon | ¼ teaspoon Ginger or |
| 1 teaspoon Poultry Seasoning | Nutmeg |
| 1 teaspoon salt | Savory Stuffing |
| 2 teaspoons Season-All | 2 tablespoons melted butter |
| ¼ teaspoon Black Pepper | or margarine |

Clean capon. Mix together poultry seasoning, salt, Season-All, pepper and ginger; rub inside the cavity and on outside of bird. Stuff neck cavity lightly with Savory Stuffing (see recipe page 204); skewer neck skin to back. Fold wing tips back and under, in toward the body. Stuff body cavity lightly with the remaining stuffing. Fasten opening with skewer; lace shut with cord. Tie legs together and fasten to tail. Brush bird lightly with melted butter. Place on a rack, breast side up, in an open roasting pan. Roast in 325°F. oven 2½ hours or 25 minutes per pound. If you use a meat thermometer, insert it so the bulb is in the center of the inside thigh muscle or thickest part of the breast, making sure the bulb does not touch bone. Thermometer should register 190°F. when bird is done. Baste several times with drippings. *Serves 4 to 5.*

# Coq au Vin

This French dish, chicken with wine, is famous the world over.

2 1½- to 2-pound chickens
¼ cup flour
1 tablespoon Season-All
½ teaspoon Paprika
¼ teaspoon Black Pepper
⅛ teaspoon Nutmeg
½ cup butter
¼ cup cognac or other brandy

12 small white onions
12 small whole mushrooms or 8-ounce can mushrooms
½ teaspoon Rosemary Leaves
¼ teaspoon Thyme Leaves
⅛ teaspoon Garlic Powder
1 teaspoon Parsley Flakes
1 cup dry red wine

Cut chicken in pieces; dredge with mixture of flour, Season-All, paprika, pepper and nutmeg. Brown slowly in hot butter. Without removing from heat, pour cognac over chicken; light immediately and flame. Add whole onions, mushrooms, remaining seasonings and wine. Cover and simmer 1 hour or until chicken is tender. May be cooked ahead of time and reheated. May also be frozen and reheated. *Serves 6 to 8.*

# Chicken Cantonese

1 buffet can pineapple tidbits
1 cup sliced celery
1 cup thinly sliced raw carrots
¼ cup Chopped Instant Onions
¼ cup toasted slivered almonds
¼ cup butter or margarine
1 tablespoon Arrowroot
¼ teaspoon Ginger
⅛ teaspoon Nutmeg

¾ cup water
1 tablespoon soy sauce
1 teaspoon lemon juice
1 teaspoon Chicken Seasoned Stock Base
1½ cups chopped, cooked chicken
1 5-ounce can water chestnuts, drained and sliced thin
Chow mein noodles or rice

186

Drain pineapple; reserve juice. Cut celery into 1-inch diagonal slices. Sauté celery, carrots, onions and almonds in butter in large skillet until onions are golden brown. Combine arrowroot, ginger, nutmeg, pineapple juice, water, soy sauce, lemon juice and seasoned stock base, mixing until well blended. Add to sautéed vegetables and cook until mixture thickens, stirring constantly. Stir in pineapple tidbits, chicken and water chestnuts. Cover and simmer 10 to 15 minutes. Serve over chow mein noodles or rice. *Serves 4.*

## Chicken Paprika

1 3-pound chicken
¼ cup flour
2 teaspoons Season-All
1½ tablespoons Paprika
¼ teaspoon Black Pepper
¼ teaspoon Ginger
⅛ teaspoon Garlic Powder
¼ teaspoon Basil Leaves
Dash Nutmeg
2 tablespoons butter or margarine

2 tablespoons shortening
¼ cup sherry or water
2 teaspoons Worcestershire sauce
1 teaspoon Chicken Seasoned Stock Base
1 4-ounce can mushrooms
1 cup commercial sour cream

Cut chicken in pieces; coat with mixture of flour, Season-All, paprika, pepper, ginger, garlic powder, basil leaves and nutmeg. Heat butter and shortening in heavy skillet. Brown chicken slowly. Combine sherry, Worcestershire sauce and seasoned stock base; pour over browned chicken. Add mushrooms. Cover and simmer 45 minutes or until tender. Remove chicken to serving platter. Blend sour cream with drippings in skillet; stir 2 to 3 minutes until sour cream is heated but do not allow it to boil. Pour sauce over the chicken; sprinkle with additional paprika. Chicken Paprika is excellent with hot buttered noodles. *Serves 4.*

# Old-Fashioned Chicken and Dumplings

1 4-pound stewing chicken
1 teaspoon Celery Flakes
½ teaspoon Onion Flakes
⅛ teaspoon MSG
1 tablespoon salt

1 teaspoon Season-All
¼ teaspoon Black Pepper
1 medium-size carrot, sliced
Dumplings
Flour

Cut chicken in pieces; put in kettle with just enough water to cover. Add seasonings and sliced carrot; cover and bring to a boil. Reduce heat and simmer until tender, about 2 hours. Let cool in broth, then remove meat from bones in as large pieces as possible. Return meat to broth; bring to a boil. Add dumplings and cook (see recipe below). Remove dumplings and thicken broth with a flour-water paste, using equal amounts of each. *Serves 6.*

**ROLLED DUMPLINGS:**

2 cups all-purpose flour
3 teaspoons baking powder
2 teaspoons Season-All

2 teaspoons Shredded Green Onions
¼ cup shortening
¾ cup milk

Sift flour, measure and sift again with baking powder and Season-All. Stir in onions. With pastry blender or two knives cut shortening into flour mixture until it resembles corn meal. Add milk and stir until dough forms ball and leaves side of bowl. Turn out on lightly floured board. Roll dough to ¼-inch thickness. Cut into ½ x 4-inch strips and drop onto chicken in boiling broth. Cover and cook 15 to 20 minutes.

**HERB DUMPLINGS:**

1½ cups all-purpose flour
2 teaspoons baking powder
2 teaspoons Bon Appétit
1 tablespoon shortening
1 teaspoon Chives

¼ teaspoon Coarse Grind Black Pepper
1 teaspoon Shredded Green Onions
¾ cup milk

Sift flour, measure and sift again with baking powder and Bon Appétit. With pastry blender or two knives cut shortening into flour until it resembles corn meal. Stir in chives, pepper and onions. Add milk and stir only enough to mix well. Drop by tablespoonfuls onto chicken in boiling broth. Cover and cook 10 minutes. Remove cover; cook 10 minutes longer.

## Fried Chicken Curry

A golden, crisp-fried chicken, with a creamy sauce pungent with curry.

| | |
|---|---|
| 1 3-pound frying chicken, cut in pieces | ¼ teaspoon Onion Powder Dash MSG |
| 2 teaspoons salt | 2 tablespoons Curry Powder |
| ⅓ cup flour | 3 cups shortening |
| ¼ teaspoon Black Pepper | 2 cups milk |

Wash chicken and wipe dry. Sprinkle with salt. Combine flour and seasonings, mixing well. Flour chicken in the seasoned flour and set aside that flour not used. Fry chicken, covered, in hot shortening in a heavy skillet or chicken fryer 15 minutes or until golden brown. Turn with tongs and fry until second side is deep golden brown. Never turn chicken more than once. Remove cover and continue cooking about 5 minutes to crisp chicken. Remove chicken to a heated platter. Pour off fat, leaving about 2 tablespoons. Stir in 2 to 3 tablespoons of the curry-seasoned flour. If you like a very hot sauce, add more curry powder. Cook 1 minute. Remove from heat; stir in milk and cook several minutes to thicken. Serve the crisp golden chicken with hot steamed rice and pass the curry sauce. *Serves 4.*

# Turkey Pot Pie

A delightful dish, with an unusual crust.

| | |
|---|---|
| 2 cups cooked turkey, cut into medium-size pieces | 1 teaspoon Bon Appétit |
| 2 tablespoons Chopped Instant Onions | ¼ teaspoon Coarse Grind Black Pepper |
| 4 tablespoons butter | 2 teaspoons Chicken Seasoned Stock Base |
| 6 tablespoons flour | 2 cups hot water |
| ½ teaspoon Poultry Seasoning | Caraway Biscuit Crust |

Put turkey and onions in a buttered 8-inch square baking dish. Melt butter; stir in flour, poultry seasoning, Bon Appétit and pepper. Cook until bubbly and remove from heat. Dissolve seasoned stock base in hot water; stir into flour mixture and cook over low heat until thickened. Pour over turkey. Place Caraway Biscuit Crust over turkey mixture, pressing down firmly around the edges. Bake in 425°F. oven 20 to 25 minutes. *Serves 4 to 6.*

## CARAWAY BISCUIT CRUST:

| | |
|---|---|
| 1 cup all-purpose flour | ¼ cup shortening |
| 1½ teaspoons baking powder | 1 teaspoon Caraway Seed |
| ½ teaspoon salt | ⅓ cup milk |
| ½ teaspoon dry Mustard | |

Sift flour, measure and sift again with baking powder, salt and dry mustard. Cut in shortening with pastry blender or two knives until mixture resembles coarse corn meal. Add caraway seed and milk. Mix until dough can be shaped into a ball. Roll out on floured board to a 9-inch square. Prick pastry with tines of fork to allow steam to escape. Carefully place over turkey mixture, sealing edges.

# Truffled Chicken Breasts Elégante

4 whole chicken breasts
4 truffles, thinly sliced
¼ teaspoon Ginger
¼ teaspoon MSG
Dash Nutmeg
¼ teaspoon Poultry Seasoning
¼ teaspoon Black Pepper

¼ teaspoon dry Mustard
¼ teaspoon Bon Appétit
1½ teaspoons salt
3 tablespoons flour
½ cup sweet butter
½ cup dry white wine
½ cup hot water

Wash and dry chicken breasts. With a sharp knife, loosen the skin from breast in 3 or 4 places on each side and insert thin slices of truffle. Wrap in aluminum foil or put in covered dish; refrigerate several hours. When ready to cook, combine spices and salt; rub into chicken, covering all sides carefully. Flour, using only enough to coat lightly. Brown slowly in hot butter in heavy skillet, turning to brown evenly. Transfer the browned chicken breasts to a baking dish. Drizzle ¼ cup of the wine over chicken. Stir 1 tablespoon flour into drippings in skillet; brown lightly, then add hot water. Mix well and pour over chicken. Cover. Bake in 325°F. oven 1 hour or until tender, basting with the remaining wine. Remove cover during the last 15 minutes to crisp chicken. Serve with wild rice, white rice or buttered noodles. Excellent with broiled bananas. *Serves 4.*

NOTE: Even without the truffles and wine this is a superb dish, real epicurean fare.

# Curried Turkey Amandine

½ cup slivered almonds
¼ cup butter or margarine
2 tablespoons flour
½ teaspoon Season-All
1 teaspoon Curry Powder
¼ teaspoon Black Pepper
1 tablespoon Instant Minced Onion

¾ cup milk
¾ cup light cream
¼ cup dry white wine
1 8-ounce can sliced mushrooms
6 thin slices cooked turkey

Slowly brown almonds in butter. Remove almonds with slotted spoon and drain on absorbent paper. To butter add flour, Season-All, curry powder, pepper and onion; stir until well blended and smooth. Gradually stir in milk and cream. Cook over low heat, stirring constantly, until mixture thickens. Add wine, mushrooms which have been drained and turkey. Simmer about 10 minutes. Serve over hot buttered rice and top each serving with almonds. *Serves 6.*

# Savory Turkey Croquettes

¼ cup butter or margarine
¼ cup flour
1 teaspoon Chicken Seasoned Stock Base
½ teaspoon Celery Salt
¼ teaspoon Black Pepper
¼ teaspoon rubbed Sage
1 teaspoon Powdered Mushrooms

1 cup milk
2 teaspoons Instant Minced Onion
2 cups ground cooked turkey
2 teaspoons Parsley Flakes
½ cup fine dry bread crumbs
1 egg, lightly beaten
2 tablespoons water
Cooking oil or shortening

Melt butter in saucepan. Blend in flour and add the next five ingredients; cook over low heat until mixture is smooth and bubbly. Remove from heat; stir in milk and onion. Bring just to a boil; reduce heat and cook 1 minute, stirring constantly. Add turkey and parsley flakes. Spread mixture out on plate. Chill. Divide chilled mixture into 8 portions; shape into cones or cylinders. Roll in bread crumbs; dip into mixture of egg and water; roll again in bread crumbs. Fry in deep fat, 375°F., 2 minutes or until golden brown. Drain on absorbent paper. Serve hot. Cream or mustard sauce goes well with croquettes. And, you will also want to serve a relish such as: Corn Relish, Dixie Relish, Pickle Relish or Chow-Chow. *Makes 8 croquettes.*

## Turkey Rolls Delicious

¼ cup butter
¼ cup flour
⅛ teaspoon Onion Salt
⅛ teaspoon Mace
⅛ teaspoon Cayenne
¼ teaspoon Poultry Seasoning
1½ teaspoons Chicken
  Seasoned Stock Base

1½ cups hot water
2 cups cubed cooked turkey
1 4-ounce can mushrooms,
  drained and chopped
5 cups soft bread crumbs
2 eggs, beaten
8 slices bacon

Melt butter; stir in flour, onion salt, mace, cayenne and poultry seasoning; cook until bubbly. Dissolve seasoned stock base in hot water; stir into flour mixture. Cook over low heat, stirring constantly, until thickened. Stir in turkey and mushrooms. Remove from heat; cool to room temperature, then chill. Shape into eight 3 x 1½-inch rolls. Roll in bread crumbs, dip in egg and, again, roll in bread crumbs. Wrap each roll with a slice of bacon; fasten with a toothpick. Bake in 375°F. oven 30 minutes or until brown. Serve piping hot. *Makes 8 rolls.*

# Canard au Grand Marnier

| | |
|---|---|
| 1 4- to 5-pound duck | ¼ teaspoon ground Thyme |
| 1½ teaspoons Bon Appétit | ¼ teaspoon Onion Powder |
| 1 teaspoon Orange Peel | ¼ teaspoon Black Pepper |
| ⅛ teaspoon rubbed Sage | 3 tablespoons Grand Marnier |

Thoroughly clean and dry duck. Remove giblets, neck and wing tips to first joint; reserve for sauce. Combine all seasonings, except Grand Marnier, and rub inside cavity and outside of duck. Tie legs together and fasten wings to body of bird. Place on rack in pan, breast side up, and roast in 450°F. oven 30 minutes. Reduce temperature to 350°F. and turn duck on its side. Roast 30 minutes; turn duck on other side and roast 30 minutes. Turn duck breast side up. During the last 30 minutes of cooking time, baste with Grand Marnier. Total cooking time is 2 hours or about 30 minutes per pound. Garnish with Spiced Figs (recipe page 425) or orange sections. *Serves 4.*

SAUCE:

| | |
|---|---|
| Wing tips, neck and giblets | 3 cups water |
| 4 tablespoons butter | 3 tablespoons sugar |
| 2 tablespoons Chopped Instant Onions | ¼ cup vinegar |
| 1 tablespoon Vegetable Flakes | 1 teaspoon Orange Peel |
| 3 teaspoons Chicken Seasoned Stock Base | ½ teaspoon Bon Appétit |
| 1 teaspoon Parsley Flakes | 2 tablespoons cornstarch |
| 1 Bay Leaf | ¾ cup port wine |
| | 3 tablespoons Grand Marnier |

While duck is roasting, brown wing tips, neck and giblets in 2 tablespoons of the butter. Add onions and vegetable flakes; cook until lightly browned. Add seasoned stock base, parsley flakes, bay leaf and water; simmer 1 hour. Strain and reduce to 2 cups of stock by boiling over high heat. Combine sugar and vinegar and cook until sugar

caramelizes to dark brown. Add stock, orange peel and
Bon Appétit. Combine cornstarch and ¼ cup of the
wine; stir into sauce and cook, stirring, until slightly
thickened. Set aside. Pour off fat from roasting pan,
leaving the browned particles and rich juices from duck.
Add the ½ cup wine to roasting pan and cook until
about 3 tablespoons liquid remains, scraping bottom of
pan to remove browned particles. Add to sauce. Stir in
Grand Marnier and the remaining 2 tablespoons butter.
Serve hot over slices of duck.

## Cornish Hens Stuffed with Wild Rice

| | |
|---|---|
| 4 1-pound Cornish hens | 2 teaspoons Parsley Flakes |
| ¾ cup wild rice | 3½ teaspoons Bon Appétit |
| 2¼ cups water | 1 tablespoon Instant Minced |
| 2 teaspoons Chicken Seasoned Stock Base | Onion |
| ½ cup melted butter | ¼ teaspoon Coarse Grind Black Pepper |
| ½ teaspoon Basil Leaves | ½ teaspoon salt |
| ¼ teaspoon Cinnamon | |

Wash and pat dry the Cornish hens; set aside. Wash rice;
add water and seasoned stock base; cover and cook until
tender and all water is absorbed, about 50 minutes. Add
¼ cup of the butter, basil leaves, cinnamon, parsley
flakes, 2 teaspoons of the Bon Appétit, onion, pepper
and salt; mix well. Fill cavities of Cornish hens with
stuffing. Cover exposed stuffing with aluminum foil during the first 30 minutes of cooking time to prevent drying.
Brush hens with a mixture of the remaining ¼ cup butter
and 1½ teaspoons Bon Appétit. Roast in 450°F. oven
20 minutes; reduce temperature to 350°F. and roast 45
minutes longer or until drumstick twists easily and birds
are nicely browned. Baste several times with seasoned
butter. Serve garnished with lettuce and pineapple slices
topped with cream cheese-filled prunes. *Serves 4.*

# Sautéed Chicken Livers

| | |
|---|---|
| 1 pound chicken livers | ¼ teaspoon Paprika |
| 3 tablespoons butter | ⅛ teaspoon Black Pepper |
| ½ teaspoon Onion Powder | ¼ teaspoon Garlic Salt |
| 2 teaspoons Chicken Seasoned Stock Base | ⅛ teaspoon Thyme Leaves |
| ⅛ teaspoon Nutmeg | ⅛ teaspoon Marjoram Leaves |

Cut chicken livers in half; pierce with tines of fork to prevent popping. Melt butter in skillet; stir in seasonings. Sauté livers in seasoned butter 5 minutes or until browned on all sides. Serve on triangles of buttered toast, in patty shells or over rice. *Serves 2 to 3.*

VARIATION:

*Sautéed Chicken Livers Rosé*—Use 1 teaspoon Chicken Seasoned Stock Base, 1 teaspoon Season-All, ¼ teaspoon Ginger, ¼ teaspoon dry Mustard and dash Mace in place of the above seasonings. Add ¼ cup rosé to the sautéed livers; cover and simmer 5 minutes.

# Duckling à l'Orange

| | |
|---|---|
| 1 3- to 4-pound duckling | ½ teaspoon dry Mustard |
| 1 teaspoon salt | ¼ teaspoon Allspice |
| ¼ teaspoon Black Pepper | ⅛ teaspoon Ginger |
| 2 tablespoons orange juice | 2 tablespoons flour |
| ¾ cup brown sugar, packed | 2 cups orange juice |
| 4 teaspoons Orange Peel | |

Clean duckling. Rub inside cavity and outside of duckling with mixture of salt and pepper. Remove wing tips to first joint. Fasten neck skin and wings to back of duckling with skewers. Close the cavity opening with skewers and tie legs together. Place on rack in roasting pan.

breast side down. Roast in 450°F. oven 30 minutes. Reduce temperature to 350°F. and turn duckling so breast side is up. Continue roasting, allowing 30 minutes per pound. The last 30 minutes of cooking time begin basting with mixture of the 2 tablespoons orange juice, brown sugar, 3 teaspoons of the orange peel, dry mustard, allspice and ginger. Continue basting with drippings from pan until duckling is tender and skin is crisp and brown. Remove to platter and keep hot. Pour off grease, leaving only brown drippings. Stir flour and the remaining 1 teaspoon orange peel into pan drippings. Add the 2 cups orange juice and cook over low heat until thickened, stirring constantly. Strain into sauce dish and serve with hot duckling. *Serves 2 to 3.*

## Country Inn Pheasant

1 2- to 3-pound pheasant,
    quartered
2 tablespoons flour
1½ teaspoons Season-All
1 teaspoon Paprika
4 tablespoons butter
2 tablespoons shortening
2 teaspoons Chicken Seasoned
    Stock Base

½ cup water
¼ cup sauterne or Chablis
1 tablespoon lemon juice
2 tablespoons Onion Flakes
    or Chopped Instant Onions
¼ teaspoon Nutmeg
1 cup sliced fresh mushrooms
    or 6-ounce can mushrooms
½ cup heavy cream

Dredge pheasant with mixture of flour, Season-All and paprika. Heat 1 tablespoon of the butter with shortening in heavy skillet. Add pheasant and brown slowly to a rich golden color on all sides. Combine seasoned stock base, water, sauterne, lemon juice, onion flakes and nutmeg; pour over pheasant. Cover and simmer 45 minutes or until tender. Remove pheasant to heated platter. To the skillet add the remaining 3 tablespoons butter; when it is melted, add mushrooms and cook 5 minutes or until tender. Remove skillet from heat, then stir in cream. Pour sauce over pheasant. Serve hot with rice. *Serves 3 to 4.*

# Roast Goose Superb

1 10-pound goose
1 teaspoon Black Pepper
2 teaspoons Bon Appétit
2 teaspoons Season-All
¼ teaspoon MSG
½ teaspoon Onion Powder
¼ teaspoon dry Mustard
⅛ teaspoon Nutmeg
1 tablespoon salt
Water or dry white wine for
   basting

¼ teaspoon Marjoram Leaves
1 tablespoon Celery Flakes
¼ teaspoon Shredded Green
   Onions
1 teaspoon Parsley Flakes
1 teaspoon Bon Appétit
⅓ cup dry white wine
1 Bay Leaf
2 cups water
Flour

Rinse goose inside and outside and pat dry. Combine pepper, the 2 teaspoons Bon Appétit, Season-All, MSG, onion powder, dry mustard, nutmeg and salt; rub inside cavity and over outside of goose. Turn the skin of the neck backward and fasten with skewer. (If desired, stuff cavity with 16 dried prunes and 4 tart apples which have been peeled, cored and quartered. Sew up the vent.) Tie the legs together loosely. Prick well all over with a 2-tined fork. Place on a rack in a roasting pan. Roast in 400°F. oven 20 minutes; reduce heat to 325°F. and continue to roast, allowing 30 minutes per pound. Baste several times with small amount of water or wine. If goose browns too rapidly, cover breast and drumsticks with cheesecloth, moistened with goose fat. Remove cheesecloth during the last hour of roasting to crisp skin. Pour off most of the fat as it accumulates in the pan. (Save every drop of the goose fat. It is a real treasure in cooking!) While goose is roasting, place the giblets and neck in a saucepan; add marjoram leaves, celery flakes, onions, parsley flakes, Bon Appétit, wine, bay leaf and water. Bring to boil and simmer 2½ to 3 hours. Strain the broth; reserve for gravy. Chop giblets. When goose is done, remove to heated platter. Pour off fat, leaving the browned bits in roasting pan; stir in 1 to 2 tablespoons flour, cooking until bubbly and lightly browned.

Gradually add the broth, stirring and scraping the bottom of pan to remove all the brown bits. Add the chopped giblets and simmer about 5 minutes. Serve gravy in sauceboat. Serve goose with stewed apples and prunes or the fruit used for stuffing. Well worth the time it takes to prepare. *Serves 8.*

---

## Roast Turkey Supreme

---

| | |
|---|---|
| 1 12-pound turkey | ½ teaspoon Poultry Seasoning |
| 2 tablespoons salt | ⅛ teaspoon Nutmeg |
| 1 teaspoon Season-All | ½ teaspoon dry Mustard |
| ¼ teaspoon MSG | Butter or oil |

Clean and rinse cavity and outside of turkey; wipe dry. Combine seasonings and rub inside and outside of turkey. (If desired, lightly fill neck and body cavities with stuffing. You will find a variety of stuffing recipes in this chapter.) Skewer neck skin to back. Fold wing tips back and under, in toward the body, or skewer to the body. Fasten body cavity with skewers and lace shut. Tie drumsticks to tail or push under bridge of skin. Place turkey on rack in shallow open pan. Rub butter or oil over entire surface of bird. If a meat thermometer is used, insert so the bulb is in the center of the inside thigh muscle or the thickest part of the breast meat. Cover top and sides with butter-moistened cheesecloth or aluminum foil. (If cheesecloth dries during cooking, moisten it with pan drippings.) Roast in 325°F. oven 5 hours or until meat thermometer registers 190°F. The bird is also sufficiently cooked when the drumsticks move easily from side to side. *Serves 8.*

NOTE: For variety, other seasonings may be used instead of the ones listed above. Some suggested seasonings are: Bon Appétit, ground Thyme, Curry Powder, rubbed Sage, Savory, Onion Powder, White Pepper, Paprika and Ginger.

# Quick 'n' Easy Stuffing

¾ cup Chopped Instant
  Onions
2 cups melted butter
5 quarts soft bread cubes
  (¼-inch square)

1 teaspoon salt
½ teaspoon Black Pepper
½ teaspoon ground Thyme
1 teaspoon Poultry Seasoning
2 tablespoons Parsley Flakes

Sauté onions in butter until lightly brown. Add remaining ingredients; mix well, tossing gently. *Makes about 3 quarts, enough stuffing for a 12- to 14-pound bird.*

# Holiday Stuffing

3½ cups chopped celery
5 tablespoons Instant Minced
  Onion
1½ cups melted butter
1 tablespoon Poultry
  Seasoning
2 teaspoons Season-All
½ teaspoon salt
½ teaspoon Black Pepper
8 cups white bread cubes

4 cups whole wheat bread
  cubes
4 cups corn bread cubes
2 eggs, lightly beaten
⅔ cup slivered toasted
  almonds
2 teaspoons Chicken Seasoned
  Stock Base
1½ cups hot water

Sauté celery and onion in butter until tender but not brown. Sprinkle poultry seasoning, Season-All, salt and pepper over bread cubes. Add celery and onion mixture, eggs and almonds. Toss. Dissolve seasoned stock base in water; pour over bread mixture. Toss lightly until well blended. Stuff bird. Put remaining stuffing in casserole; cover and bake in 300°F. oven 40 minutes, then remove cover and allow to brown. *Makes about 10 cups, enough to stuff a 10- to 12-pound bird plus an extra amount for a casserole.*

# Mushroom-Rice Stuffing

So good! Serve as a dish by itself or as a stuffing for meat or poultry.

½ cup butter or margarine
3 cups cooked rice
3 tablespoons Instant Minced Onion
2 cups diced celery
2 teaspoons Parsley Flakes
½ teaspoon ground Marjoram

2 teaspoons Powdered Mushrooms
½ teaspoon salt
⅛ teaspoon Black Pepper
⅛ teaspoon ground Thyme
1 teaspoon Chicken Seasoned Stock Base
⅔ cup chopped pecans

Melt butter in large skillet; add remaining ingredients except pecans. Sauté, stirring until lightly browned. Remove from heat and add pecans; toss gently. Use to stuff a 5- to 6-pound bird. When serving this as a side dish for meat or fowl, bake in a covered casserole in 325°F. oven 30 minutes. *Makes 6 cups.*

# Wild Rice Stuffing

1 cup wild rice
1½ teaspoons Chicken Seasoned Stock Base
1 cup chopped celery
¼ cup Chopped Instant Onions
½ cup melted butter
½ teaspoon Marjoram Leaves
¼ teaspoon Oregano Leaves

¼ teaspoon Black Pepper
1 teaspoon Season-All
¼ teaspoon Thyme Leaves
½ teaspoon salt
1 4-ounce can mushroom crowns
2 tablespoons mushroom liquid

Cook wild rice as directed on package, adding seasoned stock base to the water. Sauté celery and onions in butter. Then combine all ingredients and mix well. *Makes about 6 cups, enough to stuff a 10-pound bird.*

# Basic Bread Stuffing

½ cup Chopped Instant Onions
1½ cups chopped celery
1 cup melted butter or margarine
12 cups bread cubes, white and whole wheat bread
2 tablespoons Parsley Flakes
1½ teaspoons Poultry Seasoning
1 tablespoon Bon Appétit
½ teaspoon Black Pepper
1 teaspoon Chicken Seasoned Stock Base
½ cup hot water

Sauté onions and celery in butter in a large skillet or Dutch oven. Toss together bread cubes, parsley flakes, poultry seasoning, Bon Appétit and pepper; add to sautéed mixture and toss while lightly browning bread cubes. Dissolve seasoned stock base in water; sprinkle over stuffing, stirring lightly. Stuff loosely into neck and breast cavities of bird. *Makes about 8 cups.*

VARIATIONS:

*Herb Stuffing*—To the above recipe add one of the following: 2 teaspoons rubbed Sage, 2 teaspoons ground Thyme or 2 teaspoons ground Marjoram.

*Chestnut Stuffing*—Wash ½ pound chestnuts; cut slits on both sides of shells. Bake in 500°F. oven 15 minutes. Shell and skin nuts, then put in salted water; cover and boil 20 minutes. Drain and chop fine. (Or, if preferred, use canned chestnuts which are ready for use.) Toss with bread cubes in above recipe.

*Oyster Stuffing*—Cook ½ to 1 pint small or medium-size oysters in the oyster liquor until the edges curl. Drain and chop, or leave whole as preferred. Toss with bread cubes in above recipe.

# Sesame Stuffing

2 teaspoons Beef Flavor Base
½ cup hot water
2 tablespoons Celery Flakes
1 tablespoon Chopped Instant
  Onions
½ cup butter or margarine

⅓ cup Sesame Seed
3 cups toasted bread cubes
2 teaspoons Poultry Seasoning
¼ teaspoon Black Pepper
¼ teaspoon Ginger
1 egg, lightly beaten

Dissolve beef flavor base in hot water. Cook celery flakes and onions in butter 5 minutes. Toast sesame seed in 350°F. oven 15 minutes or until golden brown. Combine all ingredients, tossing lightly until thoroughly mixed. You will find this stuffing excellent for chicken, turkey, Cornish hens, pork chops or crown roast of pork or lamb. *Makes about 3 cups.*

# Spiced Chestnut Stuffing

½ cup chopped celery
2 tablespoons Instant Minced
  Onion
1 cup melted butter
2 cups boiled or canned
  chestnuts, sliced (2-pound
  can)
8 cups dry bread cubes
2 teaspoons salt

1 teaspoon Black Pepper
2 tablespoons Parsley Flakes
½ teaspoon rubbed Sage
½ teaspoon Rosemary Leaves
⅛ teaspoon Nutmeg
1 teaspoon Chicken Seasoned
  Stock Base
¾ cup hot water

Sauté celery and onion in butter until tender. Add chestnuts and cook 5 minutes. Mix together bread cubes, salt, pepper, parsley flakes, sage, rosemary leaves and nutmeg. Dissolve seasoned stock base in water and add to bread mixture along with chestnut mixture. Toss well. *Makes 8 cups, enough to stuff a 12- to 15-pound bird.*

# Savory Stuffing

1 tablespoon Chopped Instant Onions
¼ cup diced celery
½ cup butter or margarine
4 cups dry bread cubes
½ teaspoon salt
1½ teaspoons Poultry Seasoning
¼ teaspoon rubbed Sage
¼ teaspoon Black Pepper

Sauté onions and celery in butter until lightly browned. Add remaining ingredients; mix well, tossing gently. This stuffing is excellent for turkey, Cornish hens, whole fish, pork chops or a crown roast of lamb. *Makes about 4 cups.*

# Sausage Stuffing

An excellent stuffing to bring out the succulence of any turkey.

6 cups coarse bread crumbs
1 teaspoon Garlic Salt
1 teaspoon Season-All
1 pound bulk pork sausage
2½ cups tomatoes (No. 2 can)
2 cups cooked rice
½ cup seedless raisins
¼ cup Instant Minced Onion
2 teaspoons Poultry Seasoning
½ teaspoon Black Pepper
2 eggs, lightly beaten

Combine bread crumbs, garlic salt and Season-All. Toast in 300°F. oven, stirring occasionally, until lightly browned and crisp. Fry sausage until brown, breaking it into small pieces with a fork as it cooks. Pour off excess fat. Drain tomatoes; chop pulp very fine. (Do not use juice; save for use in other recipes.) Thoroughly mix crumbs, sausage, tomatoes, rice, raisins, onion, poultry seasoning, pepper and eggs. *Makes about 8 cups, enough to stuff a 12- to 15-pound bird.*

# Old South Corn Bread Stuffing

4 cups crumbled corn bread
3 cups crumbled biscuits
1½ cups cooked rice
¼ cup Chopped Instant Onions
½ cup water
1½ cups chopped celery
1 teaspoon Black Pepper
1 teaspoon Parsley Flakes
¼ teaspoon Poultry Seasoning
1 teaspoon Season-All
5 teaspoons Chicken Seasoned Stock Base
1½ cups hot water
1 egg
½ cup milk
½ cup butter, melted

Combine corn bread, biscuits and rice. Soak onions in the ½ cup water about 10 minutes. Add to bread mixture along with celery, pepper, parsley flakes, poultry seasoning and Season-All. Dissolve seasoned stock base in hot water. Beat egg; stir in milk. Add liquids and butter to bread mixture. Mix well. Add additional liquid if stuffing seems too dry. Spoon into a buttered shallow 3-quart baking dish and bake in 375°F. oven 40 minutes or until golden brown. *Serves about 10.*

# SEA FOODS

———— * ————

## Tuna Croquettes

2 tablespoons butter
6 tablespoons flour
¼ teaspoon dry Mustard
½ teaspoon Powdered
Mushrooms
¼ teaspoon Black Pepper
1½ teaspoons Onion Salt
Dash Cayenne or Red Pepper
1½ teaspoons lemon juice

¾ cup milk
2 7-ounce cans tuna
2 teaspoons minced pimiento
1 teaspoon Shredded Green
Onions
½ cup cracker meal
1 egg, lightly beaten
Fat for deep fat frying

Melt butter in saucepan. Remove from heat; blend in
flour, dry mustard, powdered mushrooms, pepper,
onion salt, cayenne and lemon juice. Add milk. Cook
over low heat, stirring, until mixture thickens and is very
smooth. Drain and flake tuna. Add tuna, pimiento and
shredded green onions to sauce, mixing well. Spread
mixture out on plate; chill. Divide chilled mixture into
8 to 10 portions; shape into cones or cylinders. Roll in
cracker meal, then in egg and again in cracker meal.
Chill again. Fry in deep fat, 375°F., 4 minutes or until
golden brown. Drain on absorbent paper. Serve piping
hot. For variety you may serve with one of the following:
Tasty Cream Sauce, Sour Cream Mustard Sauce, Sweet-
Sour Mustard Sauce, Mushroom Sauce or Tomato
Sauce. These recipes may be found in the sauce section.
*Makes 8 to 10 croquettes.*

# Deviled Lobster Tails

4 frozen rock lobster tails
1 tablespoon Instant Minced Onion
2 teaspoons Season-All
¼ teaspoon White Pepper
½ teaspoon Lemon Peel

½ teaspoon dry Mustard
Dash Cayenne or Red Pepper
½ cup dry bread crumbs
¾ cup mayonnaise
4 tablespoons butter, melted
Paprika

Select lobster tails weighing about 6 ounces each. Boil 9 minutes in salted water (1 teaspoon salt to each quart of water). Remove from water and drain. With scissors, cut away thin undershell and remove meat, being careful not to break shells. Cut lobster meat into bite-size pieces. Combine lobster with onion, Season-All, pepper, lemon peel, dry mustard, cayenne, bread crumbs, mayonnaise and 2 tablespoons of the melted butter. Mix well. Refill shells with the lobster mixture. Brush with remaining butter and sprinkle with paprika. Broil 5 to 6 inches from heat 10 minutes or until lightly browned. *Serves 4.*

# Savory Salmon Loaf

1 1-pound can salmon
1 cup soft bread crumbs
¾ cup milk
2 eggs, well beaten
2 tablespoons Instant Minced Onion
¼ cup sliced stuffed olives
1 teaspoon lemon juice

2 tablespoons melted butter
¾ teaspoon Celery Salt
½ teaspoon Parsley Flakes
¼ teaspoon Basil Leaves
¼ teaspoon dry Mustard
¼ teaspoon Black Pepper
1 teaspoon Lemon Peel

Drain and flake salmon; add remaining ingredients. Mix well. Pour into a greased 1½-quart loaf pan. Bake in 350°F. oven 1 hour or until top is delicately golden and loaf is firm yet moist and tender. *Serves 6.*

# Crab Imperial

1 cup milk
1 tablespoon butter
2 tablespoons flour
1 egg, well beaten
1 teaspoon dry Mustard
¼ teaspoon Cayenne
1 teaspoon Season-All
½ teaspoon Celery Salt
1 teaspoon salt
¼ teaspoon Black Pepper
1 tablespoon lemon juice
½ teaspoon Worcestershire
  sauce
4 tablespoons mayonnaise
2 pounds crab meat
2 tablespoons milk
Paprika

Heat the 1 cup milk to boiling point. Melt butter; stir in flour. Pour heated milk into flour and butter mixture, beating until smooth and creamy. Cool. Add egg, seasonings, lemon juice, Worcestershire sauce and 2 tablespoons of the mayonnaise; blend well. Add crab meat and mix well, but gently. Fill shells, ramekins or heatproof small dishes. Now mix the remaining 2 tablespoons mayonnaise with the 2 tablespoons milk and brush over tops. Sprinkle with paprika. Bake in 400°F. oven 8 minutes or until piping hot and lightly browned. You will find a slice of pimiento and a slice of green pepper make an attractive garnish. *Makes 8 servings.*

# Broiled Salmon Tarragon

½ cup butter, melted
2 teaspoons lemon juice
2 teaspoons Season-All
½ teaspoon ground
  Marjoram
1 teaspoon Tarragon Leaves
¼ teaspoon Garlic Powder
½ teaspoon Lemon Peel
Dash Cayenne or Red Pepper
2 pounds salmon steaks

Combine melted butter and lemon juice with seasonings. Arrange salmon steaks on greased broiler rack and brush with one half of the seasoned butter. Broil 2 inches from heat 5 to 10 minutes. Carefully turn and brush with remaining butter mixture. Broil steaks 7 minutes longer or until they can be flaked easily with a fork. Serve hot, garnished with stuffed olives, lemon wedges and sprigs of parsley. *Serves 4 to 6.*

VARIATION:

*Broiled Salmon with Dill*—Combine ½ cup melted butter, 2 teaspoons lemon juice, 2 teaspoons Bon Appétit, 1 teaspoon Dill Weed, ¼ teaspoon Onion Powder, ½ teaspoon Lemon Peel, ⅛ teaspoon White Pepper and dash each Oregano and Paprika. Brush mixture over salmon and cook following directions in above recipe.

---

## Superb Scalloped Oysters

---

Subtle seasoning makes the difference in this luscious version of an old favorite.

| | |
|---|---|
| 1 pint oysters | Dash Onion Powder |
| ½ cup butter or margarine | ¾ cup cream |
| 2 cups coarse cracker crumbs | ¼ cup oyster liquor |
| ½ teaspoon Season-All | 1 teaspoon Worcestershire |
| ¼ teaspoon Celery Salt | sauce |
| ¼ teaspoon Coarse Grind Black Pepper | 1 teaspoon Parsley Flakes |

Drain oysters and save liquor. Melt butter and combine with cracker crumbs, Season-All, celery salt, pepper and onion powder. Spread ⅓ of this mixture in buttered 2-quart shallow baking dish. Cover with ½ of the oysters. Make a second layer of each. Combine cream, oyster liquor and Worcestershire sauce; pour over oysters. Add parsley flakes to remaining crumbs and sprinkle over top of oysters. Bake in 350°F. oven 30 minutes or until oysters are heated through and crumbs are golden brown. *Serves 4.*

# Crab Cakes

2 slices bread
1 egg, lightly beaten
1 tablespoon mayonnaise
1 teaspoon Parsley Flakes
1½ teaspoons Celery Salt
¼ teaspoon dry Mustard
⅛ teaspoon Ginger
⅛ teaspoon Black Pepper

1 tablespoon Worcestershire
  sauce
⅛ teaspoon Cayenne or
  Red Pepper
1 tablespoon baking powder
Dash Cloves
1 pound crab meat
Shortening

Break bread into fine crumbs and mix with beaten egg.
Add mayonnaise, parsley flakes, celery salt, dry mustard,
ginger, pepper, Worcestershire sauce, cayenne, baking
powder and cloves. Mix thoroughly, then combine with
crab meat. Shape into 8 cakes. Fry in hot shortening or
deep fat at 375°F. 4 minutes or until golden brown.
*Serves 4.*

# Shrimp Sautéed in Herb Butter

These sautéed shrimp make an excellent supper.

1 pound raw shrimp
¼ cup butter
2 tablespoons lemon juice
1 teaspoon Parsley Flakes
1 teaspoon Chives
½ teaspoon Tarragon Leaves

½ teaspoon dry Mustard
¾ teaspoon Season-All
⅛ teaspoon Cayenne or
  Red Pepper
⅛ teaspoon Garlic Powder

Shell and devein shrimp. Melt butter in chafing dish or
skillet; add lemon juice and seasonings. Sauté shrimp in
hot herb butter over medium heat 8 minutes or until
pink, turning once. Serve hot. You will find this excellent
when served on a bed of rice. *Makes 2 to 3 servings.*

# Fillet Neapolitan

¼ cup flour
2 teaspoons Bon Appétit
½ teaspoon salt
¼ teaspoon Black Pepper
2 pounds fish fillets (sole,
  flounder, perch or halibut)
¼ cup olive oil
¼ cup Chopped Instant
  Onions

1 6-ounce can tomato paste
1 8-ounce can tomato sauce
½ teaspoon sugar
⅛ teaspoon Garlic Powder
2 teaspoons Parsley Flakes
½ teaspoon Italian Seasoning
¼ cup water

Combine flour, Bon Appétit, salt and pepper. Dip fish
fillets in seasoned flour, then sauté in hot oil until lightly
browned on both sides. Remove. Brown onions, then
add remaining ingredients. Mix well and simmer 10
minutes. Place fish in sauce and simmer 5 minutes longer
or until fish is heated through. Serve with lemon wedges.
*Serves 4 to 6.*

# Sole Meunière

⅓ cup flour
1 teaspoon Season-All
Dash Onion Salt
Dash dry Mustard
Dash White Pepper

2 pounds fillet of sole
½ cup butter or margarine
⅓ cup lemon juice
¼ teaspoon Dill Weed
Paprika

Combine flour, Season-All, onion salt, dry mustard and
pepper. Dip fillets in seasoned flour; sauté in butter over
medium heat until lightly browned. Remove fillets to
heated platter. Add lemon juice and dill weed to butter
in skillet; heat and pour over fish. Sprinkle with paprika.
*Serves 4.*

211

# Creamed Clams

| | |
|---|---|
| 2 7½-ounce cans minced clams | 2 tablespoons Arrowroot |
| 2 tablespoons butter | 1 cup light cream |
| ¼ teaspoon dry Mustard | 1 5-ounce can water chestnuts, sliced |
| ⅛ teaspoon Ginger | 1 teaspoon Shredded Green Onions |
| ¾ teaspoon Onion Salt | |
| Dash Cayenne | 1 tablespoon sherry |
| 1 tablespoon lemon juice | |

Simmer clams and butter 5 minutes. Stir in dry mustard, ginger, onion salt, cayenne and lemon juice; mix well. Combine arrowroot and cream. Add to clams and cook over medium heat, stirring constantly, until thickened. Add water chestnuts; just before serving add shredded green onions and sherry. Serve in patty shells or over toast. *Serves 6.*

# Sole Epicurean

Broiled in a delectable sauce until golden, this is food for gourmets.

| | |
|---|---|
| 2 pounds fillet of sole | ½ cup butter |
| 1½ teaspoons Season-All | 3 tablespoons lemon juice |
| ¼ teaspoon White Pepper | 8 Coriander Seeds, crushed |
| ⅛ teaspoon Paprika | ½ teaspoon Tarragon Leaves |

Place fillets with the thin tissue-like skin side down in broiler pan. Sprinkle with mixture of Season-All, pepper and paprika. Melt butter, carefully skimming off the white milk solids. Combine lemon juice, crushed coriander seed and tarragon leaves. Boil quickly to reduce to 1 tablespoon. Simmer the clarified butter (the clear yellow portion) over medium heat until golden brown, then slowly add lemon juice mixture. As soon as bubbling stops, the sauce is ready to use. Brush about half of it over the fillets and keep the remainder warm over hot water. Broil fillets 4 inches from heat 10 minutes or until easily flaked with a fork. Serve at once with side dish of the remaining sauce. *Serves 4.*

---

## Baked Fish with Herb Stuffing

1 4- to 5-pound whole fish (cod, red snapper, haddock, rock, halibut, bass or whitefish)
2 tablespoons Instant Minced Onion
½ cup diced celery
½ cup butter or margarine
¼ teaspoon Marjoram Leaves
½ teaspoon rubbed Sage
1 teaspoon Parsley Flakes
¼ teaspoon Tarragon Leaves
¼ teaspoon Dill Weed

1 teaspoon Bon Appétit
¼ teaspoon Lemon Peel
¼ teaspoon Savory
1 egg, beaten
3 cups soft bread crumbs, packed
¼ cup butter, melted
½ teaspoon dry Mustard
¼ teaspoon MSG
½ teaspoon Fennel Seed, crushed
1 tablespoon Bon Appétit
1 tablespoon lemon juice

Clean and wash fish. Sauté onion and celery in the ½ cup butter until onion is lightly browned. Blend in the next eight ingredients. Remove from heat; add to egg and bread crumbs, tossing lightly. Loosely fill cavity of fish with stuffing; close cavity with toothpicks or skewers, drawing edges together by lacing with string. Place fish on a piece of oiled, heavy paper or aluminum foil to prevent sticking and put in a shallow baking pan. Combine remaining ingredients and brush fish thoroughly with part of this mixture. Bake in 400°F. oven, basting occasionally with the remaining seasoned butter, until fish flakes easily with a fork, allowing 12 to 15 minutes per pound. Serve on a fish platter garnished with parsley, tomato wedges and slices of lemon centered with whole Clove. *Serves 6 to 8.*

213

# Sauteed Frogs' Legs

4 pair frogs' legs (about
  1½ pounds)
Milk to cover
1½ teaspoons Season-All
  or Bon Appétit
½ teaspoon Onion Powder
¼ teaspoon White Pepper
Flour
6 tablespoons butter

Soak frogs' legs in milk 1 hour. Remove from milk and
sprinkle with Season-All or Bon Appétit, onion powder
and pepper. Coat lightly with flour. Melt butter; as soon
as it sizzles, add frogs' legs and sauté 7 minutes on each
side or until golden brown. Remove to heated platter.
Spoon butter from skillet over frogs' legs. *Serves 2.*

VARIATIONS:

*Frogs' Legs Provençale*—Prepare frogs' legs following directions in above recipe. Remove to heated platter. To
  butter in skillet add ½ teaspoon Garlic Powder, 1
  tablespoon lemon juice and 1 teaspoon Parsley Flakes.
  Stir to mix well and pour over frogs' legs.
*Frogs' Legs aux Fines Herbes*—Prepare frogs' legs following
  directions in above recipe. Remove to heated platter.
  To butter in skillet add ¼ teaspoon Tarragon Leaves,
  ½ teaspoon Parsley Flakes, ½ teaspoon Chives and
  2 tablespoons dry white wine. Stir well and pour over
  frogs' legs.

# Fillet de Sole Véronique

6 fillets of sole
1 teaspoon salt
¼ teaspoon White Pepper
¼ teaspoon Onion Powder
1 teaspoon Chicken Seasoned
   Stock Base
1 cup hot water

½ cup dry white wine
2 Bay Leaves
4 whole Allspice
1 cup seedless white grapes
2 tablespoons butter
½ cup cream
1 tablespoon flour

Press fillets out flat; sprinkle with a mixture of the salt, pepper and onion powder, then fold in half. Place the folded fillets in a buttered, deep skillet. Dissolve seasoned stock base in hot water, then pour over fish along with wine. Drop in bay leaves and allspice. Cover. Cook gently 10 minutes or until the fish is tender and flakes easily with a fork. Carefully remove the fillets to a heated platter and garnish with grapes. Keep hot in warm oven. Reduce liquid in skillet over high heat to about ½ cup. Remove bay leaves and allspice. Stir in butter and cream. Make a thin, smooth paste by mixing together the flour with an equal amount of water. Then stir into liquid in skillet and cook, continuing to stir until sauce thickens slightly. Pour over fillets and grapes. Broil a few minutes to glaze sauce, but do not allow to brown. For an especially attractive dish sprinkle top of fillets with Paprika and garnish around sides with parsley and spiced crab apples. *Serves 6.*

# Broiled Fish Amandine

The crunchy topping of golden almonds makes this a favorite recipe.

| | |
|---|---|
| 2 12-ounce packages frozen perch or trout, or 2 pounds any fresh fish fillets | ⅛ teaspoon Black Pepper |
| | Dash Nutmeg |
| | Dash Paprika |
| 4 tablespoons melted butter | 2 tablespoons slivered blanched almonds |
| 1 teaspoon Bon Appétit | |
| ¼ teaspoon salt | 2 tablespoons lemon juice |
| Dash Onion Powder | 1 tablespoon Parsley Flakes |

If using frozen fillets, thaw just enough to separate. Brush with 2 tablespoons of the melted butter. Combine seasonings and sprinkle over fish. Place fish with the tissue-like skin side down in a well greased broiler pan. Broil 4 to 5 inches from heat 10 minutes or until fish is easily flaked with fork. Sauté almonds in the remaining butter until golden brown, then stir in lemon juice. Spoon the almonds and the lemon-butter mixture over fish. Sprinkle with parsley flakes. Serve immediately. *Serves 5 to 6.*

# Sea Food Crêpes

CRÊPES:

| | |
|---|---|
| ¾ cup sifted all-purpose flour | 2 eggs, beaten |
| 1 tablespoon sugar | 1 cup milk |
| Dash salt | 1 tablespoon cognac |
| Dash Nutmeg | 1 tablespoon melted butter |
| Dash Black Pepper | Sea Food Filling |

Sift together flour, sugar, salt, nutmeg and pepper. Combine eggs, milk and cognac and add to flour mixture. Beat until smooth. Stir in butter; cover and let batter stand 2 hours. Prepare Sea Food Filling, following recipe below. To cook crêpes, pour 3 tablespoons of the batter into a lightly buttered, hot, 7-inch skillet. Tilt pan to spread batter evenly. Brown crêpe on one side; turn and brown second side. Remove from pan and keep warm. Continue until all batter is used. Place Sea Food Filling across center of each crêpe; fold sides over to form roll. Place filled crêpes in shallow baking dish or heatproof platter. Spoon remaining sauce that was not used in filling over top of crêpes. (If sauce seems a little thick, add 2 to 3 tablespoons cream or milk.) Bake in 375°F. oven 15 minutes or until heated through, then broil a few seconds to brown top lightly. *Makes 12 crêpes.*

SEA FOOD FILLING:

| | |
|---|---|
| ¼ cup butter | Dash MSG |
| 3 tablespoons Arrowroot | 2 cups milk |
| 3 teaspoons Chicken Seasoned Stock Base | 1 egg yolk, beaten |
| ½ teaspoon dry Mustard | ¼ cup dry white wine |
| ¼ teaspoon White Pepper | ¼ cup mayonnaise |
| 4 Fennel Seeds, crushed | 1 cup crab meat |
| ¼ teaspoon Onion Powder | 1 cup finely chopped, cooked shrimp |
| 1 teaspoon Bon Appétit | 1 cup finely chopped, cooked lobster |
| Dash Cayenne | |

Melt butter; stir in arrowroot and seasonings. Remove from heat and add milk. Cook over low heat until thickened, stirring constantly. Remove from heat. Add some of the hot mixture to egg yolk while stirring briskly, then stir egg yolk mixture into hot sauce. Add wine and mayonnaise, blending well. Combine crab meat, shrimp and lobster. Mix 1 cup of the sauce into the sea food mixture. Use to fill crêpes. Reserve the remaining sauce.

217

# Scallops and Mushrooms en Brochette

2 pounds fresh scallops
½ cup olive oil
2 tablespoons lemon juice
¼ teaspoon Black Pepper
1 Bay Leaf
⅛ teaspoon Garlic Salt

8 Coriander Seeds
2 teaspoons Season-All
Dash MSG
1 8-ounce can mushroom
    crowns

Wash and drain scallops, and put in flat baking dish. Combine remaining ingredients, except mushrooms, and pour over scallops, turning them to coat all sides. Marinate in refrigerator several hours. Thread scallops onto skewers alternately with mushroom crowns, which have been drained. Place on broiler rack and broil 3 to 4 inches from heat 8 to 10 minutes. Turn and broil 8 to 10 minutes longer. Brush several times with marinade during broiling. Serve with tartare sauce. *Serves 6 to 8.*

# Deviled Crab

¼ cup flour
2 teaspoons Instant Minced
    Onion
⅛ teaspoon Cayenne or
    Red Pepper
1 teaspoon dry Mustard
1 teaspoon Powdered
    Horseradish
1 teaspoon salt

¼ cup melted butter
1 cup milk
2 egg yolks, beaten
2 teaspoons lemon juice
1 teaspoon Worcestershire
    sauce
2 cups crab meat
2 tablespoons melted butter
1 cup soft bread crumbs

Combine flour, onion, cayenne, dry mustard, powdered horseradish and salt; stir into the ¼ cup melted butter in a saucepan. Cook until bubbly, then remove from heat. Add milk and cook over medium heat until thickened, stirring constantly. Add small amount of the hot sauce to egg yolks while stirring briskly, then combine egg mixture with the remaining sauce. Cook over low heat 2 minutes, stirring. Remove from heat; add lemon juice, Worcestershire sauce and crab meat. Mix well. Place crab mixture in individual ramekins, custard cups or cleaned crab shells. Combine the 2 tablespoons melted butter and bread crumbs; sprinkle over crab mixture. Bake in 400°F. oven 20 minutes or until crumbs are delicately browned. *Serves 5 to 6.*

## *Lobster Cantonese*

6 rock lobster tails
  (6 to 8 ounces each)
¾ pound lean pork,
  coarsely ground
2 teaspoons Instant Minced
  Onion
1½ teaspoons salt
½ teaspoon Black Pepper
½ teaspoon Bon Appétit
¾ cup thinly sliced celery
¼ cup salad oil

½ cup thinly sliced
  water chestnuts
½ pound Chinese snow peas
  (fresh or frozen)
1½ teaspoons Chicken
  Seasoned Stock Base
1½ cups hot water
3 tablespoons Arrowroot
1 tablespoon soy sauce
⅓ cup water
2 eggs, well beaten

Thaw lobster, if frozen, and remove meat from shells. Cut into 1½-inch pieces. Combine ground pork, onion, salt, pepper and Bon Appétit. Sauté pork mixture and celery 1 minute in hot oil, stirring constantly. Add lobster, water chestnuts, snow peas, seasoned stock base and hot water. Cover and simmer 8 minutes, stirring once. Combine arrowroot, soy sauce and the ⅓ cup water. Stir into lobster mixture; cook 2 minutes. Add beaten eggs, stirring well, and cook 1 minute longer. Serve immediately with rice. *Serves 6.*

# Shrimp Creole

¼ cup butter or margarine
2 tablespoons Instant Minced
  Onion
1 cup chopped celery
½ cup chopped green pepper
2 tablespoons flour
1 tablespoon Season-All
1 Bay Leaf

⅛ teaspoon Cayenne or
  Red Pepper
2 teaspoons Parsley Flakes
3½ cups tomatoes
  (No. 2½ can)
½ cup water
1 pound cooked,
  cleaned shrimp

Melt butter in large skillet. Sauté onion, celery and green pepper in butter until onion is lightly browned. Blend in flour. Add remaining ingredients except shrimp; mix well. Cover and simmer 30 minutes. Stir in shrimp and continue simmering just until shrimp is heated through. Serve over hot steamed rice. *Serves 4.*

# Pan-Fried Fish

4 whole fish for frying (trout,
  perch, bass) or 1½ pounds
  fillet of sole
2 teaspoons Bon Appétit
½ teaspoon Black Pepper
1½ teaspoons Paprika

¼ teaspoon Onion Powder
¼ teaspoon dry Mustard
Dash Nutmeg
¼ cup corn meal
Shortening for frying

When using whole fish, clean and remove heads. Combine seasonings and rub over fish. Roll in corn meal. Fry fish in hot shortening, about ¼ inch deep in a heavy skillet, until crisp and brown on both sides. It should take you about 8 minutes. Serve piping hot with Tartare Sauce (see recipe page 403) and slices of lime or lemon. *Serves 4.*

# Shrimp and Lobster with Sauce Caviar

Excitingly different, superbly seasoned.

| | |
|---|---|
| 1 pound raw shrimp | 1 tablespoon Fish Garni |
| 4 rock lobster tails | 3 tablespoons lemon juice |
| ½ cup butter | Dash Nutmeg |
| ¼ teaspoon Paprika | 9 Fennel Seeds, crushed |
| ½ teaspoon Bon Appétit | ¼ teaspoon Black Pepper |
| ¼ teaspoon Onion Salt | Sauce Caviar |

Cook and clean shrimp and lobster tails; cut lobster into cubes. Thread shrimp and lobster onto skewers. Melt butter and add remaining ingredients. Brush shrimp and lobster thoroughly with this butter sauce. Broil 4 inches from heat 3 minutes. Turn; brush again and broil until delicately browned. Serve hot with Sauce Caviar. You will need, of course, to increase the amount of shrimp or lobster if you prefer to use only one of these instead of the combination. *Serves 4 to 6.*

SAUCE CAVIAR:

| | |
|---|---|
| ½ cup mayonnaise | ⅛ teaspoon salt |
| ½ cup commercial sour cream | 2 tablespoons lemon juice |
| ½ teaspoon dry Mustard | ¼ teaspoon Onion Salt |
| ⅛ teaspoon MSG | 2 tablespoons black caviar |
| ½ teaspoon Powdered | (giant grain) |
| Horseradish | 1 tablespoon cognac |
| Dash White Pepper | |

Combine all ingredients, mixing thoroughly but gently. Let stand at least 1 hour for flavors to blend. You may make this sauce ahead of time and keep in refrigerator. *Makes about 1¼ cups.*

# Fish Poached in Court Bouillon

Elegant and exquisitely seasoned, a superb fish dish.

6 fish fillets (about 2 pounds)
2 teaspoons Season-All
¼ teaspoon Garlic Powder
¼ teaspoon Celery Salt
¼ teaspoon White Pepper
1¼ cups hot water
1 teaspoon Chicken Seasoned
Stock Base
4 whole Allspice
3 whole Cloves
6 Coriander Seeds
1 Bay Leaf

1 piece whole Ginger, broken
⅓ cup lemon juice
1 4-ounce can mushrooms,
drained
2 tablespoons chopped olives
¼ cup melted butter
1 tablespoon Arrowroot
2 teaspoons Instant Minced
Onion
½ cup cream or milk
Paprika

Cut fillets lengthwise into strips 1½ inches wide. Combine Season-All, garlic powder, celery salt and pepper; sprinkle over fillet strips. Roll each strip, fasten with toothpick and place in skillet. Combine hot water and seasoned stock base; pour over fillets. Add allspice, cloves, coriander seed, bay leaf, ginger and lemon juice. Cover and simmer gently 10 minutes or just until fish is tender and flakes easily with a fork. Carefully remove rolled fillets to heated baking dish or platter; top with mushrooms and chopped olives. Drizzle with melted butter. Keep hot in warm oven. Reduce liquid in skillet to 1 cup by boiling over high heat. If desired, remove whole spices. Combine arrowroot, onion and cream; stir into hot liquid. Cook, stirring, over low heat until thickened. Spoon over fish. Sprinkle generously with paprika and serve at once. *Serves 6.*

# CASSEROLES
# SPECIAL DISHES

——— * ———

## *Brunswick Stew*

1 4- to 5-pound stewing
  chicken
3 teaspoons salt
1 teaspoon Celery Salt
1 Bay Leaf
½ cup Chopped Instant
  Onions
1 tablespoon Bell Pepper
  Flakes
¼ cup butter
2 cups tomatoes (No. 303 can)
1 tablespoon Parsley Flakes
½ teaspoon Cayenne or
  Red Pepper

⅛ teaspoon Ginger
⅛ teaspoon Cumin
½ teaspoon Lemon Peel
¼ teaspoon Black Pepper
1 tablespoon Season-All
1 tablespoon Worcestershire
  sauce
1 teaspoon sugar
1 No. 303 can whole kernel
  corn
2 cups fresh, frozen or
  canned lima beans
⅓ cup flour
½ cup water

Cover chicken with water; add 2 teaspoons of the salt, celery salt and bay leaf. Simmer until chicken is tender. Remove chicken, reserving 3 cups of the stock. Remove chicken from bone and cut into bite-size pieces. In large saucepan or Dutch oven sauté onions and pepper flakes in butter. Add tomatoes, the remaining salt, seasonings, sugar and the 3 cups stock; simmer 30 minutes. Add corn, lima beans and chicken and simmer 2 hours longer. Mix flour and water to a smooth paste and stir into stew. Continue cooking until thickened. *Makes about 3 quarts, serving 8 to 10, depending upon size of serving.*

# Eggs à la Goldenrod

A luncheon or supper dish . . . ideal during Lent.

| | |
|---|---|
| 6 hard-cooked eggs | 2 teaspoons Chicken Seasoned |
| 3 tablespoons butter | Stock Base |
| ½ teaspoon dry Mustard | 4 teaspoons Arrowroot |
| ¼ teaspoon White Pepper | 2 cups milk |
| Dash Nutmeg | 1 teaspoon vinegar |
| Dash Cayenne | 6 slices bread |
| ½ teaspoon Tarragon Leaves | Paprika |

Cut eggs in half; remove yolks. Press yolks through coarse sieve and chop whites. Melt butter in saucepan; stir in dry mustard, pepper, nutmeg, cayenne, tarragon leaves, seasoned stock base and arrowroot. Add milk; cook over medium heat, stirring, until sauce thickens. Add vinegar and chopped egg whites, blending well. Toast bread; butter if desired. Arrange toast on heated platter and pour sauce over toast. Top with sieved yolks; sprinkle with paprika. Arrange slices of Canadian bacon and tomato wedges around platter for a meal-in-one. *Serves 4 to 6.*

# Cannelloni

**PANCAKES:**

| | |
|---|---|
| 1 cup all-purpose flour | ½ cup commercial |
| 1 tablespoon corn meal | sour cream |
| ½ teaspoon Bon Appétit | 1 cup water |
| 2 eggs | 2 tablespoons oil |

Combine dry ingredients. Beat eggs; add sour cream and water and mix well. Stir in flour mixture and oil. Cook

pancakes on a lightly greased hot griddle, using about
3 tablespoons of the batter for each. *Makes about 12.*

FILLING:

1 pound raw chicken meat
½ pound veal
½ pound pork
4 slices prosciutto ham
2 tablespoons olive oil
2 tablespoons Instant Minced
  Onion
¼ teaspoon MSG
½ teaspoon salt
⅛ teaspoon Garlic Powder
¼ teaspoon Rosemary Leaves
¼ teaspoon Basil Leaves
¼ teaspoon Oregano Leaves
¼ teaspoon Thyme Leaves
2 teaspoons Season-All
¼ teaspoon Black Pepper
½ cup sherry
½ pound ricotta cheese
½ cup cream
Teleme, Monterey Jack or
  Muenster cheese
Grated Parmesan cheese

Cut meat into pieces. Sauté in hot oil about 2 minutes,
stirring to turn meat. Add seasonings; cover and simmer
slowly 45 minutes or until tender. Add sherry and cook
10 minutes longer. Remove from heat; stir in ricotta
cheese. Cool, then grind in food mill twice. Add the
broth from skillet (there should be about ½ cup) and
the cream, mixing well. Add additional broth or cream
if necessary to make a very moist, but not runny, filling.
Fill pancakes with mixture, folding sides over to make a
long roll. Place in buttered baking dish; when ready to
serve, heat in 350°F. oven about 20 minutes. Top with
a slice of teleme, Monterey Jack or Muenster cheese.
Continue baking until cheese melts. Serve with Parmesan cheese and sauce. *Serves 6.*

SAUCE:

1 cup chili sauce
1 8-ounce can tomato sauce
2 tablespoons lemon juice
2 teaspoons Instant Minced
  Onion
⅛ teaspoon Garlic Powder
⅛ teaspoon ground Oregano
Dash or two Cayenne
⅛ teaspoon MSG
2 tablespoons butter

Combine all ingredients and simmer slowly about 20
minutes.

# Eggplant Florentine with Beef

Rich, wonderful Mediterranean flavor.

1 medium-size eggplant
¼ cup butter or margarine
1 pound ground beef
1 tablespoon Instant Minced Onion
1 teaspoon Bon Appétit
⅛ teaspoon Black Pepper
1 teaspoon sugar
¼ teaspoon MSG
¼ teaspoon Basil Leaves
¼ teaspoon ground Oregano
1 8-ounce can tomato sauce
¼ cup grated Parmesan cheese
½ pound Mozzarella cheese

Wash, but do not peel eggplant; cut into ½-inch slices. Melt butter over low heat in skillet; add eggplant and brown lightly on both sides, adding extra butter if needed. Put in shallow 2-quart baking dish. To drippings in skillet, add ground beef, onion, Bon Appétit, pepper, sugar, MSG, basil leaves and oregano; mix well and cook until meat is lightly browned. Spoon meat mixture over eggplant; add tomato sauce and Parmesan cheese. Bake, uncovered, in 350°F. oven 20 minutes. Slice Mozzarella cheese and place over top of casserole. Bake 10 minutes longer or until cheese is melted. Serve hot. *Serves 6.*

# Mock Enchilada Casserole

2 tablespoons butter or
margarine
2 tablespoons Instant Minced
Onion
1 8-ounce can tomato sauce
1 4-ounce can green chili
peppers, chopped
1 teaspoon Italian Seasoning
½ teaspoon Celery Salt
¼ teaspoon White or Black
Pepper

2 eggs
1 cup light cream
6 tortillas, torn into pieces or
6-ounce package corn chips
½ pound Monterey Jack or
Muenster cheese, cubed
½ pint commercial sour
cream
½ cup grated Cheddar
cheese
Paprika

Melt butter in skillet; add onion and sauté but do not
brown. Add tomato sauce, chili peppers, Italian Seasoning, celery salt and pepper. Simmer 5 minutes. Lightly
beat eggs; add cream, mixing well. Remove tomato
mixture from heat; quickly stir in egg mixture. Cover
the bottom of a 2-quart casserole with ⅓ of the tortillas;
cover with ⅓ of the sauce and ⅓ of the cubed cheese.
Repeat layers until all tortillas, sauce and cubed cheese
have been used. Top with sour cream; sprinkle with
grated Cheddar cheese and paprika. Bake in 350°F. oven
25 minutes or until bubbly hot. Serve immediately with
a crisp tossed salad. *Makes 4 to 6 servings.*

# Paella

Saffron gives this most famous of Spanish rice dishes its special goodness.

½ pound raw shrimp
1 3- to 4-pound chicken
¼ cup olive oil
¼ pound pepperoni, sliced
2 tomatoes
¼ cup Chopped Instant Onions
⅛ teaspoon Garlic Powder
1 teaspoon Paprika
1 tablespoon Parsley Flakes
1 teaspoon Season-All
10 individual pieces Saffron
1 teaspoon salt

¼ teaspoon Black Pepper
2 teaspoons Chicken Seasoned Stock Base
1½ cups rice
3 cups water
1 9-ounce package frozen artichokes, cooked
1 pimiento, sliced
12 whole clams or about 1 cup canned minced clams
1 cup lobster pieces
1 8-ounce can peas, drained

Remove shell from the raw shrimp; set aside. Cut chicken in pieces. In large skillet, brown chicken on all sides in oil; remove. Then add pepperoni and brown. Peel and cut tomatoes into sections, then add to skillet with onions; cook until onions are lightly browned. Return chicken to pan, add shrimp and the remaining ingredients except peas. Cover and simmer 30 minutes. Add peas and cook, uncovered, 5 minutes longer. All you need to serve with Paella is plenty of salad. *Serves 6 to 8.*

# Sausage and Wild Rice Casserole

A wonderful party casserole.

¾ pound bulk pork sausage
1 tablespoon Bell Pepper
  Flakes
½ cup chopped celery
1 4-ounce can pimiento
1 cup wild rice
2 teaspoons Chicken Seasoned
  Stock Base
1½ cups hot water

1 10½-ounce can condensed
  cream of mushroom soup
1 2-ounce can mushrooms
1 tablespoon Instant Minced
  Onion
½ teaspoon Marjoram Leaves
½ teaspoon Thyme Leaves
1 cup grated American cheese

Crumble sausage and brown in a large skillet. Add pepper flakes and celery and continue cooking until celery is soft. Drain off excess fat. Drain and chop pimiento; add to sausage mixture along with remaining ingredients, mixing well. Pour into a 3-quart casserole. Cover. Bake in 325°F. oven 1½ hours or until rice is tender and dry. Rich, tasty and filling! Serve with a crisp green salad and dessert. *Serves 6 to 8.*

# Chinese Chicken Casserole

½ teaspoon Chicken Seasoned
  Stock Base
⅓ cup hot water
1 10½-ounce can condensed
  cream of mushroom soup
1 cup chopped cooked chicken

2 tablespoons Shredded
  Green Onions
½ cup whole cashew nuts
1 No. 2 can chow mein
  noodles

Dissolve seasoned stock base in water. Combine with soup, chicken, onions, nuts and half of the noodles. Put in buttered 1½-quart casserole; top with the remaining noodles. Bake in 375°F. oven 30 minutes. *Serves 4.*

# Cabbage Rolls

8 large cabbage leaves
½ cup long grain rice
1 cup water
½ teaspoon salt
1 pound ground beef
1 tablespoon Instant Minced Onion

2½ teaspoons Season-All
¼ teaspoon Black Pepper
¼ teaspoon Basil Leaves
3½ cups tomatoes (No. 2½ can)
1 tablespoon flour
¼ cup commercial sour cream

Steam cabbage leaves 8 minutes or until slightly tender. Combine rice, water and salt and cook 20 minutes or until tender. Mix together rice, beef, onion, 1½ teaspoons of the Season-All, pepper and basil leaves. Place ⅓ cup of the meat mixture in each cabbage leaf. Fold leaf over meat, tucking in ends, and fasten with toothpick. Place rolls, overlapped side down, in frying pan. Pour tomatoes over rolls and simmer 1½ hours. Remove rolls. Combine flour, sour cream and the remaining Season-All; stir into liquid in frying pan. Simmer very gently until slightly thickened but do not allow to boil. Serve cabbage rolls, steaming hot, with sauce. *Makes 8 rolls.*

# Chili con Carne

1 pound ground beef
2 tablespoons shortening
1 teaspoon salt
3 tablespoons Chili Powder
⅓ cup Onion Flakes

1 8-ounce can tomato sauce
1 No. 2 can red kidney beans
2 tablespoons vinegar
Dash Garlic Powder
Dash MSG

Crumble beef; brown in hot shortening, stirring until meat loses its pink color. Add remaining ingredients; mix well. Cover. Simmer 45 minutes, stirring occasionally. *Serves 4 to 6.*

# Party Beef Casserole

Savory beef in a red wine sauce, topped with a "crust" of mashed potato.

2 pounds beef round
  (cut into 1-inch cubes)
3 tablespoons flour
1 teaspoon Season-All
⅛ teaspoon Black Pepper
3 tablespoons bacon drippings
  or salad oil
1 cup water
1 teaspoon Beef Flavor Base
⅓ cup Chopped Instant
  Onions
½ teaspoon Garlic Powder

1 teaspoon Bon Appétit
½ teaspoon Marjoram Leaves
½ teaspoon Thyme Leaves
1 cup red wine, Burgundy
  or Bordeaux
2 cups fresh, frozen or
  canned peas
3 cups hot, stiff, mashed
  potatoes
1 tablespoon melted butter
Paprika

Dredge meat with mixture of flour, Season-All and pepper; brown on all sides in hot fat. Transfer browned meat to a 2-quart casserole. Add water to skillet and stir to loosen all the browned bits. Add beef flavor base, onions, garlic powder, Bon Appétit, marjoram leaves and thyme leaves. Simmer about 5 minutes, then add wine and mix well. Pour sauce over meat in casserole. Cover and bake in 350°F. oven 1½ hours or until meat is tender. Cook peas; drain. (Reserve several pieces of the meat and ¼ cup of the peas to use for garnishing the top if desired.) Sprinkle peas over meat. Spoon potatoes completely over top; brush with butter. Sprinkle generously with paprika. Bake 15 minutes longer or until potatoes are lightly browned. A favorite with the men. *Serves 5 to 6.*

# Lima-Sausage Casserole

1 pound bulk pork sausage
1 tablespoon Instant Minced Onion
⅛ teaspoon Garlic Powder
⅛ teaspoon MSG
¼ teaspoon Rosemary Leaves
¼ teaspoon Thyme Leaves
1 8-ounce can tomato sauce
2 No. 303 cans lima beans
¼ cup butter
1 cup dry bread crumbs
1 tablespoon Parsley Flakes

Crumble sausage; add onion, garlic powder and MSG. Cook until sausage is browned, stirring and breaking it up with a fork while cooking. Crush rosemary leaves and add to sausage along with thyme leaves and tomato sauce. Simmer 15 minutes. Drain limas; add to sausage mixture. Stir to mix well. Transfer to a 1½-quart casserole. Melt butter; stir into bread crumbs and parsley flakes, tossing lightly. Spoon over top of bean mixture. Bake in 350°F. oven 1 hour or until crumbs are golden. *Serves 4 to 6.*

# Veal and Wild Rice in Casserole

1 cup wild rice
3 cups water
1 teaspoon Chicken Seasoned Stock Base
2 pounds veal cutlet, thinly sliced
6 tablespoons butter
2 teaspoons Instant Minced Onion
½ teaspoon Chervil Leaves
¼ teaspoon ground Thyme
¼ teaspoon ground Savory
½ teaspoon Season-All
½ cup white wine
1 4-ounce can mushrooms
1 cup commercial sour cream
Paprika

Wash rice. Add water and seasoned stock base and cook, covered, until rice is fluffy and water absorbed, 45 minutes to 1 hour. Cut veal into 3- to 4-inch pieces. Brown in butter; add onion, chervil leaves, thyme, savory, Season-All and wine. Remove from heat. Stir mushrooms, including liquid, into rice; transfer to a 2-quart baking dish. Place pieces of veal over top of rice. Add sour cream to wine-herb mixture in skillet, stirring until thoroughly blended. Pour over top of veal; sprinkle with paprika. Bake in 325°F. oven 20 minutes. *Serves 4 to 5.*

## Buttered Noodles with Dill

1 8-ounce package noodles     2 teaspoons Dill Weed
½ cup melted butter

Cook noodles as directed on package; drain. Toss lightly with melted butter and dill weed. *Serves 6 to 8.*

VARIATION:

*Buttered Noodles with Poppy Seed*—In the above recipe use 2 teaspoons Poppy Seed in place of dill weed.

## Busy Day Casserole

1 pound ground beef
½ cup chopped green
  pepper
3 tablespoons oil
2 tablespoons Instant
  Minced Onion
½ cup rice

2 cups tomatoes
  (No. 303 can)
1 teaspoon Chili Powder
1 teaspoon Season-All
2 teaspoons salt
¼ teaspoon Black Pepper
⅛ teaspoon ground Thyme

Cook ground beef and green pepper in oil until beef has lost its pink color and is crumbly. Add remaining ingredients, mixing well. Pour into greased 2-quart casserole; cover and bake in 350°F. oven 45 minutes. *Serves 4 to 5.*

# Noodles Romanoff

2½ cups noodles
1 cup cottage cheese
1 cup commercial sour cream
1 teaspoon Instant Minced Onion
1½ teaspoons Season-All
⅛ teaspoon Instant Minced Garlic
1 teaspoon Worcestershire sauce
Dash Cayenne or Red Pepper
⅓ cup grated Cheddar cheese

Cook noodles as directed on package; drain. Combine noodles with remaining ingredients except grated cheese. Put in buttered 1½-quart casserole; sprinkle top with grated cheese. Bake in 350°F. oven 30 minutes or until heated through and bubbly and cheese has melted. *Serves 6.*

# Savory Stuffed Peppers

Topped with bubbly cheese to make them extra special.

6 medium-size green peppers
1 pound ground beef
1 tablespoon oil
¼ cup Chopped Instant Onions
¼ cup catchup
1 cup soft bread crumbs
½ teaspoon Basil Leaves
2 teaspoons Season-All
½ teaspoon salt
¼ teaspoon rubbed Sage
½ teaspoon Beef Flavor Base
¼ cup hot water
6 slices Muenster cheese
Paprika

Wash peppers, cut off tops and remove seed, leaving peppers whole. Steam 5 minutes. Brown beef in hot oil; add onions, catchup, bread crumbs, basil leaves, Season-All, salt and sage. Fill peppers with meat mixture and place in a baking dish. Dissolve beef flavor base in hot water and add to dish with peppers. Cover and bake in 350°F. oven 40 minutes. Place slice of cheese on top of each pepper; sprinkle with paprika and bake, uncovered, 10 minutes longer. *Serves 6.*

# Lasagne

Rich, hearty and delicious.

1 pound ground beef
2 tablespoons olive oil
3½ cups tomatoes (No. 2½ can)
2 8-ounce cans tomato sauce
2 tablespoons Instant Minced Onion
⅛ teaspoon Garlic Powder
1½ teaspoons Oregano Leaves
¼ teaspoon Rosemary Leaves
¼ teaspoon Basil Leaves
½ teaspoon MSG
2 teaspoons salt
1 teaspoon sugar
1 3-ounce can sliced mushrooms
½ pound lasagne noodles
1 pound ricotta cheese
½ pound Mozzarella cheese
½ cup grated Parmesan cheese

Sauté ground beef in hot oil until meat loses its pink color. Add tomatoes, tomato sauce, seasonings and mushrooms. Mix well; cook slowly about 2 hours or until sauce is thickened. Cook noodles following directions on package; drain, rinse in cold water and separate. In a buttered 3-quart baking dish make two layers of the noodles, meat sauce, ricotta, slices of Mozzarella cheese and Parmesan cheese, in this order, using about half of each for each layer. Bake in 350°F. oven 30 minutes or until bubbly. *Serves 6 to 7.*

NOTE: Pepperoni may be added to meat sauce if desired. You may double the recipe for sauce; use half in making the lasagne, as above, and serve the remainder, cooked down until quite thick, in a sauceboat along with the lasagne.

# Mexican Skillet Dinner

A spicy, hearty budget dish, so easy to put together.

1 pound bulk pork sausage
¼ cup Chopped Instant Onions
1 cup diced green pepper
1 8-ounce package elbow macaroni

2 cups tomatoes (No. 303 can)
1 cup buttermilk or commercial sour cream
2 tablespoons sugar
2 tablespoons Chili Powder
2 teaspoons Season-All

Brown sausage in deep heavy skillet; add onions and green pepper. Cook until onions are golden brown. Pour off excess fat. Add remaining ingredients; stir to moisten macaroni. Cover; bring to a boil, then reduce heat and cook 30 minutes. *Serves 4.*

# Indian Rice

½ cup butter
1 cup rice
2 tablespoons Instant Minced Onion
4 whole Cardamom
1 Bay Leaf
¼ teaspoon Saffron pieces
Dash Cinnamon

¼ teaspoon Coarse Grind Black Pepper
¼ cup currants or raisins
¼ cup slivered almonds
2 tablespoons Chicken Seasoned Stock Base
2 cups hot water

Melt half the butter; add rice and onion and sauté until brown. Remove the little black seed from the whole cardamom pod and crush, discarding the outer pod. Crumble the bay leaf and saffron. Then add the spices to rice along with remaining butter and other ingredients. Cover. Cook over low heat 25 to 30 minutes. Though Indian Rice may be served with any kind of meat, it is especially good with pork or chicken. *Serves 4 to 6.*

# Texas Barbecued Beef

1 pound ground beef  
3 tablespoons shortening or oil  
2 tablespoons Chopped Instant Onions  
1 tablespoon flour  

¾ cup hot water  
¾ cup chili sauce  
1 teaspoon Barbecue Spice  
1 teaspoon dry Mustard  
¼ teaspoon MSG  

Crumble beef and sauté in hot shortening until meat loses its pink color and is lightly browned. Stir in onions and flour. Add hot water and cook 5 minutes, stirring constantly. Add remaining ingredients and simmer 15 minutes. Serve piping hot over hamburger buns which have been split and toasted, or you may prefer to serve over rice or noodles. *Serves 6.*

# Saffron Rice

¼ cup butter  
½ cup slivered almonds  
1 cup rice  
1 cup chopped green pepper  
1 4-ounce can mushrooms, stems and pieces  

¼ teaspoon Saffron pieces  
¼ teaspoon Black Pepper  
1 tablespoon Instant Minced Onion  
1½ teaspoons salt  
2½ cups water  

Melt butter in skillet; add almonds and rice. Cook over low heat, stirring, until rice is delicately browned. Add remaining ingredients. Cover skillet. Bring to a boil; reduce heat and simmer about 25 minutes. Remove from heat; keep covered until ready to serve. You will find Saffron Rice excellent with chicken; but you can use it, of course, as you would plain white rice. *Serves 6.*

# Wheat Pilaf

½ cup vermicelli
5 tablespoons butter
1 cup cracked wheat
1 tablespoon Instant Minced Onion

1 teaspoon Bon Appétit
5 teaspoons Chicken Seasoned Stock Base
2 cups hot water

Break vermicelli into ½-inch pieces; then measure. Melt butter over medium heat; add vermicelli and sauté until it begins to turn in color. Add wheat and onion and continue to cook, stirring constantly, until vermicelli is golden brown. Add Bon Appétit. Dissolve seasoned stock base in hot water and pour over wheat. Cover and cook 25 minutes or until liquid is absorbed. Stir with a fork to fluff. Cook, uncovered, a few minutes to dry out. Serve immediately or cover to keep hot until ready to serve. *Serves 6.*

VARIATION:

*Rice Pilaf*—Substitute 1 cup rice for wheat in above recipe.

# Rice Gourmet

1 4-ounce can mushrooms, stems and pieces
¼ cup butter or margarine
½ cup sherry
1 teaspoon Parsley Flakes
1½ teaspoons Season-All

2 teaspoons Instant Minced Onion
⅛ teaspoon Black or White Pepper
1 cup rice
2 cups water

Drain mushrooms, reserving liquid. Sauté mushrooms in butter 2 to 3 minutes. Add sherry and seasonings and simmer slowly 5 minutes. Pour rice over mushrooms; add reserved mushroom liquid and water. Cover and cook slowly 25 to 30 minutes. *Serves 6.*

# Cheese Omelette aux Herbes

4 eggs
2 tablespoons milk
1 teaspoon Season-All
1 teaspoon Parsley Flakes
¼ teaspoon Black Pepper
½ cup grated Cheddar cheese
1 tablespoon butter

Beat together eggs, milk, Season-All, parsley flakes and pepper. Stir in cheese. Melt butter in 7- to 8-inch skillet until hot but not allowing it to brown. Tilt skillet in all directions to butter sides. Pour egg mixture into skillet; as mixture sets, lift edges with spatula or fork, allowing uncooked portion to run under cooked portion of omelette. When bottom of omelette is lightly browned and top is soft and creamy, fold in half. Immediately slip out onto plate. Especially nice with ham and Sautéed Mushrooms (see recipe page 259). *Serves 2.*

# Spanish Rice

1 cup long grain rice
½ cup Chopped Instant Onions
¼ cup butter or margarine
2 teaspoons Chicken Seasoned Stock Base
2 teaspoons Season-All
¼ teaspoon Black Pepper
1 tablespoon Bell Pepper Flakes
Dash Garlic Powder
⅛ teaspoon MSG
½ teaspoon sugar
1 tablespoon chopped pimiento
1 teaspoon Worcestershire sauce
1 cup water
3 cups tomatoes (No. 2½ can)

Sauté rice and onions in butter, stirring, until onions are lightly browned. Add remaining ingredients, cutting whole tomatoes into pieces. Cover and simmer 30 minutes. *Serves 6.*

# Spaghetti with Superb Meat Sauce

Long, slow simmering of meat and herbs produces the base for this incomparable sauce.

| | |
|---|---|
| 1 3-pound beef roast (round, chuck or rump) | ½ teaspoon Oregano Leaves |
| 3 teaspoons salt | ½ teaspoon Basil Leaves |
| ¼ cup flour | ½ teaspoon Parsley Flakes |
| ¼ cup olive oil | ½ teaspoon Rosemary Leaves, crushed |
| 2 cups hot water | ⅛ teaspoon Nutmeg |
| ¼ teaspoon Garlic Powder | 4 6-ounce cans tomato paste |
| 1 teaspoon Onion Powder | 1 quart water |
| 2 Bay Leaves | 1 cup red wine, optional |
| 1 teaspoon Celery Salt | ½ cup sliced ripe olives |
| 1 teaspoon Black Pepper | ½ cup sliced stuffed olives |
| 2 teaspoons sugar | 2 4-ounce cans mushrooms |
| ½ teaspoon Crushed Red Pepper | 8 anchovy fillets, mashed |
| 1 tablespoon Season-All | Spaghetti |
| ¼ teaspoon MSG | Grated Parmesan cheese |

Season roast with salt; dredge with flour. In Dutch oven brown slowly on all sides in hot olive oil. Add hot water; cover and cook slowly 3 hours or until meat almost falls apart. Tear into small pieces with fork. Add remaining ingredients except spaghetti and cheese. Cover tightly and simmer 2 hours longer, stirring occasionally. Remove cover and continue cooking until sauce thickens to desired consistency. Cook spaghetti following directions on package, allowing 1 pound for 4 servings. Ladle sauce over spaghetti. Top with cheese. *Makes about 3½ quarts sauce, enough for 4 pounds spaghetti.*

NOTE: Since you may not need such a large quantity of spaghetti, freeze extra sauce in half-pint, pint or quart freezer jars and use as needed.

240

# Tuna Casserole with Batter Topping

| | |
|---|---|
| ¼ cup butter | ¼ teaspoon Tarragon Leaves |
| ¼ cup flour | 1 cup hot water |
| 1 teaspoon Chicken Seasoned Stock Base | 1 cup cream or milk |
| 1 teaspoon Bon Appétit | 1 teaspoon lemon juice |
| ⅛ teaspoon White Pepper | 2 7-ounce cans tuna, drained |
| ½ teaspoon Lemon Peel | Batter Topping |

Melt butter; add flour, seasoned stock base, Bon Appétit, pepper, lemon peel and tarragon leaves. Cook until bubbly. Remove from heat; add water and cream or milk. Cook over low heat, stirring, until thickened. Add lemon juice and tuna, mixing well. Spoon into a 2-quart shallow baking dish. Cover with Batter Topping and bake in 425°F. oven 15 minutes or until golden brown. (The tuna mixture may be prepared ahead of time and refrigerated. Add Batter Topping when ready to bake and serve.) Serve piping hot. *Serves 6.*

**BATTER TOPPING:**

| | |
|---|---|
| ¾ cup all-purpose flour | 2 eggs, separated |
| ½ teaspoon Bon Appétit | ½ cup milk |
| 2 teaspoons baking powder | 1 tablespoon butter, melted |
| 2 teaspoons Shredded Green Onions | |

Sift flour, measure and sift again with Bon Appétit and baking powder. Add onions. Beat egg yolks until light; add milk and butter. Add to dry ingredients and mix lightly. Beat egg whites until stiff but not dry. Fold into batter. Pour over top of tuna mixture and bake as directed above.

# Macaroni and Cheese

½ pound sharp Cheddar cheese
4 tablespoons butter
4 tablespoons flour
1 teaspoon Chicken Seasoned Stock Base
½ teaspoon Onion Powder
¼ teaspoon White Pepper

1½ teaspoons Season-All
¼ teaspoon dry Mustard
Dash Cayenne or Red Pepper
Dash Nutmeg
2 cups milk
1 8-ounce package macaroni
Paprika

Cut cheese into ½-inch cubes. Melt butter; blend in flour, seasoned stock base and seasonings. Cook over low heat, stirring, until mixture is smooth and bubbly. Do not allow to brown. Remove from heat and stir in milk. Bring to a boil, stirring, and cook until sauce thickens. Add 1 cup of the cheese and stir until melted. Cook macaroni following directions on package; drain. Place half the macaroni in a buttered 11½ x 7½ x 1½-inch baking dish; sprinkle ½ cup cheese cubes over macaroni. Top with a second layer of macaroni and cheese. Pour cheese sauce over all. Sprinkle with paprika. Bake in 350°F. oven 30 to 40 minutes. Serve hot from baking dish. *Serves 6 to 8.*


# Herb-Broiled Sandwiches

6 slices bacon
6 slices bread
Butter or margarine

Herb Seasoning
6 slices cheese
6 slices tomato

Partially broil or fry bacon. Toast slices of bread on one side. Spread the untoasted side with butter; sprinkle with Herb Seasoning. Top each with a slice of cheese, tomato and bacon. Broil until bacon is crisp and cheese begins to melt. *Makes 6 open-faced sandwiches.*

# Snappy Cheese-wiches

4 English muffins, split
½ pound grated sharp
  cheese
½ teaspoon Onion Salt
⅛ teaspoon Nutmeg
⅛ teaspoon Allspice
⅛ teaspoon Cayenne
2 teaspoons prepared
  mustard

1 teaspoon Worcestershire
  sauce
1 teaspoon Powdered
  Horseradish
1 teaspoon lemon juice
¼ cup mayonnaise
  or salad dressing

Toast split sides of muffins under broiler until lightly
browned. Combine remaining ingredients, mixing well;
spread mixture over toasted side of muffins. Broil 4 inches
from heat 5 minutes or until cheese is bubbly and lightly
browned. *Makes 8 open-faced sandwiches.*

# Salmon Luncheon Pie

1 unbaked 10-inch pastry
  shell
1 1-pound can salmon
1 tablespoon lemon juice
¼ cup Chopped Instant
  Onions
1 tablespoon Parsley Flakes

2 tablespoons butter
6 eggs, lightly beaten
1½ cups milk
1 teaspoon Season-All
¼ teaspoon White or Black
  Pepper

Prick pastry shell with tines of a fork; bake in 450°F.
oven 5 minutes. Drain salmon, reserving liquid. Remove
bones and skin. Flake salmon and place in bottom of
pastry shell. Sprinkle with lemon juice. Sauté onions and
parsley flakes in butter; sprinkle over salmon. Mix liquid
from salmon with eggs, milk, Season-All and pepper.
Pour over salmon. Bake in 350°F. oven 50 minutes or
until firm. Serve hot. *Serves 6.*

# Italian Pizza

SAUCE:

3½ cups tomatoes
(No. 2½ can)
1 6-ounce can tomato paste
½ teaspoon Oregano Leaves
¼ teaspoon Basil Leaves
1 teaspoon Garlic Salt

¼ teaspoon crushed
Rosemary Leaves
¼ teaspoon Crushed Red
Pepper
½ teaspoon Coarse Grind
Black Pepper

Press tomatoes, including juice, through a sieve, then combine with remaining ingredients in saucepan. Cook over medium heat, stirring occasionally, until mixture is reduced to one half the original volume, leaving about 2 cups sauce.

CRUST:

1 package hot roll mix
½ teaspoon ground Oregano
½ teaspoon Onion Powder
⅛ teaspoon Garlic Powder
2 tablespoons oil

1 8-ounce package sliced
Mozzarella cheese
Toppings: anchovies,
pepperoni, mushrooms
or sliced olives

Prepare pizza dough as directed on package of hot roll mix, adding oregano, onion powder and garlic powder to the yeast-water mixture. Divide dough in half; roll each half to fit a 14-inch pizza pan and arrange dough in pans. Brush with oil, spread with sauce and top with cheese and one or more of the toppings. Bake in 450°F. oven 15 to 20 minutes. *Serves 4 to 6 as a luncheon or supper dish.*

VARIATION:

*Herb Pizza*—Make pizza as in recipe above. Before baking sprinkle top with any one or a combination of the following herbs: Basil Leaves, Oregano Leaves, Marjoram Leaves, Thyme Leaves or Italian Seasoning.

# Easter Egg Casserole

Here is how those pretty Easter eggs may be used to make a gay supper dish for Easter Monday.

1 cup rice
2 cups water
1 teaspoon salt
8 individual pieces Saffron
2 cups medium White Sauce
   Supreme

1 cup diced ham
8 small slices ham
Stuffed Eggs

Combine rice, water, salt and saffron; bring to a boil. Cover; reduce heat and simmer 20 minutes or until rice absorbs all the water. Make White Sauce Supreme (see recipe page 385). Mix rice with diced ham and 1 cup of the white sauce; spoon into a buttered shallow 2-quart baking dish. Pour the remaining white sauce over rice. Arrange ham slices on top and place a stuffed egg on each slice. Bake in 325°F. oven 30 minutes. You might like to serve with green peas tossed with toasted slivered almonds and a relish tray to round out the meal. *Serves 4 to 8.*

STUFFED EGGS:

4 hard-cooked eggs
¼ cup mayonnaise
1 teaspoon vinegar
2 teaspoons Instant Minced
   Onion

¼ teaspoon dry Mustard
½ teaspoon salt
Dash Black Pepper
Paprika

Slice eggs lengthwise. Remove yolks; mash and mix with remaining ingredients except paprika. Stuff whites. Sprinkle tops with paprika.

# Fried Rice

¼ cup Instant Minced
  Onion
¼ cup oil or butter
3 cups cold, cooked rice
2 eggs, lightly beaten
¼ teaspoon Black Pepper

2 teaspoons Beef Flavor Base
2 tablespoons soy sauce
1 cup chopped, cooked meat
  (chicken, pork, beef,
  shrimp, lobster, sausage
  or bacon)

Sauté onion in hot oil until golden brown. Add rice; heat
thoroughly, stirring often. Stir in beaten eggs, pepper,
beef flavor base and soy sauce. Sauté 3 minutes, continuing to stir. Add meat and continue heating until
mixture is steaming hot. *Serves 6.*

# Cheese Soufflé

3 tablespoons butter
  or margarine
3 tablespoons flour
2 teaspoons Bon Appétit
Dash MSG
½ teaspoon dry Mustard

⅛ teaspoon Cayenne
  or Red Pepper
1¼ cups milk
½ pound Cheddar cheese,
  grated
5 eggs, separated

Melt butter; stir in flour, Bon Appétit, MSG, dry
mustard and cayenne. Cook until bubbly but do not
allow to brown. Remove from heat; stir in milk. Cook
over low heat, stirring until thickened. Add cheese and
stir until melted. Beat egg yolks; add a little of the cheese
sauce to beaten yolks, then stir egg yolk mixture into
remaining cheese sauce. Beat egg whites until stiff but not
dry. Slowly pour cheese sauce into egg whites, carefully
folding until evenly combined. Pour into 2-quart ungreased casserole. Bake in 300°F. oven 45 minutes or
until set. Serve immediately. Excellent with crisp bacon
and Herb Broiled Tomatoes (see recipe page 265).
*Serves 5 to 6.*

# Beef and Noodle Casserole

2 cups (½ pound) noodles
1 tablespoon oil
¼ cup Instant Minced Onion
1 pound ground beef
1½ teaspoons Season-All
½ teaspoon Thyme Leaves
¼ teaspoon MSG

¼ teaspoon Black Pepper
1 10½-ounce can condensed
   cream of celery soup
½ cup water
½ cup evaporated milk
1 cup grated sharp cheese
2 eggs, beaten

Cook noodles as directed on package; drain and rinse. Put oil, onion, beef, Season-All, thyme leaves, MSG and pepper in large skillet and cook until meat loses its red color but is not brown. Combine soup, water and milk. In 2-quart casserole put ⅓ of the noodles, ½ of the meat mixture and ½ of the soup mixture. Repeat. Put remaining noodles on top. Sprinkle grated cheese over noodles and pour beaten eggs over cheese. Bake, uncovered, in 350°F. oven 1 hour or until thoroughly heated and bubbly and top is very crisp. *Serves 6.*

# Welsh Rabbit

1 teaspoon Worcestershire
   sauce
⅛ teaspoon Paprika
½ teaspoon dry Mustard
Dash MSG
Dash Cayenne

Dash Onion Powder
½ cup flat beer
   or light cream
1 pound sharp Cheddar
   cheese, crumbled

Combine Worcestershire sauce, paprika, dry mustard, MSG, cayenne and onion powder; mix to smooth paste. Combine with beer or cream in top pan of chafing dish over hot water. (May be made in double boiler.) Adjust flame to keep water hot but not boiling. Heat until beer or cream is hot. Add cheese and stir constantly until cheese melts. Serve hot over toast or waffles. Garnish with bacon if desired. *Serves 4.*

# Princess Omelette

4 eggs
¼ cup commercial sour cream
2 teaspoons Instant Minced Onion
¼ teaspoon Crushed Red Pepper
½ teaspoon salt
1 3-ounce package cream cheese
1 tablespoon butter
8 asparagus spears, canned or cooked

Beat together eggs, sour cream, onion, pepper and salt. Cut cheese into ¼-inch cubes; stir into egg mixture. Melt butter in 7- to 8-inch skillet until hot but not allowing it to brown. Tilt skillet in all directions to butter sides. Pour egg mixture into skillet; as mixture sets, lift edges with spatula or fork, allowing uncooked portion to run under cooked portion of omelette. When bottom of omelette is lightly browned and top is soft and creamy, arrange asparagus spears across the center with stem ends together and spears toward outside edge. Fold sides over asparagus and slide from skillet onto plate. Serve garnished with crisp bacon, tomato wedges and water cress. *Serves 2.*

# Viennese Noodles au Gratin

½ pound noodles
1 tablespoon Poppy Seed
½ pound Cheddar cheese, grated
1 pint commercial sour cream
Paprika

Cook noodles in boiling salted water following directions on package. Drain well. Toss gently with poppy seed and cheese until well mixed. Alternate layers of noodle mixture and sour cream in a buttered 2-quart casserole, ending with sour cream on top. Sprinkle with paprika. Bake in 350°F. oven 20 minutes or until bubbly hot. *Serves 6 to 8.*

# VEGETABLES

——— * ———

## Cauliflower with Creamy Cheese Sauce

1 large cauliflower
2 teaspoons Chicken
 Seasoned Stock Base
1 cup warm water
2 tablespoons butter
1 tablespoon Arrowroot

¼ teaspoon salt
¼ teaspoon White Pepper
½ teaspoon dry Mustard
½ teaspoon Onion Powder
1 cup milk or light cream
¾ cup grated sharp cheese

Wash cauliflower and cut off heavy stalks and leaves. Put in saucepan. Combine 1 teaspoon of the seasoned stock base with water; pour over cauliflower. Cover and bring to boil then simmer 25 minutes or until tender. Drain. Melt butter; stir in the remaining 1 teaspoon seasoned stock base, arrowroot, salt, pepper, dry mustard and onion powder. Add milk and cook over low heat, stirring constantly, until sauce thickens. Stir in cheese and continue cooking until cheese melts. Pour over cauliflower in serving dish. Garnish with radish roses, or you may prefer to sprinkle with Paprika or toasted livered almonds. *Serves 4.*

# Ginger Glazed Carrots

The spiciest carrots you can imagine, marvelous with pork.

1 bunch carrots
1 teaspoon Chicken
    Seasoned Stock Base
1 teaspoon Bon Appétit
1 teaspoon sugar
¾ cup water

4 tablespoons butter
1 tablespoon lemon juice
3 tablespoons honey
½ teaspoon Ginger
¼ teaspoon Nutmeg
Parsley Flakes

Clean carrots and cut into rounds. Put in skillet with seasoned stock base, Bon Appétit, sugar, water and 1 tablespoon of the butter. Cover; cook 12 minutes; drain. Add the remaining butter, lemon juice, honey, ginger and nutmeg to carrots. Cook, uncovered, over medium heat 2 to 3 minutes, tossing frequently to thoroughly glaze carrots. Sprinkle with parsley flakes just before serving. *Serves 4.*

# Eggplant Parmigiana

1 large or 2 medium
    eggplant
Oil for frying
2 cups tomatoes
    (No. 303 can)
1 6-ounce can tomato paste
¼ teaspoon Garlic Powder
1½ teaspoons Season-All

⅛ teaspoon Black Pepper
1 tablespoon Parsley Flakes
1 Bay Leaf
½ cup grated Parmesan
    cheese
2 cups soft bread crumbs
½ pound Mozzarella cheese,
    sliced

Cut eggplant into ½-inch slices and peel. Sauté in oil 5 minutes or until tender and lightly browned. Remove and keep warm. In skillet combine tomatoes, tomato paste, garlic powder, Season-All, pepper, parsley flakes and bay leaf. Cover and simmer 15 minutes. Remove bay leaf; add Parmesan cheese and bread crumbs, mixing well. Place a layer of eggplant in buttered, shallow 2-quart baking dish. Cover with half the tomato sauce then with half the Mozzarella cheese. Repeat layers. Bake in 350°F. oven 20 minutes or until cheese melts and is lightly browned. Serve at once. You will find this dish excellent for Lent. *Serves 5 to 6.*

## Old-Fashioned Baked Beans

1 pound dried marrow, navy or pea beans
½ teaspoon soda
2 cups dark brown sugar, packed
4 cups tomato juice
2 teaspoons Bon Appétit
¼ teaspoon Cloves

⅛ teaspoon Cardamom
2 tablespoons Instant Minced Onion
½ teaspoon dry Mustard
1½ teaspoons Powdered Horseradish
⅛ teaspoon Black Pepper
8 slices bacon

Wash beans; cover with cold water and soak overnight. Drain; cover with fresh water and add soda. Bring to a boil and cook 35 minutes or until beans are tender. Drain and rinse with cold water. Combine brown sugar, tomato juice and seasonings; pour over beans. Cut bacon into 1- to 2-inch pieces; add to beans and mix thoroughly. Put beans in a 3-quart bean pot or casserole. Cover. Bake in 300°F. oven 5 hours or until tender. Add hot water if beans become dry during baking. Remove cover during last 30 minutes of baking. This is a favorite patio food that is excellent to serve with baked ham or broiled chicken. *Makes about 2 quarts.*

**VARIATION:**

*Barbecued Baked Beans*—Add 1 tablespoon Barbecue Spice to the above recipe and proceed as directed.

# Parsley Buttered Potatoes

1½ pounds small whole
  potatoes
½ cup water
1 teaspoon Chicken
  Seasoned Stock Base

¼ cup butter
1 teaspoon Parsley Flakes
1 teaspoon Season-All

Wash and peel potatoes. Put in saucepan with water and seasoned stock base. Bring to a boil; reduce heat and cook until tender, 20 to 25 minutes. Drain. Melt butter; add seasonings. Pour over potatoes. Serve hot. *Serves 4 to 6.*

VARIATION:

*Dill Buttered Potatoes*—Substitute ½ teaspoon Dill Weed for parsley flakes in above recipe.

# Asparagus Oriental

1½ pounds fresh asparagus
  or 1 10-ounce package
  frozen asparagus spears
3 tablespoons butter
1 teaspoon Chicken
  Seasoned Stock Base

1 teaspoon Season-All
⅛ teaspoon Celery Salt
⅛ teaspoon Ginger
Dash White Pepper
Dash MSG
1 teaspoon soy sauce

When using fresh asparagus, wash and break off stalks as far down as they snap easily. Slice either fresh or the frozen spears at an extreme angle to make diagonal slices about ¼ inch thick. Melt butter in skillet; add seasoned stock base, Season-All, celery salt, ginger, pepper and MSG, mixing well. Add asparagus; toss gently. Cover and cook over high heat 2 minutes or until crisp-tender, stirring two or three times. Add soy sauce and mix well. Serve piping hot. *Serves 4 to 5.*

# Sauerkraut Caraway

1 No. 2½ can sauerkraut
½ cup port wine
2 teaspoons Caraway Seed
½ teaspoon Powdered
  Horseradish

½ teaspoon dry Mustard
1 teaspoon Instant Minced
  Onion
1 tablespoon sugar

Combine all ingredients in a saucepan; cover. Simmer 2 hours. A favorite with sausage, frankfurters, spareribs and roast pork. In a few sections of the country this is a traditional dish served with the Thanksgiving turkey. *Serves 4.*


# Brussels Sprouts with Chestnuts

Rich and wonderful for holiday dinners.

1½ cups canned chestnuts
  or ½ pound chestnuts
2 tablespoons melted butter
½ teaspoon Season-All
⅛ teaspoon Savory
¼ teaspoon Basil Leaves
Dash Nutmeg

½ cup water
1½ teaspoons Chicken
  Seasoned Stock Base
¼ teaspoon Black Pepper
1 pint fresh Brussels sprouts
  or 1 package frozen
  Brussels sprouts

Drain chestnuts and put in shallow pan; cover with mixture of butter, Season-All, savory, basil leaves and nutmeg. (When fresh chestnuts are used, make a slit in skin. Cover with water and boil 25 minutes; cool and peel before using.) Bake in 325°F. oven 20 minutes, stirring once. Add water, seasoned stock base and pepper to Brussels sprouts. Cook 10 minutes or until tender; drain. Carefully toss together chestnuts and Brussels sprouts; serve hot. *Serves 4.*

# Broccoli Soufflé

3 tablespoons butter
3 tablespoons flour
2 teaspoons Instant Minced Onion
1 teaspoon salt
⅛ teaspoon Black Pepper
⅛ teaspoon Nutmeg

Dash Cayenne
1 cup milk
1 cup minced, cooked broccoli
1 tablespoon lemon juice
4 eggs, separated
¼ teaspoon Cream of Tartar

Melt butter; stir in flour, onion, salt, pepper, nutmeg and cayenne. Cook until bubbly then remove from heat. Stir in milk and cook over low heat until thickened, stirring constantly. Remove from heat; add broccoli and lemon juice. Beat egg yolks until thick and add to broccoli mixture, stirring quickly. Cool slightly. Beat egg whites with cream of tartar until stiff but not dry. Fold into broccoli mixture; pour into buttered 1½-quart casserole. Bake in pan of hot water in 350°F. oven 40 minutes or until silver knife inserted in center comes out clean. You will find this good with any meal but especially ideal to serve with ham, chicken, turkey, beef or veal. *Makes 6 servings.*

# Okra Southern Style

1 10-ounce package frozen okra or 2 cups sliced, fresh okra
¼ cup corn meal
1 teaspoon Season-All

¼ teaspoon Onion Powder
¼ teaspoon Black Pepper
Dash MSG
¼ teaspoon Celery Salt
½ cup salad oil

Trim ends off okra. Cut into ¼-inch slices. Dredge in mixture of corn meal and seasonings. Fry in hot oil 15 minutes or until crisp and brown. Drain on absorbent paper. If preferred, you may leave okra in whole pods and fry exactly as above. *Serves 4.*

# Stewed Tomatoes with Oregano

1 quart tomatoes
  (2 No. 303 cans)
½ teaspoon Oregano Leaves
¼ teaspoon Basil Leaves
2 tablespoons Chopped
  Instant Onions
1 teaspoon salt

Dash Black Pepper
1 tablespoon sugar
1 tablespoon butter
1 tablespoon Arrowroot
1 tablespoon cold water
1 slice bread, optional

Cut whole tomatoes into pieces; add oregano leaves, basil leaves, onions, salt, pepper and sugar. Bring to a boil, reduce heat and simmer, uncovered, 15 minutes. Add butter. Mix together arrowroot and cold water and stir into tomatoes. Continue cooking to thicken. If a still thicker consistency is desired, remove crust from bread; cut bread into small cubes and add to tomatoes just before serving. This is a wonderful vegetable to serve with any starchy food, such as potatoes au gratin, macaroni and cheese, rice or noodles, as well as many fish dishes. *Serves 5 to 6.*

# Creamed Spinach

1 10-ounce package frozen
  chopped spinach
¼ teaspoon Onion Salt
½ teaspoon Bon Appétit

Dash MSG
Dash Mace
½ cup commercial
  sour cream

Place spinach in saucepan. Do not add water. Cover and bring to boil; separate with fork. Simmer until just tender, about 2 minutes. Drain thoroughly. Combine with seasonings and sour cream and purée in a blender. If you do not have a blender, you may put spinach through a coarse sieve, food mill or food grinder, then combine with seasonings and sour cream. This dish will be liked by those who think they don't like spinach. Excellent with steaks and chops. *Serves 3 to 4.*

# Italian Style Peas

1 tablespoon Instant Minced Onion
1 teaspoon Parsley Flakes
¼ teaspoon Basil Leaves
2 slices boiled ham, shredded (about ½ cup)
1 tablespoon olive oil
½ cup water
1 teaspoon Chicken Seasoned Stock Base
⅛ teaspoon Black Pepper
1 10-ounce package frozen peas or 2 cups fresh or canned peas
1 tablespoon butter

Sauté onion, parsley flakes, basil leaves and shredded ham in olive oil over low to medium heat about 5 minutes, stirring frequently. Add water, seasoned stock base and pepper; stir. (Tap the package of peas on edge of cabinet to break peas apart.) Add peas and butter. Cover. Bring to a boil and simmer slowly 25 minutes or until peas are tender. An excellent and different way to serve peas. Especially good with chicken, veal, beef or omelettes. *Serves 4.*

# Zucchini Sauté

4 medium-size zucchini
¼ teaspoon White Pepper or Black Pepper
2 teaspoons Season-All
Dash Garlic Powder
2 teaspoons Parsley Flakes
½ teaspoon ground Oregano
1 teaspoon Instant Minced Onion
¼ cup olive oil

Wash zucchini but do not peel. Slice in rounds about ¼ inch thick. Mix together remaining ingredients except olive oil. Sprinkle over zucchini and toss until seasoning is well distributed. Heat oil in skillet; add zucchini and sauté until browned on both sides, about 10 minutes. Drain on absorbent paper. This is a quick and tasty way to cook zucchini and it goes well with any meat. *Serves 4.*

# Corn Pudding

So good you can make a meal of it.

1 12-ounce can corn niblets
2 No. 303 cans cream-style corn
5 eggs, lightly beaten
½ cup sugar
3 tablespoons Arrowroot
1½ teaspoons Season-All

½ teaspoon dry Mustard
1 teaspoon Instant Minced Onion
Dash Cayenne or White Pepper
½ cup milk
½ cup melted butter

If the vacuum packed niblets are not available, 1 No. 303 can whole kernel corn, drained, may be used. Mix together corn and eggs. Combine sugar, arrowroot, Season-All, dry mustard, onion and cayenne; stir into corn mixture. Add milk and butter, mixing well. Pour into a buttered 2½- to 3-quart casserole. Bake, uncovered, in 400°F. oven 1 hour or until silver knife comes out clean when inserted near center. Stir once after 30 minutes cooking. Serve immediately from the casserole in which it was cooked. *Serves 8.*

---

# Lima Bean Casserole

1 10-ounce package frozen lima beans
¼ cup water
1 tablespoon Instant Minced Onion

½ teaspoon Lemon Peel
1 teaspoon Bon Appétit
¼ teaspoon Black Pepper
1 10½-ounce can condensed cream of mushroom soup

Cook beans in water 15 minutes or until just tender. Drain. Put beans in 1-quart casserole and sprinkle with onion, lemon peel, Bon Appétit and pepper. Spoon undiluted soup over top. Cover. Bake in 350°F. oven 45 minutes. Excellent with most meats. *Serves 4.*

# Clove-Studded Onions

1 No. 303 can whole onions
Whole Cloves
1 teaspoon Season-All

½ teaspoon Chicken
Seasoned Stock Base
1 tablespoon butter

Empty can of onions with liquid into small saucepan. Stud each onion with a whole clove. Add Season-All and seasoned stock base. Bring to a boil; lower heat and simmer about 15 minutes. Drain. Toss with butter. For added color you may sprinkle with Paprika. *Serves 4.*

# Corn and Pepper Stroganoff

Deliciously different. An excellent side dish—good with sandwiches too.

4 ounces sausage
(about 3 links or 3 patties)
1 No. 303 can whole kernel
corn, drained
2 tablespoons Bell Pepper
Flakes

¼ teaspoon MSG
½ teaspoon Bon Appétit
1 8-ounce can tomato sauce
1 cup commercial sour
cream

Cut sausage into small pieces; fry until browned. Pour off grease. Add drained corn, pepper flakes, MSG, Bon Appétit and tomato sauce; mix well. Cover and simmer 15 minutes. Cool a few minutes then stir in sour cream. Place over a low, low heat 15 minutes, but do not let it simmer or boil to prevent curdling. *Serves 4.*

NOTE: The first steps may be prepared well in advance, setting aside until time to serve, then add sour cream and heat very slowly, never allowing mixture to come to a boil.

# Sautéed Cabbage and Apples

2 large tart apples
⅓ cup butter
8 cups coarsely shredded
  cabbage
¼ cup Chopped Instant
  Onions
1 teaspoon Season-All

½ teaspoon Nutmeg
3 tablespoons cider vinegar
2 teaspoons sugar
Dash Cayenne
¼ cup chopped pecans
  or walnuts, optional

Peel, core and chop apples. Melt butter (bacon drippings may be used if you prefer); add apples, cabbage, onions, Season-All and nutmeg. Mix well. Cover and cook over low heat 20 minutes, stirring frequently. Combine vinegar, sugar and cayenne; add to cabbage. Cook 5 minutes longer. Stir in nuts or serve with nuts sprinkled over top. This is one of those dishes you will find even better when reheated. Excellent served with pork, duckling, goose and game. *Serves 4 to 5.*

# Sautéed Mushrooms

½ pound fresh mushrooms
2 teaspoons lemon juice
2 tablespoons butter
  or margarine

¼ teaspoon salt
¼ teaspoon Season-All
⅛ teaspoon Black Pepper
⅛ teaspoon MSG

Wash, dry and slice mushrooms. Sprinkle with lemon juice. Melt butter and stir in seasonings. Add mushrooms and sauté about 7 minutes until delicately browned, stirring frequently. You may serve as a main vegetable or as an accompaniment to steaks, chops, sautéed chicken livers, roast beef or omelettes. *Serves 2 to 4, depending on how used.*

# Sweet Potato Pudding

An old-time favorite, spicy and good.

¼ cup butter or margarine
¾ cup sugar
2 eggs
½ teaspoon Pumpkin Pie Spice

¼ teaspoon salt
1½ cups milk (use part cream for richer flavor)
2½ cups grated, raw sweet potatoes

Cream butter and sugar. Mix in eggs, pumpkin pie spice, salt and milk. Fold in grated sweet potatoes. Pour into a buttered, shallow 2-quart baking dish and bake in 400°F. oven 1 hour. You will want to take the pudding right from the oven to table and serve with pork roast, baked ham or chicken. *Serves 4 to 6.*

# Country-Good Baked Squash

2 pounds small yellow squash
3 tablespoons Instant Minced Onion
¼ cup water
¼ cup butter, melted
½ cup milk

2 eggs, beaten
½ teaspoon salt
¼ teaspoon Black Pepper
1 teaspoon Parsley Flakes
½ teaspoon Tarragon Leaves
2 tablespoons butter, melted
½ cup cracker crumbs

Wash, but do not peel, squash and cut into small pieces. Add onion and water. Cook about 10 minutes or until just tender, taking care not to overcook. Drain squash and transfer to 1½-quart baking dish. Pour the ¼ cup melted butter over squash. Combine milk, eggs and seasonings and pour over all. Combine the 2 tablespoons melted butter and cracker crumbs; sprinkle over top. Bake in 450°F. oven 20 minutes. *Serves 6 to 8.*

# Baked Acorn Squash

2 acorn squash
½ cup water
¼ cup brown sugar, packed
¼ cup butter

¼ teaspoon Black Pepper
½ teaspoon Season-All
¼ teaspoon Basil Leaves,
  crumbled

Wash squash and cut in half; remove seed. Place cut side down in shallow baking dish containing water. Bake in 350°F. oven 45 minutes. Turn cut side up. Put 1 tablespoon brown sugar and 1 tablespoon butter in each half. Sprinkle with pepper, Season-All and basil leaves. Return to oven and bake 15 minutes longer. *Serves 4.*

# Apple Cider Squash

The seasonings make frozen squash extra special.

1 package frozen cooked
  squash (1¼ cups)
2 tablespoons butter
½ teaspoon salt

⅛ teaspoon Mace
⅛ teaspoon Cinnamon
Dash Black Pepper
⅓ cup apple cider

Place frozen squash in buttered 1½-quart casserole. Add butter, salt, mace, cinnamon and pepper. Pour cider over squash. Cover and bake in 350°F. oven 45 minutes, stirring once during baking period. *Serves 4.*

# Sweet Potatoes——Pineapple Rings

2 cups cooked, mashed sweet potatoes
⅔ cup brown sugar, packed
¼ cup butter, melted
½ cup orange juice
1 teaspoon Pumpkin Pie Spice
1 teaspoon Orange Peel
¼ cup chopped pecans
½ cup raisins
1 No. 2 can sliced pineapple
Miniature marshmallows

Combine sweet potatoes, brown sugar, butter, orange juice, pumpkin pie spice, orange peel, pecans and raisins, mixing well. Drain pineapple slices and place in baking dish. Mound ⅓ cup of the sweet potato mixture on top of each pineapple slice. Bake in 375°F. oven 20 minutes. Top with marshmallows and bake 5 minutes longer. *Makes 10 servings.*

# Candied Sweet Potatoes

2 pounds sweet potatoes
½ cup brown sugar, packed
1 cup orange juice
1 tablespoon Orange Peel
1 teaspoon Pumpkin Pie Spice
⅓ cup sherry
2 tablespoons butter

Boil potatoes in salted water 30 minutes or until almost tender. Drain; peel and cut into serving-size pieces. (Or dry-packed canned sweet potatoes may be used if preferred.) Place potatoes in shallow 1½-quart baking dish. Combine remaining ingredients and bring to a boil, stirring; boil 3 minutes. Pour over potatoes. Bake in 350°F. oven 1 hour, basting often to glaze well. *Serves 4.*

VARIATION:

*Candied Sweet Potatoes and Apples*—Peel, core and quarter 2 medium-size cooking apples. Place along with sweet potatoes in baking dish and continue as in above recipe.

# Carrots Vichy

6 medium-size carrots
½ cup water
1 teaspoon Chicken Seasoned
  Stock Base
Dash Onion Powder

Dash MSG
2 tablespoons lemon juice
2 tablespoons butter
1 teaspoon Parsley Flakes

Scrape carrots and cut into thin slices. Add water, seasoned stock base, onion powder and MSG. Cook 15 minutes or until tender; drain. Add remaining ingredients and toss gently. *Serves 4 to 5.*

# Fresh Corn Sauté

A summertime treat.

4 cups fresh corn
  (5 to 6 ears)
2 tablespoons butter
1 teaspoon Instant Minced
  Onion
2 teaspoons Arrowroot

¼ teaspoon White Pepper
1½ teaspoons Bon Appétit
½ teaspoon salt
1 teaspoon sugar
¾ cup milk

Cut corn from cob and measure. Melt butter; add onion and corn. Cook 1 minute, stirring. Mix in arrowroot, pepper, Bon Appétit, salt and sugar. Pour milk into corn mixture. Simmer 20 minutes, stirring frequently to prevent corn from sticking. Garnish with strips of pimiento if desired. *Serves 4 to 5.*

# Creamed Onions

This is a favorite holiday dish.

2 tablespoons butter
2 tablespoons flour
1 teaspoon salt
⅛ teaspoon White Pepper
1 teaspoon Bon Appétit

¼ teaspoon dry Mustard
Dash MSG
1 cup milk
1 No. 303 can whole white
  onions, drained

Melt butter in saucepan; stir in flour and seasonings. Cook over low heat, allowing to bubble 1 minute. Remove from heat and add milk. Return to heat and cook, stirring, until thickened. Add onions and continue cooking until onions are heated through. *Serves 4.*

# Harvard Beets

1 No. 303 can sliced or
  whole beets
¼ cup cider vinegar
¼ cup sugar

4 teaspoons Arrowroot
½ teaspoon Orange Peel
⅛ teaspoon Cloves
1 tablespoon butter

Drain beets, reserving the juice. Combine beet juice, vinegar, sugar, arrowroot, orange peel and cloves in small saucepan. Cook over medium heat, stirring constantly, until sauce thickens. Stir in beets and butter; simmer 5 minutes or until beets are thoroughly heated. This sweet-sour vegetable adds sparkle to any meal. *Serves 4.*

# Herb Broiled Tomatoes

4 tomatoes
¼ cup butter, melted
1 teaspoon Season-All
½ teaspoon Herb Seasoning

¼ teaspoon Oregano Leaves
¼ teaspoon MSG
½ teaspoon sugar
½ cup soft bread crumbs

Wash tomatoes; slice in half and place in broiler pan, cut side up. Brush with 1 tablespoon of the butter. Combine Season-All, Herb Seasoning, oregano leaves, MSG and sugar. Sprinkle over tomatoes. Broil 4 inches from heat 5 to 7 minutes. Pour remaining butter over bread crumbs and toss well. Spoon bread crumbs evenly over top of tomatoes and continue to broil 5 minutes or until bread crumbs are toasted. Excellent served with steaks or chops. *Serves 8.*

# Herb Seasoned Broccoli

1 10-ounce package frozen or
   2 pounds fresh broccoli
   spears
½ cup hot water
1 teaspoon Chicken
   Seasoned Stock Base

½ teaspoon Marjoram
   Leaves
½ teaspoon Basil Leaves
¼ teaspoon Onion Powder
Dash Nutmeg
1 tablespoon butter

Place broccoli in saucepan. Combine water and seasoned stock base; pour over broccoli, then sprinkle with the seasonings. Cover and bring to a boil; separate broccoli spears with fork. Simmer 6 minutes or until tender; drain. Add butter. Serve with Creamy Lemon-Butter Sauce (see recipe page 402). *Serves 3 to 4.*

# Green Beans with Dill

1 9-ounce package frozen
green beans
¼ cup water
1 teaspoon Dill Weed
or Dill Seed

1 teaspoon Beef Flavor Base
¼ teaspoon salt
2 tablespoons butter
or margarine

Place frozen beans in saucepan with water, dill weed or seed, beef flavor base and salt. Cover; bring to a boil. Separate beans with fork, reduce heat and simmer 10 minutes or until tender. Drain. Toss lightly with butter. *Serves 3 to 4.*

NOTE: In place of the frozen beans, you may use 2 cups fresh or canned green beans (1 No. 303 can).

# Minted Peas

1 10-ounce package frozen
peas
¼ cup water
1 3½-ounce bottle cocktail
onions, drained
1 tablespoon butter

½ teaspoon Mint Flakes,
crushed
¼ teaspoon MSG
1½ teaspoons Chicken
Seasoned Stock Base

Combine all ingredients in saucepan. Cover. Bring to a boil then reduce heat to low and cook 5 to 7 minutes. Minted Peas go well with any meat, but are especially good with lamb chops and leg of lamb. *Serves 4.*

NOTE: In place of the frozen peas, you may use 2 cups fresh or canned peas (1 No. 303 çan).

# Sweet-Sour Red Cabbage

The German favorite, perfect with roast goose or fresh ham.

½ cup butter
2 tablespoons Chopped Instant Onions
¼ cup brown sugar, packed
1 teaspoon salt
½ teaspoon Black Pepper

1 teaspoon Allspice
¼ teaspoon Cloves
1 2-pound red cabbage, finely shredded
½ cup boiling water
½ cup wine vinegar

Melt butter in skillet; sauté onions until golden brown. Add sugar, seasonings and shredded cabbage; mix lightly. Add water, cover and simmer 1 hour. Add vinegar and simmer 10 minutes longer. This is pleasantly tart; should you prefer it milder, use only ¼ cup vinegar. Serve hot. *Serves 8.*

# Delectable Green Beans

1 9-ounce package frozen French-style green beans
¼ cup water
¼ teaspoon Instant Minced Onion
2 tablespoons butter
2 tablespoons flour

1¼ teaspoons Bon Appétit
¼ teaspoon Savory
⅛ teaspoon Black Pepper
½ cup commercial sour cream
¼ cup shredded Swiss cheese

Place beans, water and onion in saucepan. Cover. Simmer 8 minutes or until just tender; drain. Melt butter; blend in flour, Bon Appétit, savory and pepper. Add sour cream and cook until thickened, stirring constantly. Do not allow to boil. Fold in beans. Pour into lightly buttered 1-quart casserole and sprinkle cheese over top. Broil 4 inches from heat 4 minutes or until cheese melts. *Serves 3 to 4.*

# Asparagus Parmesan

½ cup water
3½ teaspoons Season-All
2 pounds fresh asparagus or
   2 10-ounce packages
   frozen asparagus spears
1 cup coarse cracker crumbs
3 tablespoons butter
3 tablespoons flour

⅛ teaspoon Onion Powder
¼ teaspoon Black Pepper
¼ teaspoon dry Mustard
1½ cups milk
1 4-ounce can mushroom
   crowns
Parmesan cheese

Add water and 1½ teaspoons of the Season-All to asparagus. (When you use fresh asparagus, break stalks off as far down as they snap easily; wash well.) Cook about 10 minutes or until tender. Drain. Sprinkle cracker crumbs evenly over bottom of buttered 1½-quart shallow baking dish. Top with asparagus. Melt butter in saucepan. Stir in flour, onion powder, pepper, dry mustard and the remaining Season-All; cook until bubbly. Remove from heat; add milk, mixing well. Cook over low heat, stirring, until thickened. Stir in mushrooms including liquid and pour over asparagus. Sprinkle with Parmesan cheese. Bake in 350°F. oven 30 minutes. This dish lends itself to entertaining. Can be made ahead, refrigerated and cooked just before serving. *Serves 6 to 8.*

# Celery and Carrots in Parsley Cream

2 cups tender celery stalks,
   cut in 2-inch lengths
1 carrot, thinly sliced
½ teaspoon Rosemary
   Leaves, crushed
2 teaspoons Chicken
   Seasoned Stock Base
½ cup hot water

2 tablespoons butter
1½ teaspoons Arrowroot
¼ teaspoon salt
Dash Black Pepper
1 tablespoon Chopped
   Instant Onions
1 cup milk
½ teaspoon Parsley Flakes

Put celery, carrot and crushed rosemary in saucepan. Combine seasoned stock base and water; pour over vegetables. Cover; bring to a boil then simmer 10 minutes or until tender. Drain vegetables and keep warm. Melt butter; stir in arrowroot, salt, pepper, onions and milk. Cook over medium heat, stirring, until sauce thickens. Stir in parsley flakes then pour over vegetables, mixing gently. *Serves 3 to 4.*

---

## Potatoes au Gratin

---

| | |
|---|---|
| 1 teaspoon Chicken Seasoned Stock Base | 1 teaspoon Season-All |
| | ¼ teaspoon dry Mustard |
| 1 cup hot water | ⅛ teaspoon Nutmeg |
| 4 large potatoes, peeled | 2 cups milk |
| 3 tablespoons butter | 1½ cups grated sharp cheese |
| 2 tablespoons Arrowroot or ¼ cup flour | 1 cup soft bread crumbs |
| | 2 tablespoons melted butter |
| ¼ teaspoon salt | Paprika |
| ¼ teaspoon White Pepper | |

Dissolve seasoned stock base in water and pour over potatoes which have been quartered. Bring to a boil then simmer 20 minutes or until tender. Drain; cut into cubes and place in a buttered 1½-quart baking dish. Melt the 3 tablespoons butter in saucepan; stir in arrowroot, salt, pepper, Season-All, dry mustard and nutmeg. Add milk and cook over medium heat, stirring constantly, until smooth and thickened. Stir in 1 cup of the cheese and continue cooking until cheese melts. Pour over potatoes. Toss bread crumbs with the 2 tablespoons melted butter; spoon evenly over all. Top with the remaining cheese and sprinkle generously with paprika. Bake in 350°F. oven 20 minutes. You will find this a favorite of the men in your family. *Serves 4 to 6.*

# Baked Stuffed Eggplant

1 large eggplant
3 tablespoons Chopped
Instant Onions
1 green pepper, finely
minced
1 large tomato, finely
chopped
3 tablespoons butter
1 teaspoon Chicken
Seasoned Stock Base
¼ cup water

½ teaspoon salt
¼ teaspoon Black Pepper
¼ teaspoon MSG
¼ teaspoon Herb Seasoning
1½ cups finely minced or
ground ham or any other
leftover meat
¾ cup grated sharp cheese
½ cup bread crumbs
1 tablespoon melted butter

Cut eggplant in half lengthwise; remove inside pulp leaving a firm shell about ¼ inch thick. Cover shells with salted water and set aside while preparing filling. Dice eggplant pulp and put in skillet along with onions, green pepper, tomato, the 3 tablespoons butter, seasoned stock base and water. Mix well. Cover and cook 15 minutes or until tender. Remove cover and continue cooking until all liquid is gone. Add salt, seasonings, ham and ½ cup of the cheese; mix well. Drain shells; fill with ham mixture. Bake in 350°F. oven 30 minutes. Remove from oven; sprinkle top with the remaining ¼ cup grated cheese. Toss bread crumbs with the 1 tablespoon melted butter; sprinkle over top. Continue baking 15 minutes longer or until crumbs are lightly browned. *Serves 4 to 6.*

# Broiled Bananas

A new way to serve bananas.

| | |
|---|---|
| 6 bananas | 1 tablespoon sugar |
| ¼ cup lemon | ½ teaspoon Cinnamon |
|   or lime juice | ⅛ teaspoon Mace |
| ¼ cup melted butter | ¼ teaspoon Allspice |

Peel bananas; brush entire surface with lemon juice and place in a shallow baking pan or in the bottom of a broiler pan. Brush with butter. Combine sugar and spices; spoon on top of bananas. Drizzle with butter. Broil 4 to 5 inches from heat 10 minutes or until nicely browned. Baste with juices in pan once while broiling. Serve with ham, chicken, veal, pork, lamb or curried dishes. *Serves 6.*

# BREADS

——— * ———

## Hot Cross Buns

1 package hot roll mix
1 teaspoon Cinnamon
¼ teaspoon Allspice
¼ teaspoon Cardamom

½ cup seedless white raisins
¾ cup powdered sugar
¾ teaspoon Lemon Extract
3 teaspoons water

To the flour mixture in the hot roll mix add cinnamon, allspice, cardamom and raisins; mix well. Then prepare mix as directed on package. After first rising shape dough into 18 2-inch balls and place on greased baking sheet. Set in warm place and let rise to double in bulk. Bake in 400°F. oven 15 minutes. Cool. Combine sugar, lemon extract and water; drizzle in shape of cross on top of each bun. *Makes 18 buns.*

## Sesame Ring

1 package hot roll mix
Sesame Seed

Prepare hot roll mix as directed on package. After first rising, shape dough into 9 balls about 2 inches in diameter. Place balls side by side in well greased 1½-quart ring mold. Set in warm place and let rise to double in bulk. Sprinkle sesame seed on top. Bake in 350°F. oven 30 to 35 minutes. *Makes 1 ring.*

# Holiday Confetti Bread

1 cup milk
½ cup sugar
1½ teaspoons salt
6 tablespoons butter
1 teaspoon Lemon Peel
½ teaspoon Allspice
½ teaspoon Ginger
1 package active dry yeast

¼ cup lukewarm water
2 eggs, well beaten
4 cups sifted all-purpose
  flour
1½ cups mixed candied
  fruits, cut into small pieces
2 tablespoons flour
½ cup slivered almonds

Scald milk; add sugar, salt, butter and spices. Cool to lukewarm. Dissolve yeast in water. Stir in beaten eggs and milk mixture. Add the 4 cups flour and stir until moistened. Cover and set in warm place and let rise until double in bulk, about 1½ hours. Dredge fruit with the 2 tablespoons flour. Add fruit and almonds to batter; beat 2 minutes (an electric mixer set on low speed may be used). Push into greased 2-quart mold or 9 x 3½-inch tube pan. Set in warm place and let rise until double in bulk, about 1 hour. Bake in 350°F. oven 1 hour. *Makes 1 loaf.*

# Corn Sticks Rosemary

1 teaspoon Rosemary Leaves
1 package corn bread mix

Add rosemary leaves to corn bread mix. Prepare according to directions on package. Spoon into well greased corn stick pans filling almost full. Bake in 400°F. oven 15 minutes or until golden brown. You may want to vary shape and use muffin pans instead of corn stick pans. *Makes 14 to 16 corn sticks.*

273

# Oregano Batter Bread

| | |
|---|---|
| 1 package active dry yeast | 2 teaspoons Oregano Leaves |
| ¼ cup warm water | 1 egg |
| ¾ cup milk | 1 tablespoon oil |
| 1 tablespoon sugar | 3 cups all-purpose flour |
| 1½ teaspoons salt | 2 teaspoons Fennel Seed |

Dissolve yeast in warm water in large mixing bowl. Scald milk, then cool to lukewarm. Add milk, sugar, salt, oregano leaves, egg, oil and 2 cups of the flour to yeast. Beat on high speed with electric mixer 3 minutes (beat longer if beating by hand). Stir in remaining flour. Set in warm place free from draft and let rise to double in bulk, about 1 hour. Stir well. Put in greased 9¼ x 5¼ x 2¾-inch loaf pan. Push dough so that it fills corners of pan. Brush top lightly with oil and sprinkle with fennel seed. Set in warm place and let rise to double in bulk, about 30 minutes. Bake in 375°F. oven 50 minutes. *Makes 1 loaf.*


# Herb Croutons

For interesting variations in flavor use different combinations of spices and herbs.

| | |
|---|---|
| 1 cup bread cubes | Dash Herb Seasoning |
| (about ½-inch cubes) | Dash Season-All |
| 2 tablespoons butter | Dash Garlic Salt |

Toast bread cubes in 300°F. oven until dry and crisp and golden brown. Sauté in butter seasoned with Herb Seasoning, Season-All and garlic salt. Use in Caesar salad, potato dumplings; spoon on top of soups or use as topping for vegetables and casseroles. *Makes 1 cup.*

# Rum Buns

1 package hot roll mix
1 1-ounce bottle Rum
  Extract
2 cups powdered sugar

4 teaspoons water
3 tablespoons soft butter
Cinnamon

Prepare roll mix as directed on package. After first rising, roll dough into a 10 x 12-inch rectangle. Combine rum extract, powdered sugar and water; mix until smooth. Spread soft butter and half of the powdered sugar mixture over dough. Sprinkle with cinnamon. Roll as jelly roll, starting with long side. Cut into 12 1-inch slices. Put into greased muffin cups, cut side down. Set in warm place and allow to rise until double in bulk. Bake in 350°F. oven 25 minutes. Remove from pans. Drizzle remainder of the powdered sugar mixture over buns. *Makes 12.*

# Cinnamon-Pineapple Buns

1 8½-ounce can crushed
  pineapple
½ cup butter, melted
½ cup brown sugar, packed
1 teaspoon Cinnamon
¼ teaspoon Nutmeg

¼ cup chopped pecans
2 cups biscuit mix
4 tablespoons sugar
½ cup milk
⅓ cup melted butter

Drain pineapple. Mix together thoroughly the pineapple, ½ cup melted butter, brown sugar, cinnamon, nutmeg and pecans. Spoon into 12 muffin cups. Combine remaining ingredients and spoon over cinnamon-pineapple mixture. Bake in 425°F. oven 15 to 20 minutes. Immediately turn upside down on rack or tray to remove buns. Serve warm. *Makes 12.*

# Danish Pastry

2 packages active dry yeast
¼ cup warm water
⅓ cup sugar
Dash Cardamom
1 egg, beaten

1 cup milk
3½ cups all-purpose flour
½ pound butter, softened
Filling

Dissolve yeast in water; add sugar, cardamom, egg and milk. Stir in flour to make soft dough. (If dough seems too soft, add extra flour.) Roll out on floured board to 14-inch square. Spread one half of the butter over center third of dough. Fold one side over butter, then fold other side over first side, making three layers. Give dough a quarter turn and roll out to 14-inch square. Spread remaining butter over center and fold once more as directed above. Turn, roll and fold dough again. Chill 1 hour. Again, roll, fold and turn dough three times. Chill 1 hour. Roll dough to ⅛-inch thickness. Cut into 4-inch squares. Put 1 tablespoon filling in center of each. Shape. (For *envelopes*—bring two opposite ends of square to center and overlap; seal edges. For *pockets*—bring all four corners of square to center and overlap; seal edges. For *cockscombs*—cut dough into 5 x 10-inch pieces; put filling on one end of rectangle. Fold other half of dough over filling; seal edges, then cut 4 to 5 deep slashes along one side of pastry.) Chill 2 hours. Bake in 350°F. oven 15 minutes or until golden brown. *Makes about 36 rolls.*

RASPBERRY FILLING:

1 10-ounce package frozen
raspberries
1 tablespoon sugar

⅛ teaspoon Cardamom
¼ teaspoon Almond Extract
2 teaspoons cornstarch

Combine all ingredients. Cook, stirring, until slightly thickened. Cool. *Makes filling for 18 pastries.*

276

**APRICOT FILLING:**

1 8-ounce package dried
   apricots, cooked and
   mashed

3 tablespoons sugar
¼ teaspoon Cardamom

Combine all ingredients; mix well. *Makes filling for 18 pastries.*

**POPPY SEED FILLING:**

⅓ cup Poppy Seed
½ cup milk
1 egg yolk
1 teaspoon Orange Peel

¼ cup sugar
¼ cup bread crumbs
1 tablespoon honey

Add poppy seed to milk; bring to a boil. Remove from heat and let stand 1 hour. Drain. Combine poppy seed with remaining ingredients. *Makes filling for 18 pastries.*

---

## *Parsley Biscuits*

---

2 cups all-purpose flour
3 teaspoons baking powder
1 teaspoon salt
2 teaspoons Parsley Flakes

5 tablespoons shortening
¾ cup milk
Sesame Seed, Poppy Seed
   or Caraway Seed

Sift flour, measure and sift again with baking powder and salt. Add parsley flakes. Using pastry blender or two knives cut shortening into flour until the mixture is consistency of coarse corn meal. Add milk and stir until mixture forms ball and leaves side of bowl. Turn out on lightly floured board. Roll to ¼-inch thickness. Cut with biscuit cutter and put on lightly greased baking sheet. Sprinkle tops with seed and lightly press into biscuits. Bake in 425°F. oven 10 to 12 minutes. *Makes 16 2-inch biscuits.*

# Cardamom Crescent

½ cup milk, scalded
1 cake compressed yeast
1 egg, beaten
3 tablespoons sugar
1 teaspoon salt
½ teaspoon ground
  Cardamom

1 teaspoon Lemon Peel
2 cups all-purpose flour
6 tablespoons soft butter
Cardamom Fruit Filling
1 tablespoon melted
  shortening
Glaze

Cool milk to lukewarm. Crumble in yeast; stir to dissolve. Add egg, sugar, salt and spices. Gradually beat in flour, mixing to a moderately stiff dough. (If dough is too soft, add about ¼ cup more flour.) Turn out on lightly floured board and knead just until smooth. Put in greased bowl; cover and let stand in warm place until double in bulk, about 1½ hours. Turn out on lightly floured board; roll to rectangle about 12 x 15 inches. Spread with 4 tablespoons of the butter. Fold one end to middle and overlap second end to make 3 layers. Roll out again to 12 x 15 inches and spread with remaining butter; fold again as before. Cover and let stand 15 minutes. Roll out dough to 10 x 16 inches. Spread with cooled Cardamom Fruit Filling; roll up as jelly roll, starting from long side. Seal lengthwise seam and ends. Place seam side down on lightly greased baking sheet and shape into crescent. With scissors make cuts ⅔ of way through crescent at about 1-inch intervals. Brush surface of dough with melted shortening. Set in warm place and let rise until double in bulk, 50 to 60 minutes. Bake in 350°F. oven 25 to 30 minutes. Cool on wire rack. Glaze. *Makes 1 large crescent.*

CARDAMOM FRUIT FILLING:

¼ cup sugar
¼ teaspoon ground
  Cardamom
⅛ teaspoon salt
1 cup chopped dates

⅓ cup water or orange juice
1 tablespoon butter
  or margarine
¼ cup chopped nuts

Combine sugar, cardamom, salt, dates and water. Cook, stirring, over medium heat until mixture becomes thick. Remove from heat; stir in butter and nuts. Cool before using.

GLAZE:

Combine 1 cup sifted powdered sugar and 4 teaspoons milk or water. Drizzle over top of crescent.

## Sticky Spice Buns

Old-fashioned goodness, sweet and mouth-watering.

| | |
|---|---|
| 1 package hot roll mix | 2½ teaspoons Pumpkin Pie |
| ½ cup butter | Spice |
| 2¼ cups brown sugar, | ½ cup raisins |
| packed | 1 cup light corn syrup |

Prepare hot roll mix as directed on package. After first rising, roll dough to 18 x 20-inch rectangle. With pastry blender or two knives cut ¼ cup of the butter into ¾ cup of the brown sugar and pumpkin pie spice. Add raisins. Sprinkle this mixture evenly over the dough. Roll as jelly roll, starting from long side. Seal edge. Cut into 18 equal pieces. Combine the remaining ¼ cup butter and 1½ cups brown sugar with corn syrup. Cook over low heat until sugar dissolves. Pour syrup into two buttered 9-inch layer pans. Cool slightly. Place nine slices of the dough, cut side down, in each pan. Set in warm place and allow to rise to double in bulk. Bake in 350°F. oven 30 to 35 minutes. Cool 10 minutes. Turn out onto plate. *Makes 18 buns.*

# Quick Coffee Cake

**CAKE BATTER:**

3 tablespoons butter
  or margarine
⅓ cup sugar
1 egg
1 teaspoon Lemon Peel

1½ cups all-purpose flour
3 teaspoons baking powder
½ teaspoon salt
⅔ cup milk

Cream together butter and sugar; add egg and lemon peel. Sift flour, measure and sift again with baking powder and salt. Add to creamed mixture alternately with milk and mix lightly. Spread in greased and floured 8-inch square pan. Sprinkle Streusel Topping over batter. Bake in 400°F. oven 25 to 30 minutes. *Makes 9 servings.*

**STREUSEL TOPPING:**

3 tablespoons soft butter
  or margarine
½ cup sugar
2 teaspoons Pumpkin Pie
  Spice

2 tablespoons flour
⅛ teaspoon salt
1 teaspoon Lemon Peel
½ cup chopped nuts,
  optional

Blend together all ingredients and sprinkle over top of cake batter.

# Old-Fashioned Herb Bread

1 cup warm water
1 package active dry yeast
1½ teaspoons salt
2 teaspoons sugar
1 tablespoon soft shortening
1 teaspoon Marjoram Leaves
¾ teaspoon Dill Weed

¾ teaspoon Thyme Leaves
½ teaspoon Rosemary
  Leaves
3 cups sifted all-purpose
  flour
Poppy Seed

Pour water into bowl; sprinkle yeast on top. Stir until dissolved. Add salt, sugar, shortening and herbs; stir. Add flour to make a soft dough. Turn dough out on lightly floured board and knead until smooth and elastic, 5 to 7 minutes. Put dough in greased bowl; turn to bring greased side up. Cover; set in warm place and allow to rise to double in bulk, about 1½ hours. Shape dough into a roll 18 inches long. Place on greased baking sheet. With sharp knife make ¼-inch deep slashes in top of loaf, about 1½ inches apart. Brush with water. Set in warm place and allow to rise to double in bulk, about 1 hour. Brush again with water. Bake in 425°F. oven 15 minutes. Brush a third time with water and sprinkle poppy seed on top. Bake 15 minutes longer. *Makes 1 loaf*.

# Party Biscuits

Delightful flavor and made in minutes.

| | |
|---|---|
| 1 can refrigerator biscuits | Seasoning, Orange Peel |
| 1 teaspoon of one of the following: Barbecue Spice, Curry Powder, Herb | or 2 teaspoons Lemon Peel |
| | 2 tablespoons butter, melted |

Pull each biscuit to about 6 inches in length. Stir one of the spices into melted butter. Dip each length of dough in seasoned butter; twist. Place on ungreased baking sheet. Bake in 475°F. oven 8 minutes. *Makes 10*.

NOTE: For added flavor when using Herb Seasoning, roll dough in Parmesan cheese after dipping in the butter mixture.

# Fun with Waffles

2 cups waffle mix
2 tablespoons brown sugar
2 tablespoons melted butter
1 teaspoon pure Vanilla Extract
1 tablespoon Lemon Peel or 1 teaspoon Allspice

Prepare the 2 cups waffle mix as directed on package, adding brown sugar, butter, vanilla and lemon peel or allspice. Bake. *Makes 3 9-inch square waffles.*

**VARIATIONS:**

*Herb Waffles*—Add 2 teaspoons Parsley Flakes and 1 teaspoon Herb Seasoning to 2 cups waffle mix. Prepare as directed on package. Serve with creamed dishes; excellent, too, as a hot bread.

*Mace Waffles*—Add 1 teaspoon Mace to 2 cups waffle mix. Prepare as directed on package.

*Sage Waffles*—Add 2 teaspoons rubbed Sage to 2 cups waffle mix. Prepare as directed on package. Excellent with creamed dishes.

*Sesame Waffles*—Prepare waffle mix as directed. After pouring batter on waffle iron, sprinkle generously with Sesame Seed. Bake.

# Garlic Cheese Bread

1 loaf French bread
¼ teaspoon Garlic Powder
½ cup butter or margarine
1 cup grated sharp cheese or Parmesan cheese

Cut bread into 1-inch slices. Heat garlic powder and butter slowly until butter is melted. Brush each slice of bread on both sides with garlic butter and place on baking sheet. Sprinkle with cheese and bake in 425°F. oven 10 minutes or until cheese melts. Serve hot. *Serves 6.*

# Spicy Banana Nut Bread

⅓ cup shortening
⅔ cup sugar
2 eggs
1 teaspoon pure Vanilla
  Extract
1¾ cups all-purpose flour
2 teaspoons baking powder

½ teaspoon salt
1 teaspoon Cinnamon
⅛ teaspoon Cardamom
⅛ teaspoon Mace
1 cup mashed bananas
½ cup chopped nuts

Cream shortening and sugar until light and fluffy. Add eggs and vanilla and beat well. Sift flour, measure and sift again with baking powder, salt, cinnamon, cardamom and mace. Add alternately with bananas to creamed mixture. Stir in nuts. Grease bottom of 9¼ x 5¼ x 2¾-inch loaf pan. Pour batter into pan. Bake in 350°F. oven 1 hour to 1 hour and 10 minutes. Serve warm or cold at any meal. You will find this especially good with fruit salads, spread with butter or cream cheese for sandwiches and is a school lunch box favorite. *Makes 1 loaf.*

---

# Cinnamon-Pecan Biscuits

Quick and Easy!

2 tablespoons butter
3 tablespoons honey
1 teaspoon Cinnamon
1 teaspoon Orange Peel

½ cup chopped pecans
1 package refrigerator
  biscuits

Melt butter; add honey, cinnamon and orange peel. Stir until well blended. Add pecans and cook over medium heat until pecans are glazed, stirring constantly. Put biscuits on baking sheet and flatten slightly. Spoon pecan mixture over top of biscuits. Bake as directed on package. *Makes 10 biscuits.*

# Doughnuts

½ cup sugar
1 teaspoon salt
¼ cup butter
¾ cup scalded milk
2 packages active dry yeast
½ cup warm water

1 egg, beaten
2 teaspoons Lemon Peel
4 cups all-purpose flour
½ teaspoon Cinnamon
1 teaspoon Nutmeg
Fat for frying

Add sugar, salt and butter to scalded milk and cool to lukewarm. Dissolve yeast in warm water. Add egg, lemon peel and cooled milk mixture; mix well. Sift flour, measure and sift again with cinnamon and nutmeg. Stir into yeast mixture. Turn out on lightly floured board and knead until smooth and dough no longer sticks to board, about 10 minutes. Put in greased bowl; turn dough over to coat with grease. Cover and set in warm place free from draft and let rise until double in bulk, about 1 hour. Punch down. Roll on lightly floured board to ¼-inch thickness. Cut with doughnut cutter. Spread cloth over baking sheet. Put doughnuts on cloth and set in warm place and let rise to double in bulk, about 1 hour. Fry in deep fat, 375°F., until golden brown. Remove and drain on absorbent paper. Glaze (see recipe page 320). *Makes 3 dozen.*

# Quick Cinnamon Twists

1 can refrigerator biscuits
2 tablespoons butter, melted
½ cup finely chopped nuts

2 tablespoons Cinnamon
  Sugar

Pull each biscuit to about 6 inches in length. Dip in melted butter, then in mixture of nuts and cinnamon sugar. Twist. Place on ungreased baking sheet. Bake in 475°F. oven 8 minutes. Quick to make and wonderful with coffee or tea. *Makes 10.*

# Muffins

2 cups all-purpose flour
3 teaspoons baking powder
½ teaspoon salt
3 tablespoons sugar
1 egg

1 cup milk
1 teaspoon pure Vanilla
    Extract
3 tablespoons shortening,
    melted

Grease well the bottoms of muffin cups or line with paper baking cups. Sift flour, measure and sift again with dry ingredients. Beat egg lightly; stir in milk, vanilla and melted shortening. Add to dry ingredients. Mix just until dry ingredients are moistened, 10 to 15 strokes. Spoon into muffin cups and bake in 425°F. oven 20 to 25 minutes. Serve hot. *Makes 12 muffins.*

### VARIATIONS:

*Mace-Blueberry Muffins*—Add ¼ teaspoon Mace to dry ingredients and substitute 1 cup blueberries for ¼ cup of the milk in above recipe.

*Orange Muffins*—Add 2 teaspoons Orange Peel to dry ingredients in above recipe and proceed as directed. Mix together ½ cup powdered sugar, ½ teaspoon Orange Peel, ½ teaspoon Orange Extract and 2 teaspoons water. Drizzle over top of hot baked muffins.

*Spice Muffins*—Add 1 teaspoon Pumpkin Pie Spice to dry ingredients in above recipe. For even greater variety you will find it fun and exciting to vary the flavor of Spice Muffins. Add ¼ teaspoon Cinnamon, Ginger, Nutmeg or Cardamom in place of Pumpkin Pie Spice.

*Cinnamon-Streusel Muffins*—Mix together 1 tablespoon butter and ¼ cup Cinnamon Sugar. Sprinkle over top of muffin batter before baking.

# Easy Saffron Bread

1 cup milk
3 tablespoons sugar
2 tablespoons butter
or margarine
2 teaspoons Instant Minced
Onion
2 teaspoons salt

⅛ teaspoon crushed Saffron
pieces
2 packages active dry yeast
1 cup warm water
4½ cups all-purpose flour
Caraway Seed

Scald milk. Stir in sugar, butter, onion, salt and crushed saffron. Cool to lukewarm. Sprinkle yeast over warm water in a large mixing bowl. Stir until dissolved, then add milk mixture. Add flour; stir until well blended. Cover and set in warm place. Let rise to more than double in bulk, about 40 minutes. Stir batter down and beat vigorously ½ minute. Turn into greased 1½-quart round casserole; sprinkle top with caraway seed. Bake in 375°F. oven 1 to 1¼ hours. *Makes 1 loaf*.

# Dill Ring

1 package hot roll mix
¼ cup melted butter

1 teaspoon Dill Weed
Poppy Seed

Prepare roll mix as directed on package. After first rising, roll out dough on lightly floured board to ¼-inch thickness. Cut approximately 30 rounds with a 2-inch biscuit cutter. Dip each round in a mixture of melted butter and dill weed. Arrange the rounds upright (on edge) next to each other in a 9½-inch ring mold. Set in warm place and let rise to double in bulk, about 30 minutes. Sprinkle top with poppy seed. Bake in 375°F. oven 20 minutes. *Makes 1 ring*.

# Rye Herb Bread

1 tablespoon Parsley Flakes
⅛ teaspoon Garlic Powder
1 teaspoon Bon Appétit
¼ teaspoon Black Pepper
¼ teaspoon dry Mustard
¼ teaspoon Rosemary Leaves

¼ teaspoon rubbed Sage
¼ teaspoon Tarragon Leaves
¼ teaspoon ground Thyme
½ cup butter, creamed
1 loaf light rye bread, sliced

Add seasonings to creamed butter; mix well. Spread mixture generously on each slice of bread and reassemble loaf. Wrap in aluminum foil and heat in 400°F. oven 15 to 20 minutes. You will find this good with almost any dish but is especially good with spaghetti, eggs or cheese dishes. *Serves 8 to 10.*

# Blueberry Pancakes

1 egg, well beaten
1½ cups buttermilk
1 teaspoon pure Vanilla
　Extract
1¼ cups sifted all-purpose
　flour
2 teaspoons sugar
½ teaspoon soda

1 teaspoon baking powder
½ teaspoon salt
¼ teaspoon Allspice
2 tablespoons melted
　shortening
1 cup blueberries (thaw and
　drain frozen berries)

Combine beaten egg, buttermilk and vanilla; beat until well blended. Sift together flour, sugar, soda, baking powder, salt and allspice. Add to egg mixture along with melted shortening and beat until smooth. Stir in blueberries. Pour batter onto heated griddle. Cook until full of bubbles and brown. Turn and brown other side. *Makes 10 to 12 pancakes.*

# Whole Wheat Salt Sticks

1 package active dry yeast
¾ cup warm water
¼ cup molasses
1 tablespoon sugar
2 teaspoons salt
1 tablespoon oil

1 teaspoon Anise Seed
1 tablespoon Caraway Seed
1 cup whole wheat flour
1½ cups all-purpose flour
Salad Salt

Dissolve yeast in warm water. Add molasses, sugar, salt, oil, anise seed and caraway seed; stir well. Stir in whole wheat flour. Sift all-purpose flour, measure and add to dough, mixing well. (If dough seems too soft, add ¼ to ½ cup additional all-purpose flour.) Turn out on lightly floured board and knead until smooth and elastic, about 10 minutes. Shape into a ball and put into greased bowl. Turn dough over to bring greased side up; cover with a cloth. Set in warm place free from draft and allow to rise until double in bulk, about 3 hours. Punch down. Roll on lightly floured board into a circle ¼ inch thick. Cut into 10 pie-shaped pieces. Roll up tightly, beginning at wide end. Seal point firmly. Put on lightly greased baking sheet with point underneath. Set in warm place and allow to rise to double in bulk, 30 to 45 minutes. Brush with water and sprinkle with salad salt. Bake in 425°F. oven 15 minutes. *Makes 10 rolls.*

# DESSERTS

— ✳ —

---

## Spicy Meringues

---

8 egg whites
½ teaspoon Cream of Tartar
¼ teaspoon salt
2 cups superfine sugar

1 teaspoon pure Vanilla
Extract
¼ teaspoon Cardamom

Have egg whites at room temperature. Add cream of tartar and salt to egg whites; beat until soft peaks form. Continue beating, adding sugar one tablespoon at a time, then add vanilla and cardamom. Beat 5 minutes longer. Drop by spoonfuls on brown paper or a piece of lightly greased aluminum foil placed on baking sheet. Shape into circles and with the back of a spoon form a well in center of each. Put in 450°F. oven and immediately turn off heat. Let stand several hours until oven is cold or overnight. Do not open oven door. Remove from paper and place on serving plate. Just before serving fill with ice cream or whipped cream and top with fruit or a tasty sauce. For interesting variations in flavor you may substitute Mace or Allspice for cardamom. Meringues can be made in any desired shapes, such as: puffs, mushrooms, ribbon strips, swans or hollow shells. *Makes 20 large or 40 small meringues.*

# Ginger Dessert Waffles

| | |
|---|---|
| ½ cup butter or margarine | 2½ cups all-purpose flour |
| 1 cup sugar | 1 tablespoon Ginger |
| 2 eggs | 1 teaspoon Cinnamon |
| 1 teaspoon pure Vanilla Extract | ¼ teaspoon salt |
| | 1 teaspoon soda |
| 1 teaspoon Orange Peel | ⅔ cup buttermilk |

Cream butter and sugar until light and fluffy. Add eggs, one at a time, beating well after each addition. Add vanilla and orange peel. Sift flour, measure and sift again with ginger, cinnamon, salt and soda. Add flour and buttermilk alternately to butter mixture. Bake in waffle iron. Serve with ice cream, whipped cream or syrup. *Serves 6 to 8.*

# Chocolate Mousse

Rich, smooth, luscious.

| | |
|---|---|
| 1½ teaspoons unflavored gelatine | ¼ teaspoon Mace |
| 2 tablespoons cold water | 1 cup milk |
| 2 1-ounce squares unsweetened chocolate | 2 cups heavy cream |
| | 1 teaspoon pure Vanilla Extract |
| ¾ cup sugar | |

Soften gelatine in cold water. Put chocolate, ½ cup of the sugar, mace and milk in saucepan or in top of double boiler. Heat thoroughly over low heat until chocolate melts. Do not boil. Beat until smooth with rotary beater. Add gelatine; stir until melted. Pour into a bowl and chill until mixture thickens; then beat until light and fluffy. Whip cream, adding remaining sugar and vanilla. Fold into chocolate mixture. Pour into a 2-quart mold. Freeze. Remove from mold onto serving plate. *Serves 6 to 8.*

# Coffee Torte

An elegant Viennese dessert—impressive, very special.

**MERINGUES:**

6 egg whites
¼ teaspoon Cream of Tartar
1 cup sugar
1½ cups sifted powdered
  sugar

1 teaspoon Almond Extract
Dash Allspice
Dash Mace

Beat egg whites until foamy; add cream of tartar.
Continue beating until egg whites hold a stiff peak.
Slowly add sugar and powdered sugar, one tablespoon
at a time, beating well after each addition. Add extract,
allspice and mace; beat 2 minutes longer. Cut four 8-
inch circles from heavy brown paper. Divide meringue
into 4 parts and spread evenly over the circles of paper.
Place on baking sheets. Bake in 250°F. oven 1 hour 15
minutes. Remove from oven; cool. Then remove paper
from bottom of meringue layers.

**FILLING:**

6 egg yolks
½ cup sugar
½ cup cold strong coffee
1 tablespoon flour

½ cup soft butter
½ pint heavy cream,
  whipped

Combine egg yolks, sugar, coffee and flour in top of
double boiler. Cook over boiling water, stirring constantly, until mixture thickens. Cool to lukewarm. Add
butter; stir until well blended. Spoon and spread filling
over top of meringue layers, stacking as a layer cake.
Decorate with rosettes of whipped cream. Chill. *Serves
8 to 10.*

# Spiced Bread Pudding

| | |
|---|---|
| 2 cups dry bread cubes | ½ teaspoon Cinnamon |
| 4 cups milk, scalded | ¼ teaspoon Ginger |
| ¾ cup sugar | 4 eggs, lightly beaten |
| 1 tablespoon butter | 2 teaspoons pure Vanilla |
| ¼ teaspoon salt | Extract |
| ⅛ teaspoon Nutmeg | ¼ cup raisins |

Soak bread in milk 5 minutes. Add sugar, butter, salt, nutmeg, cinnamon and ginger. Pour slowly over eggs. Add vanilla and raisins; mix well. Pour into buttered 1½-quart casserole or baking dish. Bake in pan of hot water in 350°F. oven 1 hour or until silver knife comes out clean when inserted in center. You may serve with lemon or orange sauce or Crème Anglaise (see recipe page 407), if desired. *Makes 8 to 10 servings.*

# Homemade Vanilla Ice Cream

There is no dessert more delicious than old-fashioned homemade ice cream flavored with pure vanilla.

| | |
|---|---|
| 2 cups milk | 4 egg yolks |
| ½ cup sugar | 2 teaspoons pure Vanilla |
| 1 tablespoon Arrowroot | Extract |
| ¼ teaspoon salt | 2 cups heavy cream |

Scald milk. Combine sugar, arrowroot and salt. Beat egg yolks and gradually add sugar mixture, beating until sugar dissolves. Slowly add milk to egg mixture while beating. Cook in top of double boiler or over lowest heat, stirring constantly, until mixture thickens and coats a metal spoon. Strain and chill. Stir in vanilla and cream. Freeze in 2-quart ice cream freezer. Excellent served with fresh fruits. *Makes about 1½ quarts.*

*Spiced Coffee Ice Cream*—Blend 2 tablespoons instant coffee (dry), ¼ teaspoon Cinnamon, ⅛ teaspoon Nutmeg and dash Cloves into hot custard before chilling. Proceed as in above recipe.

*Cinnamon-Nut Ice Cream*—Add 1½ teaspoons Cinnamon with the sugar in recipe for Homemade Vanilla Ice Cream and stir in ½ cup chopped nuts just before freezing.

---

# *Creamy Rice Pudding*

---

Nutmeg is essential to give this old-time favorite its special goodness.

| | |
|---|---|
| ½ cup rice | 1 teaspoon pure Vanilla |
| 4 cups milk | Extract |
| ¼ cup butter | ¼ teaspoon salt |
| 3 eggs | ½ teaspoon Nutmeg |
| ¾ cup sugar | |

Combine rice and 2 cups of the milk in top of double boiler; cover and cook over hot water until rice is tender. Add butter. Beat eggs; mix in sugar, vanilla, salt and remaining milk. Add hot rice mixture, mixing well. Pour into a buttered 2-quart baking dish. Sprinkle with nutmeg. Bake in 350°F. oven 50 minutes or until silver knife comes out clean when inserted near center. *Serves 6.*

VARIATION:

*Cardamom Rice Pudding*—Add ⅛ teaspoon Cardamom when adding sugar in the above recipe.

# Crêpes Suzette

Make the crêpes ahead, then heat in luscious sauce just before serving with a grand flourish.

CRÊPES:

| | |
|---|---|
| 1 cup milk | ¾ teaspoon baking powder |
| 2 tablespoons butter | ½ teaspoon salt |
| 2 eggs, well beaten | ¼ teaspoon Cinnamon |
| ½ cup sifted all-purpose flour | Dash Mace |

Heat milk and butter to just below boiling point. Do not boil. Cool slightly. Combine eggs, flour, baking powder, salt, cinnamon and mace; beat into milk mixture. Pour 2 generous tablespoons batter into lightly buttered 6- to 7-inch fry pan and cook over medium heat 1 minute or until lightly browned on bottom. Turn and brown other side. Remove to plate; set aside until ready to serve. Repeat until batter is used. (These may be made ahead of time.) When ready to serve follow one of the recipes below. *Makes 12 crêpes.*

SUZETTE SAUCE:

| | |
|---|---|
| ⅓ cup butter | 1 teaspoon Orange Peel |
| ¼ cup Cointreau | ¼ cup brandy |
| ⅓ cup orange juice | |

Melt butter in chafing dish; add Cointreau, orange juice and orange peel. Heat until mixture comes to a boil. Add crêpes, one at a time, and baste with sauce. Fold crêpes in quarters and move to one side of pan until all are heated. Pour brandy over all and flame. Serve three to each person. *Serves 4.*

VARIATION:

*Ginger Crêpes*—Make crêpes following above recipe. When ready to serve proceed as directed below.

24 small pieces Crystallized Ginger
1 cup Grand Marnier
⅓ cup sweet butter

4 tablespoons sugar
Juice of 1 orange
Few drops lemon juice

Put ginger in ¼ cup of the Grand Marnier and heat a few minutes. Set aside. Melt butter in chafing dish or skillet. Sprinkle sugar into pan; cook until sugar begins to melt and turns golden in color. Add orange juice, lemon juice and ¼ cup of the Grand Marnier. Bring to a boil. Place crêpes in sauce, baste, then carefully turn crêpes over. Put 2 pieces of the ginger in center of each; fold each crêpe in quarters. Push to one side of pan. Continue until all crêpes are folded, then sprinkle with remaining Grand Marnier and flame. Serve with a scoop of vanilla ice cream on one side of the plate. *Serves 4.*

---

## Steamed Date Pudding

---

¼ cup butter
¼ cup shortening
¾ cup sugar
3 eggs
1¼ cups sifted cake flour
1 teaspoon salt
⅛ teaspoon Mace

¾ teaspoon Allspice
1 cup milk
3 cups soft bread crumbs
¾ cup chopped dates
¼ cup chopped walnuts
1 teaspoon Lemon Peel
2 teaspoons Orange Peel

Cream together butter, shortening and sugar until light and fluffy. Add eggs, one at a time, mixing after addition of each. Sift together flour, salt, mace and allspice; add alternately to creamed mixture with milk. Fold in remaining ingredients. Spoon into a 1½-quart mold or eight individual 7-ounce molds, filling ⅔ full. Cover tightly with lid or aluminum foil. Place molds on rack in large kettle. Add enough boiling water to come half way up side of mold. Cover. Steam 1 hour or longer, depending on size mold used. You may use frozen juice cans in place of individual molds. *Makes 16 servings.*

# Cinnamon Ice Cream

An easy way to create a brand new dessert.

1 quart vanilla ice cream     1 teaspoon Cinnamon

Soften ice cream just enough to stir. Add cinnamon; mix thoroughly. Spoon into freezer tray and immediately refreeze. A delight with apple pie. *Makes 1 quart.*

# Spiced Soufflé

| | |
|---|---|
| 2 tablespoons butter | 2 teaspoons Lemon Peel |
| 1 tablespoon Arrowroot | 2 teaspoons pure Vanilla |
| ½ cup milk |    Extract |
| 5 egg yolks | 6 egg whites |
| ¼ cup sugar | Dash salt |
| ½ teaspoon Ginger | ¼ teaspoon Cream of Tartar |
| ½ teaspoon Cinnamon | 1 tablespoon sugar |
| ¼ teaspoon Mace | Soufflé Sauce Grand Marnier |

In small saucepan melt butter; remove from heat. Stir in arrowroot and milk. Cook over medium heat, stirring, until sauce thickens. Beat egg yolks lightly with the ¼ cup sugar, ginger, cinnamon, mace and lemon peel. Gradually add hot sauce to beaten yolks. Stir in vanilla; continue stirring until sugar dissolves. Beat egg whites until foamy; add salt and cream of tartar and continue beating until stiff but not dry. Add the 1 tablespoon sugar during the last minutes of beating; gently fold into cooked mixture. Pour into a 2½-quart soufflé dish or casserole which has been buttered and sugared. Bake in 375°F. oven 30 minutes or until puffy and browned. Dust top with powdered sugar if desired, and serve immediately, with side dish of Soufflé Sauce Grand Marnier. *Serves 4 to 6.*

SOUFFLÉ SAUCE GRAND MARNIER:

| | |
|---|---|
| 4 eggs | 1 cup heavy cream |
| ½ cup sugar | 1 cup milk, scalded |
| ¼ teaspoon salt | 3 tablespoons Grand |
| 1 teaspoon pure Vanilla | Marnier |
| Extract | |

Beat eggs until light and fluffy. Gradually beat in sugar. Add salt, vanilla and ½ cup of the cream; mix well. Slowly add scalded milk, beating briskly. Cook over very low heat or in top of double boiler, stirring constantly, until it is thick enough to coat a silver spoon. Chill. Stir in Grand Marnier. Whip remaining cream and fold into sauce. For a real gourmet touch, separate 2 or 3 orange sections by pulling apart the tiny tear-shaped cells which make up each orange section. Stir into sauce. Serve spooned over dessert soufflé. *Makes about 1 quart.*

---

## *Banana Fritters*

---

| | |
|---|---|
| 1 cup all-purpose flour | ½ cup milk |
| 2 teaspoons baking powder | 2 teaspoons melted |
| 1 teaspoon salt | shortening |
| ¼ cup sugar | 3 firm bananas |
| ¼ teaspoon Mace | Fat for deep fat frying |
| 1 egg, well beaten | ½ cup heavy cream, |
| 1 teaspoon pure Vanilla | whipped |
| Extract | Cinnamon |

Sift flour, measure and sift again with baking powder, salt, sugar and mace. Combine egg, vanilla, milk and melted shortening; mix well. Stir into dry ingredients and beat until smooth. Peel bananas and cut each into 3 or 4 pieces. Dip banana pieces into batter. Fry in deep fat, 375°F., until golden brown. Top hot fritters with whipped cream and sprinkle with cinnamon. *Makes 9 to 12 fritters.*

# Baked Apples

¾ cup sugar
1½ cups water
2 teaspoons Lemon Peel
1½ teaspoons Cinnamon
¼ teaspoon Red Food Color
6 baking apples

Mix together sugar, water, lemon peel, cinnamon and food color. Bring to a boil, stirring to dissolve sugar. Core apples and remove peel from the top third of apple. Arrange in baking dish and pour syrup over apples. Bake in 350°F. oven about 1 hour. Cook longer if a very soft apple is desired. Baste frequently with syrup. Serve warm or cold and you may serve with cream. Good for breakfast, too! *Serves 6.*

# Floating Island Meringues

4 egg whites
¼ teaspoon Cream of Tartar
¼ teaspoon salt
¾ cup superfine sugar
1 teaspoon pure Vanilla Extract
Dash Nutmeg

Have egg whites at room temperature. Add cream of tartar and salt; beat until soft peaks form. Beat in sugar, adding 1 tablespoon at a time. Add vanilla and beat 5 minutes. Drop by spoonfuls as "islands" on steaming hot water in a large baking dish or pan. Sprinkle with nutmeg. Bake in 400°F. oven 5 minutes or until delicately browned. Carefully remove with a slotted spoon or two forks. Put in serving bowls or saucers. Pour Crème Anglaise sauce (see recipe page 407) over tops when ready to serve. For variations in flavor, add ⅛ teaspoon Cardamom, ¼ teaspoon Mace or 1 teaspoon Lemon Peel to meringue mixture when you add vanilla. *Makes 10 to 12 meringues.*

# Curried Fruit Medley

Exotically different, a delightful conclusion for a company dinner.

1 No. 2 or No. 303 can each
    pear halves, peach halves
    and pineapple slices
½ cup butter or margarine

1 cup brown sugar, packed
1 tablespoon Curry Powder
¼ teaspoon salt

Drain fruit well; arrange in a 2-quart baking dish. Melt butter; add sugar, curry powder and salt. Heat until sugar is dissolved. Pour over fruit. Bake in 350°F. oven 25 to 30 minutes. Serve hot. You will find sour cream is just right with this fruit. *Serves 8 to 10.*

# Peach Cobbler Supreme

A surprise cobbler, batter rises to the top during cooking and forms a golden crust.

¼ cup butter
1 cup sifted all-purpose flour
1 cup sugar
⅛ teaspoon salt
1 tablespoon baking powder

⅔ cup milk
1 No. 2½ can sliced peaches
¼ teaspoon Nutmeg
¼ teaspoon Cinnamon
½ teaspoon Lemon Peel

Melt butter in a 7 x 11-inch shallow baking dish. Sift together dry ingredients; add milk and stir well. Pour this mixture into the baking dish. Do not stir. Top with peaches, including juice. Sprinkle nutmeg, cinnamon and lemon peel over peaches, but do not stir. Bake in 350°F. oven 40 minutes or until golden brown. Serve warm with cream. *Serves 6 to 8.*

# Strawberry-Rhubarb Crisp

⅔ cup sugar
2 tablespoons Arrowroot
⅛ teaspoon Cloves
Dash Cardamom
1 10-ounce package frozen
  strawberries, thawed
3 cups diced rhubarb
Red Food Color
⅓ cup soft butter

⅔ cup brown sugar, packed
½ cup all-purpose flour
½ cup quick-cooking rolled
  oats
1½ teaspoons Lemon Peel
½ teaspoon Nutmeg
2 tablespoons Cinnamon
  Sugar

Combine sugar, arrowroot, cloves and cardamom; add strawberries, rhubarb and a few drops food color. (If frozen rhubarb is used, thaw, then drain thoroughly and use only ⅓ cup sugar.) Mix well and pour into a buttered 1½-quart baking dish. Mix remaining ingredients with pastry blender or fork until crumbly. Sprinkle over strawberries and rhubarb. Bake in 350°F. oven 40 to 45 minutes. *Serves 6.*

# Spiced Bavarian

3½ cups milk
2 envelopes unflavored
  gelatine
6 eggs, separated
¾ cup sugar
¼ teaspoon salt

¼ teaspoon Mace
⅛ teaspoon Cardamom
½ teaspoon Ginger
1½ teaspoons pure Vanilla
  Extract
1 cup heavy cream, whipped

Scald 3 cups of the milk and soak gelatine in remaining ½ cup milk. Beat together egg yolks, sugar, salt and spices. Slowly add scalded milk to egg yolk mixture. Cook over low heat or in a double boiler, stirring constantly, until custard becomes thick and coats a silver spoon. Add softened gelatine, stirring until gelatine melts. Cool. Add vanilla and chill until slightly thickened. Fold the stiffly beaten egg whites and whipped cream into custard. Spoon into 2½-quart mold. Chill until firm. Remove from mold and garnish with whipped cream and fresh strawberries or any fruit you may desire. *Makes 10 servings.*

---

## English Plum Pudding

1½ cups all-purpose flour
½ teaspoon soda
¼ teaspoon salt
½ teaspoon Cinnamon
¼ teaspoon Ginger
¼ teaspoon Nutmeg
¼ teaspoon Allspice
½ cup dry bread crumbs
1 cup brown sugar, packed
1 teaspoon Lemon Peel
1 teaspoon Orange Peel
½ pound suet, ground
1 cup currants, plumped
1 cup raisins, plumped
½ cup chopped candied citron
½ cup chopped candied lemon peel
1 cup chopped apple
½ cup chopped nuts
4 eggs
¾ cup milk
1 teaspoon pure Vanilla Extract
1 tablespoon Rum Extract

In large bowl sift together flour, soda, salt, cinnamon, ginger, nutmeg and allspice. Add bread crumbs, brown sugar, lemon peel, orange peel, ground suet, fruits and nuts; mix well. Beat eggs; add milk, vanilla and rum extract. Stir into dry ingredients, mixing well. Pour into two well-greased 1-quart molds or one 2-quart mold. Fill to about one inch from top. Cover tightly and place on rack in large kettle. Add boiling water to come half way up side of mold. Cover kettle and steam 4½ to 6 hours, depending on size of mold. Remove from mold and serve hot with Spiced Hard Sauce (see recipe page 401). Pudding may be made weeks in advance and stored in a cool place or frozen. To serve, return pudding to mold or wrap in heavy cloth and steam 2 to 3 hours. *Serves 12 to 14.*

# Orange Bread Custard

¼ cup sugar
2 tablespoons melted butter
1 egg, lightly beaten
½ teaspoon salt
1 teaspoon pure Vanilla
Extract

½ teaspoon Orange Peel
2 cups scalded milk
1 cup bread cubes
½ cup seedless raisins

Mix together sugar, butter, egg, salt, vanilla and orange peel. Gradually add scalded milk, stirring constantly. Add bread cubes and raisins; mix well. Pour into a 1-quart buttered baking dish. Place dish in a pan of warm water. Bake in 350°F. oven 1 hour or until a silver knife comes out clean when inserted in center. *Serves 4.*

# Apricot Pudding

1 cup sugar
¼ cup soft butter
1 egg
2 cups chopped apricots,
fresh or cooked, dried
1 cup all-purpose flour

1 teaspoon soda
1 teaspoon Cinnamon
½ teaspoon Nutmeg
¼ teaspoon salt
½ cup chopped nuts

Gradually add sugar to butter, creaming well. Add egg and beat hard. Mix in apricots. Sift flour, measure and sift again with dry ingredients. Stir into apricot mixture. Add nuts and mix well. Bake in greased 8-inch square pan in 350°F. oven about 45 minutes. Cut into squares. Serve warm with Pudding Sauce (see recipe page 392), hard sauce, custard sauce or whipped cream. Good reheated. This pudding keeps well and it may also be frozen. *Serves 9.*

# Heavenly Hash

1 11-ounce can Mandarin
  orange sections
1 8-ounce bottle red
  maraschino cherries
1 8-ounce bottle green
  maraschino cherries
2 buffet cans pineapple
  tidbits

1 pound marshmallows
1 pint heavy cream
⅛ teaspoon Cardamom
¾ teaspoon Ginger
1 teaspoon Orange Peel

Drain fruit. Cut marshmallows in half. Whip cream; add cardamom, ginger and orange peel. Gently fold all ingredients together. Refrigerate several hours before serving. *Serves 8 to 10.*

# Peaches Zanzibar

1 No. 2½ can peach halves
2 pieces whole Ginger
2 3-inch pieces Cinnamon
8 whole Allspice
4 whole Cardamom

6 whole Cloves
1 pint vanilla ice cream
½ pint heavy cream,
  whipped
Red and green cherries

Drain peaches, cut ginger into small pieces and add with other spices to the juice. Simmer 15 minutes. Arrange peaches in baking dish and pour spiced juice over top. Cover and chill several hours or overnight. Put scoop of ice cream in coupe or dessert dish. Place peach half over ice cream and spoon juice over peach. Garnish with whipped cream and pieces of red and green cherries. *Serves 5 to 6.*

# *Cheesecake Elégante*

CRUST:

1½ cups graham cracker
  crumbs
¼ cup powdered sugar

1 teaspoon ground Allspice
⅓ cup melted butter

Combine all ingredients. Spread in bottom of a 9-inch spring-form pan, pressing some of the crumbs up the sides to form a rim about 1 inch high.

CHEESE LAYER:

2 8-ounce packages cream
  cheese, at room
  temperature
2 eggs, lightly beaten

⅔ cup sugar
2 teaspoons pure Vanilla
  Extract

Beat cheese until soft and creamy. Add eggs, sugar and vanilla, beating until thoroughly creamed and smooth. Pour into crust. Bake in 350°F. oven 25 minutes then top with sour cream layer.

SOUR CREAM LAYER:

1½ cups commercial sour
  cream
¼ cup sugar

2 teaspoons pure Vanilla
  Extract or Rum Extract

Combine sour cream, sugar and extract. Spread over cheese layer. Return to oven; increase temperature to 450°F. and bake 7 minutes. Remove from oven and cool, then chill. This is very rich so you will want to serve small pieces. *Serves 10 to 12.*

# Choux Glacés à la Crème

Petite cream puffs with a spicy cream filling, colorfully glazed.

½ cup butter
⅛ teaspoon salt
1 cup boiling water
¼ teaspoon Allspice

1 cup sifted all-purpose
  flour
4 eggs
Spiced Cream Filling
Gay Tinted Glaze

Add butter and salt to boiling water and stir until mixture boils again. Sift together allspice and flour. Add all at once to boiling mixture and beat vigorously until mixture leaves side of pan. Remove from heat and add eggs, one at a time, beating hard after each addition. Drop by tablespoonfuls on baking sheet. Bake in 450°F. oven 8 minutes; reduce heat to 350°F. and continue baking 10 minutes or until puffs are lightly browned. Remove from baking sheet immediately, cutting small slit in side of each puff. Cool; fill with Spiced Cream Filling and glaze tops using Gay Tinted Glaze (see recipe page 321). If you want to make very crisp puffs, as soon as puffs are removed from oven, cut off tops and pull out soft centers. Bake shells and tops a few minutes longer. *Makes about 40.*

SPICED CREAM FILLING: To one package instant vanilla pudding add one of the following: 1 teaspoon Ginger, ¼ teaspoon Mace, ¼ teaspoon Cardamom or 1 teaspoon Lemon Peel. Prepare pudding as directed on package.

# *Apple Dumplings*

Pastry for two-crust pie
¼ teaspoon Nutmeg
1 teaspoon Lemon Peel
4 medium-size cooking
   apples
4 teaspoons butter
4 teaspoons Cinnamon Sugar
½ cup brown sugar, packed

½ cup white corn syrup
1 teaspoon Cinnamon
¼ teaspoon Nutmeg
⅛ teaspoon Allspice
⅛ teaspoon Cloves
1½ cups water
2 tablespoons butter

Prepare pastry adding ¼ teaspoon nutmeg and the lemon peel. Roll dough about ⅛ inch thick; cut into 4 equal squares. Peel and core apples. Put an apple in center of each pastry square. Fill center of each apple with 1 teaspoon butter and 1 teaspoon cinnamon sugar. Bring opposite ends of pastry over top of apple, overlap and seal edges. Place about 1 inch apart in buttered baking dish. Combine remaining ingredients and bring to a boil. Bake dumplings in 500°F. oven 10 minutes. Reduce heat to 350°F.; bake 45 minutes longer, basting frequently with syrup. Serve warm with cream or ice cream. *Makes 4 dumplings.*

# CAKES
# FROSTINGS

—— * ——

## Ginger Peach Upside-Down Cake

⅓ cup butter
½ cup brown sugar, packed
1 teaspoon Ginger
1 teaspoon Lemon Peel
1 No. 2 can sliced peaches

Maraschino cherries
Pecan halves
½ package yellow cake mix
1 teaspoon pure Vanilla
    Extract

Melt butter in heavy 10-inch skillet with ovenproof handle or 9-inch square pan. Add brown sugar, ginger and lemon peel; mix well. Spread this mixture evenly over bottom of pan. Drain peaches, saving juice. Arrange peaches, cherries and pecans over sugar mixture in an attractive design. Divide cake mix in half. Prepare cake mix as directed on package being sure to divide all ingredients in half and substituting peach juice for the liquid. Stir in vanilla. Carefully spoon batter over peaches. Bake in 375°F. oven 35 minutes. Turn out on plate. Serve hot or cold and you may top with whipped cream. *Serves 9.*

VARIATION:

*Pineapple Upside-Down Cake*—Make cake following recipe
    above using 1 teaspoon Cinnamon, ¼ teaspoon
    Allspice and 1 No. 2 can sliced pineapple, drained,
    instead of the ginger, lemon peel and peaches.

307

# Cardamom Ripple Cake

1 package white cake mix
¼ teaspoon ground
  Cardamom

1 teaspoon pure Vanilla
  Extract
14 drops Red Food Color

To cake mix add cardamom and vanilla. Prepare cake as directed on package. Pour half the batter into another bowl and tint with food color. Spoon white and pink batters alternately into two greased and floured 8- or 9-inch layer cake pans. Cut through batter with knife several times for rippled effect. Bake as directed on package. Frost with Pink Perfection Frosting (see recipe page 321).

# Golden Saffron Cake

½ cup butter or margarine
1 cup sugar
8 individual pieces Saffron
2 eggs
1 teaspoon pure Vanilla
  Extract

2½ cups sifted cake flour
¼ teaspoon salt
1 tablespoon baking powder
1 cup milk

Cream butter and sugar until light and fluffy. Add saffron which has been finely crushed. Add eggs, one at a time, beating well after each addition. Stir in vanilla. Sift flour, salt and baking powder together; add to butter mixture alternately with milk. If using mixer, set at low speed when mixing in flour. Pour batter into two greased and floured 8-inch cake pans. Bake in 375°F. oven 25 minutes. Remove from pans and when cool frost with Lemon Frosting (see recipe page 324). Decorate with Poppy Seed, Multicolored Décors or Yellow Crystal Décors for added interest.

# Lane Cake

1 cup butter or margarine
2 cups sugar
2 teaspoons pure Vanilla
  Extract
3¼ cups sifted cake flour
3½ teaspoons baking powder

½ teaspoon salt
¼ teaspoon Mace
1 cup milk
8 egg whites, stiffly beaten
Lane Filling

Cream butter and sugar together until light and fluffy; add vanilla. Sift together flour, baking powder, salt and mace. Add flour mixture and milk alternately to butter mixture. Fold in stiffly beaten egg whites. Pour into three greased and floured 9-inch layer cake pans. Bake in 375°F. oven 20 minutes or until cake tests done. Turn out on cake racks; cool. Spread Lane Filling between layers and on top of cake. Store in covered container in cool place about 3 days, allowing cake to ripen. Each day spoon filling that has run off back onto cake.

**LANE FILLING:**

8 egg yolks
1¼ cups sugar
½ cup butter
1 teaspoon Orange Peel
¼ teaspoon Mace
⅛ teaspoon Cardamom
¼ teaspoon salt

1 cup chopped pecans
1 cup finely chopped
  candied pineapple
1 cup finely chopped
  candied cherries
1 cup shredded coconut
⅓ cup bourbon

Beat egg yolks lightly; add sugar, butter, orange peel, mace, cardamom and salt. Cook, stirring constantly, 5 minutes or until sugar melts and mixture thickens slightly. Remove from heat and add remaining ingredients. Cool before spreading on cake. *Makes enough for tops of three 9-inch cake layers.*

# Lemon Angel Food Cake

1½ cups sifted cake flour
2 cups superfine sugar
½ teaspoon salt
1½ teaspoons Cream of Tartar
1½ cups (11 or 12) egg whites

2 teaspoons Lemon Peel
1½ teaspoons pure Vanilla Extract
½ teaspoon Almond Extract
½ teaspoon Lemon Extract

Sift flour and 1 cup of the sugar together three times. Set aside. Add salt and cream of tartar to egg whites; beat until stiff but not dry. Add the remaining cup of sugar, 2 tablespoons at a time; if using mixer, set at low speed. Continue beating until meringue holds stiff peaks. Do not use mixer from this point, but fold with wire whip or spatula. Mix in lemon peel and extracts. Fold in the sugar-flour mixture, 2 tablespoons at a time, mixing well but gently. Push batter into ungreased 10-inch tube pan. Cut through batter with knife to remove any large air bubbles. Bake in 375°F. oven 30 minutes or until no imprint remains when lightly touched. Invert pan on funnel or bottle until cake is completely cooled; remove from pan. Drizzle Lemon Glaze (see recipe page 320) over top.

# Excellent Prune Cake

1 cup coarsely chopped prunes
½ cup butter
1 cup sugar
1 teaspoon Cinnamon
¼ teaspoon Nutmeg
¼ teaspoon Allspice
2 eggs

2 cups all-purpose flour
3 teaspoons baking powder
¼ teaspoon soda
1 teaspoon salt
¼ cup prune juice
½ cup milk
1 cup chopped walnuts

removed from oven, brush with additional syrup and decorate with candied fruits reserved for top. You may bake in two 10-inch tube pans, baking 5 to 6 hours. *Makes 12 to 14 pounds fruit cake.*

---

## Devil's Food Cake

---

3 eggs, separated
1½ cups sugar
½ cup butter
1 teaspoon Cinnamon
¼ teaspoon Nutmeg
2 teaspoons Brandy Extract
3 1-ounce squares
  unsweetened chocolate,
  melted

2 cups sifted cake flour
1 teaspoon soda
½ teaspoon salt
1 cup commercial sour
  cream

Beat egg whites until almost stiff; gradually add ½ cup of the sugar. Continue beating until stiff peaks form; set aside. Cream together butter, the remaining 1 cup sugar and spices until light and fluffy. Add egg yolks, one at a time, beating well after each addition. Stir in extract and melted chocolate. Sift together flour, soda and salt. Add to creamed mixture alternately with sour cream. Gently fold in the stiffly beaten egg whites. Pour into two greased and floured 8-inch square or 9-inch round layer cake pans. Cut through batter with a knife to remove large air bubbles. Bake in 350°F. oven 30 to 35 minutes. Good frosted with Mint Julep Frosting (see recipe page 319). Decorate with Chocolate Décors if desired.

# Pound Cake

3½ cups cake flour
1 teaspoon baking powder
½ teaspoon salt
¼ teaspoon Mace
1¾ cups butter (3½ sticks)
2 cups superfine sugar

8 eggs
1 teaspoon pure Vanilla
  Extract
½ teaspoon Almond Extract
½ teaspoon Lemon Extract

Sift flour, measure and sift twice with baking powder, salt and mace. Cream butter until light and fluffy. Add sugar slowly, beating hard. Continue beating until butter-sugar mixture resembles whipped cream. Add eggs, one at a time, beating well after addition of each. Stir in about half the flour using the lowest position on electric mixer or beat by hand. Add extracts and remaining flour. Pour the batter into two greased and floured 9¼ x 5¼ x 2¾-inch loaf pans or one 10 x4- inch tube pan. Cut through the thick batter several times with a knife to break air bubbles. Bake in 325°F. oven 1 hour to 1 hour and 10 minutes. Remove from pan immediately and let cool on cake rack. This cake will probably have a characteristic rough crack down the center. *Makes 2 loaf cakes or 1 tube cake.*

# Cinnamon Luncheon Cake

1 package yellow cake mix
2 tablespoons butter
  or margarine

¼ cup powdered sugar
2 teaspoons Cinnamon

Prepare the cake as directed on package. When removed from pan, brush top of cake with melted butter. Sprinkle with powdered sugar and cinnamon which have been sifted together. Serve warm. It's good cold too! You will find this cake quick and easy. *Makes 16 servings.*

# Spice Chiffon Cake

2¼ cups sifted cake flour
1½ cups sugar
3 teaspoons baking powder
1 teaspoon salt
1 teaspoon Cinnamon
½ teaspoon Nutmeg
½ teaspoon Allspice

½ teaspoon Cloves
½ cup salad oil
5 egg yolks
¾ cup cold water
1 teaspoon Orange Peel
½ teaspoon Cream of Tartar
1 cup egg whites (7 or 8)

Sift flour, sugar, baking powder, salt and spices into a bowl. Make a well and add oil, egg yolks, water and orange peel. Beat with spoon until smooth. Add cream of tartar to egg whites; beat until stiff but not dry. Pour egg yolk mixture slowly over egg whites, folding just until blended. Do not stir. Pour into ungreased 10-inch tube pan. Bake in 325°F. oven 55 minutes, then increase temperature to 350°F. and bake 10 minutes longer. Invert pan on funnel or bottle until cake is completely cooled; remove from pan. Glaze with Lemon Glaze (see recipe page 320) if desired.

# Gingerbread

¼ cup butter
½ cup brown sugar, packed
1 egg
½ cup molasses
1½ cups all-purpose flour

1 teaspoon soda
1 teaspoon Ginger
½ teaspoon Cinnamon
⅛ teaspoon Cardamom
½ cup buttermilk

Cream butter and sugar until light and fluffy. Add egg, then molasses; beat well. Sift flour, measure and sift again with soda and spices. Add alternately with buttermilk to creamed mixture. Pour into greased 8- or 9-inch square pan. Bake in 350°F. oven 30 minutes. Serve hot or cold with Crème Anglaise (see recipe page 407), lemon sauce or whipped cream. *Serves 6 to 8.*

# Welsh Pork Cake

An old, old recipe, seldom found in cookbooks—excellent.

| | |
|---|---|
| 1 pound bulk pork sausage | 3 cups boiling water |
| 1 pound seedless raisins | 6 cups all-purpose flour |
| 1 pound dates, chopped | 1 tablespoon soda |
| 1 cup nuts, chopped | 2 tablespoons Cinnamon |
| 4 cups brown sugar, packed | 1 tablespoon ground Cloves |
| 1 tablespoon Orange Peel | 2 teaspoons Nutmeg |

Combine sausage, raisins, dates, nuts, sugar, orange peel and boiling water; mix thoroughly. Sift flour, measure and sift again with soda and spices. Add to sausage mixture and mix well. Pour into two 9¼ x 5¼ x 2¾-inch loaf pans which have been greased and lined with paper. Bake in 350°F. oven 1½ hours. Cool; remove from pans. Store in tight containers 3 to 4 weeks. Moisten cakes with brandy at frequent intervals if desired. *Makes 2 cakes.*

# Applesauce Cake

| | |
|---|---|
| ½ cup butter or margarine | ½ teaspoon Nutmeg |
| 1½ cups sugar | ½ teaspoon Cloves |
| 2 eggs, well beaten | 1 cup applesauce |
| 2 cups all-purpose flour | 1 cup chopped golden |
| 1 teaspoon baking powder | seedless raisins |
| ½ teaspoon soda | 1 tablespoon flour |
| ¼ teaspoon salt | 1 cup pecans, chopped |
| 1 teaspoon Cinnamon | |

Cream butter and sugar until light and fluffy. Add eggs, beating well. Sift the 2 cups flour, measure and sift again with baking powder, soda, salt, cinnamon, nutmeg and cloves. Add to butter mixture alternately with apple-sauce. Dredge raisins in the 1 tablespoon flour. Stir raisins and pecans into batter. Pour into well-greased and floured 9¼ x 5¼ x 2¾-inch loaf pan. Bake in 350°F. oven 1 hour. Remove from pan; cool on rack. Serve plain, or you may glaze or frost cake. *Makes 1 loaf cake.*

---

## *Raisin Spice Cupcakes*

---

1 cup raisins
½ cup water
½ teaspoon soda
½ cup butter or shortening
1 cup sugar
1 teaspoon salt
¾ teaspoon Cinnamon
⅛ teaspoon Nutmeg

⅛ teaspoon Allspice
2 eggs
½ teaspoon pure Vanilla
  Extract
2 cups all-purpose flour
½ teaspoon baking powder
½ cup chopped walnuts
Cinnamon Sugar

Boil raisins in water 5 minutes. Drain, reserving ¼ cup liquid (if necessary add water to make ¼ cup). Cool; then add soda to cooled liquid and set aside. Cream butter, sugar, salt, cinnamon, nutmeg and allspice at low speed until thoroughly creamed. Add eggs and vanilla and beat at high speed until light and fluffy. Sift flour, measure and sift again with baking powder. Add about ¼ flour mixture at a time alternately with small amount of the raisin liquid, mixing just until smooth after each addition. Stir in walnuts and drained raisins. Spoon into muffin cups which have been greased and floured or lined with paper baking cups, filling two thirds full. Sprinkle tops generously with cinnamon sugar. Bake in 350°F. oven 20 to 25 minutes. *Makes about 20 cupcakes.*

# Old-Fashioned Spice Cake

2½ cups sifted cake flour
2 teaspoons baking powder
½ teaspoon soda
½ teaspoon salt
¼ teaspoon Cloves
¼ teaspoon Nutmeg
  or Mace
½ teaspoon Allspice
1 teaspoon Cinnamon
½ cup shortening
1¼ cups brown sugar,
  packed
3 eggs
1 cup buttermilk

Sift flour, baking powder, soda, salt and spices together. Cream shortening and sugar until light and fluffy. Add eggs, one at a time, beating well after addition of each. Add flour mixture alternately with buttermilk. Pour batter into two greased and floured 9-inch layer cake pans. Bake in 350°F. oven 30 minutes. Remove from pan; cool on racks. Frost with Cinnamon Frosting (see recipe page 322). Decorate with walnut halves.

# Poppy Seed Cake

4 eggs, separated
1 cup butter or margarine
1 cup commercial sour
  cream
1½ cups sugar
⅓ cup Poppy Seed
1 teaspoon soda
2 cups sifted cake flour

Have eggs, butter and sour cream at room temperature. Beat egg whites until almost stiff; gradually beat in ½ cup of the sugar. Continue beating until stiff peaks form; set aside. Cream together butter and the remaining sugar until light and fluffy. Add egg yolks, one at a time, beating well after each addition. Stir in poppy seed. Combine soda and sour cream; add to creamed mixture

318

alternately with flour. (Add about ¼ of the flour first, then ⅓ of the cream, and repeat until all is used, mixing just until smooth after each addition.) Gently fold in the stiffly beaten egg whites. Spoon into an ungreased 9-inch tube pan (line bottom with paper if desired). Bake in 350°F. oven 1 hour. Loosen around sides and carefully turn out on rack to cool. Delicious served while still warm.

## Mint Julep Frosting

2 egg whites
1½ cups sugar
½ teaspoon Cream of Tartar
Dash salt
⅓ cup water

1 teaspoon Mint Extract
or Mint and Peppermint
Extract
Green Food Color

Put all ingredients, except extract and food color, in top of double boiler. Beat 1 minute with electric mixer or rotary beater. Cook over boiling water, beating constantly, 7 minutes or until peaks form. Remove from heat; add extract and a few drops food color. Continue beating until spreading consistency is reached. *Makes enough to frost one 10-inch tube cake or tops and sides of two 9-inch cake layers.*

# Fluffy Snow Peak Frosting

A divinity type frosting—delicately spiced.

2 cups sugar
2 tablespoons light corn
  syrup
¾ cup hot water
2 egg whites

⅛ teaspoon Cardamom
¼ teaspoon Nutmeg
½ teaspoon pure Vanilla
  Extract

Combine sugar, corn syrup and hot water. Cook over low heat, stirring, until sugar is dissolved. Wash down sides of pan with water to prevent crystals forming. Cook to 240° on candy thermometer (soft ball stage). Beat egg whites until stiff but not dry; beat in spices. Slowly add hot syrup to egg whites, continuing to beat. Add vanilla and continue beating until frosting loses its gloss and holds a stiff peak. *Makes enough to frost tops and sides of two 8- or 9-inch cake layers.*

# Lemon Glaze

Glazes are easy—festive too!

2 cups sifted powdered sugar
2 teaspoons Lemon Peel

½ teaspoon Lemon Extract
3 tablespoons hot water

Combine all ingredients and mix well. Drizzle over top of cakes, doughnuts, sweet rolls, pastries or cream puffs. *Makes about ¾ cup.*

VARIATIONS:

*Cinnamon Glaze*—Use ½ teaspoon Cinnamon in place of lemon peel and lemon extract in above recipe.

*Nutmeg Glaze*—Use ¼ teaspoon Nutmeg in place of lemon peel and lemon extract in above recipe.

*Allspice Glaze*—Use ⅛ teaspoon Allspice in place of lemon peel and lemon extract in above recipe.

*Orange Glaze*—Use ½ teaspoon Orange Peel and ¼ teaspoon Orange Extract in place of lemon peel and lemon extract in above recipe.

*Gay Tinted Glaze*—Add several drops Red, Yellow, Green or Blue Food Color, or a combination of these colors to obtain desired shade or color in Lemon Glaze recipe.

# Sour Cream Frosting

An unusually good frosting.

2 pounds powdered sugar
⅛ teaspoon Cream of Tartar
2 egg whites
¼ cup (white) vegetable shortening
¼ cup commercial sour cream
1 teaspoon pure Vanilla Extract

Sift sugar; reserve about 2 cups. Add cream of tartar to egg whites; beat until very stiff. Cream shortening until light and fluffy; add sugar alternately with sour cream and egg whites. Stir in vanilla. Add part or all of the reserved sugar until the desired spreading consistency is reached. *Makes about 3½ cups, enough to frost tops and sides of two 9-inch cake layers or three 8-inch cake layers.*

VARIATION:

*Pink Perfection Frosting*—Make frosting following recipe above, reducing vanilla to ½ teaspoon and adding 2 teaspoons Strawberry, Raspberry or Cherry Extract and about 8 drops Red Food Color. Tint part of the frosting a deeper shade for decorating cake.

# Spiced Whipped Cream Topping

Melt-in-your-mouth flavor, superb on lemon or orange cakes.

1 cup heavy cream
1 cup powdered sugar
1 teaspoon pure Vanilla
  Extract

½ teaspoon Pumpkin Pie
  Spice

Whip cream until it forms soft peaks. Stir in sugar, vanilla and pumpkin pie spice. Beat until well blended and stiff. Spread on top of an 8- or 9-inch cake layer. Serve immediately, or chill until ready to serve. This topping is excellent when served on chocolate, spice, applesauce, white or yellow cake. You will also find this delicious on waffles, stewed fruits or as a topping for fruit pies. *Makes 1⅔ cups.*

**VARIATION:**

*Orange Whipped Cream Topping*—Use 1 teaspoon Orange
  Peel and omit pumpkin pie spice in above recipe.


# Cinnamon Frosting

1 pound powdered sugar
1 tablespoon Cinnamon
¼ cup melted butter

1 egg white
Dash salt
3 tablespoons milk

Sift sugar and cinnamon together. Add about one third of it to butter, creaming with mixer or by hand. Beat in egg white and salt. Add the remaining sugar and enough milk to get the desired spreading consistency. Beat hard. Use to frost spice or applesauce cakes. *Makes enough to frost tops and sides of two 8- or 9-inch cake layers.*

# Broiled Spice Topping

A tasty and quick way to frost a layer of cake.

⅓ cup soft butter
⅔ cup brown sugar, packed
¼ cup cream
¾ teaspoon pure Vanilla
  Extract

½ teaspoon Orange Peel
1 teaspoon Cinnamon
¼ teaspoon Nutmeg
⅛ teaspoon Cloves
1 cup flake coconut

Thoroughly combine all ingredients. Spread evenly over warm cake before removing from pan. Broil 4 inches from heat 3 minutes or until lightly browned. Especially good on a white or yellow cake and is an easy topping to make when using a cake mix. *Makes enough to frost one 9-inch square cake.*

# Spicy Chocolate Frosting

3 1-ounce squares
  unsweetened chocolate
¼ cup melted butter
2½ tablespoons hot water
1 teaspoon pure Vanilla
  Extract

1½ cups powdered sugar
¼ teaspoon Mace
¼ teaspoon Cinnamon
⅛ teaspoon Allspice
3 egg yolks

Melt chocolate in top of double boiler or over lowest heat. Remove from heat; stir in butter, hot water and vanilla. Sift sugar and combine with spices; gradually beat into chocolate mixture alternately with egg yolks. Beat hard. *Makes 1½ cups frosting, enough to frost tops and sides of two 8- or 9-inch cake layers or one 9- or 10-inch tube cake.*

# Lemon Frosting

2 egg whites
1½ cups sugar
½ teaspoon Cream of Tartar
1 teaspoon Lemon Peel
Dash salt

¼ cup water
2 tablespoons lemon juice
1 teaspoon pure Vanilla
   Extract
Yellow Food Color, optional

Combine egg whites, sugar, cream of tartar, lemon peel, salt and water in top of double boiler. Beat 1 minute with electric mixer or rotary beater. Add lemon juice and cook over boiling water, beating constantly, 7 minutes or until peaks form. Remove from heat; add vanilla and a few drops food color. Beat until spreading consistency is reached. *Makes enough to frost tops and sides of two 9-inch cake layers.*

NOTE: For an even creamier frosting, transfer the frosting from the double boiler to a mixing bowl as soon as you remove it from the heat. Add extract and food color and continue as above.

# PIES

—— * ——

---
## Blackberry Cobbler
---

1 pastry recipe for
  two-crust pie
6 cups fresh blackberries
2 teaspoons quick-cooking
  tapioca
¾ cup sugar

½ teaspoon Cinnamon
1 teaspoon pure Vanilla
  Extract
2 tablespoons butter
1 tablespoon Arrowroot
1 tablespoon sugar

Prepare pastry; roll out half of it and line 1½-quart shallow baking dish. Cook blackberries just until heated through. Remove 1 cup of the juice and set aside. Combine blackberries and the remaining juice with tapioca, the ¾ cup sugar and cinnamon. Pour into pastry-lined baking dish; sprinkle with vanilla and dot with butter. Make lattice top using 1-inch wide strips of pastry. Bake in 425°F. oven 15 minutes; reduce temperature to 350°F. and bake 30 minutes longer. Combine the 1 cup reserved juice and arrowroot and cook, stirring, over medium heat until thickened. Remove from heat and stir in the 1 tablespoon sugar. Serve cobbler in bowls with sauce spooned over top. You may like to serve with cream, whipped cream or ice cream. *Serves 8.*

# Blueberry Crumble

Easier than rolling out pie crust, deliciously good.

2½ cups fresh blueberries
or 2 10-ounce packages
frozen unsweetened
blueberries
½ cup sugar
¼ teaspoon Orange Peel
Dash Mace

⅛ teaspoon Cardamom
1 cup pie crust mix
1 tablespoon butter
2 teaspoons lemon juice
½ teaspoon pure Vanilla
Extract

Place blueberries in buttered 1¼-quart shallow baking
dish. Combine sugar, orange peel, mace and cardamom.
Sprinkle sugar mixture and pie crust mix in alternate
layers over blueberries. Continue until all is used. Dot
with butter. Drizzle lemon juice and vanilla over all.
Bake in 350°F. oven 45 minutes. Serve with cream if
desired. *Serves 4 to 6.*

# Pumpkin Pie

Pastry for 9-inch pie shell
2 eggs
1½ cups mashed, cooked
pumpkin
½ cup brown sugar, packed

1 tablespoon Pumpkin Pie
Spice
1½ teaspoons Arrowroot
½ teaspoon salt
1½ cups milk

Line a 9-inch pie plate with pastry. Beat eggs until light
and fluffy; stir in pumpkin. Combine sugar, pumpkin pie
spice, arrowroot and salt. Add to pumpkin mixture,
mixing thoroughly. Gradually stir in milk. Part light
cream or half and half makes a richer filling and may be
used if desired. Pour into pastry shell. Bake in 450°F. oven
15 minutes. Reduce temperature to 350°F. and continue
baking 40 minutes or until silver knife inserted in center

comes out clean. Serve plain or topped with whipped cream. *Serves 6 to 8.*

NOTE: If desired, make your own spice blend to use in place of pumpkin pie spice in above recipe. For a spicy pie use 1½ teaspoons Cinnamon, ½ teaspoon Ginger, ½ teaspoon Nutmeg, ¼ teaspoon Cloves and ¼ teaspoon Allspice. For a milder spice note use 1 teaspoon Cinnamon, ¼ teaspoon Ginger, ¼ teaspoon Nutmeg and ⅛ teaspoon Allspice. Of course, you may use other spices in varying amounts as desired.

## *Deep Dish Apple Pie*

| | |
|---|---|
| 1 pastry recipe for one-crust pie | ¼ teaspoon Nutmeg |
| | ¼ teaspoon Cloves |
| 6 cups sliced tart apples | 2 tablespoons water |
| ¾ cup sugar | 1 teaspoon Brandy Extract |
| ¼ cup flour | 2 tablespoons butter |
| 1 teaspoon Cinnamon | Cinnamon Sugar |

Prepare pastry; set aside. Toss together apples, sugar, flour, cinnamon, nutmeg and cloves. In place of the spices listed above, you may use 1½ teaspoons Apple Pie Spice if desired. Put in buttered 1½-quart shallow baking dish. Sprinkle with water and extract; dot with butter. Roll pastry to ⅛-inch thickness. Place on top of baking dish. Trim, leaving ½-inch overhang. Fold the overhang back and under; flute edges. Cut two or three steam vents in top of pastry. Sprinkle top with cinnamon sugar. Bake in 425°F. oven 15 minutes; reduce temperature to 350°F. and bake 30 minutes longer or until top is nicely browned. Serve warm or cold with cream or ice cream. *Serves 8.*

327

# Strawberry Patch Pie

**MERINGUE CRACKER CRUST:**

3 egg whites
1 cup sugar
⅛ teaspoon Mace
1 teaspoon pure Vanilla
   Extract

12 soda crackers,
   crushed
1 teaspoon baking powder
¾ cup chopped nuts

Beat egg whites until stiff. Combine sugar and mace; add, one tablespoon at a time, to egg whites, beating well after each addition. Add vanilla. Combine crushed soda crackers, baking powder and nuts. Fold into egg white mixture. Spoon into a buttered 10-inch pie plate, pushing mixture to conform to shape of pie plate. Bake in 350°F. oven 30 minutes. Cool. You will find this crust excellent for chiffon or ice cream pie.

**STRAWBERRY FILLING:**

1½ cups crushed fresh
   strawberries
¼ cup sugar
1 teaspoon Lemon Peel

1 envelope unflavored
   gelatine
¼ cup cold water
30 whole fresh strawberries

Combine crushed strawberries, sugar and lemon peel. Soften gelatine in cold water, then melt over hot water. Add to crushed berry mixture. Chill until mixture begins to thicken. Spread half of the mixture over bottom of cooled crust. Add enough whole berries, placing them stem end down and close together to fill the pie. Carefully spoon remaining crushed berry mixture around whole berries. Chill until firm. You may serve with whipped cream if desired. *Makes one 10-inch pie.*

# Wonderful Apple Pie

Pastry for 9- or 10-inch
  pie shell
1 cup light brown sugar,
  packed
½ cup all-purpose flour
1 teaspoon Cinnamon
⅛ teaspoon Allspice
⅛ teaspoon Cloves
⅛ teaspoon Nutmeg
½ teaspoon Lemon Peel
½ cup butter
6 medium-size apples
  or 2 No. 2 cans
  pie-sliced apples

Line pie plate with pastry. Mix sugar, flour, spices and butter with pastry blender until crumbly. You may use 1½ teaspoons Apple Pie Spice in place of above spices if desired. Spread one third of this mixture over bottom of unbaked pastry. Peel apples, core and cut into slices; put in crust. Spoon remaining sugar and spice mixture over apples. Bake in 400°F. oven 50 to 55 minutes. *Serves 6 to 8.*

# Deep Dish Peach Pie

1 pastry recipe for
  two-crust pie
6 cups sliced peaches
¾ cup sugar
¼ cup flour
¼ teaspoon Nutmeg
¼ teaspoon Allspice
Dash Cardamom
2 tablespoons water
2 tablespoons butter
Cinnamon Sugar

Prepare pastry; roll out half of it and line 1½-quart shallow baking dish. Toss together peaches, sugar, flour, nutmeg, allspice and cardamom. Place in pastry-lined baking dish. Sprinkle with water and dot with butter. Cover with a lattice top and sprinkle with cinnamon sugar. Bake in 425°F. oven 15 minutes; reduce temperature to 350°F. and bake 50 minutes longer. Especially good served with cream. *Serves 8.*

# Raspberry Cloud Pie

2 10-ounce packages frozen
  raspberries, thawed
2 cups vanilla wafer crumbs
¼ cup sugar
1 teaspoon Cinnamon
5 tablespoons melted butter

1 envelope unflavored
  gelatine
¼ cup cold water
½ teaspoon Lemon Peel
½ pint heavy cream
1 teaspoon pure Vanilla
  Extract

Drain raspberries, reserving 1 cup of the juice. Combine crumbs, sugar, ½ teaspoon of the cinnamon and the butter; pat into a 10-inch pie plate. Bake in 375°F. oven 8 to 10 minutes; cool. Soften gelatine in water. Mix the reserved raspberry juice, the remaining ½ teaspoon cinnamon and lemon peel and heat to boiling. Remove from heat; add gelatine and stir until melted. Chill until mixture just begins to thicken. Whip cream; add vanilla. Fold raspberries, gelatine mixture and whipped cream together. Pour into pie shell. Chill. You may decorate with additional whipped cream if desired. *Serves 6 to 8.*

# Spicy Custard Pie

Pastry for 9-inch pie shell
4 eggs
6 tablespoons sugar
¼ teaspoon salt
¼ teaspoon Mace

1 teaspoon pure Vanilla
  Extract
2¾ cups milk
Dash Nutmeg

Line a 9-inch pie plate with pastry. Break eggs into bowl, removing enough of one egg white to lightly brush the bottom of the pastry shell. Beat eggs lightly; add sugar, salt, mace, vanilla and milk, mixing well. Pour custard into pie shell; sprinkle top with nutmeg. Bake in 450°F. oven 10 minutes. Reduce heat to 300°F. and bake 45 minutes longer or just until silver knife inserted in center of pie comes out clean. Caution: You will find overbaking makes custard watery. *Serves 6 to 8.*

# Cherry Pie

1 pastry recipe for
  two-crust pie
2 No. 2 cans red tart
  pitted cherries
4 tablespoons cornstarch
1 cup sugar
⅛ teaspoon Nutmeg

⅛ teaspoon Allspice
½ teaspoon Lemon Peel
¼ teaspoon salt
1 tablespoon butter
  or margarine
½ teaspoon Almond Extract

Line 9-inch pie plate with pastry. Drain cherries, saving juice. Combine cornstarch with ½ cup of the cherry juice; bring to a boil and cook, stirring constantly, until thick and clear. Remove from heat. Add sugar, nutmeg, allspice, lemon peel, salt, butter and extract. Mix well. Carefully stir in cherries to prevent crushing. Fill pie shell. Make lattice top and a stand-up fluted rim. Bake in 425°F. oven 35 minutes. *Serves 6 to 8.*

---

# Elegant Peach Pie

Sesame Seed Pastry
¾ cup brown sugar, packed
3 tablespoons quick-cooking
  tapioca
½ teaspoon Lemon Peel

¾ teaspoon Ginger
4 cups sliced fresh peaches
2 tablespoons butter
¼ teaspoon Almond Extract

Prepare Sesame Seed Pastry (see recipe page 334) and line 9-inch pie plate. Combine brown sugar, tapioca, lemon peel and ginger. Sprinkle half of this mixture over bottom of pastry. Arrange peaches over sugar mixture. Sprinkle remaining sugar mixture over peaches; dot with butter. Drizzle almond extract over all. Cover with a lattice top. Bake in 425°F. oven 10 minutes; reduce temperature to 350°F. and continue baking 30 minutes. For variety serve à la mode. *Serves 6 to 8.*

# Cranberry Chiffon Pie

| | |
|---|---|
| 1 baked 10-inch pastry shell | ¼ teaspoon Cream of Tartar |
| 1 envelope unflavored gelatine | 8 drops Red Food Color |
| ½ cup water | 2 cups crushed raw cranberries |
| 4 eggs, separated | ½ pint heavy cream |
| 2 tablespoons lemon juice | 2 tablespoons powdered sugar |
| 1 cup sugar | |
| 1 teaspoon Orange Peel | |

Bake and cool pastry shell. Soften gelatine in ¼ cup of the water. Beat egg yolks lightly; mix in the remaining ¼ cup water, lemon juice, ½ cup of the sugar and orange peel. Cook in double boiler, stirring, until thick. Add softened gelatine; stir until melted. Set aside to cool. Add cream of tartar to egg whites and beat until stiff. Gradually beat in the remaining ½ cup sugar. Blend in food color. Fold cooled mixture into egg whites, then fold in crushed cranberries. Pour into pie shell; chill until firm. Whip cream, gradually adding powdered sugar. Spread on top of pie before serving. *Serves 6 to 8.*

# Coconut Crust

| | |
|---|---|
| 1½ cups flake coconut | ¼ cup finely chopped pecans |
| 2 tablespoons melted butter | ¼ teaspoon Pumpkin Pie Spice |
| ¼ cup finely crushed graham cracker crumbs | ½ teaspoon Orange Peel |
| 2 tablespoons sugar | |

Combine coconut and butter; mix well. Add remaining ingredients, mixing thoroughly. Press firmly over bottom and around sides of 9-inch pie plate. Bake in 375°F. oven 8 minutes or until lightly browned. Chill. Fill with ice cream, chiffon or cream pie filling. *Makes one 9-inch crust.*

# Black Bottom Pie

24 small gingersnaps
¼ cup melted butter
  or margarine
2 teaspoons unflavored
  gelatine
¼ cup cold water
2 eggs, separated
2 cups milk, scalded
1 cup sugar
1½ tablespoons Arrowroot
⅛ teaspoon salt

2 1-ounce squares
  unsweetened chocolate,
  melted
⅛ teaspoon Mace
1 teaspoon pure Vanilla
  Extract
¼ teaspoon Rum Extract
1 teaspoon Cream of Tartar
1 cup heavy cream
1 tablespoon powdered sugar
1 tablespoon shaved bitter
  or semi-sweet chocolate

Roll gingersnaps into fine crumbs; you should have about 1½ cups. Blend in butter; press evenly into bottom and around sides of 10-inch pie plate. Bake in 350°F. oven 5 minutes. Cool. Soak gelatine in water. Beat egg yolks; slowly add scalded milk, stirring constantly. Mix together ¾ cup of the sugar, arrowroot and salt; stir into milk-egg yolk mixture. Cook over low heat, stirring constantly, until mixture thickens and coats a metal spoon. Remove from heat. To one cup of the custard mixture add the melted chocolate, mace and vanilla; mix well. Spoon into crust and allow to cool. To the remaining custard mixture add gelatine, stirring until melted. Cool. Stir in rum extract. Add cream of tartar to egg whites and beat until stiff but not dry. Gradually add the remaining ¼ cup sugar, beating constantly. Fold into gelatine-custard mixture; spread over chocolate layer in pie crust. Chill. Before serving whip cream until stiff. Add powdered sugar, mixing well. Spread whipped cream on pie and sprinkle with chocolate shavings. Or, you may want to use Chocolate Décors. *Serves 6 to 8.*

# Plain Pastry

**ONE-CRUST:**

1 cup sifted all-purpose flour  
½ teaspoon salt  

⅓ cup shortening  
2 tablespoons cold water

**TWO-CRUST:**

2 cups all-purpose flour  
1 teaspoon salt  

⅔ cup shortening  
4 tablespoons cold water

Sift flour and salt into a bowl. Remove about ¼ cup of the mixture; set aside. With pastry blender or two knives cut in shortening until particles are the size of peas. (For a shorter, richer pastry, increase shortening 1 tablespoon for each cup flour.) Make a paste of the ¼ cup flour and water; sprinkle over flour-shortening mixture. Using a fork, quickly blend together until the flour is moistened and can be pressed into a ball; overmixing causes pastry to be tough. Roll out on lightly floured board to ⅛-inch thickness. Line pie plate. For a baked pastry shell, prick thoroughly with tines of a fork. Bake in 475°F. oven 8 minutes or until golden brown.

**VARIATIONS:**

*Sesame Seed Pastry*—Toast Sesame Seed in 350°F. oven 15 minutes or until golden; cool. Add 2 tablespoons Sesame Seed to flour-shortening mixture for one-crust pastry and 4 tablespoons for two-crust pastry.

*Lemon Pastry*—Add ¾ teaspoon Lemon Peel to flour-shortening mixture for one-crust pastry and 1¼ teaspoons Lemon Peel for two-crust pastry.

*Poppy Seed Pastry*—Add 2 teaspoons Poppy Seed to flour-shortening mixture for one-crust pastry; 4 teaspoons Poppy Seed for two-crust pastry.

*Spicy Pastry*—Add ⅛ to ¼ teaspoon Nutmeg, Allspice, Mace, Cardamom or Cloves to flour-shortening mixture for one-crust pastry and ¼ to ½ teaspoon of any one of these spices for two-crust pastry.

---

## Spiced Coconut Chiffon Pie

---

1 baked 9- or 10-inch pastry
  shell
1½ cups flake coconut
1 teaspoon Cinnamon
¼ teaspoon Ginger
⅛ teaspoon Cardamom
1 envelope unflavored
  gelatine
¼ cup cold water

4 eggs, separated
½ cup sugar
¼ teaspoon salt
1 cup milk, scalded
1 teaspoon pure Vanilla
  Extract
¼ teaspoon Cream of Tartar
1 pint heavy cream

Bake and cool pastry shell. Combine 1 cup of the coconut with spices. If desired ¾ teaspoon Pumpkin Pie Spice and ⅛ teaspoon Mace may be substituted for the above spices. Spread in a shallow pan. Toast in 350°F. oven 8 minutes or until brown, stirring occasionally. Soften gelatine in water. Beat egg yolks; stir in sugar and salt. Slowly add scalded milk, stirring constantly. Cook over low heat, stirring, until mixture thickens. Add gelatine; stir until melted. Cool. Stir in vanilla and the remaining ½ cup coconut. Add cream of tartar to egg whites and beat until stiff but not dry. Whip ½ pint of the cream until stiff. Fold egg whites and whipped cream into egg yolk mixture. Line bottom of pie shell with half the toasted coconut. Pour filling into shell. Chill. Before serving, whip remaining cream and spoon on top of pie; sprinkle with remaining toasted coconut. *Serves 6 to 8.*

# Festive Lime Pie

**GINGER CRACKER CRUST:**

¼ cup finely minced
  Crystallized Ginger
1½ cups crushed graham
  crackers

½ cup powdered sugar
¼ cup melted butter
  or margarine
Dash Nutmeg

Mix the finely minced ginger, cracker crumbs and powdered sugar so that the pieces of ginger will be evenly distributed throughout. Add melted butter; mix well. Press mixture into bottom and around sides of 9-inch pie plate; sprinkle with one or two dashes of nutmeg. Bake in 325°F. oven 10 minutes. Cool.

**LIME CHIFFON FILLING:**

1 envelope unflavored
  gelatine
2 tablespoons cold water
4 eggs, separated
1 cup sugar

¼ teaspoon salt
½ cup lime juice
½ teaspoon grated lime rind
Green Food Color

Soften gelatine in cold water. Beat egg yolks in top of double boiler or saucepan. Stir in ½ cup of the sugar, salt and lime juice, mixing well. Cook over boiling water or lowest heat, stirring constantly, until mixture thickens slightly. Remove from heat. Add gelatine and lime rind. Continue stirring until gelatine melts. Set aside to cool. Beat egg whites until soft peaks form. Add the remaining sugar, 1 tablespoon at a time, and 6 to 8 drops green food color. Beat 3 to 4 minutes longer. Fold the cooled gelatine mixture into egg whites, folding gently but thoroughly. You may also fold in one half cup heavy cream, whipped, if desired. Pour into pie shell and chill. Garnish with paper-thin slices of lime. *Serves 6 to 8.*

# Fried Pies

2 cups all-purpose flour
½ teaspoon Nutmeg
¼ teaspoon Cloves
½ teaspoon salt
½ teaspoon soda
½ cup shortening

1 tablespoon vinegar
5 tablespoons cold water
Filling
Fat for frying
Cinnamon Sugar

Sift flour, measure and sift again with nutmeg, cloves, salt and soda. With pastry blender or two knives cut shortening into flour until particles are size of peas. Add vinegar and water and mix until dry ingredients are moist. Chill. Roll out thin and cut into 4-inch squares. Put one tablespoon filling on one half of each pastry square; moisten edges. Fold other half of pastry over filling to form triangle. Seal edges well, pressing with the tines of a fork. Chill. Fry in deep fat, 375°F., until golden brown. Drain on absorbent paper. Sprinkle with cinnamon sugar. *Makes about 16 pies.*

APPLE FILLING:

1 8-ounce package
   dried apples
½ teaspoon Nutmeg

½ teaspoon Cinnamon
1 teaspoon Lemon Peel
1 tablespoon sugar

Simmer apples in small amount of water until soft. Drain and mash or cut into small pieces. Combine with remaining ingredients. Cool. *Makes filling for 16 pies.*

APRICOT FILLING:

1 8-ounce package
   dried apricots
1 tablespoon sugar

1 teaspoon Orange Peel
¼ teaspoon Coriander Seed,
   crushed

Simmer apricots in small amount of water until soft. Drain. Cut into small pieces. Combine with remaining ingredients. Cool. This is a tart filling and you may prefer to add more sugar. *Makes filling for 16 pies.*

337

# Sweet Potato–Pecan Pie

Out of the Old South, a memorable pastry.

Pastry for 9-inch pie shell
1 cup brown sugar, packed
½ teaspoon salt
2 teaspoons Pumpkin Pie
  Spice

3 eggs
1½ cups milk
1½ cups cooked mashed
  sweet potatoes
Pecan Topping

Line 9-inch pie plate with pastry and make a high fluted edge. Mix sugar, salt and pumpkin pie spice; stir in eggs, mixing well. Add milk and sweet potatoes and mix thoroughly. Pour into pie shell. Bake in 425°F. oven 10 minutes; reduce heat to 300°F. and bake 30 minutes. Cover top of pie with Pecan Topping. Bake 30 minutes longer or until silver knife comes out clean when inserted in center. *Serves 6 to 8.*

PECAN TOPPING:

2 tablespoons melted butter
¼ cup dark brown sugar,
  packed

1 cup chopped pecans
1 teaspoon Pumpkin Pie
  Spice

Combine all ingredients; mix well. Spoon over pie.

# Spicy Lemon Angel Pie

Spiced Graham Cracker
  Crust
1 envelope unflavored
  gelatine
2 tablespoons cold water
1 15-ounce can sweetened
  condensed milk

3 eggs, separated
½ teaspoon Lemon Peel
¼ teaspoon Ginger
¼ teaspoon Mace
1 cup heavy cream
¾ cup lemon juice

Make Spiced Graham Cracker Crust for a 10-inch pie (see recipe page 340). Soak gelatine in cold water to soften; then set over hot water to melt. Combine milk, egg yolks, lemon peel, ginger and mace. Heat over boiling water or lowest heat on range, beating with a rotary beater until slightly warm. Stir in melted gelatine, mixing well. Beat egg whites in a large bowl until stiff. Whip cream. Add lemon juice to gelatine mixture, beating with rotary beater until thoroughly mixed. Gently fold beaten egg whites, whipped cream and gelatine mixture together. Pile into crust. Chill. Serve plain or you may decorate top with rosettes of whipped cream. *Serves 8.*

## Banbury Tarts

| | |
|---|---|
| 1 pastry recipe for two-crust pie | 1 tablespoon butter, melted |
| ½ teaspoon Lemon Peel | ⅛ teaspoon salt |
| 1 cup raisins | ¼ teaspoon Nutmeg |
| 1 cup sugar | 2 tablespoons Lemon Peel |
| 3 tablespoons cracker meal | 2 tablespoons lemon juice |
| 2 egg yolks | ½ cup chopped nuts |

To a plain pastry recipe for a two-crust pie or packaged mix add the ½ teaspoon lemon peel. Soak raisins in warm water 15 minutes; drain. Put raisins through food grinder, or chop fine, and combine with remaining ingredients. Roll pastry thin. Cut 5-inch circles or squares. Put a heaping tablespoon of the filling on one half of each pastry circle or square; moisten edges. Fold other half of pastry over filling and seal edge by pressing with tines of a fork. Prick top of tarts and put on baking sheet. Bake in 400°F. oven 15 minutes or until lightly browned. Serve plain or with lemon sauce for dessert. You will also find these excellent for picnics or lunch box surprises. *Makes about 14 tarts.*

# Easy Mincemeat Pie

Add your own fresh spices to prepared mincemeat for real homemade flavor.

Pastry for 9-inch pie shell
1 1-pound 12-ounce jar
  prepared mincemeat
1 medium-size apple, grated
½ teaspoon Cinnamon

⅛ teaspoon Allspice
⅛ teaspoon Nutmeg
⅛ teaspoon Ginger
2 tablespoons Brandy Extract

Line a 9-inch pie plate with pastry. Combine all remaining ingredients and pour into unbaked pastry shell. If mincemeat seems quite moist, bring to boil and cook to reduce moisture before filling pastry. Add top crust or make lattice top if desired. Bake in 425°F. oven 30 to 35 minutes. For a festive dinner, you may like to serve this pie topped with hard sauce or whipped cream. *Serves 6 to 8.*

# Spiced Graham Cracker Crust

1½ cups graham cracker
  crumbs (about 20 squares)
¼ cup soft or melted butter
  or margarine

¼ cup sugar
⅛ teaspoon Nutmeg

Combine all ingredients in 9- or 10-inch pie plate. Mix thoroughly with fingers. If a fork or pastry blender is used, it is better to mix in a bowl and transfer to pie plate. Press crumbs evenly over bottom and around sides of pie plate. Bake in 350°F. oven 8 minutes. Cool. If you are making an ice cream pie, freeze crust before filling. *Makes 9- or 10-inch pie crust.*

NOTE: For intriguing spice variations, add one of the following in place of nutmeg:

⅛ teaspoon Mace  
⅛ teaspoon Cloves  
¼ teaspoon Allspice  

½ teaspoon Cinnamon  
½ teaspoon Ginger  
⅛ teaspoon Cardamom  

---

## Chocolate-Mace Cream Pie

1 baked 9-inch pastry shell  
1½ cups sugar  
½ teaspoon salt  
5 tablespoons cornstarch  
1 tablespoon flour  
¼ teaspoon Mace  
3 cups milk  
3 1-ounce squares  
  unsweetened chocolate,  
  melted  

3 eggs, separated  
1 tablespoon butter  
1½ teaspoons pure Vanilla  
  Extract  
¼ teaspoon Cream of Tartar  
6 tablespoons sugar  

Bake and cool pastry shell. In a saucepan blend together the 1½ cups sugar, salt, cornstarch, flour and mace. Gradually stir in milk and melted chocolate. Cook over medium heat, stirring constantly, until thickened. Remove from heat. Gradually stir part of this hot mixture into the lightly beaten egg yolks. Blend the two mixtures; add butter. Return to heat and continue cooking until thick, stirring constantly. Remove from heat; cool. Stir in vanilla. Pour into pastry shell. Add cream of tartar to egg whites and beat until peaks form. Add the 6 tablespoons sugar, 1 tablespoon at a time. Beat hard 5 minutes. Spoon meringue over top of chocolate filling, being sure to bring meringue to edge of crust. Bake in 400°F. oven 8 minutes or until lightly browned. Chill several hours before serving. *Serves 6 to 8.*

341

# Velvety Pumpkin Chiffon Pie

| | |
|---|---|
| 1 baked 10-inch pastry shell | 2 teaspoons Pumpkin Pie |
| 1 envelope unflavored | Spice |
|   gelatine | ½ teaspoon salt |
| ¼ cup cold water | ½ cup milk |
| 3 eggs, separated | ¼ teaspoon Cream of Tartar |
| ¾ cup brown sugar, packed | 6 tablespoons sugar |
| 1⅓ cups mashed, cooked | 1 cup heavy cream, whipped |
|   pumpkin | |

Bake and cool pastry shell. Soften gelatine in water. Beat egg yolks; add brown sugar, pumpkin, pumpkin pie spice and salt. (You may increase the pumpkin pie spice to 3 teaspoons for a delightful heavy spice note.) Mix well, then stir in milk. Cook over medium heat, stirring, until it begins to boil. Then cook 2 minutes, stirring constantly. Remove from heat. Add softened gelatine, stirring until melted. Cool. Add cream of tartar to egg whites and beat until soft peaks form. Add the 6 tablespoons sugar, 1 tablespoon at a time, beating until stiff but not dry. Beat cooled pumpkin mixture until smooth, then gently fold in egg whites. Spoon into crust. Chill. Top with whipped cream. *Serves 6 to 8.*

VARIATION:

*Harvest Pumpkin Chiffon Pie*—In the above recipe, after beating the pumpkin mixture until smooth, add ¼ cup slivered almonds, ¼ cup chopped dates and 3 tablespoons thinly sliced Crystallized Ginger, mixing well. Then fold in beaten egg whites and spoon into crust. Chill and top with whipped cream.

# Rhubarb Custard Pie

Pastry for 9-inch pie shell
1½ cups sugar
3 tablespoons flour
¼ teaspoon salt
½ teaspoon Nutmeg
1 teaspoon Orange Peel

¼ teaspoon Allspice
2 eggs, beaten
2 tablespoons cream
3 cups 1-inch pieces rhubarb
2 tablespoons butter
   or margarine

Line a 9-inch pie plate with pastry. Combine sugar, flour, salt, nutmeg, orange peel and allspice. Add beaten eggs and cream; mix well. Add rhubarb and pour into pastry-lined pie plate. Dot with butter. Pastry strips may be arranged over top in lattice fashion if desired. Bake in 400°F. oven 20 minutes; reduce heat to 350°F. and bake 25 minutes longer or until custard is firm and pastry is golden brown. *Makes one 9-inch pie.*

# Sesame Pecan Pie

Pastry for 9-inch pie shell
¼ cup Sesame Seed
3 eggs
¾ cup sugar
¼ teaspoon salt

⅓ cup melted butter
1 cup light corn syrup
1½ teaspoons pure
   Vanilla Extract
1 cup pecan halves

Line a 9-inch pie plate with pastry. Toast sesame seed in 350°F. oven 15 minutes or until golden brown. Sprinkle evenly over bottom of pastry shell. Beat eggs with rotary beater or electric mixer until light and fluffy. Add sugar, salt, butter, corn syrup and vanilla; continue to beat until well mixed. Gently stir in pecan halves. Pour into pastry. Bake in 350°F. oven 1 hour or until set and pastry is nicely browned. Serve slightly warm or cold. *Serves 6 to 8.*

# COOKIES
# CONFECTIONS

———— ✳ ————

## *Frosted Nutmeg Logs*

| | |
|---|---|
| 1 cup butter or margarine | 2 teaspoons pure Vanilla |
| ¾ cup sugar | Extract |
| 1¼ teaspoons Nutmeg | 3 cups all-purpose flour |
| 1 egg | Vanilla-Rum Frosting |
| 2 teaspoons Rum Extract | |

Cream butter and sugar. Add nutmeg, egg and extracts, mixing thoroughly. Sift flour and measure; stir into creamed mixture. Shape into rolls ½ inch in diameter and 3 inches long. Place, about 2 inches apart, on ungreased baking sheet. Bake in 350°F. oven 15 minutes or until lightly browned. Cool. Frost with Vanilla-Rum Frosting. *Makes 3 to 4 dozen.*

VANILLA-RUM FROSTING:

| | |
|---|---|
| ¼ cup soft butter | 1 teaspoon Rum Extract |
| 3 cups powdered sugar | 2 tablespoons cream |
| 1 teaspoon pure Vanilla | Nutmeg |
| Extract | |

Cream butter until soft and fluffy. Add part of the sugar and extracts, mixing well. Add remaining sugar and enough of the cream to obtain the desired spreading consistency. Frost cookies and run the tines of a fork down frosting. Sprinkle with nutmeg. *Makes 1⅓ cups frosting.*

# Fancy Decorated Cookies

½ cup butter
¾ cup sugar
1 egg
1½ teaspoons pure Vanilla
   Extract
1½ cups all-purpose flour

1 teaspoon baking powder
¼ teaspoon salt
Décors
Food Color
Frosting or glaze
Tinted coconut

Cream butter and sugar until light and fluffy. Add egg and vanilla and beat hard. Sift flour, measure and sift again with baking powder and salt. Stir into creamed mixture. (This makes a soft dough to work with. If you prefer a stiffer dough, add 2 to 4 tablespoons additional flour.) Chill dough 1 hour or longer. Roll out thin on floured cloth or board, working with only part of the dough at a time. Cut with cookie cutters. Place on lightly greased baking sheet. Bake in 350°F. oven 6 to 8 minutes. Remove immediately to cooling racks. Number of cookies depends on size and shape of cookie cutters. *Makes about 7 dozen 2-inch cookies.*

TO DECORATE COOKIES:

Sprinkle with décors, nonpareils and colored crystal
   sugars before baking.
Tint dough before baking.
Make pinwheels of white and tinted dough.
Frost or glaze cookies, then decorate using frosting in a
   decorating tube or with décors.
Tint coconut with food color and decorate.

# Filled Cookies

½ cup butter  
1 cup sugar  
2 eggs  
1½ teaspoons pure Vanilla  
   Extract  

3 cups all-purpose flour  
1 teaspoon baking powder  
1 teaspoon ground  
   Cardamom  
Jam or jelly  

Cream butter and sugar until light and fluffy. Add eggs, one at a time, beating after each addition. Stir in vanilla. Sift flour, measure and sift again with baking powder and cardamom; add to butter mixture. Mix well. Chill dough. Roll out on floured board to ⅛-inch thickness. Cut out with 2½-inch cutters. Using center of doughnut cutter or small fancy cutters, cut centers from half the cookies. Put the whole cookies on greased baking sheet and top with cookies which have had centers removed. Fill center of each cookie with jam. Bake in 350°F. oven 12 to 15 minutes. *Makes about 3 dozen.*

# Filled Fancies

¾ cup butter  
1½ cups sugar  
2 eggs  
2 teaspoons pure Vanilla  
   Extract  
4¾ cups all-purpose flour  

½ teaspoon soda  
¼ teaspoon salt  
¾ cup commercial sour  
   cream  
Filling  

Cream butter and sugar until light and fluffy. Add eggs and vanilla; beat well. Sift flour, measure and sift again with soda and salt. Add dry ingredients to creamed mixture alternately with sour cream. (This makes a soft dough. If you prefer to work with a stiffer dough, add 2 to 4 tablespoons more flour.) Thoroughly chill dough. Roll out on floured cloth or board to ⅛-inch thickness.

Cut with 2½-inch cutters of any desired shape. Cut 2 alike for each cookie, putting them together with a spoonful of filling between each. Use one of the fillings below or mincemeat. Press edges together. (For interesting decorative effect, centers may be cut from top pieces with small, fancy cutters.) Bake on lightly greased baking sheet in 400°F. oven 10 to 12 minutes. *Makes about 6 dozen.*

### APRICOT FILLING:

| | |
|---|---|
| 1 8-ounce package dried apricots | ¼ teaspoon Mace |
| | Dash Allspice |
| ½ cup sugar | ¼ teaspoon Almond Extract |
| 1 cup water | ¼ cup finely chopped pecans |

Combine apricots, sugar, water, mace and allspice in saucepan. Cover and simmer until apricots are soft and mixture is thickened. Cool; stir in almond extract and pecans. *Makes enough filling for about 3 dozen cookies.*

### FIG FILLING:

| | |
|---|---|
| 2 cups chopped dried figs | ½ teaspoon Cinnamon |
| ¾ cup water | 2 teaspoons Lemon Peel |
| ½ cup sugar | 2 tablespoons lemon juice |
| ¼ teaspoon Ginger | Dash Allspice |

Combine all ingredients in saucepan. Cover and cook until figs are tender. *Makes enough filling for about 3 dozen cookies.*

### POPPY SEED-CHEESE FILLING:

| | |
|---|---|
| 1 8-ounce package cream cheese | 2 teaspoons Rum Extract |
| | 2 teaspoons Poppy Seed |

Have cream cheese at room temperature; thoroughly blend with extract and poppy seed. *Makes enough filling for about 2 dozen cookies.*

# Fruit Cake Cookies

½ pound candied pineapple
1 pound candied cherries
1 pound pitted dates
3 tablespoons flour
4 cups pecan pieces
¼ cup butter
½ cup dark brown sugar,
  packed
2 eggs

1½ cups all-purpose flour
1½ teaspoons soda
¼ teaspoon Cloves
¼ teaspoon Allspice
½ teaspoon Cinnamon
¼ teaspoon Nutmeg
1 tablespoon milk
4 tablespoons orange juice

Cut fruit into medium-size pieces. Sprinkle lightly with the 3 tablespoons flour and toss to coat fruit. Add pecans and mix well. Cream butter and sugar until light and fluffy; add eggs, one at a time, beating well after each addition. Sift flour, measure and sift again with soda and spices; add to creamed mixture alternately with milk and orange juice. Stir in fruits and pecans, mixing well. Drop by teaspoonfuls onto greased and floured baking sheet. For more colorful cookies you may want to top with half a red or green cherry. Bake in 350°F. oven 15 minutes. *Makes about 9 dozen cookies.*

# Southern Praline Cookies

1 cup brown sugar, packed
1 egg white, stiffly beaten
½ teaspoon pure Vanilla
  Extract

¼ teaspoon salt
¼ teaspoon Cinnamon
2 cups pecan halves

Stir brown sugar into stiffly beaten egg white. Add remaining ingredients, mixing well. Drop from a teaspoon onto a greased baking sheet, allowing 2 or 3 pecans to each cookie. Bake in 250°F. oven 30 minutes. Remove to rack or paper immediately. *Makes 3 to 4 dozen cookies.*

# Old-Fashioned Tea Cakes

½ cup butter
½ cup granulated sugar
½ cup brown sugar, packed
1 egg
½ teaspoon pure Vanilla
  Extract

3 cups all-purpose flour
½ teaspoon baking powder
¼ teaspoon soda
¼ teaspoon Nutmeg
¼ cup buttermilk

Cream butter, granulated sugar and brown sugar until light and fluffy. Add egg and vanilla. Sift flour, measure and sift again with baking powder, soda and nutmeg. Add dry ingredients and buttermilk alternately to creamed mixture. Chill dough. Roll out to ⅛-inch thickness on lightly floured board. Cut with cookie cutters. Bake on lightly greased baking sheet in 400°F. oven 8 minutes. *Makes about 6 dozen 2-inch cookies.*

# Gingersnaps

¾ cup shortening
1 cup sugar
¼ cup molasses
1 egg
2 cups all-purpose flour

¼ teaspoon salt
2 teaspoons soda
1 teaspoon Cinnamon
1 teaspoon Cloves
1 teaspoon Ginger

Cream shortening and sugar together. Add molasses and egg; beat well. Sift flour, measure and sift again with remaining ingredients. Add to butter mixture and mix thoroughly. Roll into small balls and dip into additional granulated sugar or leave plain. Place two inches apart on greased baking sheet. Bake in 375°F. oven 10 to 12 minutes. *Makes 6 to 7 dozen.*

# Date Nut Cookies

2 cups all-purpose flour
2 cups pitted dates
½ teaspoon salt
½ teaspoon soda
1 teaspoon Pumpkin Pie
  Spice
½ cup butter or margarine

1 cup brown sugar, packed
1 egg
1 teaspoon pure Vanilla
  Extract
½ cup buttermilk
½ cup chopped pecans

Sift and measure flour. Slice dates; dredge with 2 tablespoons of the flour. Sift remaining flour with salt, soda and pumpkin pie spice. Cream butter and sugar thoroughly. Add egg and vanilla; beat hard. Add flour mixture alternately with milk. Stir in dates and pecans. Drop by teaspoonfuls onto greased baking sheets. Bake in 375°F. oven 8 to 10 minutes. These cookies should be soft and not too brown. *Makes about 5 dozen.*

# Refrigerator Spice Cookies

½ cup butter
1 cup dark brown sugar,
  packed
1 egg
1 teaspoon pure Vanilla
  Extract

2¼ cups all-purpose flour
½ teaspoon soda
¼ teaspoon salt
1 teaspoon Cinnamon
½ teaspoon Nutmeg
1 cup nuts, finely chopped

Cream butter and sugar until light and fluffy. Beat in egg and vanilla. Sift flour, measure and sift again with soda, salt, cinnamon and nutmeg. Stir into butter-sugar mixture. Add nuts, mixing well. Shape into roll; wrap in waxed paper and chill. Cut into thin slices and bake on lightly greased baking sheet in 350°F. oven 8 to 10 minutes. *Makes 6 to 7 dozen cookies.*

# Rocks

1 cup butter or margarine
1½ cups brown sugar, packed
3 eggs
3 cups all-purpose flour
1 teaspoon soda
¼ teaspoon Cloves
¼ teaspoon Allspice
1 teaspoon Cinnamon
Dash Nutmeg
2 cups seedless raisins
1½ cups chopped walnuts

Cream butter and sugar until light and fluffy. Add eggs, one at a time, beating well after each addition. Sift and measure flour; reserve 2 tablespoons. Sift remaining flour with soda and spices and stir into creamed mixture. Dredge raisins in the 2 tablespoons flour, then stir into batter along with walnuts. Drop by tablespoonfuls onto lightly greased baking sheet. Bake in 375°F. oven 8 to 10 minutes. *Makes about 6 dozen.*

# Cinnamon Sandies

1 cup butter or margarine
1½ cups powdered sugar
2 teaspoons pure Vanilla Extract
1 tablespoon water
2 cups sifted all-purpose flour
1 cup finely chopped nuts
2 teaspoons Cinnamon

Cream butter and ½ cup of the sugar; stir in vanilla and water. Add flour, mixing well. Stir in nuts. Shape small pieces of dough into crescents. Bake on an ungreased baking sheet in 300°F. oven 20 minutes or until very lightly browned. Sift the remaining 1 cup powdered sugar and cinnamon together. Roll hot cookies in this mixture. Allow cookies to cool, then roll again in the sugar-spice mixture. *Makes about 5 dozen.*

# Pecan Cookie Balls

| | |
|---|---|
| 1 cup butter or margarine | 2 teaspoons pure Vanilla Extract |
| 2½ cups sifted powdered sugar | 2 cups sifted all-purpose flour |
| ⅛ teaspoon salt | 2 cups finely chopped pecans |
| ½ teaspoon Nutmeg | |

Cream butter until soft; add ½ cup of the powdered sugar, salt, nutmeg and vanilla; continue creaming until thoroughly mixed. Stir in flour and pecans. Shape dough into small balls. Place on baking sheet and bake in 350°F. oven 15 minutes. Remove from baking sheet and quickly roll the hot cookies in the remaining 2 cups powdered sugar. Cool; roll again in powdered sugar. Store in tight container. *Makes 4 to 5 dozen cookies about 1 inch in diameter.*

# Poppy Seed Goodies

| | |
|---|---|
| ½ cup butter | ½ teaspoon soda |
| ½ cup brown sugar, packed | ¼ teaspoon salt |
| ¼ cup honey | ¼ teaspoon Mace |
| 1 egg | 2 tablespoons Poppy Seed |
| 1 teaspoon pure Vanilla Extract | 1½ cups quick-cooking rolled oats |
| 1 cup all-purpose flour | |

Cream butter, brown sugar and honey until light and fluffy. Add egg and vanilla; beat well. Sift flour, measure and sift again with soda, salt and mace. Add to creamed mixture along with poppy seed and rolled oats, mixing well. Drop by teaspoonfuls onto greased baking sheet. Bake in 400°F. oven 10 minutes or until lightly browned. Cool slightly before removing from baking sheet. *Makes about 4½ dozen.*

# Gingerbread Boys

½ cup shortening
½ cup sugar
1 cup molasses
1 egg, beaten
3½ cups all-purpose flour

1 teaspoon soda
1½ teaspoons Cinnamon
1½ teaspoons Ginger
¼ teaspoon salt
Raisins

Heat shortening, sugar and molasses until shortening is melted, stirring constantly. Cool; add egg and mix well. Sift flour, measure and sift again with soda, spices and salt. Stir into molasses mixture. Chill well. Roll out dough on lightly floured board to ¼-inch thickness; and cut with 3- to 4-inch gingerbread-boy cutter. Carefully place on lightly greased baking sheet. Decorate with raisins. Bake in 350°F. oven 10 minutes. Carefully remove and cool on rack. *Makes about 24 gingerbread boys.*

# Sesame Macaroons

½ cup Sesame Seed
¼ teaspoon Cream of Tartar
¼ cup egg whites (about 2)

¼ cup sugar
½ teaspoon Almond Extract

Toast sesame seed in 350°F. oven 15 minutes or until golden brown. Pulverize in blender or with mortar and pestle. Add cream of tartar to egg whites; beat until stiff. Gradually add sugar, beating well after each addition. Fold in sesame seed and almond extract. Drop by teaspoonfuls onto lightly greased baking sheet. Bake in 250°F. oven 30 minutes. Remove at once from baking sheet. *Makes about 3 dozen.*

# Spiced Mixed Nuts

| | |
|---|---|
| 1½ cups walnut halves | ½ teaspoon Cloves |
| 2 cups boiling water | 1 teaspoon Allspice |
| 2 cups superfine sugar | 2 teaspoons Orange Peel |
| 1 teaspoon salt | 2 egg whites |
| 1 teaspoon Nutmeg | 2 tablespoons water |
| 2 tablespoons Cinnamon | 1 cup pecan halves |
| 2 teaspoons Ginger | ½ cup blanched almonds |

Drop walnuts into boiling water and simmer 10 minutes. Drain. Sift sugar, salt and spices together 2 or 3 times to blend well. Beat egg whites until frothy; add the 2 tablespoons water and mix well. Add walnuts, pecans and almonds; stir to coat well with egg white mixture. Drain in colander. Make a shallow layer of the spiced sugar, using about half of it, in a 15½ x 10½ x 1-inch jelly roll pan. Add nuts to the remaining sugar mixture and mix well. Separate nuts and spread in a single layer over sugar in pan. Bake in 200°F. oven 2½ to 3 hours. Be sure the oven is not over 200°F. Remove from oven and while warm break into small pieces, allowing 2 to 3 nuts to each piece. *Makes about 4 cups.*

# Spiced Divinity

A new treat in Divinity!

| | |
|---|---|
| 2 cups superfine sugar | ¼ teaspoon Mace |
| ½ cup light corn syrup | ⅛ teaspoon Allspice |
| ½ cup water | 1 teaspoon pure Vanilla |
| ⅛ teaspoon Cream of Tartar | Extract |
| 2 egg whites | 1½ cups chopped nuts |

Combine sugar, corn syrup and water. Bring to a boil, stirring until sugar dissolves. Cook to 252° on candy thermometer (hard ball stage), washing down sides of saucepan to prevent crystals forming. Add cream of tartar to egg whites; beat until stiff. Pour the hot syrup in a thin stream over egg whites, beating vigorously. Continue beating until the mixture just begins to thicken, then add mace, allspice and vanilla. Continue beating until it begins to hold its shape and loses its high gloss. Stir in nuts. Drop quickly from tip of spoon in individual pieces onto waxed paper; or spread in a buttered pan and cut into squares when firm. *Makes 3 to 4 dozen pieces, depending on size.*

## Mincemeat Refrigerator Cookies

¾ cup shortening
1 cup sugar
1 egg
1 teaspoon Lemon Peel
¼ teaspoon crushed
  Coriander Seed
½ teaspoon pure Vanilla
  Extract
2½ cups all-purpose flour

½ teaspoon soda
½ teaspoon salt
1 teaspoon Cinnamon
Dash Nutmeg
¼ teaspoon Cloves
¼ teaspoon Ginger
½ cup mincemeat
½ cup chopped nuts

Cream shortening and sugar until fluffy. Add egg; beat well. Stir in lemon peel, crushed coriander seed and vanilla. Sift flour, measure and sift again with soda, salt, cinnamon, nutmeg, cloves and ginger. Add to creamed mixture, mixing thoroughly. Stir in mincemeat and nuts. Shape into rolls 1½ inches in diameter and wrap in waxed paper. Chill. Cut thin slices and place on baking sheet. Bake in 375°F. oven 9 to 10 minutes. *Makes 8 to 9 dozen.*

# Date Sticks

½ cup butter
1 cup sugar
1 egg
1 teaspoon pure Vanilla
   Extract
1 teaspoon Lemon Peel
2 cups all-purpose flour

½ teaspoon baking powder
¼ teaspoon soda
1 teaspoon Cinnamon
⅛ teaspoon Nutmeg
¼ teaspoon salt
1 cup chopped dates

Cream butter; gradually add sugar, beating until light and fluffy. Add egg, vanilla and lemon peel, beating well. Sift flour, measure and sift again with baking powder, soda, cinnamon, nutmeg and salt. Slowly add the dry ingredients to creamed mixture. Stir in dates. Shape cookies into thin sticks about 1½ inches long. Place on a greased baking sheet; bake in 350°F. oven 15 to 20 minutes. *Makes about 6 dozen.*


# Spicy Oatmeal Cookies

1 cup raisins or currants
⅔ cup shortening
1½ cups sugar
2 eggs, lightly beaten
½ cup milk
1 teaspoon pure Vanilla
   Extract
2 cups sifted all-purpose flour

½ teaspoon soda
1 teaspoon salt
1 teaspoon baking powder
½ teaspoon Cinnamon
¼ teaspoon Nutmeg
¼ teaspoon Allspice
2½ cups quick-cooking
   rolled oats

Rinse and drain raisins. Cream together shortening and sugar until fluffy. Stir in eggs, milk, vanilla and raisins. Sift together flour, soda, salt, baking powder and spices; combine with rolled oats. Stir into creamed mixture, mixing well. Drop by teaspoonfuls onto greased baking sheet. Bake in 350°F. oven 15 minutes or until lightly browned. *Makes 5 to 6 dozen cookies, depending on size.*

# Cinnamon Sledges

2 cups all-purpose flour
3 teaspoons Cinnamon
1 cup butter

1 cup sugar
1 egg, separated
½ cup chopped pecans

Sift flour, measure and sift again with cinnamon. Cream butter and sugar until light and fluffy. Add egg yolk; beat well. Add flour and cinnamon, mixing until well blended. Spread this stiff mixture to about ¼-inch thickness on a 12 x 15-inch baking sheet, leaving a border about 1½ inches around the edge to allow for spreading. Beat egg white until foamy and brush over top of dough. Sprinkle with nuts and press in lightly. Bake in 300°F. oven 45 to 50 minutes. Cut into bars while still hot and remove from baking sheet. *Makes 3 to 4 dozen, depending on size.*

# Chocolate Nut Brownies

4 1-ounce squares
  unsweetened chocolate
¾ cup butter
4 eggs
2 cups sugar
¼ teaspoon salt

¼ teaspoon Mace
1 teaspoon pure Vanilla
  Extract
1 cup sifted all-purpose flour
1 cup pecan or walnut pieces

Melt chocolate over hot water; add butter. Beat eggs until light and fluffy; gradually add sugar, salt and mace. Stir in vanilla; beat until light. Stir in chocolate mixture, then flour, beating until smooth. Add nuts and mix well. Pour into a greased and floured 15½ x 10½ x 1-inch jelly roll pan. Bake in 350°F. oven 30 minutes. When cool cut into oblong pieces or squares. Makes a moist brownie. *Makes 32 to 40.*

# Pfeffernüsse

German Christmas cookie meaning Peppernuts.

2 eggs
1 cup brown sugar, packed
2 teaspoons Lemon Peel
½ cup finely chopped citron
2 cups sifted all-purpose flour
1 teaspoon baking powder
½ teaspoon salt
1 teaspoon Cinnamon

⅛ teaspoon Nutmeg
⅛ teaspoon Cloves
⅛ teaspoon Mace
¼ teaspoon Black Pepper
⅛ teaspoon Cardamom
½ cup chopped nuts
Brandy Extract
 or Rum Extract

Beat eggs until thick; add brown sugar and lemon peel. Continue beating until well blended. Stir in citron. Sift flour with baking powder, salt and spices and add to egg mixture. Stir in nuts. Shape into roll 1 inch in diameter. Chill. Cut into ½-inch slices and place on baking sheet; allow to dry overnight. Turn cookies over and put 1 to 2 drops extract in center of each cookie. Bake in 375°F. oven 12 to 15 minutes. Store in tightly covered container several days to mellow. *Makes about 6 dozen.*

# Sesame Toffee Bars

¼ cup Sesame Seed
1 cup butter or margarine
1 cup dark brown sugar, packed
1 egg
1 teaspoon pure Vanilla Extract
2 cups sifted all-purpose flour

¼ teaspoon Cinnamon
¼ teaspoon Allspice
⅛ teaspoon Nutmeg
½ cup finely chopped or ground nuts
2 6-ounce packages semi-sweet chocolate pieces

Toast sesame seed in 350°F. oven 15 minutes or until golden brown. Cream butter and sugar. Add egg and vanilla and mix well. Sift flour with spices. Add to creamed mixture and mix well. Stir in nuts. Spread ¼ inch thick into a 13 x 15-inch rectangle on a baking sheet. Bake in 350°F. oven 20 minutes. While baking, melt chocolate pieces over hot water or on lowest heat. Spread chocolate over cookies while hot. Sprinkle top with sesame seed and cut into bars while warm. *Makes about 4 dozen.*

---

## Cinnamon Chocolate Fudge

---

Everyone likes chocolate fudge—and this one is extra special.

| | |
|---|---|
| 4 1-ounce squares unsweetened chocolate | 4 tablespoons butter or margarine |
| 3 cups sugar | 1 teaspoon pure Vanilla Extract |
| 2 teaspoons Cinnamon | 2 cups pecans or walnuts, broken |
| 2 tablespoons light corn syrup | |
| 1¼ cups milk | |

Melt chocolate in 3-quart saucepan on lowest heat or over hot water. Stir in sugar, cinnamon, corn syrup and milk. Increase heat to medium and cook, stirring until sugar dissolves. Wash crystals from side of pan. Cook to 236° on candy thermometer (soft ball stage). Remove from heat; add butter and, without stirring, let cool to 110° or lukewarm. Add vanilla and beat until mixture begins to thicken. Stir in nuts and continue beating until candy holds its shape. Drop from spoon onto buttered waxed paper or pour into buttered pans. When cool, cut into squares. *Makes about 3 pounds.*

# Holiday Chews

Double-decker cookie bars the children will adore.

½ cup butter or margarine
½ cup brown sugar, packed
1 cup sifted all-purpose flour
½ teaspoon Pumpkin Pie
  Spice
½ teaspoon Ginger
1 cup brown sugar, packed
2 eggs
2 tablespoons flour

1 teaspoon Orange Peel
¼ teaspoon salt
1 teaspoon pure Vanilla
  Extract
1 cup chopped nuts
1½ cups shredded coconut
½ teaspoon baking powder
¼ teaspoon Mace

With a pastry blender or two knives thoroughly blend together butter, the ½ cup brown sugar, the 1 cup flour, pumpkin pie spice and ginger. Pat into a greased, shallow 8 x 12-inch pan. Bake in 375°F. oven 20 minutes or until crisp. Remove from oven and reduce temperature to 350°F. Thoroughly mix remaining ingredients and spoon over baked mixture. Return to oven and bake 25 minutes longer or until topping is brown and bubbly. Cool and cut into 1 x 1½-inch bars. *Makes 32.*


# Sugared Nuts

1 cup sugar
1 teaspoon Cinnamon
1 teaspoon Orange Peel
⅛ teaspoon Mace
½ cup milk

1 teaspoon butter
1 teaspoon pure Vanilla
  Extract
2 cups walnut halves

Combine sugar, cinnamon, orange peel and mace. Stir in milk; cook to 236° on candy thermometer (soft ball stage). Remove from heat; add butter. Let stand 2 to 3 minutes, then add vanilla and nuts. Stir mixture until thick and begins to hold its shape. Immediately turn out on waxed paper and, working quickly, separate the nuts. *Makes about 70 halves.*

## Sesame Wafers

½ cup Sesame Seed
1 cup butter
⅔ cup sugar
¼ teaspoon salt

1 tablespoon milk
½ teaspoon Almond Extract
1⅔ cups sifted all-purpose
   flour

Toast sesame seed in 350°F. oven 15 minutes or until golden brown. Cream butter, sugar and salt until light and fluffy. Add remaining ingredients, mixing well. Chill. Shape into small balls. Place on ungreased baking sheet 2 to 3 inches apart. Bake in 350°F. oven 15 minutes or until lightly browned. Cool slightly before removing from pan. *Makes 4 dozen.*

## Anise Cookies

½ cup butter
1 cup sugar
1 egg
½ teaspoon pure Vanilla
  Extract

1¾ cups sifted all-purpose
   flour
½ teaspoon salt
1½ teaspoons baking powder
1½ teaspoons Anise Seed

Cream butter; add sugar and continue beating until light and smooth. Add egg and vanilla, mixing well. Sift together flour, salt and baking powder. Gradually add dry ingredients and anise seed, beating hard after each addition. Shape dough into a roll. Wrap in waxed paper and chill. Cut into thin slices. Place on a lightly greased baking sheet and bake in 400°F. oven 8 minutes or until golden brown. *Makes about 5 dozen.*

# Lebkuchen

German Christmas Honey Cakes.

½ cup honey
½ cup molasses
1 cup sugar
⅓ cup butter
2 teaspoons lemon juice
1 egg
2 teaspoons Lemon Peel
1 teaspoon Orange Peel
3¼ cups all-purpose flour
¾ teaspoon soda
¼ teaspoon salt
1 teaspoon Cinnamon

1 teaspoon Allspice
1 teaspoon Cloves
¾ teaspoon Mace
¼ teaspoon Cardamom
½ cup chopped mixed
    candied fruits
½ cup slivered blanched
    almonds
3 cups powdered sugar
¼ cup boiling water
½ teaspoon Almond Extract

Combine honey, molasses and sugar in saucepan; bring to a boil. Remove from heat; add butter, then cool. Beat in lemon juice, egg, lemon peel and orange peel. Sift flour, measure and sift again with soda, salt and spices. Add to honey-molasses mixture, mixing well. Stir in candied fruits and almonds. Chill dough overnight. Roll out on floured board to ¼-inch thickness, using one fourth of the dough at a time. Cut into rectangles, 1½ x 2½ inches. Place on greased baking sheet and bake in 400°F. oven 10 minutes or until brown. To make glaze, thoroughly blend powdered sugar, boiling water and extract. Brush glaze over cookies as soon as they are removed from oven. Immediately remove from baking sheet. Store in tight container a few days to mellow. You may add a sliced apple or orange for added moisture. *Makes about 5 dozen cookies.*

# Fondant

2½ cups sugar  
1½ cups water  
⅛ teaspoon Cream of Tartar

Extract, any flavor  
Food Color

Combine sugar, water and cream of tartar. Cook over medium heat, stirring until sugar dissolves. Wash down side of pan. Cook to 238° on candy thermometer. (This is near the highest degree for soft ball stage. A little syrup when dropped in cold water forms a ball which will just hold its shape when picked up.) Immediately pour onto platter or marble slab. Do not scrape syrup from pan. When mixture has cooled to lukewarm, begin working with wide spatula, scraping fondant from outside edge toward center. Continue working, using a wooden spoon if necessary, until the fondant is white, creamy and firm; then knead well, until smooth but not flaky. Put in a bowl; cover and set aside 12 to 24 hours to ripen. To all or part of fondant add few drops of any desired extract to taste, using about 1 teaspoon per pound. Tint with a few drops of food color if desired. *Makes about 1 pound.*

VARIATION:

*Fondant Tipped Almonds*—Toast 2 cups whole blanched almonds. After Fondant, recipe above, has ripened, put it in top of double boiler and melt over hot water. Stir in 1 teaspoon Mint Extract or Mint and Peppermint Extract and tint using Red, Green, Yellow or Blue Food Color. For an assortment of colors, divide fondant into small amounts, tinting each a different shade or color. Dip large end of almond into melted fondant and place on waxed paper to dry. *Makes about 1½ pounds.*

# Prune-Filled Squares

PRUNE FILLING:

1½ cups chopped, cooked prunes
2 tablespoons liquid from prunes
2 tablespoons lemon juice
1 teaspoon Orange Peel

3 tablespoons sugar
⅛ teaspoon Cloves
¼ teaspoon Ginger
Dash Nutmeg
Dash salt

Combine all ingredients. Cook over low heat, stirring occasionally, 8 minutes or until thickened. Cool to room temperature. Prepare crumb layer.

CRUMB LAYER:

1¼ cups all-purpose flour
½ teaspoon Cinnamon
½ teaspoon salt
¾ cup brown sugar, packed

1 cup quick-cooking rolled oats
1 tablespoon Poppy Seed
½ cup butter or margarine

Sift flour, then measure. Add cinnamon and salt and sift again into a large bowl. Stir in brown sugar, rolled oats and poppy seed. Using a pastry blender or 2 knives, cut in butter until mixture resembles coarse meal. Spread half this mixture evenly over the bottom of a well-greased 8-inch square pan. Press down firmly. Cover with prune filling, spreading it evenly to edges and into corners. Sprinkle remaining crumb mixture over filling. Carefully press down crumbs to make smooth top. Bake in 400°F. oven 30 minutes or until top is browned. Cool in pan on cake rack. Cut into squares. Store in tightly covered container. These cookies keep well. *Makes about 16.*

VARIATION:

*Apricot Squares*—Use 1½ cups chopped, cooked, dried apricots in place of prunes. Proceed as in recipe above.

# Chewy Popcorn Balls

A sure way to delight the younger generation. These are fine to offer for trick-or-treats, too.

1 cup sugar
1 cup light corn syrup
½ teaspoon salt
½ teaspoon Cinnamon
¼ teaspoon Ginger
⅛ teaspoon Mace
2 tablespoons butter
½ cup water

1 teaspoon pure Vanilla
Extract
½ teaspoon Almond Extract
3 quarts crisp salted
popped corn
1½ cups chopped mixed
nuts

Combine sugar, corn syrup, salt, spices, butter and water in saucepan. Cook over low heat, stirring until sugar dissolves. Wash crystals from side of pan. Cook over medium heat to 245° on candy thermometer (firm ball stage). Remove from heat; stir in extracts. Pour slowly over mixture of popped corn and nuts, stirring to mix well. Shape, with buttered hands, into balls. *Makes about 2 dozen balls, 2 inches in diameter.*

VARIATIONS:

*Holiday Popcorn Balls*—In the above recipe, add ½ cup minced candied cherries (mixture of red and green) to popped corn and nuts. Pour hot syrup over this mixture and proceed as directed.
*Crunchy Popcorn Balls*—In recipe for Chewy Popcorn Balls use only 2 quarts popped corn instead of 3 quarts; make syrup following directions, cooking to 290° on candy thermometer (hard crack stage). Pour over popped corn and nuts. Shape into balls if desired, or spread in thin layer on aluminum foil. When cool, break into small pieces.

# Orange Butter Gems

1 cup butter
1 cup powdered sugar
2½ cups all-purpose flour
¼ teaspoon Mace

¼ teaspoon salt
1 egg
2 teaspoons Orange Peel
2 teaspoons Orange Extract

Cream butter and sugar until light and fluffy. Sift flour, measure and sift again with mace and salt. Add 1 cup of the flour mixture to the butter-sugar mixture. Beat in egg, orange peel and orange extract. Add remaining flour mixture. Put dough into cookie press and form cookies on ungreased baking sheet. Bake in 375°F. oven 10 minutes or until lightly browned. Decorate with tinted frosting if desired. *Makes about 6 dozen.*

**VARIATION:**

*Lemon Butter Gems*—Substitute 2 teaspoons Lemon Peel and 2 teaspoons Lemon Extract for orange peel and orange extract in the above recipe.

# Czechoslovakian Cookies

1 cup butter or margarine
1 cup sugar
2 egg yolks
1 teaspoon pure Vanilla
   Extract
⅛ teaspoon Cardamom

¼ teaspoon Allspice
2 cups sifted all-purpose
   flour
1 cup chopped walnuts
   or pecans
½ cup strawberry jam

Cream butter until soft. Add sugar gradually, beating until light and fluffy. Add egg yolks and vanilla; beat hard. Sift cardamom and allspice with flour; gradually add to butter mixture, mixing thoroughly. Stir in chopped nuts. Spoon half of the dough into a greased 8-inch square cake pan; spread evenly. Top with strawberry jam. Cover with remaining dough. Bake in 325°F. oven 1 hour or until lightly browned. Cool. Cut into about 1½-inch squares. *Makes about 2 dozen.*

## Date Roll

3 cups sugar
1 tablespoon light corn syrup
½ teaspoon salt
1 cup milk
1 teaspoon Orange Peel
½ teaspoon Cinnamon
¼ teaspoon Nutmeg
⅛ teaspoon Allspice

1 8-ounce package dates, cut into pieces
2 tablespoons butter
1 teaspoon pure Vanilla Extract
1 cup chopped pecans or walnuts

Combine sugar, corn syrup, salt and milk. Cook over low heat, stirring until sugar dissolves. Wash down sides of pan to prevent crystals forming. Continue cooking to 236° on candy thermometer (soft ball stage). Add orange peel, spices and dates and continue cooking to 238°. Remove from heat and add butter. Do not stir. Let cool to 110° or lukewarm. Add vanilla and beat until mixture just begins to thicken. Add nuts and continue beating until it begins to hold its shape. Turn out onto damp cheesecloth and shape into a roll 2 inches in diameter. Set aside and when firm cut into thin slices as needed. *Makes about 2 pounds.*

# Cardamom Butter Cookies

| | |
|---|---|
| 1 cup butter | 1 teaspoon baking powder |
| 1¼ cups sugar | ½ teaspoon salt |
| 2 eggs | 1 teaspoon Cardamom |
| 1 teaspoon pure Vanilla Extract | ½ teaspoon Cinnamon |
| 3 cups sifted all-purpose flour | ¼ teaspoon Allspice |

Cream butter and sugar until light and fluffy. Add eggs and vanilla and beat well. Sift together remaining ingredients; stir into creamed mixture and mix well. Chill dough, roll and cut with cookie cutters. Or, if you prefer, shape dough into two rolls and wrap in waxed paper. Chill. Cut into thin slices. Bake in 350°F. oven 8 to 10 minutes, depending on thickness of cookies. *Makes 8 dozen thin cookies.*

# Sesame Pralines

A delightfully different version of the famous New Orleans confection.

| | |
|---|---|
| ¼ cup Sesame Seed | 1 cup cream |
| 1 cup dark brown sugar, packed | 2 tablespoons butter or margarine |
| 1 cup granulated sugar | 2 cups pecan halves |

Toast sesame seed in 350°F. oven 15 minutes or until golden brown. In a 3-quart saucepan combine both sugars and cream. Cook over medium heat, stirring until sugar dissolves. Wash crystals from side of pan. Cook to 230° on candy thermometer. Add butter, pecans and sesame seed; continue cooking, stirring occasionally, to 234° (soft ball stage). Remove from heat. Cool 2 to 3 minutes, then stir 2 minutes or until slightly thickened.

Drop from spoon, working fast, onto buttered waxed paper, aluminum foil or marble slab. *Makes about 15, depending on size.*

---

## Sugared Vanilla Wafers

---

1 cup butter or margarine
1½ cups sugar
2 eggs
3 teaspoons pure Vanilla
  Extract

3 cups sifted all-purpose flour
2 teaspoons baking powder
2 tablespoons milk
Sugar for sprinkling
Cinnamon Sugar, optional

Cream butter and the 1½ cups sugar thoroughly; add eggs and vanilla and beat well. Sift together flour and baking powder; add to creamed mixture. Stir in milk and chill several hours. Lightly flour a board and sprinkle with 1 tablespoon sugar. Roll out chilled dough very thin and cut with cookie cutters. Place on lightly greased baking sheet. Sprinkle with sugar or cinnamon sugar. Bake in 400°F. oven 6 to 8 minutes. *Makes about 5 dozen 2-inch cookies.*

## Traditional Wassail Bowl

Merrie Olde England's Christmas cup of cheer.

3 apples
1 cup water
1 cup sugar
½ teaspoon Nutmeg
1 piece whole Ginger,
broken
1 3-inch piece Cinnamon
3 whole Cloves

3 whole Allspice
4 Coriander Seeds
2 whole Cardamom
½ teaspoon Mace
Rind of 1 lemon
⅘ quart sherry
3 12-ounce cans ale
3 eggs, separated

Wash apples; place in baking dish. Roast in 350°F. oven 45 minutes. Combine water, sugar, nutmeg, ginger, cinnamon, cloves, allspice, coriander seed, cardamom, mace and lemon rind. Bring to a boil; reduce heat and simmer 10 minutes. Pour sherry and ale into spice mixture. Heat to just under boiling point but do not boil. Strain. Beat egg whites until stiff. Beat yolks until thick; stir beaten whites into yolks. Slowly add spice mixture to eggs, beating constantly. Pour into silver or heatproof punch bowl. Float roasted apples on top. Serve hot. *Makes about 2 quarts.*

# Holiday Cranberry Punch

¼ teaspoon Cinnamon
¼ teaspoon Nutmeg
¼ teaspoon Allspice
4 pints cranberry juice
cocktail

1 6-ounce can frozen orange
juice, reconstituted
6 12-ounce bottles ginger ale

Combine all ingredients except ginger ale. Mix well and bring to a boil. Strain through cheesecloth if desired. Chill. Add chilled ginger ale just before serving. *Makes about 5 quarts, or 42 4-ounce servings.*

# Hot 'n' Spicy Punch

2 6-ounce cans frozen grape
juice concentrate
1 6-ounce can frozen orange
juice concentrate
7½ cups water

½ cup sugar
4 3-inch pieces Cinnamon
1 teaspoon whole Cloves
Juice of 2 lemons

Combine all ingredients except lemon juice; stir to dissolve sugar. Boil 5 minutes. Remove from heat; strain to remove spices and add lemon juice. Serve hot in punch cups or chill and serve over ice cubes. *Makes about 2 quarts.*

# Cinnamon-Vanilla Milk Shake

1 cup cold milk
1 teaspoon pure Vanilla
   Extract

1 pint vanilla ice cream
¼ teaspoon Cinnamon
Dash Nutmeg

Mix all ingredients except nutmeg in a blender or beat with a mixer or rotary beater until light and fluffy. Pour into chilled glasses and top each with dash nutmeg. *Makes 2 milk shakes.*

# Party Punch

For extra sparkle add champagne.

1 46-ounce can pineapple-
   grapefruit juice
1 quart apple juice
3 6-ounce cans frozen
   orange juice concentrate
1 can frozen lemon juice
   (5¾-ounce can)
24 whole Cloves

4 3-inch pieces Cinnamon
½ teaspoon Ginger
½ teaspoon ground Allspice
½ teaspoon Mace
6 whole Cardamom
½ cup sugar
4 quarts ginger ale
   (13 or 14 7-ounce bottles)

Combine fruit juices. Tie whole cloves in cheesecloth bag and add to juice with other spices and sugar; mix well to dissolve sugar. Let stand several hours. When ready to serve, remove spice bag; stir well. Pour into punch bowl over ice; add ginger ale. (If you want to mix small amount at a time, use 1 cup fruit juice mixture to 1 cup or 1 7-ounce bottle ginger ale.) Float a Spice-Fruit Ring (see following recipe) in punch bowl. *Makes 2 gallons, or about 64 4-ounce servings.*

# Spice-Fruit Ring

An attractive way to chill punch without diluting the flavor.

Pineapple spears
Pineapple slices
Red maraschino cherries
with stems
Green maraschino cherries
Lemon slices, cut ¼ inch
thick

Orange slices, cut ¼ inch
thick
Whole Cloves
Whole Cardamom
1 quart ginger ale
Whole Ginger
Cinnamon Sticks
Whole Allspice

Drain pineapple; rinse cherries. Stud outer edges of lemon and orange slices with whole cloves and place whole cardamom in center. Pour enough ginger ale into ring mold or interestingly shaped mold to cover bottom; freeze. Arrange fruits and whole spices in an attractive design over frozen ginger ale and pour enough ginger ale over fruits and spices to just cover. Freeze. Pour remaining ginger ale into ring mold and freeze until solid. When ready to serve, remove from mold and float in punch bowl. *Makes 1 ring.*

# Hot Cranberry Punch

4 pints cranberry
juice cocktail
4 6-ounce cans frozen
lemonade, undiluted

½ teaspoon salt
1 teaspoon ground Allspice
4 cups water
15 3-inch pieces Cinnamon

Combine all ingredients except cinnamon. Simmer 10 to 15 minutes; do not boil. Serve hot in mugs, using cinnamon sticks as stirrers. *Makes 15 1-cup servings.*

# Tropical Delight

| | |
|---|---|
| 1 46-ounce can grapefruit juice, unsweetened | 1 cup water |
| 1 12-ounce can apricot juice | ½ cup sugar |
| 1 12-ounce can papaya juice | 4 whole Cardamom |
| 1 12-ounce can guava nectar | 1 3-inch piece Cinnamon |
| 1 12-ounce can pear nectar | ⅛ teaspoon Mace |
| | 4 7-ounce bottles ginger ale |

Combine juices. Bring water, sugar, cardamom, cinnamon and mace to a boil; reduce heat and simmer 10 minutes. Cool and strain into juices. Add ginger ale and serve over ice. *Makes about 1 gallon, or 32 4-ounce servings.*

# Café Diable

| | |
|---|---|
| 1 orange | 1 thin slice lemon |
| Whole Cloves | 1½ cups Myers rum |
| 4 tablespoons sugar | or cognac |
| 2 3-inch pieces Cinnamon, broken in half | 2 cups strong coffee |

Peel orange, being careful to keep peeling in one long piece. Stud peel with whole cloves, putting them about 1 inch apart down the full length of orange peel. Put sugar, 2 whole cloves and cinnamon in café diable dish or chafing dish (remove the water pan when using chafing dish). Heat until sugar melts and just begins to turn golden. Drop in lemon slice and orange peel; pour in rum. Dip up a ladleful of the hot rum; set afire and lower the flaming ladle into the dish. Slowly pour in the coffee. With a long-handled fork or pair of tongs hold the orange peel up by one end; ladle the flaming rum mixture over peel until flame dies. Serve in café diable or demitasse cups. When flaming, turn lights down. *Serves 6.*

# Glögg

The traditional Swedish Christmas drink.

| | |
|---|---|
| 6 whole Cardamom | 2 cups dry red wine |
| 1 3-inch piece Cinnamon | 1 cup water |
| 1 piece whole Ginger, broken | ½ cup seedless raisins |
| 5 whole Cloves | ½ cup blanched almonds |
| 1 tablespoon Orange Peel | ½ cup sugar |
| 2 cups port wine | 1 cup brandy |

Open white cardamom pods and remove the little black seed. Tie seed in a bag along with cinnamon, ginger, cloves and orange peel. Combine all ingredients except brandy. Heat to just under boiling point and hold at this temperature for 15 minutes. Remove spice bag. Carefully pour brandy into mixture. Light and flame. Serve in cups or mugs. *Makes about 6 cups.*


# Tea House Punch

| | |
|---|---|
| ½ cup sugar | 3 Tea Bags |
| ¼ teaspoon Nutmeg | ¼ cup orange juice |
| ¼ teaspoon Allspice | ¼ cup lemon juice |
| ¼ teaspoon Cinnamon | 2 cups cold water |
| 2 cups hot water | |

Combine sugar, spices and hot water in saucepan; boil 1 minute and pour while boiling hot over tea bags. Steep 5 minutes. Strain; mix with fruit juices and cold water. Delicious either hot or cold. *Makes about 1 quart.*

# Cranberry Wassail Bowl

Delightful holiday punch—teen-agers will especially enjoy.

½ cup blanched almonds
1 cup seedless raisins
Rind of 1 orange
Rind of 1 lemon
1 teaspoon whole Cloves
¼ teaspoon Coriander Seed
6 whole Cardamom

2 3-inch pieces Cinnamon
½ teaspoon whole Allspice
1 quart water
2 quarts cranberry juice
  cocktail
2 No. 2 cans pineapple-
  grapefruit juice

Combine all ingredients except fruit juices in saucepan. Cover. Bring to a boil, then reduce heat and simmer 15 minutes. Cool. Chill fruit juices. If desired, strain spiced mixture; and just before serving, pour with chilled juices over a block of ice in large punch bowl. Or, you may serve hot in mugs, using Cinnamon Sticks as stirrers. *Makes about 1 gallon.*

# Autumn Spiced Cider

A marvelous drink for teen-age parties.

4 quarts apple cider
1 cup orange juice
½ cup sugar
2 teaspoons Orange Peel
1 teaspoon whole Allspice
½ teaspoon Mace

¼ teaspoon salt
1 teaspoon Coriander Seed
2 teaspoons whole Cloves
2 tablespoons Cinnamon
  Décors

Combine all ingredients in large saucepan. Cover. Bring to boiling point, then simmer 30 minutes. Strain. Delicious hot as a mulled drink, or you may serve it iced as a cold cider punch. *Makes 1 gallon.*

# Island Fruit Punch

4 pieces whole Ginger
8 cups water
¼ cup Mint Flakes
1 tablespoon whole Allspice
1 tablespoon whole Cloves
5 cups sugar

2 quarts orange juice
2 cups lemon juice
2 46-ounce cans pineapple-
    grapefruit juice
2 cups guava juice,
    optional

Pound ginger root to bruise or cut into several pieces. Boil with 4 cups of the water 10 minutes or until a strong ginger flavor is obtained. Add mint flakes, allspice and whole cloves and steep until cool. Strain through a cloth. Boil sugar with the remaining 4 cups water to make a syrup. Cool. Combine with all other ingredients. Mix well. Chill and pour over ice ring made of frozen juice, using any one or a mixture of juices listed above. *Makes about 2 gallons.*

# Spiced Tea

4 cups boiling water
4 Tea Bags
½ cup orange juice
¼ cup lemon juice
½ cup sugar

3 3-inch pieces Cinnamon
8 whole Cloves
Dash Nutmeg
7 slices lemon

Pour boiling water over tea bags in a heated teapot and steep 5 minutes. Remove tea bags and pour tea into a saucepan, preferably glass or stainless steel. Add orange juice, lemon juice, sugar, cinnamon, cloves and nutmeg. Keep hot, not simmering, for at least 30 minutes before serving, so that flavors may blend. Hold longer if desired. Serve hot with a paper-thin slice of lemon floating in each cup. *Makes about 7 servings.*

## Apple Blossom Cooler

1 cup water
⅓ cup sugar
2 teaspoons Mint Flakes

1 3-inch piece Cinnamon
1 quart apple juice
½ cup lemon juice

Bring water, sugar, mint flakes and cinnamon to a boil; reduce heat and simmer 10 minutes. Cool. Combine apple juice and lemon juice. Strain syrup into juice mixture. Chill. *Makes about 5 cups.*

## Mint Tea Hawaiian

4 cups boiling water
6 Tea Bags
½ teaspoon Mint Flakes
¼ cup sugar

⅓ cup lemon juice
¼ cup pineapple juice
Pineapple spears

Pour boiling water over tea bags and mint flakes in heated teapot. Cover and steep 5 minutes. Strain; combine with sugar, lemon juice and pineapple juice and mix well. Chill. Serve over ice cubes garnished with a spear of fresh or canned pineapple. *Makes 1 quart.*

## Eggnog

3 eggs, separated
1 cup milk
1 teaspoon pure Vanilla
  Extract

1 teaspoon Rum Extract
1 teaspoon Brandy Extract
1 pint vanilla ice cream
Nutmeg

Beat egg yolks until light; mix in milk and extracts. Beat egg whites until stiff but not dry. Fold egg whites and

378

softened ice cream into milk mixture. Sprinkle with
nutmeg. *Makes 5 cups.*

# Spiced Grape Punch

A subtle blending of fruit juice and spices.

1½ cups reconstituted
  frozen limeade
½ teaspoon ground Allspice
½ teaspoon ground
  Cinnamon
½ teaspoon ground Nutmeg
3 6-ounce cans frozen grape
  juice concentrate
6 12-ounce bottles ginger ale

Combine limeade and spices in saucepan. Boil 3 minutes.
Add spice mixture to grape juice concentrate and ginger
ale. Chill. *Makes 25 4-ounce servings.*

# Mexican Chocolate with Marshmallows

2 1-ounce squares
  unsweetened chocolate
2 tablespoons hot water
½ cup sugar
¼ teaspoon salt
2 teaspoons Cinnamon
2 cups hot strong coffee
3 cups hot milk
8 marshmallows
1½ teaspoons pure Vanilla
  Extract

Put chocolate and water in a 2-quart saucepan; melt
over low heat, stirring. Combine sugar, salt and cinnamon and slowly stir into melted chocolate. Add coffee,
stirring until smooth; cook a few minutes longer. Stir in
milk; add marshmallows. Heat until marshmallows
melt; add vanilla and beat until frothy. Serve hot. *Makes
8 servings.*

# French Hot Chocolate

4 1-ounce squares
  unsweetened chocolate
¼ cup water
1 quart milk
½ cup cream
½ cup sugar
¼ teaspoon salt
¼ teaspoon Mace

⅛ teaspoon Allspice
1 teaspoon pure Vanilla
  Extract
½ teaspoon Almond Extract
⅛ teaspoon Nutmeg
½ cup heavy cream,
  whipped

Place chocolate and water in saucepan; stir over low heat until melted and smooth. Slowly stir in milk, then add cream, sugar, salt, mace and allspice. Cook over medium heat, stirring occasionally, until milk is hot; stir in vanilla and almond extract. Carefully blend nutmeg into whipped cream. Top each cup of hot chocolate with a spoonful of the whipped cream. *Makes 6 servings*.

VARIATION:

*French Mint Chocolate*—To the above recipe, add ½ teaspoon Mint or Mint and Peppermint Extract in place of almond extract.

# Banana Frost

3 large ripe bananas
1 tablespoon lemon juice
1 tablespoon sugar
¼ teaspoon Cinnamon

⅛ teaspoon Cloves
⅛ teaspoon Mace
1 cup milk
1 cup soft vanilla ice cream

Peel and thoroughly mash bananas with fork. Sprinkle with lemon juice, then combine with remaining ingredients. Beat until smooth using rotary beater, electric mixer or blender. Pour into frosted glasses. *Makes 3 servings*.

# Lime-Mint Cooler

A teen-age favorite, cool and refreshing.

2 10-ounce bottles
  quinine water
½ cup lime juice
¼ teaspoon Mint Extract
  or Mint and Peppermint
  Extract

3 tablespoons sugar
Green Food Color
Ice cubes
Lime sherbet

Chill quinine water. Combine lime juice, extract and sugar, stirring to dissolve sugar. Tint to a delicate green with food color. Add quinine water and ice cubes. Mix well. Pour into tall glasses. Top each with a scoop of lime sherbet. Garnish with red maraschino cherry, sprig of mint or thin slice of lime. *Serves 4.*

# Mulled Wine

1 cup sugar
1 cup water
2 3-inch pieces Cinnamon
12 whole Allspice

12 whole Cloves
Dash Nutmeg
1 lemon
3 cups red wine

Combine sugar, water and spices in saucepan. Peel lemon and drop whole peel into sugar mixture. Stir to dissolve sugar. Simmer 5 minutes. Remove from heat and let stand 30 minutes. Strain. Add wine and heat slowly to just under boiling point. Serve hot. *Makes about 6 servings.*

381

# Cocoa with a Hint of Spice

¼ cup cocoa
3 tablespoons sugar
½ teaspoon ground
  Cinnamon
Dash Cloves

Dash Allspice
Dash salt
¼ cup water
3 cups milk
4 3-inch pieces Cinnamon

Combine cocoa, sugar, ground cinnamon, cloves, allspice, salt and water; mix well. Cook over medium heat 2 minutes. Stir in milk and heat to just below boiling point but do not boil. Serve hot in cups using a stick of cinnamon as a stirrer. *Serves 4.*

# Minted Mocha Float

2 1-ounce squares
  unsweetened chocolate
3 cups strong coffee
½ cup sugar
Dash Cardamom

1 teaspoon pure Vanilla
  Extract
1 teaspoon Mint Flakes
2 cups milk
1 cup light cream
1 pint vanilla ice cream

Combine chocolate and ¼ cup of the coffee in saucepan. Cook over lowest heat, stirring, until chocolate is melted. Stir in sugar, cardamom and vanilla. Add mint flakes to milk and cream. Scald. Strain into chocolate mixture, stirring to mix well. Chill. Place a scoop of ice cream in each chilled glass and fill with chilled mocha drink. You may also serve hot omitting the ice cream. *Serves 6.*

# Iced Viennese Coffee

A gay, delightful summer drink.

3 cups boiling water
2 tablespoons instant coffee
2 3-inch pieces Cinnamon

3 whole Cloves
5 whole Allspice
Whipped cream

Pour boiling water over coffee, cinnamon, cloves and allspice. Let stand one hour. Strain and pour over ice in tall glasses. Sweeten if desired. Top with whipped cream. *Serves 4.*

# Ginger Peach Freeze

2 12-ounce packages frozen
    sliced peaches
1 pint vanilla ice cream
½ teaspoon Ginger

¼ teaspoon Allspice
¼ teaspoon Cinnamon
1 teaspoon Lemon Peel

Thaw peaches. Have ice cream soft enough to spoon easily. Mash peaches with a fork. Add spices and mix well. Add ice cream. Beat with rotary beater or an electric mixer until smooth. You will find this ideal to make in a blender. Serve in chilled glasses. *Makes 4 servings.*

# Zippy Tomato Juice

1 No. 2 can tomato juice (about 2 cups)
¼ teaspoon Onion Powder
¼ teaspoon Powdered Horseradish

½ teaspoon Celery Salt
⅛ teaspoon dry Mustard
1 teaspoon lemon juice

Combine all ingredients and mix well. Chill at least two hours before serving to allow flavors to blend. Serve over ice cubes in glasses for a refreshing summer beverage that children will love with hamburgers or at barbecues. Wonderful pick-me-up at breakfast too. *Makes about 2 cups.*

# SAUCES

— * —

## White Sauce Supreme

THIN SAUCE:

1 tablespoon butter
1 tablespoon flour
1 teaspoon Chicken
  Seasoned Stock Base

¼ teaspoon dry Mustard
⅛ teaspoon White Pepper
1 cup milk or cream

MEDIUM SAUCE:

In above recipe increase both butter and flour to 1½ to 2 tablespoons.

THICK SAUCE:

In above recipe increase both butter and flour to 3 to 4 tablespoons.

Melt butter in saucepan over low heat. Stir in flour, seasoned stock base, dry mustard and pepper. Let mixture bubble 1 minute. Remove from heat. Stir in milk or cream, mixing well. Cook over medium heat, stirring constantly, until sauce thickens. *Makes 1 cup.*

Use thin sauce for creamed vegetables, creamed dried beef or as a base for thin creamed soups.
Use medium sauce for gravies, sauces for fish or egg dishes or creamed and scalloped dishes.
Use thick sauce for base for soufflés, croquettes and deviled crab.

# Holiday Nutmeg Sauce

| 1 egg yolk | 1 teaspoon Nutmeg |
| ½ cup sugar | 1 teaspoon Arrowroot, |
| 1 cup milk | optional |

Beat together egg yolk, sugar and milk. Heat to the boiling point, stirring constantly. Remove from heat and add nutmeg. (Should you want a thicker sauce, make a thin, smooth paste by mixing together arrowroot with an equal amount of water. Stir into sauce and cook, stirring, until thickened.) Serve over apple pie, apple dumplings, steamed puddings, gingerbread or mincemeat pie. *Makes 1⅓ cups.*

# Beurre Noir

The classic French brown butter sauce.

| ¾ cup butter (1½ sticks) | 4 tablespoons fresh lemon |
| 1 teaspoon Parsley Flakes | juice |
| ⅛ teaspoon White Pepper | 1 tablespoon dry white wine, |
| | optional |

Melt butter in a heavy saucepan over medium to low heat. Skim off the foam and pour the clear yellow liquid into a small bowl. Be sure it is free of the milky residue at the bottom of the pan. (Strain if any particles of the milk solids should mix with the clear butter.) Wash and dry saucepan; return the clarified butter to it. Set over low to medium heat until butter turns deep golden brown; pour into a small heated bowl or saucepot. Stir in parsley flakes and pepper. Boil lemon juice to reduce to 1 tablespoon. (If wine is used, add to lemon juice before boiling to reduce volume.) Stir into butter. Keep butter sauce warm over hot, but not boiling, water until ready to serve. Serve over vegetables, fish, sautéed sweetbreads, shirred eggs, veal or chicken. *Makes about ½ cup.*

---

## Sour Cream Mustard Sauce

1 cup commercial sour cream
1 teaspoon dry Mustard
⅛ teaspoon White Pepper

½ teaspoon Onion Salt
¼ teaspoon salt
¼ teaspoon Turmeric

Combine all ingredients. Heat in top of double boiler or over very low heat, stirring several times. Serve on fish, corned beef, boiled beef, frankfurters, hamburgers or luncheon meats. This sauce is easy to make; use it as a dunk for meat balls, cocktail franks, shrimp, fried scallops or oysters. *Makes 1 cup.*

---

## Quick 'n' Easy Barbecue Sauce

1 cup catchup
½ cup wine vinegar
1 teaspoon Worcestershire sauce
½ teaspoon Season-All

1 teaspoon Instant Minced Onion
¼ teaspoon Barbecue Spice
⅛ teaspoon Garlic Salt
⅛ teaspoon Black Pepper

Combine all ingredients and mix well. Use to baste grilled or broiled chicken, frankfurters, hamburgers as well as many other meats. *Makes 1½ cups.*

387

# Tomato Sauce

An excellent tangy sauce!

| | |
|---|---|
| 2 cups tomatoes (No. 303 can) | ⅓ teaspoon Thyme Leaves |
| | 1 teaspoon Parsley Flakes |
| 1 8-ounce can tomato sauce | 1 Bay Leaf |
| 1 tablespoon Instant Minced Onion | Dash MSG |
| | 1 teaspoon Season-All or Bon Appétit |
| 1 teaspoon Bell Pepper Flakes | |
| | 2 whole Cloves |
| ⅛ teaspoon Black Pepper | 2 tablespoons butter |
| ¼ teaspoon Garlic Powder | 1 teaspoon sugar |

Cut tomatoes into small pieces. Combine all ingredients, mixing well. Bring to a boil and simmer 20 minutes. Serve on meat loaf, hamburgers, fish, frankfurters, boiled beef, veal or omelettes. *Makes 3 cups.*

# Coconut Mace Sauce

| | |
|---|---|
| ⅓ cup butter or margarine | ¼ teaspoon Mace |
| 1 cup shredded coconut | Dash salt |
| ½ cup light brown sugar, packed | ¾ cup evaporated milk |
| | ½ teaspoon pure Vanilla Extract |
| 2 tablespoons corn syrup | |

Melt butter; add coconut and sauté until golden brown. Lift out coconut and set aside. To the butter in pan, add sugar, corn syrup, mace and salt. Cook over low heat, stirring constantly, until mixture boils vigorously. Stir in milk; simmer 1½ minutes. Remove from heat, then add vanilla and coconut. Serve warm or cold on ice cream, cakes, puddings or custards. *Makes about 1½ cups.*

# Honey Spice Butter

½ cup butter (1 stick)
2 teaspoons honey

½ teaspoon Cinnamon
⅛ teaspoon Nutmeg

Let butter soften at room temperature. Add remaining ingredients, mixing well. This makes an excellent spread for date nut bread, graham crackers, muffins, biscuits, banana bread, waffles, toast or pancakes. *Makes ½ cup.*

VARIATION:

*Orange Butter*—Add 2 teaspoons Orange Peel and dash Cloves in place of cinnamon and nutmeg in above recipe.

# Creamy Mustard Sauce

3 tablespoons butter
  or margarine
2 tablespoons flour
1 teaspoon dry Mustard
½ teaspoon salt

Dash White Pepper
1 egg yolk
1 cup milk
1 tablespoon lemon juice

Melt butter; stir in flour, dry mustard, salt and pepper. Mix well and cook until bubbly, about 1 minute. Remove from heat. Beat egg yolk; add milk and mix well. Stir into butter-flour mixture. Cook, stirring constantly, 3 minutes or until smooth and thickened. Remove from heat. Just before serving stir in lemon juice, mixing well. Serve hot over cauliflower, green beans or broccoli; or with fish, ham or boiled beef. *Makes about 1¼ cups sauce.*

# Spaghetti Sauce

3½ cups plum tomatoes (No. 2½ can)
1 6-ounce can tomato paste
3 cups water
2 tablespoons Instant Minced Onion
½ teaspoon Garlic Powder
½ teaspoon Oregano Leaves
1 teaspoon Bon Appétit
1 Bay Leaf

1½ teaspoons salt
¼ teaspoon Black Pepper
1 teaspoon sugar
¼ teaspoon MSG
¼ teaspoon Crushed Red Pepper
2 tablespoons olive oil or salad oil[1]
1 tablespoon Arrowroot, optional

Force tomatoes through a coarse sieve to purée and remove seed. Combine the tomato purée and remaining ingredients, except arrowroot, in glass or stainless steel saucepan. Bring to boil; reduce heat and simmer, uncovered, 1 hour. Remove bay leaf. For a thicker sauce, simmer 20 minutes longer; or thicken by making a thin, smooth paste of the arrowroot and an equal amount of water. Stir into sauce and cook, continuing to stir, until thickened. Serve over cooked spaghetti topped with grated Parmesan cheese. Meat balls, sautéed chicken livers, clams or calamari (very small whole squid) may be added to the sauce or served on the side. *Makes 5 cups sauce or enough for 1 pound spaghetti.*

VARIATION:

*Pizza Sauce*—Make sauce following above recipe but simmer 1 hour and 30 minutes or until sauce is quite thick. Spread over pizza dough; top with grated Parmesan cheese, slices of Mozzarella cheese and any of the following: anchovies, sliced mushrooms, thin slices pepperoni or salami, or sliced olives. You may also sprinkle with Oregano Leaves. Bake; serve hot. *Makes enough for two 12-inch pizzas.*

# Brown Sauce

A rich basic brown sauce, having many uses.

| | |
|---|---|
| 3 tablespoons butter | ⅛ teaspoon Black Pepper |
| 2 tablespoons flour | ⅛ teaspoon MSG |
| 1 teaspoon Beef Flavor Base | Dash Nutmeg |
| ⅛ teaspoon Onion Powder | 1 cup water |

Heat butter in small heavy saucepan or skillet until browned. Stir in flour and blend well. Cook over low heat, stirring constantly, until flour is deep brown. Remove from heat; add beef flavor base, onion powder, pepper, MSG and nutmeg; mix well. Gradually stir in water. Return to heat and bring to a boil, stirring constantly. Boil 1 minute. Serve this sauce or its variations over rice, meat loaf, leftover meats, omelettes, chops, steaks, tongue or hamburgers; or use as a base for many casserole dishes. *Makes about 1 cup.*

VARIATIONS:

*Onion Sauce*—Sauté 1 to 2 tablespoons Chopped Instant Onions in 1 tablespoon butter until golden brown, watching carefully to prevent burning. Add to above recipe and let stand 10 to 15 minutes before serving to allow onions to soften.

*Sauce Champignon (Mushroom Sauce)*—Stir ½ teaspoon Powdered Mushrooms into Brown Sauce (recipe above); simmer 3 minutes longer.

*Horseradish-Vegetable Sauce*—Simmer ½ teaspoon Powdered Horseradish and 2 tablespoons Vegetable Flakes in ¼ cup water 20 minutes. Stir into Brown Sauce (recipe above) and simmer 3 minutes longer.

*Herbed Giblet Sauce*—Stir ¼ teaspoon Poultry Seasoning and ¼ cup chopped cooked giblets into Brown Sauce (recipe above) and simmer 3 minutes longer.

# Creamy Chocolate Sauce

4 1-ounce squares
   unsweetened chocolate
2 cups sugar
1 tall can (14½ ounce)
   evaporated milk

1 teaspoon pure Vanilla
   Extract
Dash Mace

Melt chocolate over low heat, stirring. Add remaining ingredients; mix well. Cook over low heat, stirring constantly, until smooth and thickened. Serve warm over ice cream or cake. *Makes 2½ cups.*

# Pudding Sauce

¼ cup butter or margarine
1 cup sugar
½ cup cream or evaporated
   milk

1½ teaspoons pure Vanilla
   Extract or Rum Extract
Dash Nutmeg

Combine butter, sugar and cream in saucepan. Cook over low heat, stirring occasionally, 10 minutes or until slightly thickened. Do not allow sauce to boil. Stir in extract and nutmeg. Serve hot or cold over ice cream, bread pudding, gingerbread, rice pudding, vanilla pudding, mincemeat pie or squares of warm cake. *Makes 1½ cups.*

# Tasty Cream Sauce

3 tablespoons butter
2 tablespoons flour
1½ teaspoons Instant
 Minced Onion
½ teaspoon Season-All

1 teaspoon Chicken
 Seasoned Stock Base
⅛ teaspoon White Pepper
1 cup milk or light cream

Melt butter. Add flour, onion, Season-All, seasoned stock base and pepper. Stir until smooth and cook until bubbly but do not brown. Add milk, stirring constantly; cook until thickened. Serve over vegetables and top with toasted slivered almonds, or use as base for creamed dried beef, chicken, tuna or other creamed dishes. *Makes 1 cup.*

# Mint Sauce for Desserts

1 cup sugar
2 tablespoons Arrowroot
⅛ teaspoon salt
2 cups boiling water

¼ teaspoon Mint Extract
 or Mint and Peppermint
 Extract
2 drops Green Food Color

Combine sugar, arrowroot and salt in a saucepan. Gradually add boiling water, stirring constantly. Continue stirring and simmer over low heat 5 minutes or until clear and thickened. Remove from heat; mix in extract and food color. Serve hot. If a thicker sauce is desired, increase the arrowroot to 3 tablespoons. Delicious and colorful to serve over ice cream, vanilla pudding, plain cake, pound cake, angel food cake, chocolate brownies or chilled fruits. *Makes 2 cups.*

# Hot Exotic Curry Sauce

This sauce is well worth your time and effort to prepare.

¼ cup Instant Minced Onion
⅛ teaspoon Garlic Powder
2 Bay Leaves
⅛ teaspoon ground Thyme or Thyme Leaves
¼ cup Celery Flakes
3 tablespoons Indian or Madras Curry Powder
1½ teaspoons Season-All
2 tablespoons butter

2 carrots, cut into slices
¼ cup grated coconut
1 tart apple, chopped
3 tablespoons chutney
2 tablespoons tomato paste or 1 fresh tomato, chopped
4 teaspoons Chicken Seasoned Stock Base
4 cups water
2 tablespoons Arrowroot

Combine all ingredients except arrowroot. Stir to mix well. Bring to a boil; reduce heat and simmer 2 hours. Strain through a sieve, pressing as much of the fruit and vegetables through as possible. Make a thin, smooth paste of arrowroot and an equal amount of water. Stir into sauce; cook over medium heat, stirring, until thickened. Serve over chicken, lamb, beef or rice; or add meats, chicken, shrimp, eggs or any leftover meat to sauce and serve over rice. *Makes about 3½ cups sauce.*

# Nutmeg Sauce

1 cup sugar
1 tablespoon Arrowroot
¼ teaspoon salt

1 cup boiling water
1 teaspoon butter
1 teaspoon Nutmeg

Mix sugar, arrowroot and salt; slowly add boiling water, stirring constantly. Add butter and cook 5 minutes. Remove from heat; add nutmeg. Serve hot on apple, date or other fruit puddings. *Makes 1⅓ cups.*

# Paprika Butter

½ cup soft butter (1 stick)    ¼ teaspoon salt
1 teaspoon Paprika    Dash Black Pepper
1 teaspoon lemon juice      or White Pepper

Combine all ingredients, mixing well with a fork. Let stand 30 minutes for flavors to blend. Spread over chicken, lobster, shrimp or fish before broiling. You will also find this excellent with steaks and chops. This is a must in seasoning vegetables such as cauliflower, onions or potatoes. *Makes ½ cup.*

# Mushroom Sauce

2 tablespoons butter    Dash MSG
3 tablespoons flour    1 4-ounce can mushrooms
1 teaspoon Beef Flavor Base    1 teaspoon Parsley Flakes
⅛ teaspoon Black Pepper    1 tablespoon Madeira

Melt butter; stir in flour. Cook, stirring constantly, until mixture is golden brown. Remove from heat; add beef flavor base, pepper and MSG, stirring well. Drain mushrooms and set aside; save liquid. Add enough water to liquid to make 1 cup. Stir into flour mixture and cook, stirring, over low heat until thickened. Add mushrooms and parsley flakes; cook until mushrooms are heated through. Just before serving, stir in Madeira. Serve over roast beef, filet mignon, sirloin steak, ham, chicken livers or omelettes. *Makes about 1½ cups.*

# Creamy Horseradish Sauce

½ cup heavy cream
¼ cup commercial sour
cream

1 teaspoon Bon Appétit
1 tablespoon Powdered
Horseradish

Combine heavy cream and sour cream; whip until stiff. Stir in Bon Appétit and powdered horseradish. Let stand 30 minutes to 1 hour in refrigerator for flavors to blend. Serve with roast beef, boiled beef or corned beef. *Makes about 1½ cups sauce.*

# Red Cocktail Sauce

1 cup catchup
1 cup chili sauce
1½ teaspoons Powdered
Horseradish
½ teaspoon Bon Appétit

¼ teaspoon MSG
2 tablespoons lemon juice
¼ cup finely minced celery
1 teaspoon capers, optional

Combine all ingredients, mixing well. Sauce improves in flavor if allowed to stand an hour or longer before using. Keeps well in refrigerator. Serve with shrimp, crab, oysters or any sea food. *Makes about 2 cups.*

# Garlic Butter

½ cup soft butter (1 stick)
¼ teaspoon Garlic Powder

¼ teaspoon salt
Dash Black Pepper

Combine all ingredients, mixing well with a fork. Cover. Let stand 30 minutes for flavors to blend. Chill slightly if desired. Use to season green beans, stewed tomatoes, frogs' legs, steak, hamburgers, broiled fish, sautéed shrimp or lamb; or use as a spread for canapés. *Makes ½ cup.*

## Sour Cream Topping

1 cup commercial sour cream
1½ teaspoons Hickory
 Smoked Salt
⅛ teaspoon Onion Powder
1 teaspoon Chives

Mix together all ingredients; allow to stand at least 1 hour for flavors to blend. Serve over baked potatoes, broccoli, green beans or boiled onions; or toss with water cress or cucumbers. *Makes 1 cup.*

## Sauce Rémoulade

2 cups mayonnaise
6 tablespoons tomato paste
1 tablespoon prepared
 mustard
¼ teaspoon Celery Salt
⅛ teaspoon Cayenne
4 anchovy fillets, washed
 and mashed
½ teaspoon Parsley Flakes
½ teaspoon Chervil Leaves
¼ teaspoon Tarragon Leaves
3 teaspoons Instant
 Minced Onion
1 tablespoon chopped capers
2 tablespoons minced sour
 pickles

Combine all ingredients; mix well. Let stand several hours to allow flavors to blend. Serve with cold shrimp, crab or lobster. You will find this makes an excellent topping for head lettuce, tossed salad or sliced avocado. Keeps well in refrigerator. *Makes 3 cups.*

# Hot Chinese Mustard

¼ cup dry Mustard        2 tablespoons cold water

Put dry mustard in cup or small bowl. Gradually add cold water, stirring until thoroughly mixed. Make only the amount needed at a time, for it dries on standing. Serve with appetizers such as egg roll, sliced pork, shrimp or cubes of cheese and ham. Flat beer may be used in place of water. You will find this quite hot so use cautiously. *Makes about ¼ cup.*

# Sauce Piquant

1 8-ounce package cream cheese
½ teaspoon salt
⅛ teaspoon White Pepper
¼ teaspoon dry Mustard

⅛ teaspoon Cayenne
2 eggs
2 tablespoons lemon juice
½ cup commercial sour cream

Have cream cheese at room temperature. Add salt, pepper, dry mustard and cayenne. Cream thoroughly. Beat in eggs, one at a time, then add lemon juice and sour cream. Mix well. Set over simmering, but not boiling, water until heated thoroughly; stir often. Serve over asparagus, green beans, broccoli or poached or broiled fish; or serve with artichokes. *Makes 2 cups.*

# Whipped Maple-Cinnamon Butter

½ cup sweet butter, softened  
1 teaspoon Maple Extract  
1 teaspoon Cinnamon  

2 tablespoons powdered sugar

Whip butter until very light and fluffy. Add remaining ingredients and continue whipping until thoroughly mixed. Serve on pancakes, coffee cake, French toast, waffles or breads. *Makes ½ cup.*

# Creamy Curry Sauce

2 tablespoons butter  
  or margarine  
2 teaspoons Curry Powder  
2 tablespoons all-purpose flour  

¼ teaspoon salt  
¼ teaspoon White Pepper  
1¼ cups milk

Melt butter; stir in curry powder. (Curry powder may be decreased or increased according to individual taste.) Cook over low heat, stirring, 2 to 3 minutes. Add flour, salt and pepper, mixing until well blended and smooth. Cook until bubbly, stirring constantly. Remove from heat; stir in milk. Cook, continuing to stir, until thickened. To this sauce you will want to add cooked shrimp, chicken, lamb cubes or chopped hard-cooked eggs. Serve hot over rice. Curry is usually served with several condiments such as: slivered almonds, minced onion, chopped hard-cooked eggs, raisins, sliced Crystallized Ginger, chutney, mashed banana, grated coconut or crumbled crisp bacon. *Serves 4 to 6.*

# Herb Butter

½ cup butter
¼ teaspoon Tarragon Leaves
1 teaspoon Parsley Flakes
½ teaspoon Savory
⅛ teaspoon Thyme
Dash Black Pepper

Let butter soften at room temperature. Add remaining ingredients, mixing well. Use to season vegetables, fish or meats; or use as a spread for hot breads or sandwiches. *Makes ½ cup.*

# Whipped Lemon Butter

½ cup soft butter (1 stick)
1 teaspoon dry Mustard
4 teaspoons lemon juice
Dash Paprika

Whip all ingredients with rotary beater or electric mixer until smooth. Use with vegetables, fish, meats or breads. *Makes ½ cup.*

# Dill Sauce

2 tablespoons butter
1 tablespoon Arrowroot
1 teaspoon Bon Appétit
¼ teaspoon MSG
⅛ teaspoon White Pepper
1 teaspoon Chicken
  Seasoned Stock Base
½ cup water
1 cup commercial sour cream
1 tablespoon Dill Weed

Melt butter; blend in arrowroot, Bon Appétit, MSG, pepper, seasoned stock base and water. Cook over low heat, stirring, until mixture thickens. Remove from heat. Stir in sour cream and dill weed. Heat but do not allow to boil. Serve over boiled potatoes, broccoli, green beans, cauliflower, peas, asparagus or carrots. *Makes 1½ cups.*

# Caper Sauce

| | |
|---|---|
| 4 tablespoons butter | 1 teaspoon Parsley Flakes |
| 4 tablespoons flour | 4 whole Allspice |
| ½ teaspoon Onion Powder | 2 Bay Leaves |
| ⅛ teaspoon MSG | 2 whole Cloves |
| 3 teaspoons Chicken | Dash Cayenne |
| Seasoned Stock Base | 1 cup water |
| ⅛ teaspoon White Pepper | 1½ cups milk |
| Dash Nutmeg | ½ cup heavy cream |
| ⅛ teaspoon Turmeric | 2 tablespoons capers, chopped |

Melt butter; stir in flour and cook over low heat, stirring, 2 minutes. Do not let it brown. Add seasonings; mix well, then stir in water and milk. Cook, stirring constantly, until sauce thickens. Reduce heat and simmer, uncovered, 20 minutes. Add cream and cook 5 minutes longer. Strain. Stir in capers. Delicious served hot with fish, broiled chicken, roast lamb, lobster, tongue, cauliflower or asparagus. *Makes 3 cups.*

**VARIATION:**

*Truffle Sauce*—Make sauce following recipe above except use ¼ cup thinly sliced truffles in place of capers. Superb on poached eggs and over sliced turkey on rice.

# Spiced Hard Sauce

| | |
|---|---|
| ½ cup butter | ¼ teaspoon Cardamom |
| 2 cups powdered sugar | ¾ teaspoon Cinnamon |
| ¼ teaspoon Mace | ¼ teaspoon Allspice |

Cream butter until light and fluffy. Beat in sugar and spices. Chill. A must for plum pudding! Also good with fruit cobblers, mincemeat pie, bread puddings and other steamed puddings. *Makes about 1⅓ cups.*

# Raspberry Sauce

2 10-ounce packages frozen
   raspberries
3 tablespoons Arrowroot
½ cup sugar

¼ teaspoon salt
⅛ teaspoon Allspice
¼ teaspoon Mace
2 tablespoons butter

Thaw raspberries just enough to drain syrup. Measure syrup and add water to make 1½ cups. Mix arrowroot, sugar, salt, allspice and mace; stir into liquid. Cook, stirring, over medium heat until sauce thickens. Add drained raspberries and butter. (If you prefer a smoother sauce, press berries through fine sieve to remove seed and purée the fruit.) Simmer 3 minutes longer. Cool. Excellent topping for vanilla pudding, ice cream, ice cream pies, cheesecake or butter, angel food, pound or chiffon cake. *Makes 2½ cups.*

# Creamy Lemon-Butter Sauce

¾ cup soft butter
¼ teaspoon salt
Dash Cayenne

½ teaspoon Lemon Peel
1½ tablespoons lemon juice
3 egg yolks

Put butter in top of double boiler; before placing over hot water beat with rotary beater until creamy. Add salt, cayenne and lemon peel, mixing well. Gradually add lemon juice, beating constantly. Add egg yolks, one at a time, beating after addition of each. Continue beating until mixture is light and fluffy, then place sauce over hot water for a few minutes, beating constantly until glossy. Serve immediately. This is an excellent sauce over broccoli, asparagus, green beans, cauliflower or broiled or poached fish. *Makes 1⅓ cups.*

# Tartare Sauce

¾ cup mayonnaise
3 tablespoons minced pickle
2 teaspoons Instant Minced
  Onion

1 tablespoon lemon juice
¼ teaspoon dry Mustard
¼ teaspoon Celery Salt
1 teaspoon capers, minced

Combine all ingredients and mix well. Refrigerate 1 hour, allowing flavors to blend. Serve with baked, broiled or fried fish and sea food or salmon or tuna croquettes. *Makes 1 cup*.


# Hollandaise Sauce

1 cup butter
4 egg yolks
2 tablespoons lemon juice
¼ teaspoon salt

⅛ teaspoon Cayenne
⅛ teaspoon White Pepper
¼ teaspoon dry Mustard

Divide butter into three equal parts. Put ⅓ of the butter, egg yolks and lemon juice in top of double boiler. (Never allow water in bottom of boiler to boil or to touch the bottom of top boiler.) Cook over hot water, stirring constantly, until butter melts. Add ⅓ of the butter; continue to stir until butter melts. Remove from heat and stir in remaining butter and seasonings. If sauce is not thick enough, continue cooking over hot water, stirring constantly. Should it start to separate, add 1 or 2 teaspoons boiling water; beat briskly until smooth. Serve warm over asparagus, broccoli or poached fish; or use in making Eggs Benedict. *Makes 1½ cups*.

# Teriyaki Sauce

1 cup soy sauce
¼ cup brown sugar, packed
¼ teaspoon Garlic Powder
¼ teaspoon Onion Powder
2 tablespoons lemon juice

1 teaspoon ground Ginger
or 10 to 12 pieces
whole Ginger
about size of
shelled peanut

Combine all ingredients in jar. Shake to mix well and to dissolve sugar. For a marinade, let stand in sealed jar overnight. Pour over beef cubes, steak, pork chops or disjointed chicken and let marinate 2 hours or longer. Broil, brushing meat with marinade 2 or 3 times while cooking. For a sauce to be used in a side dish, simmer 10 minutes. Use for dunking shrimp, meat balls, bite-size pieces of meat or chicken, broiled pineapple cubes or French fried sweet potatoes; or serve over rice. Refrigerate extra sauce in a tightly sealed jar for future use. *Makes about 1 cup*.

# Sweet-Sour Mustard Sauce

1 cup brown sugar, packed
¼ cup dry Mustard
2 teaspoons Arrowroot
¼ teaspoon salt

1 teaspoon Beef Flavor Base
½ cup hot water
½ cup vinegar
2 eggs, beaten

Mix together sugar, dry mustard, arrowroot and salt. Dissolve beef flavor base in hot water; add to sugar mixture. Stir in vinegar. Add beaten eggs, mixing well. Cook over low heat, stirring constantly, until it thickens. Cool. Serve in a sauce bowl. Excellent with ham, cold meats and fried shrimp. *Makes 2 cups*.

# Parsley-Almond Sauce

¼ cup butter or margarine
¼ cup slivered almonds
1 teaspoon Parsley Flakes

½ teaspoon Season-All
¼ teaspoon Black Pepper
3 tablespoons lemon juice

Melt butter. Add almonds and brown lightly, then add remaining ingredients. Serve hot over fish fillets, cauliflower, green beans or carrots. *Makes about ½ cup.*

# Spicy Barbecue Sauce

Do not let the long list of spices frighten you. You will probably have most of them on your shelf.

3 6-ounce cans tomato paste
3 cans water (2¼ cups)
¼ cup vinegar
3 tablespoons Worcestershire sauce
3 tablespoons butter
2 tablespoons Onion Flakes
2 tablespoons Celery Flakes
1 teaspoon Black Pepper
½ teaspoon Allspice
½ teaspoon Cinnamon

½ teaspoon Chili Powder
1 teaspoon Paprika
1 teaspoon dry Mustard
½ teaspoon Nutmeg
2 teaspoons Season-All
2 teaspoons Barbecue Spice
½ teaspoon Garlic Salt
Dash MSG
¼ teaspoon Red Pepper
    or Cayenne, optional

Combine all ingredients in saucepan and mix well; cover. Slowly bring to a boil; reduce heat and simmer 1 hour or longer if time permits. Use to baste spareribs, pork chops, bologna roll or chicken. *Makes about 5 cups.*

NOTE: This sauce will be one of your favorites and you will find it keeps weeks in the refrigerator and may also be frozen.

# Sauce Béarnaise

A renowned French sauce, superb with beef.

¼ cup wine vinegar
1 teaspoon Shredded Green
  Onions
1½ teaspoons Tarragon
  Leaves
1 teaspoon Chervil Leaves

⅛ teaspoon Coarse Grind
  Black Pepper
¼ teaspoon salt
Dash Cayenne
3 egg yolks
2 tablespoons cold butter
½ cup melted butter

Combine vinegar, onions, 1 teaspoon of the tarragon leaves, chervil leaves, pepper, salt and cayenne. Boil until mixture is reduced to 2 tablespoons; strain. Beat egg yolks in top of double boiler until thick. Add vinegar and 1 tablespoon of the cold butter. Cook over hot, not boiling, water until mixture is thickened, stirring constantly. Remove from heat and add the remaining tablespoon of cold butter; stir to blend. Slowly add melted butter, stirring constantly. Add the remaining ½ teaspoon tarragon leaves. Serve warm with châteaubriand, filet mignon, sirloin steaks, roast leg of lamb or broiled or poached fish. *Makes about 1 cup.*

# Tangy Butter

½ cup butter (1 stick)
1 teaspoon Herb Seasoning

3 dashes Cayenne
  or Red Pepper

Let butter soften at room temperature. Mix in remaining ingredients. You may like this hotter and more pungent; if so, increase the amount of cayenne. Serve on hamburgers, meat loaf, grilled meats, broiled or fried fish, baked or mashed potatoes, green beans or hot bread. *Makes ½ cup.*

# Crème Anglaise

A delicate custard sauce.

| | |
|---|---|
| 1½ cups milk | ¼ teaspoon salt |
| 4 egg yolks | 1 teaspoon pure Vanilla |
| Dash Mace | Extract |
| ¼ cup sugar | Dash Nutmeg |

Scald milk in top of double boiler. In a small bowl beat together the egg yolks, mace, sugar and salt. Gradually stir in scalded milk. Return to double boiler. (Do not have the water in the bottom boiler touching the top boiler.) Cook, stirring constantly, until sauce thickens and forms a thin coating on a metal spoon. Remove from heat. Cool quickly. Stir in vanilla and chill thoroughly. Serve in dessert glasses topped with whipped cream; or use as a sauce over gingerbread, Floating Island Meringues (see recipe page 298) or other desserts. Top with dash of nutmeg. *Makes about 1½ cups.*

# Onion Butter

| | |
|---|---|
| ⅓ cup melted butter | ⅛ teaspoon Herb Seasoning |
| 1 teaspoon Instant Minced | Dash Cayenne |
| Onion | or Red Pepper |
| 1 teaspoon lemon juice | |

Combine all ingredients and mix well. Excellent served over peas, green beans, boiled potatoes, carrots, chops, steaks, liver, sweetbreads, or baked or broiled fish. *Makes about ⅓ cup.*

# Curry Butter

A quick way to add exciting new flavor to sandwiches, canapés and entrées.

½ cup soft butter (1 stick)
1 teaspoon Indian or Madras
  Curry Powder

¼ teaspoon salt
Dash Black Pepper

Combine all ingredients, mixing well with a fork. Let stand 30 minutes to 1 hour for flavors to blend. Use as a base for canapés, as a substitute for regular butter in making sandwiches; or serve on meats, fish, sea food, vegetables, noodles or rice. *Makes ½ cup.*

# Spiced Raisin Sauce

1 pound seedless raisins
Water to cover
½ cup vinegar
¾ cup brown sugar, packed

½ teaspoon Cinnamon
½ teaspoon Ginger
¼ teaspoon Allspice
1 teaspoon Orange Peel

Soak raisins in water 2 hours. Boil slowly until water is reduced to about one half. Add remaining ingredients and simmer until only a small amount of liquid is left and sauce is syrupy in appearance. Serve with baked ham, roast pork, leg of lamb, pork chops, duckling or tongue. *Makes about 3 cups.*

# Tropical Barbecue Sauce

1 cup water
1 cup brown sugar, packed
3 tablespoons catchup
1 tablespoon soy sauce
1 teaspoon dry Mustard

1 cup crushed pineapple
2 tablespoons Bell Pepper
 Flakes
1 tablespoon Arrowroot
¼ cup cold water

Mix together the 1 cup water and brown sugar. Add catchup, soy sauce, dry mustard, pineapple and pepper flakes. Bring to a boil; simmer 10 minutes. Dissolve arrowroot in the ¼ cup water; add to sauce and cook, stirring, until sauce thickens. Serve hot with spareribs, pork, lamb, ham, shrimp or chicken; or serve as a dip for meat hors d'oeuvres. This sauce adds excellent flavor to oven roasted or broiled meats. *Makes 2½ cups.*

# CANNING

— ❋ —

## *Sweet Cucumber Pickles*

5 pounds small whole
  cucumbers
1 cup rock salt
2 quarts cold water
½ teaspoon powdered Alum

2 quarts boiling water
5 cups cider vinegar
2 tablespoons Pickling Spice
5 cups sugar

Wash cucumbers and place in stone crock or enamel container. If you cannot purchase small whole cucumbers, you may use 5 pounds large cucumbers, sliced; the yield may vary since slices pack more compactly than whole cucumbers. Mix salt with the 2 quarts cold water; pour over cucumbers. Let stand one week, weighting cucumbers with a glass plate so they are completely covered with brine at all times. Remove scum each day. At end of week, drain and rinse well. Mix alum with the 2 quarts boiling water; pour over cucumbers. Let stand 24 hours; drain. Combine vinegar, pickling spice and 3 cups of the sugar and bring to a boil; pour over pickles. Let stand 24 hours. Drain liquid into a saucepan; add ½ cup of the sugar and bring to a boil. Pour over pickles. Let stand 24 hours. Repeat draining, adding ½ cup sugar and boiling each day for three more days. On the third and last day, pack pickles in hot sterilized jars; cover with hot syrup, leaving ½-inch head space. Seal. *Makes 6 to 7 pints.*

# Spicy Peach Butter

26 medium-size ripe
  peaches
2 cups sugar

1¼ teaspoons Lemon Peel
½ teaspoon Cinnamon
¼ teaspoon Cardamom

Peel and slice peaches. Cook in small amount of water until peaches are soft. Mash and strain. Measure 4 cups pulp and combine with remaining ingredients. Cook until mixture thickens, about 45 minutes, stirring often. Fill hot sterilized jars, leaving ¼-inch head space. Seal at once. *Makes 2 pints.*

# Chow-Chow

3 large heads of cabbage
12 large green peppers
3 bunches celery
18 large onions
12 large green tomatoes
10 large sweet cucumber
  pickles
5 tablespoons Celery Seed
4 tablespoons Turmeric
2 tablespoons ground Ginger

4 tablespoons Cinnamon
4 tablespoons salt
1 pound Mustard Seed
⅛ teaspoon Cayenne
2 tablespoons Mace
1 tablespoon ground
  Allspice
2½ quarts vinegar
3 pounds brown sugar

Cover cabbage, peppers and celery with cold water and let stand 30 minutes to crisp. Drain. Chop vegetables and pickles medium fine and include seed of two of the green peppers. Place mixture in cheesecloth; squeeze out juice from vegetables, then discard juice. Add remaining ingredients to vegetables and bring to a rapid boil. Boil 15 minutes. Fill hot sterilized jars, leaving ¼-inch head space. Seal. *Makes about 14 quarts.*

# Chili Sauce

24 large red-ripe tomatoes
8 large onions, chopped
6 green peppers, chopped
2 cups vinegar
1 tablespoon salt
1 teaspoon Cinnamon
1 teaspoon Cloves

1 teaspoon Ginger
1 tablespoon Celery Seed
1 teaspoon Crushed Red
  Pepper
1 teaspoon dry Mustard
3 cups sugar

Peel, core and chop tomatoes; combine with remaining ingredients. Boil gently, uncovered, 4 hours or until thickened. Stir frequently to prevent sticking. Fill hot sterilized jars, leaving ¼-inch head space. Seal. *Makes about 6½ pints.*

# Corn Relish

1 cup chopped sweet red
  pepper
1½ cups chopped cabbage
1 cup chopped celery
1 cup chopped onion
1 cup sugar
1½ cups white vinegar
1 tablespoon Celery Seed

2 teaspoons dry Mustard
2 teaspoons Turmeric
1 tablespoon salt
2 No. 303 cans whole kernel
  yellow corn, drained
2 tablespoons flour
¼ cup water

Wash and prepare vegetables; cut into ¼-inch cubes or pieces, then measure. Put in large saucepan and add sugar, vinegar, spices and salt. Boil 20 minutes. Add drained corn and cook 5 minutes longer or until corn is thoroughly heated. Blend flour with water then stir into relish. Cook 10 minutes or until slightly thickened. Fill hot sterilized jars, leaving ½-inch head space. Seal. *Makes 3 pints.*

# Pickle Relish

24 medium to large
  cucumbers
10 medium-size onions
3 tablespoons salt
2 cups sugar
3 cups vinegar

1 tablespoon ground
  Turmeric
1 tablespoon Celery Seed
1 tablespoon Mustard Seed
1 tablespoon ground Ginger

Wash cucumbers and cover with ice water; let stand 3 hours. Drain; slice cucumbers and onions paper-thin and sprinkle with salt. Allow to stand 3 hours. Drain, reserving 1 cup of the juice. Combine this juice with remaining ingredients; add vegetables. Boil gently until vegetables are clear and transparent, about 40 minutes. Fill hot sterilized jars, leaving ¼-inch head space; seal. *Makes 5 pints.*

# Kosher Dill Pickles

7 pounds medium-size
  cucumbers
4 tablespoons Dill Seed
¾ teaspoon Instant Minced
  Garlic
3 teaspoons Crushed Red
  Pepper

6 thick onion slices
1 quart vinegar
2 quarts water
½ cup salt

Wash cucumbers and pack into 6 hot sterilized quart jars. To each jar add 2 teaspoons dill seed, ⅛ teaspoon instant minced garlic, ½ teaspoon crushed red pepper and 1 slice onion. For a stronger garlic flavor, use ¼ teaspoon instant minced garlic in each jar. Combine remaining ingredients and bring to a boil. Pour, boiling hot, over cucumbers, leaving ¼-inch head space. Seal at once. *Makes 6 quarts.*

# Cantaloupe Pickles

3 pints cantaloupe cubes
2 tablespoons coarse salt
4 quarts water
3 tablespoons powdered Alum
1 tablespoon ground Ginger
1½ cups white vinegar

3 cups light brown sugar, packed
2 tablespoons Celery Seed
2 tablespoons Mustard Seed
1 3-inch piece Cinnamon
1 tablespoon whole Cloves

Peel cantaloupe, remove seed and cut into 1-inch cubes; measure. Put in stone crock or glass bowl and let stand 24 hours in a solution of coarse salt and 2 quarts of the water. Wash and drain. Let stand 24 hours in a solution of alum and 1 quart of the water. Wash and drain. Cover with water and let stand 24 hours. Drain. Add ginger to the remaining 1 quart of water and bring to a boil; add cantaloupe and boil 30 minutes. Drain. Make syrup of vinegar, brown sugar and the remaining spices tied in a cheesecloth bag. Add cantaloupe and cook 30 minutes or until cantaloupe is clear and tender. Pack, hot, into hot sterilized jars. Remove spice bag and pour the hot syrup into jars, leaving ¼-inch head space. Seal. *Makes 2 pints.*

# Dill Pickles

4 pounds cucumbers, about 4 inches long
1 cup Dill Seed
21 Peppercorns

3½ teaspoons Mustard Seed
3 cups white vinegar
3 cups water
6 tablespoons salt

Cut cucumbers in half lengthwise. Pack into hot sterilized pint jars. To each jar add about 2 tablespoons dill seed, 3 peppercorns and ½ teaspoon mustard seed. Bring the vinegar, water and salt to a boil. Pour, boiling hot, over cucumbers, leaving ¼-inch head space. Seal. Process 10 minutes. *Makes 7 pints.*

# Tomato Relish

24 large ripe tomatoes
7 medium-size onions
½ cup salt
1 teaspoon Cayenne
2 teaspoons ground Allspice
2 teaspoons ground Cloves
2 teaspoons ground Ginger

2 teaspoons dry Mustard
1 quart vinegar
1 green pepper, cut fine
2 cups sugar
¼ pound (⅔ cup) Mustard
  Seed

Peel tomatoes and cut in half. Peel and slice onions. Sprinkle vegetables with salt and let stand overnight. Drain well and add cayenne, allspice, cloves, ginger, dry mustard, vinegar and green pepper. Simmer, uncovered, 2 hours. Add sugar and mustard seed; cook 10 minutes longer or until syrupy. Fill hot sterilized jars, leaving ¼-inch head space. Seal. *Makes about 7 pints.*

---

# Colorful Spiced Pineapple

1 No. 2½ can pineapple
  chunks
¾ cup vinegar
1¼ cups sugar
6 whole Cloves

1 3-inch piece Cinnamon
2 whole Allspice
Green Food Color
  or Red Food Color

Drain pineapple and save syrup. Combine syrup, vinegar, sugar, cloves, cinnamon and allspice. Bring to a boil; reduce heat and simmer 10 minutes. Add about ¼ teaspoon food color, mixing well. Add pineapple and bring back to a boil. Fill hot sterilized jar, leaving ¼-inch head space. Seal. If you would like to have both red and green pineapple, tint half red and half green. Pack into half-pint jars. Use as a garnish, on a relish tray, as an appetizer or as an accompaniment to meat or poultry. *Makes 1 pint.*

# Mango Chutney

The king of chutneys—highly prized as an accompaniment with curry.

1 pint cider vinegar
3½ cups brown sugar, firmly packed (1½ pounds)
2 medium-size onions, chopped
1 lemon, sliced thin
⅛ teaspoon Instant Minced Garlic
1½ cups seedless raisins or currants
¼ teaspoon Cayenne
1½ teaspoons salt

1 tablespoon Mustard Seed
4 ounces Crystallized Ginger, thinly sliced
6 tomatoes, peeled and cut into eighths
1 green pepper, chopped
6 whole Cloves
¼ teaspoon Nutmeg
6 medium-size apples, peeled, cored and sliced
4 large mangoes, peeled and sliced

Combine all ingredients, except apples and mangoes, in a large kettle. Cook 1 hour or until liquid is clear and syrupy. Add apples and mangoes; continue cooking until fruit is tender. Fill hot sterilized jars, leaving ½-inch head space. Seal. *Makes about 5 pints.*

# Mint-Apple Jelly

12 medium-size cooking apples
3 cups sugar
1 teaspoon Mint Extract or

Mint and Peppermint Extract
3 drops Green Food Color

Quarter apples; remove stem and blossom ends. Add just enough water to cover. Cook, covered, 20 minutes or until apples are tender. Put apples, including juice, into jelly bag or 4 thicknesses of cheesecloth. Allow juice to drip from bag. (For clear jelly do not squeeze bag.)

Combine 4 cups of the juice with sugar and boil rapidly to jellying point, 220°F. to 222°F., or until two drops of jelly will run together off side of spoon. Add extract and food color. Remove from heat. Pour into hot sterilized jelly glasses or jars. Seal. You will find this to be excellent with lamb. *Makes about 4 half-pints.*

## Crystal Pickles

7 pounds cucumbers
  or green tomatoes
2 cups slaked lime
2 gallons water
¾ cup powdered Alum
  (4 ounces)
2 gallons water
½ cup ground Ginger
  (1⅛ ounces)

2 gallons water
5 pounds sugar
2 quarts cider vinegar
1 teaspoon ground Cinnamon
1 teaspoon whole Cloves
1 teaspoon whole Allspice
1 teaspoon Celery Seed

Wash cucumbers or tomatoes and slice medium thin, then weigh. Place in stone crock or enamel container. Dissolve slaked lime in the first 2 gallons water; pour over cucumbers. With a glass plate, weight cucumbers so they are completely covered with brine at all times. Let stand 24 hours. Drain; wash well. Dissolve alum in the second 2 gallons water; pour over cucumbers. Let stand 24 hours. Drain; wash well. Stir ginger into the third 2 gallons water; pour over cucumbers. Let stand 6 hours. Drain and wash well. Make a syrup of the sugar, vinegar and spices. Pour over cucumbers and let stand 4 hours, then bring to a boil and boil 10 minutes. Fill hot sterilized jars with pickles. Bring syrup back to a boil and pour over pickles, leaving ½-inch head space. If necessary make additional syrup to cover pickles. Seal. *Makes 10 to 12 pints.*

# Mixed Pickles

4 cups cucumber pieces
2 cups carrot pieces
1 cauliflower
2 sweet red peppers
2 cups pickling onions
3 4-ounce cans mushroom
   crowns
1 cup salt

1 gallon water
2 cups sugar
2 quarts vinegar
4 tablespoons Mustard Seed
3 tablespoons Celery Seed
1 tablespoon Crushed Red
   Pepper
1 tablespoon Pickling Spice

Wash, rinse and drain vegetables. Before measuring, quarter cucumbers and cut into 1-inch lengths. Cut carrots into ½-inch pieces; measure. Break cauliflower into small flowerets. Seed and chop peppers; peel onions. Drain mushrooms. Put all the vegetables in a stone crock. Dissolve salt in water; pour over vegetables. Let stand 18 hours; drain. Combine sugar, vinegar, mustard seed, celery seed, crushed red pepper and pickling spice; boil 3 minutes. Add vegetables; simmer until thoroughly heated, then bring to a rolling boil. Pack, boiling hot, into hot sterilized jars, leaving ¼-inch head space. Seal at once. *Makes about 4 pints.*

# Thousand Island Pickles

4 quarts sliced cucumbers
4 medium-size onions, sliced
2 sweet red peppers, cut
   into strips
1 green pepper, cut into
   strips

3 cups sugar
3 cups vinegar
1 tablespoon dry Mustard
1 tablespoon Turmeric
¼ cup salt
2 tablespoons Mustard Seed

Combine all ingredients. Heat to just below the boiling point but do not boil. Fill hot sterilized jars, leaving ½-inch head space. Seal. *Makes about 7 pints.*

# Mustard Pickles

2 quarts medium-size
   cucumbers
1 quart green tomatoes
1 large cauliflower
2 sweet red peppers
1 quart pickling onions
1 cup salt
3 quarts water

6 tablespoons dry Mustard
1 tablespoon Turmeric
1 cup flour
¾ cup water
2 cups sugar
2 quarts cider vinegar
2 tablespoons Celery Seed
1 tablespoon Peppercorns

Wash and drain vegetables. Cut cucumbers into ½-inch cubes, tomatoes into wedges and cauliflower into small flowerets. Remove seed from peppers and cut peppers into small pieces. Peel onions and cut in half. Dissolve salt in the 3 quarts water and pour over vegetables. Let stand 12 hours. Rinse; drain 1 hour. Combine dry mustard, turmeric and flour. Gradually add the ¾ cup water, stirring until smooth. Add sugar, vinegar, celery seed and peppercorns. Cook over medium heat until sauce coats a silver spoon. Add vegetables and simmer 15 minutes. Pack, boiling hot, into hot sterilized jars, leaving ¼-inch head space. Seal. Process 10 minutes in boiling water bath. *Makes 12 pints.*

# Pear-Pineapple Butter

4 cups grated pears
   (8 to 10 medium-size pears)
2 cups sugar

2 3-inch pieces Cinnamon
1 No. 2 can crushed
   pineapple

Combine pears, sugar and cinnamon in saucepan and boil 5 minutes, stirring often. Add pineapple and boil 30 minutes longer, stirring occasionally. Fill hot sterilized jars, leaving ¼-inch head space. Seal. *Makes 2½ pints.*

419

## Cinnamon Peach Preserves

2 pounds quartered
  peaches (8 to 10)
3 cups sugar

1½ cups water
2 3-inch pieces Cinnamon

Peel, remove pit and quarter peaches; weigh. Make syrup of 1½ cups of the sugar, water and cinnamon. While boiling, add peaches and cook 15 minutes. Remove from heat and let peaches stand in syrup 1 hour. Add remaining 1½ cups sugar and bring to a boil. Cook rapidly to jelly stage, 220°F. to 222°F. Fill hot sterilized jars, leaving ¼-inch head space. Seal. *Makes 1½ pints*

## Dilled Green Beans

2 pounds green beans
  (young and tender)
1 teaspoon powdered Alum
1 gallon water
½ teaspoon Instant
  Minced Garlic
4 teaspoons Dill Seed

2 teaspoons Mustard Seed
1 teaspoon Crushed Red
  Pepper
2 cups water
2 cups vinegar
¼ cup salt

Wash beans and trim ends; place in stone crock or glass container. Dissolve alum in the 1 gallon water; pour over beans and let stand 24 hours. Drain and wash. Put beans in saucepan; add about 1 cup water. Cover and boil 5 minutes then drain. Pack beans, lengthwise, into hot sterilized jars. To each jar add ⅛ teaspoon instant minced garlic, 1 teaspoon dill seed, ½ teaspoon mustard seed and ¼ teaspoon crushed red pepper. Combine remaining ingredients and bring to a boil. Pour over beans, leaving ¼-inch head space. Seal at once. *Makes 4 pints.*

# Dixie Relish

1 quart ground cabbage
1 pint ground white onions
1 pint ground sweet red
  peppers
½ cup salt
4 tablespoons Mustard Seed
3 tablespoons Celery Seed

1 quart cider vinegar
3 cups sugar
1 tablespoon salt
1 3-inch piece Cinnamon
1 tablespoon whole Cloves
1 tablespoon whole Allspice

Mix vegetables with the ½ cup salt and let stand 4 to 5 hours. Put mixture in cheesecloth and squeeze until free of juice. Put vegetables in large saucepan; add remaining ingredients, tying cinnamon, cloves and allspice in a cheesecloth bag for easy removal. Slowly bring to a boil then simmer 10 minutes. Remove spice bag. Fill hot sterilized jars, leaving ½-inch head space. Seal. *Makes 5 pints.*

# Apple Chutney

8 cups chopped apples
2 cups chopped dried apricots
½ cup Chopped Instant
  Onions
1 pound brown sugar
1 pint vinegar
1 tablespoon ground Ginger
1 tablespoon Mint Flakes

2 teaspoons ground Allspice
2 teaspoons salt
1 tablespoon Mustard Seed
1 teaspoon Cayenne
  or Red Pepper
⅛ teaspoon Instant
  Minced Garlic

Peel and core apples. Coarsely chop apples and apricots, then measure. Combine with remaining ingredients. Simmer 1 hour or until thickened. Fill hot sterilized jars, leaving ¼-inch head space. Seal at once. Apple Chutney is delicious with lamb, pork, capon or duckling. *Makes about 2 pints.*

# Basil-Apple Jelly

12 medium-size
  cooking apples

3 cups sugar
1 tablespoon Basil Leaves

Quarter apples, removing stem and blossom ends. Add just enough water to cover. Cook, covered, until apples are tender, about 20 minutes. Put apples, including juice, into jelly bag or 4 thicknesses of cheesecloth. Allow juice to drip from bag. (For clear jelly do not squeeze bag.) Combine 4 cups of the juice with sugar. Tie basil leaves in cheesecloth bag and add to juice. Boil rapidly to jellying stage, 220°F. to 222°F., or until two drops of jelly will run together off side of spoon. Remove basil leaves. Pour into hot sterilized jelly glasses or jars. Seal. *Makes about 4 half-pints.*

# Spiced Pickled Peaches

10 pounds peaches
Whole Cloves
4 pounds brown sugar

1 pint cider vinegar
2 3-inch pieces Cinnamon

Peel peaches; stick 2 or 3 whole cloves in each. Cover peaches with brown sugar and let stand overnight. Drain off syrup and combine with vinegar and cinnamon; bring to boil. Drop peaches into boiling syrup, a few at a time, and cook 20 minutes or until tender. As peaches are cooked, pack into hot sterilized jars. When all have been cooked, pour hot syrup over peaches in jars, leaving ¼-inch head space. Seal at once. You will find these excellent served with ham, roast poultry or game. *Makes 3 quarts.*

# Mango Marmalade

½ large lemon
½ large orange
½ cup orange juice
5 cups diced, ripe mangoes

3 cups sugar
12 whole Cloves
4 whole Allspice
2 whole Cardamom

Slice lemon and orange into paper-thin slices; cut each slice in half. Combine with orange juice, diced mangoes and sugar in a large heavy saucepan. Tie spices in a cheesecloth bag and add to mixture. Bring to a boil, stirring gently. Boil rapidly almost to, or to, the jellying point, 220°F. to 222°F., stirring often to prevent sticking. Remove spice bag. Pour boiling hot marmalade into hot sterilized jars, leaving ¼-inch head space. Seal at once. *Makes about 2 pints.*

# Apple Butter

15 medium-size apples
  (4 to 5 pounds)
1½ quarts cider
1½ pounds (3 cups) sugar

1 teaspoon Cinnamon
1 teaspoon Allspice
1 teaspoon Cloves
¼ teaspoon Nutmeg

Select firm, tart cooking apples. Wash and slice; do not remove core, seed or peel. Add cider and boil 15 minutes or until apples are soft. Press through sieve. (You should have about 3 quarts pulp.) Gently boil the pulp 1 hour or until it begins to thicken, stirring occasionally. Stir in spices and continue cooking slowly 3 hours or until thickened, stirring frequently. Pour into hot sterilized jars, leaving ¼-inch head space. Seal. *Makes about 3½ pints.*

# Peach Chutney

2 quarts peaches
4 tart apples
1 lemon
4 ounces Crystallized Ginger
1 cup raisins
1 pound brown sugar
1 pint vinegar
½ cup Chopped Instant Onions
⅛ teaspoon Instant Minced Garlic

1 teaspoon ground Ginger
2 teaspoons salt
2 tablespoons Mustard Seed
1 teaspoon ground Cloves
½ teaspoon Cayenne or Red Pepper
½ teaspoon ground Cinnamon

Peel and slice peaches. Peel apples and chop coarsely. Cut lemon into thin slices. Chop crystallized ginger. Combine all ingredients and simmer 1½ hours. Fill hot sterilized jars, leaving ¼-inch head space. Seal at once. Excellent served as a condiment with curry; or serve with lamb, beef or duckling. Adds an interesting note to tuna or chicken salad. *Makes 5 pints.*

# Bread and Butter Pickles

40 medium-size cucumbers
1 pound small white onions
1 green pepper
1 sweet red pepper
½ cup rock salt
3 quarts ice water

6 cups sugar
5 cups cider vinegar
2 tablespoons Mustard Seed
2 teaspoons Celery Seed
1 teaspoon ground Turmeric
½ teaspoon ground Cloves

Slice cucumbers and onions ⅛ inch thick. Cut peppers into ¼-inch strips. Dissolve salt in ice water; pour over vegetables and let stand 3 hours. Drain. Mix the remaining ingredients; add vegetables. Heat to boiling and immediately fill hot sterilized jars, leaving ½-inch head space. Seal. *Makes 8 to 9 pints.*

# Watermelon Pickles

4½ pounds peeled watermelon
   rind (about 4 quarts)
2 tablespoons rock salt
3 quarts water
2 tablespoons powdered Alum

1 quart white vinegar
9 cups sugar
¼ cup whole Cloves
2 3-inch pieces Cinnamon

Peel and cut rind into desired shapes; put in stone crock and let stand 24 hours in a solution of the salt and 2 quarts of the water. Drain thoroughly. Let stand 24 hours in a solution of alum and the remaining quart of water. Drain thoroughly. Add fresh water to cover and let stand 24 hours. Bring to a boil and cook until tender, about 30 minutes; drain. Make syrup of vinegar, sugar and spices tied in a cheesecloth bag. Add watermelon rind and cook until clear and tender, about 20 minutes. Remove rind from syrup and pack into hot sterilized jars. Cook syrup 15 minutes longer; remove spice bag. Fill jars with hot syrup, leaving ¼-inch head space. Seal at once. *Makes 5 to 6 pints.*

# Spiced Figs

3 quarts white or black figs
Boiling water
1 cup water
6 cups sugar

1 cup vinegar
¼ cup Pickling Spice
3 3-inch pieces Cinnamon
8 whole Cloves

Wash and stem figs; cover with boiling water and let stand 5 minutes. Make syrup of the 1 cup water, sugar, vinegar and spices which have been tied in a cheesecloth bag. Drain figs and add to syrup. Boil gently 10 minutes but do not boil hard. Remove from heat; cover and let stand 24 hours. Repeat boiling process for 3 consecutive days. On the third day pack in hot sterilized jars, leaving ¼-inch head space. Seal. *Makes about 5 pints.*

# Old-Time Mincemeat

1 3-pound rump roast
1 tablespoon salt
1 cup water
1 No. 303 can red tart
pitted cherries
1 pound brown sugar
1 pound dark seedless raisins
1 pound golden seedless
raisins
1 11-ounce box currants
8 ounces candied citron,
finely chopped
1½ cups chopped orange
pulp
⅓ cup minced, fresh orange
peel

¼ cup lemon juice
2 teaspoons grated lemon rind
½ pound ground suet
1 cup tart jelly
1 cup dark molasses
3 cups sweet cider
1 tablespoon Cinnamon
1 teaspoon Nutmeg
1 teaspoon Cloves
1 teaspoon Allspice
1 teaspoon Mace
½ teaspoon Ginger
½ teaspoon Black Pepper
3 quarts chopped, tart apples
(about 4 pounds)
2 tablespoons Brandy Extract

Sprinkle beef with salt; simmer, covered, in water 2 hours or until tender. Remove meat, reserving the liquid. When meat is cool, put through food grinder using fine blade; you should have 5 to 7 cups ground beef. Drain cherries, reserving juice. In a large saucepan or kettle, combine cherry juice, sugar, raisins, currants, citron, orange pulp, orange peel, lemon juice, lemon rind, suet, jelly, molasses, cider and the spices. Mix well. Slowly bring to a boil, stirring occasionally. Then stir in ground beef, cherries, apples and brandy extract. Cook until mixture comes to a boil. Fill hot sterilized jars, leaving 1-inch head space. (Caution: Take care in filling to distribute as equally as possible the amount of liquid and solids.) Seal. *Makes eight 1½ pints or enough for eight 9-inch pies.*

# OUTDOOR COOKING

— ✳ —

## Rolled Rump Roast

1 6-pound rolled rump roast  
2 cups water  
2 cups vinegar  
¼ cup Instant Minced  
    Onion  
1 lemon, thinly sliced  
4 whole Allspice

12 whole Cloves  
3 Bay Leaves  
10 Peppercorns  
3 teaspoons Season-All  
2 teaspoons Hickory  
    Smoked Salt  
¼ teaspoon MSG

Have roast rolled and securely tied. It should be about 5 inches in diameter and 10 to 12 inches long. Combine remaining ingredients; mix well and pour over roast. Marinate in refrigerator 24 hours; turn meat several times. Cook on a spit over hot coals about 2 hours, basting frequently with marinade. Cooking time depends on distance from fire and heat of coals. Carve into thin slices. *Serves 8 to 10.*

NOTE: You will find a meat thermometer is helpful when cooking large pieces of meat on a spit. Caution should be taken when inserting the meat thermometer so the end is as near the center as possible but does not rest against the spit, the locking tines or bone.

# Chuck Wagon Franks

1 8-ounce can tomato sauce
1 6-ounce can tomato paste
½ cup catchup
¼ cup brown sugar, packed
2 tablespoons butter
  or margarine
3 tablespoons vinegar
2 tablespoons Worcestershire
  sauce
1 tablespoon Season-All

2 teaspoons Barbecue Spice
1 tablespoon prepared
  mustard
2 teaspoons Instant Minced
  Onion
2 teaspoons Celery Flakes
Dash Black Pepper
Dash Cayenne, optional
12 frankfurters

Combine all ingredients, except frankfurters, in a saucepan. Cover and slowly bring to a boil; reduce heat, then
simmer 1 hour. If you want a thinner sauce, add 1 cup
water. Grill frankfurters 4 inches from coals, turning
occasionally, 10 minutes or until nicely browned. Brush
often with sauce while cooking. A complete meal when
served with lots of baked beans and coleslaw. Adults as
well as children enjoy this treat. *Serves 6.*

# Chicken Legs Waikiki

½ cup pineapple juice
¼ cup soy sauce
2 tablespoons lemon juice
½ cup salad oil
1 teaspoon Ginger
2 teaspoons Season-All
¼ teaspoon MSG
1 teaspoon Rosemary
  Leaves, crushed

½ teaspoon Black Pepper
½ teaspoon Onion Powder
¼ teaspoon crushed Mint
  Flakes
½ cup Chablis, optional
8 chicken legs
  (drumstick and thigh)

Combine all the ingredients except chicken; mix well.
Arrange chicken in a single layer in flat baking dish.

428

Pour sauce over chicken and marinate in refrigerator several hours or overnight, turning several times. Cook on grill, 5 to 6 inches from coals, about 1 hour, turning and basting frequently with sauce. Excellent served with a tossed green salad and hot bread. *Serves 8.*

---

## Grilled Fish Fennel

---

Really an outdoor fish feast.

4 small whole fish  
  (about 2 pounds each)  
½ cup butter

¼ cup lemon juice  
4 teaspoons salt  
2 teaspoons Fennel Seed

Clean fish and cut three diagonal slashes on each side. Melt butter; add lemon juice and 2 teaspoons of the salt. Brush part of this mixture over fish. Combine remaining salt and fennel seed; rub inside and over outside of fish. Place fish in a basket grill and cook about 5 inches from coals 30 minutes or until fish flakes easily with fork; cooking time will vary depending on thickness of fish and heat of coals. Baste frequently with remaining butter mixture and turn once or twice during cooking time. Serve hot! *Serves 4.*

VARIATIONS:

*Dill Grilled Fish*—In above recipe use 4 teaspoons Dill Weed in place of fennel seed. Cook as directed.

*Grilled Tarragon Fish*—In above recipe use 4 teaspoons Tarragon Leaves in place of fennel seed. Cook as directed.

*Grilled Fish with Thyme*—In above recipe use 2 teaspoons Thyme Leaves in place of fennel seed. Cook as directed.

# Chinese Style Spareribs

½ cup salad oil
1½ cups brown sugar, packed
½ cup orange juice
½ cup lemon juice
1 teaspoon Ginger
1 teaspoon dry Mustard
¼ teaspoon MSG

¼ teaspoon Cloves
½ teaspoon Onion Powder
⅛ teaspoon Garlic Powder
2 teaspoons salt
¼ cup soy sauce
4 pounds spareribs
  (loin back ribs)

Combine all ingredients except spareribs. Place spareribs, rounded side up, on grill; sear on both sides. Raise grill to 6 inches from coals. Cook over medium heat 30 minutes or until nicely browned and thickest part of the meat tests well done, turning and basting frequently with sauce. For a longer and slower method, cook ribs over very low coals 1 hour or longer, turning and basting frequently. *Serves 3 to 4.*

# Pork Chops Luau

The Polynesian sauce adds exotic flavor.

½ cup pineapple juice
½ cup salad oil
¼ cup soy sauce
2 tablespoons lemon juice
1 teaspoon dry Mustard

½ teaspoon Ginger
⅛ teaspoon Mace
¼ cup brown sugar, packed
8 pork chops,
  cut 1 inch thick

Combine all ingredients, except pork chops, and mix well. Marinate pork chops in sauce in a flat baking dish several hours, turning once or twice. Place chops on grill 6 inches from coals; sear on both sides. Cook slowly, basting frequently with sauce, 40 minutes or until well done. May be served with grilled pineapple slices, peach halves or applesauce. *Serves 4.*

# Fish Fillets in a Package

2 fish fillets (about 1 pound)     Dash Mace
½ teaspoon Onion Salt              2 tablespoons soft butter
¾ teaspoon Season-All             1 tablespoon lemon juice

Place fillets on a piece of heavy duty aluminum foil.
Thoroughly blend together onion salt, Season-All, mace,
butter and lemon juice. Spread over top of fillets. Fold
aluminum foil to make a package; seal edges. Place
package on grill about 5 inches from coals. Cook 20
minutes or until fish can be flaked easily with a fork. Turn
package over after 10 minutes cooking time. *Serves 2.*

VARIATIONS:

*Dilled Fish Fillets*—In the above recipe, use ¾ teaspoon
    salt, ½ teaspoon Dill Weed, ⅛ teaspoon Black Pepper
    and dash MSG in place of onion salt, Season-All and
    mace. Proceed as in above recipe.
*Herbed Fish Fillets*—In the above recipe use ¾ teaspoon
    salt, ¼ teaspoon crushed Rosemary Leaves, ⅛ tea-
    spoon Tarragon Leaves, ⅛ teaspoon crushed Fennel
    Seed and dash Black Pepper in place of onion salt,
    Season-All and mace. Proceed as in above recipe.

# Grilled Garlic Bread

1 loaf French bread               ½ cup butter or margarine,
¼ teaspoon Garlic Powder             softened

Slice bread but not through the bottom crust. Add garlic
powder to butter and blend thoroughly. Spread between
slices and over top of bread. Wrap in aluminum foil;
seal edges. Heat on back of grill 45 minutes to 1 hour,
depending on heat of coals. Serve hot. *Serves 6 to 8.*

# Curried Lamb Chops Bengal

½ cup salad oil
2 tablespoons sugar
3 tablespoons lemon juice
1 teaspoon salt
1 teaspoon Instant Minced
   Onion

1 teaspoon Season-All
½ teaspoon Black Pepper
2 teaspoons Curry Powder
¼ teaspoon Garlic Salt
8 lamb chops,
   cut 1 inch thick

Combine all ingredients, except lamb chops, in saucepan. Bring to a boil, then simmer 10 minutes. Arrange chops on grill 5 to 6 inches from hot coals. Sear on both sides. Continue cooking, basting frequently with the curry sauce, 30 minutes or until chops are browned and done. *Serves 4.*

# Bonfire Green Beans

1 9-ounce package frozen
   French-style green beans
2 tablespoons butter
1 teaspoon Onion Salt

½ teaspoon Powdered
   Mushrooms
1 tablespoon lemon juice

Place green beans, frozen or partially thawed, on piece of aluminum foil. Dot with butter, then sprinkle with onion salt, powdered mushrooms and lemon juice. Seal foil. Place on grill 5 inches from coals. Cook 1 hour or until crisp-tender, turning occasionally. *Serves 3 to 4.*

VARIATION:

*Camper's Green Beans*—In the above recipe use 1 teaspoon Season-All in place of onion salt, powdered mushrooms and lemon juice. Cook as directed above.

# Charcoal Grilled Steak

4 club steaks, cut 1 inch thick
½ cup salad oil
2 tablespoons lemon juice
⅛ teaspoon Garlic Powder
1 teaspoon Onion Salt
¼ teaspoon Black Pepper
½ teaspoon Season-All
1 teaspoon Worcestershire sauce

Place steaks in shallow baking dish. Combine remaining ingredients and pour over steaks, being sure to coat all sides. Marinate several hours in refrigerator, turning once. Place on grill and sear on both sides. Raise grill to about 5 inches from coals. Cook 15 minutes, turning once, or until the desired degree of doneness is reached. *Serves 4.*

# Vegetable Kebabs

4 small whole onions
4 mushrooms
4 cherry tomatoes
4 pineapple chunks
4 ripe olives
4 jumbo stuffed olives
¼ cup melted butter
2 teaspoons Barbecue Spice
1 teaspoon salt
¼ teaspoon Black Pepper
1 teaspoon Bon Appétit
Dash Nutmeg

Peel and cook onions in boiling salted water 10 minutes or until slightly tender. Thread vegetables, pineapple and olives alternately onto skewers. (Small canned potatoes and pieces of raw green pepper, squash and eggplant may also be used.) Combine remaining ingredients; mix well. Brush vegetables with seasoned butter. Adjust grill 4 to 5 inches from coals. Place skewers on grill. Cook vegetables 10 minutes, turning and basting frequently with seasoned butter. *Serves 4.*

# Onion Rounds Delicious

3 large onions
¼ cup melted butter
¼ teaspoon Coarse Grind
  Black Pepper

1 teaspoon Season-All
¼ teaspoon Celery Salt
1 teaspoon Barbecue Spice

Peel and cut onions into ½-inch slices; do not break apart. Grill 6 inches from coals 10 minutes on each side or until tender and brown; brush often with a mixture of the remaining ingredients. *Serves 6 to 8.*

# Barbecued Bologna Roll

1 4-pound bologna roll
Whole Cloves
½ cup chili sauce
2 tablespoons lemon juice

1 teaspoon Barbecue Spice
1 teaspoon Powdered
  Horseradish
½ teaspoon dry Mustard

Score bologna roll, cutting diagonal lines ⅛ inch deep, to form a diamond pattern. Stud each diamond with a whole clove. Insert spit through center of roll and cook about 5 inches from coals, basting frequently with sauce made by combining the remaining ingredients. Cook 30 minutes or until heated through. Slice and serve with potato or macaroni salad, baked beans, coleslaw or your favorite relish. *Serves 8 to 10.*

# Ham Slice Delicious

1 ham slice, cut 1½ inches
    thick
2 tablespoons melted butter
3 tablespoons brown sugar,
    packed

1 tablespoon dry Mustard
1 teaspoon Orange Peel
Dash Paprika
1 tablespoon lemon juice

Trim most of the outside fat from ham. Adjust grill to about 5 inches from coals and place ham on grill. Brown on one side; turn. Begin basting with mixture of the remaining ingredients. Cook 25 minutes, turning and basting frequently. Pineapple-Yam Kebabs (see recipe page 438) are a must with this ham. *Serves 4 to 6.*

# Grilled Tomatoes

4 tomatoes, cut in half
2 tablespoons melted butter
    Season-All, Oregano,

Thyme, Celery Salt
    or Herb Seasoning

Brush cut side of tomatoes with butter. Sprinkle with one of the seasonings. Place tomatoes on grill over low coals and cook about 15 minutes or until soft. You will find these tomatoes a perfect accompaniment to any meat, sea food, fish or chicken. *Serves 8.*

# Shish Kebabs

4 pounds lean lamb
1 medium-size onion
2 green peppers
4 tablespoons wine vinegar
½ cup lemon juice
½ cup olive or salad oil
½ teaspoon Garlic Salt
½ teaspoon Onion Salt

1 tablespoon Season-All
½ teaspoon Black Pepper
¼ teaspoon Thyme Leaves
¼ teaspoon Basil Leaves
¼ teaspoon Marjoram
   Leaves
⅛ teaspoon MSG

Cut lamb into 1½- to 2-inch cubes, removing gristle and most of the fat. Peel onion, separate and cut into large pieces. Cut peppers into pieces. Combine remaining ingredients; mix well. Pour over lamb, onion and pepper; stir to coat with marinade. Cover and let marinate 12 to 24 hours. When ready to cook, thread skewers, alternating lamb, onion and pepper. Cook 5 inches from coals about 25 minutes, turning and basting often with marinade. *Makes 6 large kebabs, serving about 8.*

# Baked Beans Bar-B-Q

4 cups canned baked beans
½ cup catchup
¼ cup molasses
2 tablespoons brown sugar
2 teaspoons dry Mustard
2 teaspoons Barbecue Spice

½ teaspoon MSG
½ teaspoon Onion Powder
½ teaspoon Ginger
¼ teaspoon Black Pepper
2 teaspoons Sherry Extract
4 slices bacon

Mix together all ingredients, except bacon, in a heavy pot. Cut bacon into 1-inch pieces; place over top of beans. Cover and set on back of grill and cook over a slow fire, stirring occasionally, 45 minutes to 1 hour. If you prefer, you may bake beans in an oven and keep hot on back of grill. *Serves 8 to 10.*

# Celery Seed Rolls

A delicious way of adding new flavor to hot rolls.

| | |
|---|---|
| ¼ cup soft butter | Dash Season-All |
| ½ teaspoon Celery Seed | 6 ready-to-serve fan-tan rolls |

Blend together butter, celery seed and Season-All. Break rolls apart from the top and spread butter mixture between sections. Wrap rolls in aluminum foil. Place on grill and heat 10 minutes, turning once or twice. *Serves 3 to 6.*

**VARIATIONS:**

*Oregano Rolls*—Substitute ½ teaspoon Oregano Leaves, ¼ teaspoon Onion Salt and dash Paprika for seasonings in above recipe.

*Dill Rolls*—Substitute ½ teaspoon Dill Weed and dash Garlic Powder for seasonings in above recipe.

*Kräuterbutter Rolls*—Substitute 1 teaspoon Kräuterbutter Seasoning for seasonings in above recipe.

# Grilled Bananas

| | |
|---|---|
| 6 whole, unpeeled bananas | ¼ teaspoon Ginger |
| ¼ cup melted butter | ⅛ teaspoon Cloves |
| 2 tablespoons lemon juice | Cinnamon or Nutmeg |

Put the whole, unpeeled bananas on grill 4 inches from heat; cook 4 minutes or until peel turns black. Turn and cook 4 minutes on other side. Combine butter, lemon juice, ginger and cloves. When ready to serve, peel one side of each banana and spoon the spiced butter over top. Sprinkle each with cinnamon or nutmeg. Serve piping hot with grilled chicken, barbecued pork or ham. *Serves 6.*

# Barbecued Chicken

3 broilers, split in
  half lengthwise
1 6-ounce can tomato paste
½ cup catchup
¼ cup unsulphured molasses
½ cup water
1 tablespoon prepared
  mustard
1 tablespoon vinegar
1 tablespoon Worcestershire
  sauce
2 tablespoons butter
  or margarine
1 teaspoon Instant Minced
  Onion
1 teaspoon Season-All
¼ teaspoon Barbecue Spice
¼ teaspoon Garlic Salt
¼ teaspoon Black Pepper
¼ teaspoon MSG

Clean and dry chicken. Combine remaining ingredients,
mixing well; bring to a boil and boil 1 minute. Adjust
grill 5 to 6 inches from coals. Place chicken, skin side
down, on grill; brown on both sides, then begin basting
with sauce. Continue cooking, turning and basting
frequently, 45 minutes or until chicken is tender. *Serves 6.*

# Pineapple-Yam Kebabs

4 sweet potatoes
Pineapple cubes
4 apples, cut in quarters
½ cup melted butter
2 teaspoons Cinnamon
¼ teaspoon Cloves
¼ teaspoon Nutmeg
2 tablespoons lemon juice

Scrub and cook sweet potatoes in salted water 25 minutes
or until just tender. Peel and cut into large pieces.
Thread on skewers, alternating potatoes, pineapple and
apple quarters. Brush with mixture of remaining
ingredients. Grill over hot coals, turning and basting
frequently, until lightly browned. You will find these
especially good with pork or chicken. *Serves 4 to 6.*

438

# Scampi on a Skewer

A wonderful outdoor appetizer.

1½ pounds fresh
   or frozen shrimp
½ cup soy sauce
½ cup olive oil
2 tablespoons lemon juice
   or vinegar

½ teaspoon Ginger
½ teaspoon Garlic Salt
1 teaspoon Italian Seasoning

Wash shrimp thoroughly; do not remove shells. Mix together remaining ingredients to make marinade; pour over shrimp and let stand 1 to 2 hours in refrigerator. Thread shrimp onto skewers. Cook over hot coals about 10 minutes, turning several times. Serve hot from grill. *Serves 4.*

# Canadian Bacon on a Spit

A favorite from 6 to 60!

1 4-pound roll Canadian
   bacon
¼ cup honey
2 tablespoons wine vinegar
½ teaspoon Powdered
   Horseradish

1 teaspoon Hickory Smoked
   Salt
¼ teaspoon ground Cloves

Tie Canadian bacon in two or three places. Insert spit through center of roll and roast 5 to 6 inches from coals. Combine remaining ingredients and baste Canadian bacon frequently with this mixture. Cook about 30 minutes or until heated through. You will find this is an unusual outdoor treat. May be served either as an appetizer or as the main course. *Serves 6 to 8.*

# Rolled Rib Roast

| | |
|---|---|
| 1 rolled rib roast of beef (4 to 5 pounds) | ¼ teaspoon Ginger |
| ⅛ teaspoon Garlic Powder | 2 teaspoons Season-All |
| ½ teaspoon Onion Salt | 1 teaspoon salt |
| ¼ teaspoon dry Mustard | ½ teaspoon Coarse Grind Black Pepper |

Trim off most of the outside fat from roast. Combine seasonings and rub into all surfaces of the roast. Place on spit, 5 to 6 inches from coals, and cook 1½ hours or until desired degree of doneness is reached. You'll find leftover roast makes excellent sandwiches. *Serves 6 to 8.*

VARIATIONS:

*Rosemary Roast*—Rub 1 teaspoon Rosemary Leaves into roast along with above seasonings.

*Thyme Roast*—Rub ½ teaspoon Thyme Leaves into roast along with above seasonings.

NOTE: You will find a meat thermometer is helpful when cooking large pieces of meat on a spit. Caution should be taken when inserting the meat thermometer so the end is as near the center as possible but does not rest against the spit, the locking tines or bone.

# Patio Potatoes

| | |
|---|---|
| 2 medium-size potatoes | 1 teaspoon Barbecue Spice |
| ¼ cup soft butter | |

Parboil potatoes until just tender. Drain and cool. Slice potatoes into ¼-inch rounds; place on a piece of aluminum foil. Dot with butter and sprinkle with barbecue spice. Fold foil to make a package, sealing edges, and place on grill 5 inches from medium coals. Heat 25 minutes or until potatoes are steaming hot. *Serves 2 to 3.*

VARIATIONS:

*Hickory Smoked Potatoes*—In the above recipe use 1 teaspoon Hickory Smoked Salt and ½ teaspoon Cracked Black Pepper in place of barbecue spice. Cook as directed.

*Herbed Potatoes*—In the above recipe use ½ teaspoon Herb Seasoning, ¼ teaspoon salt, dash MSG and dash Cayenne in place of barbecue spice. Cook as directed.

*Dill Flavored Potatoes*—In the above recipe use ½ teaspoon Dill Weed, ½ teaspoon salt and dash Black Pepper in place of barbecue spice. Cook as directed.

*Potatoes with Marjoram*—In the above recipe use ½ teaspoon Marjoram Leaves, ¾ teaspoon Onion Salt, ¼ teaspoon Paprika and dash Black Pepper in place of barbecue spice. Cook as directed.

## Flank Steak Western Style

| | |
|---|---|
| 1 1½-pound flank steak | ½ teaspoon Coarse Grind |
| ½ cup oil | or Cracked Black Pepper |
| 2 tablespoons lemon juice | ½ teaspoon Onion Powder |
| ½ teaspoon Celery Salt | 1 teaspoon Season-All |

Put steak in shallow dish. Combine remaining ingredients and pour over steak, coating entire surface. Marinate several hours. Grill 4 inches from coals 15 to 20 minutes, turning once. Baste often with marinade. Carve into thin slices on extreme diagonal against the grain. *Serves 4.*

# Roasted Dilly Corn

6 ears of corn, in husks
½ cup soft butter
1 teaspoon salt
5 Coriander Seeds, crushed

1 teaspoon Dill Weed
Dash MSG
Dash Nutmeg

Loosen husks of corn enough to remove silk. Soak in cold water 30 minutes or longer. When ready to roast, drain well. Combine remaining ingredients and spread generously over corn. Rewrap husks, then wrap in aluminum foil. Place on grill about 5 inches from coals; cook 25 minutes, turning several times. Remove foil and husks. Serve piping hot. *Serves 6.*

VARIATION:

*Roasted Fiesta Corn*—Use 1 teaspoon Season-All and a dash dry Mustard in place of salt and seasonings in above recipe. Prepare and cook following directions above.

# Outdoor Chefs' Grillburgers

2 pounds ground beef
1 tablespoon Instant Minced Onion
¼ teaspoon Garlic Salt
½ teaspoon Barbecue Spice

½ teaspoon dry Mustard
¼ teaspoon Black Pepper
1½ teaspoons Bon Appétit
Hickory Smoked Salt
Charcoal Seasoning

Combine beef, onion, garlic salt, barbecue spice, dry mustard, pepper and Bon Appétit, being careful not to overmix. Shape into burgers; sprinkle with hickory smoked salt or charcoal seasoning. Grill over coals about 3 minutes on each side for rare or longer, depending on degree of doneness preferred. Serve on buns with your favorite relish and sauce. *Makes 8.*

# Grilled Chuck Steak

1 4-pound chuck steak,
  cut 1½ inches thick
2 teaspoons Meat Tenderizer

Charcoal Seasoning
Coarse Grind Black Pepper

Sprinkle steak on both sides with meat tenderizer; pierce surface with tines of a fork. Let stand 1 hour. Place on grill and sear on both sides. Sprinkle each side with charcoal seasoning and pepper. Raise grill to about 6 inches from coals and cook 35 minutes, turning once, or until desired degree of doneness is reached. Cut into thin slices and serve. Your whole family will enjoy this juicy and tender steak. *Serves 4 to 6.*

# Peppered Steak

An excellent steak for family and friends! Black Pepper gives the good flavor.

1 T-bone steak, cut 1½
  inches thick
2 teaspoons Coarse Grind
  or Cracked Black Pepper

⅛ teaspoon Garlic Salt
⅛ teaspoon MSG
1 teaspoon salt

Place steak on grill and sear each side. Combine remaining ingredients and sprinkle one half of the pepper mixture over each side of steak, pressing down firmly with spatula. Cook 4 to 5 inches from coals 12 minutes on each side or until desired degree of doneness is reached. For a very rare steak decrease cooking time; increase for well done steak. Cooking time varies with heat of coals and distance from coals. *Serves 2 to 3*

# Hamburgers

| | |
|---|---|
| 1 pound ground beef | 1 tablespoon Instant Minced |
| ½ teaspoon salt | Onion |
| ¼ teaspoon Black Pepper | ⅛ teaspoon Garlic Salt |

Thoroughly mix together all ingredients but do not overmix. Shape into 4 patties. Place on grill 3 inches from coals. Cook 3 minutes on each side or until desired degree of doneness is reached.

**VARIATIONS:**

*Savory Burgers*—Add ¼ teaspoon Savory to above recipe.

*Pepper Burgers*—Soak 4 teaspoons Bell Pepper Flakes in water 5 minutes. Add to above recipe.

*Sesame Burgers*—Toast ¼ cup Sesame Seed in 350°F. oven 15 minutes. Add to above recipe.

*Red Hot Burgers*—Add 1 teaspoon Crushed Red Pepper to above recipe.

*Oriental Burgers*—Add ¼ teaspoon Ginger, 1 teaspoon Lemon Peel and 1 teaspoon soy sauce to above recipe.

*Dill Burgers*—Add ½ teaspoon crushed Dill Seed and ¼ cup chopped olives or sweet pickles to above recipe.

*Herb Burgers*—Add ¼ teaspoon Marjoram, ⅛ teaspoon Thyme, ½ teaspoon Celery Salt and 1 teaspoon Parsley Flakes to above recipe.

*Chili-Cheese Burgers*—Add 1 cup grated cheese, ¼ cup milk and ½ teaspoon Chili Powder to above recipe.

*Hot 'n' Tangy Burgers*—Omit salt in above recipe and add 1 teaspoon Season-All and 1 teaspoon Barbecue Spice.

*Spice Burgers*—Add ½ teaspoon dry Mustard and ¼ teaspoon Nutmeg to above recipe.

# SPICE INDEX

———— * ————

445

447

449

453

456

462

469

470

471

## Extracts, Décors, Food Colors and Tea

473

# GENERAL INDEX

———— * ————

475

476

478

479

481

482

493

494

*To:*
McGraw-Hill Book Co.
Attn: Department PL
General Books—35th Floor
1221 Avenue of the Americas
New York, New York 10020

I enclose full payment for ...... copy(ies) of the regular hard cover edition of *Spices of the World Cookbook Revised Edition* by McCormick @ **$16.95** per copy, plus sales taxes required in my community. (Check or money order payable to *Spices of the World Cookbook*.)

**Please send the book to:**

**Name** ................................................

**Address** ..............................................

**City** ................ **State** ............ **Zip Code** ......

(The regular hard cover edition of *Spices of the World Cookbook Revised Edition* is a publication of McGraw-Hill Book Company.)